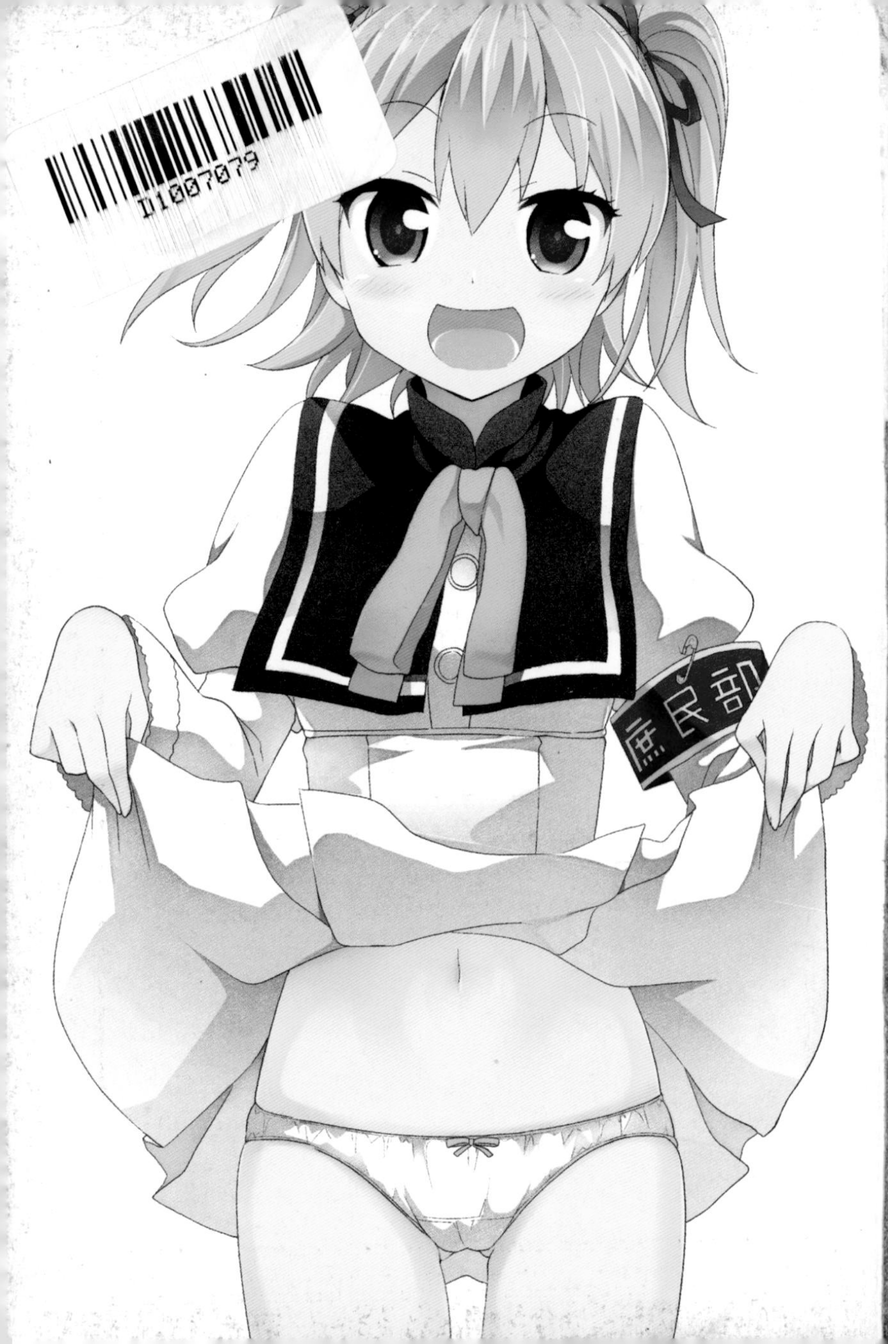
庶民部

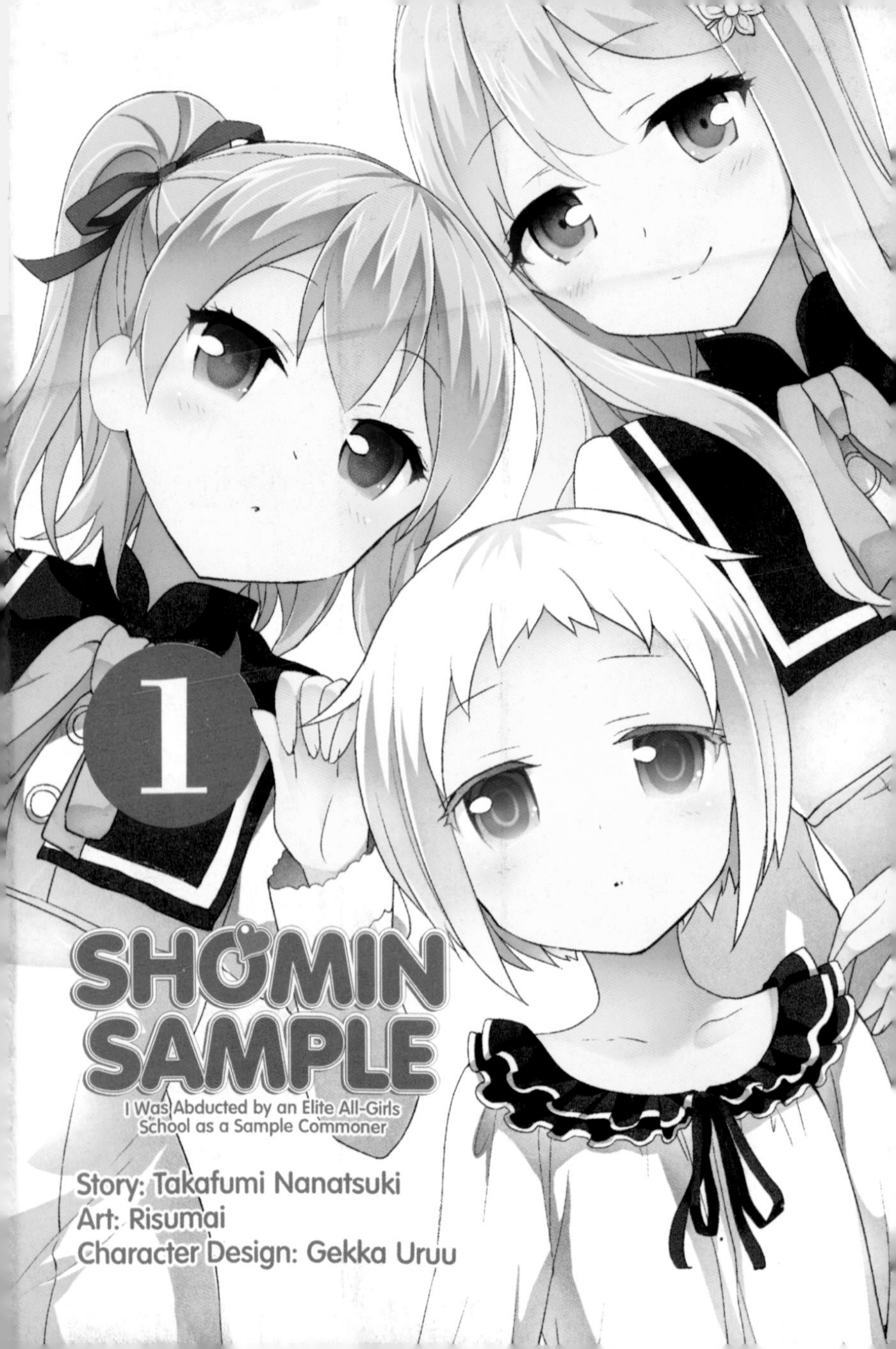

1

SHOMIN SAMPLE

I Was Abducted by an Elite All-Girls School as a Sample Commoner

Story: Takafumi Nanatsuki
Art: Risumai
Character Design: Gekka Uruu

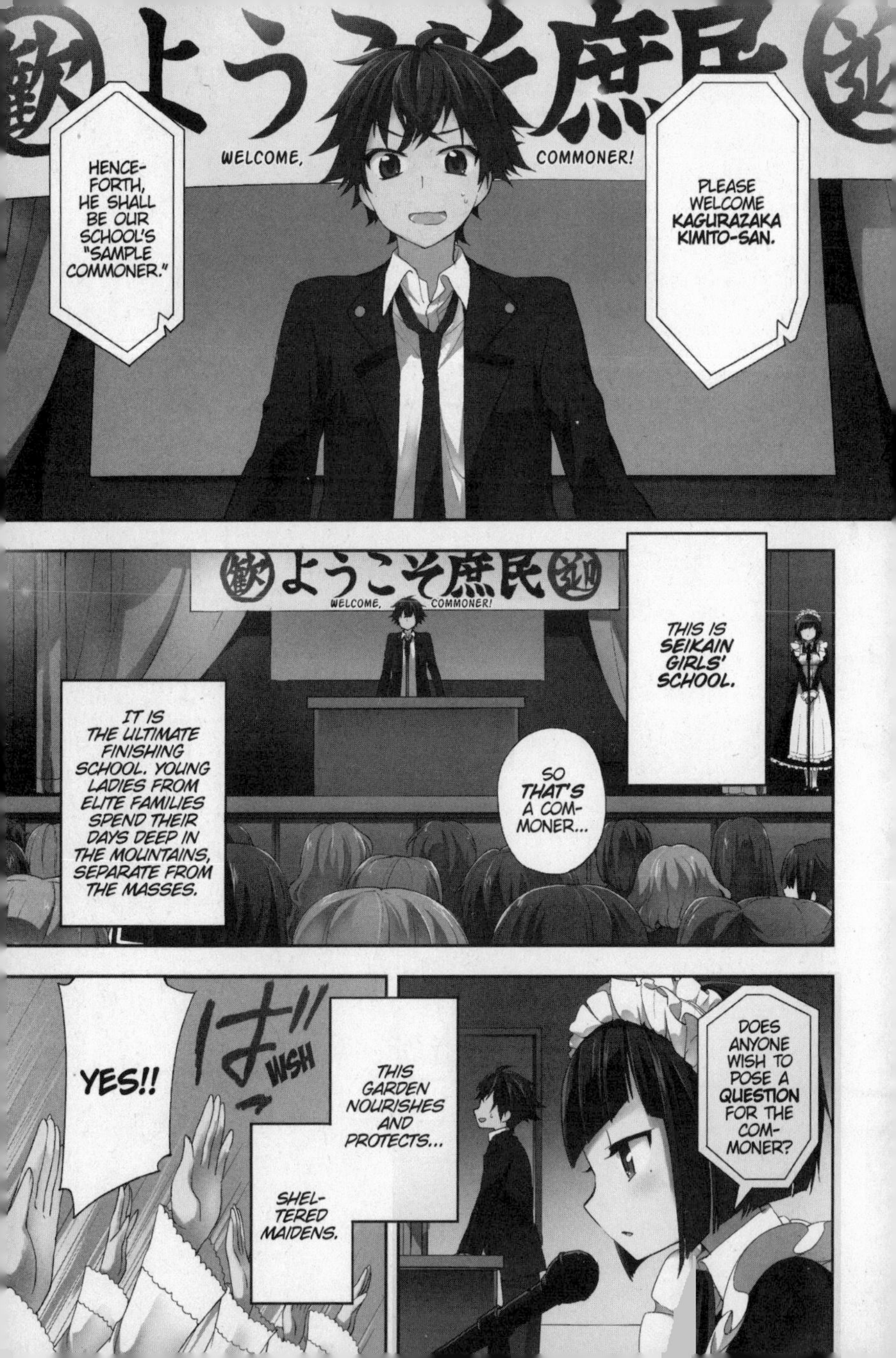
PLEASE WELCOME KAGURAZAKA KIMITO-SAN.
WELCOME, COMMONER!
HENCE-FORTH, HE SHALL BE OUR SCHOOL'S "SAMPLE COMMONER."
歓 ようこそ庶民 迎
WELCOME, COMMONER!
THIS IS SEIKAIN GIRLS' SCHOOL.
SO THAT'S A COMMONER...
IT IS THE ULTIMATE FINISHING SCHOOL. YOUNG LADIES FROM ELITE FAMILIES SPEND THEIR DAYS DEEP IN THE MOUNTAINS, SEPARATE FROM THE MASSES.
DOES ANYONE WISH TO POSE A QUESTION FOR THE COMMONER?
THIS GARDEN NOURISHES AND PROTECTS...
SHELTERED MAIDENS.
ば
WISH
YES!!

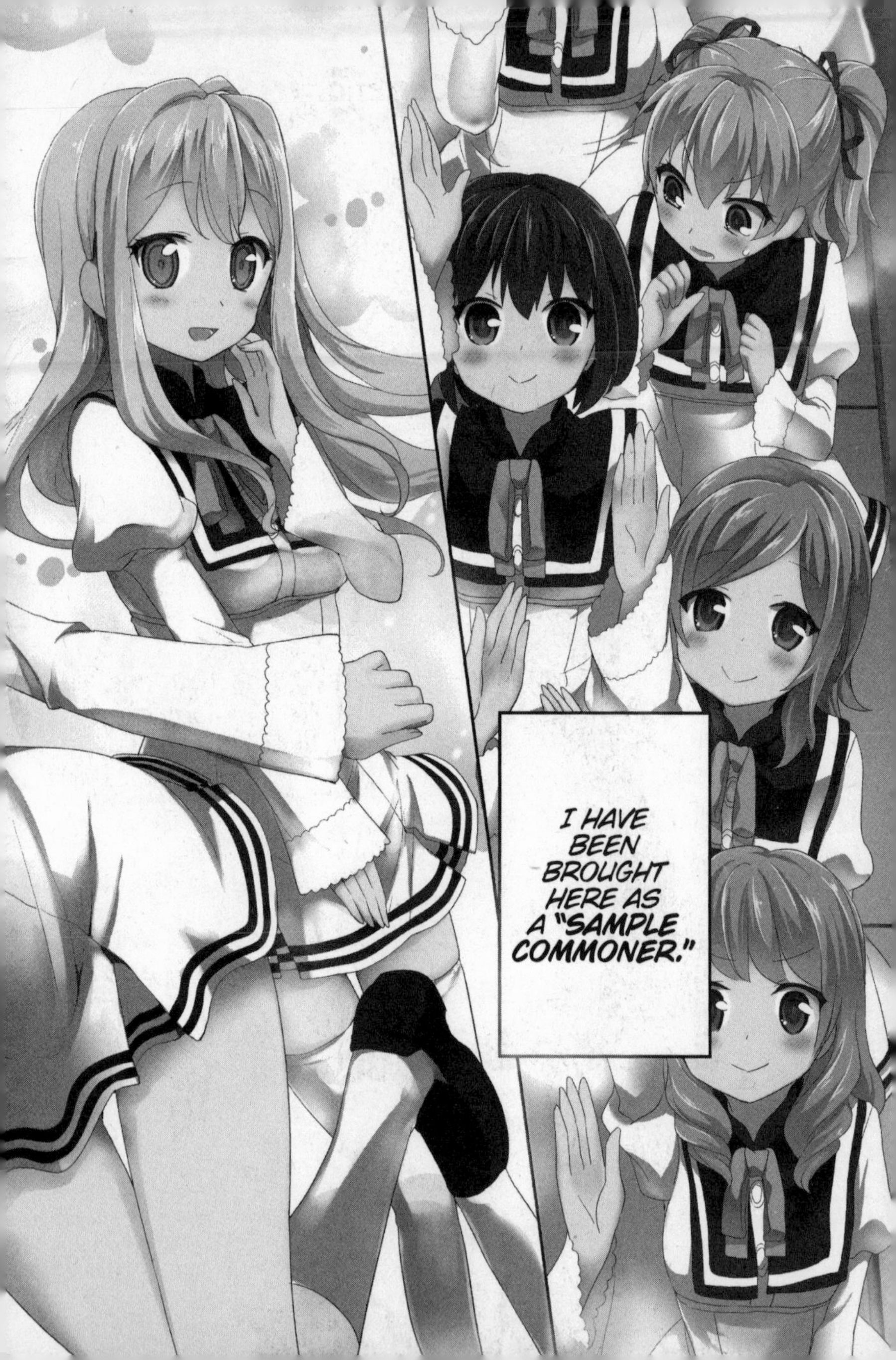
I HAVE BEEN BROUGHT HERE AS A "SAMPLE COMMONER."

Chapter 1 ✿ Welcome, Commoner

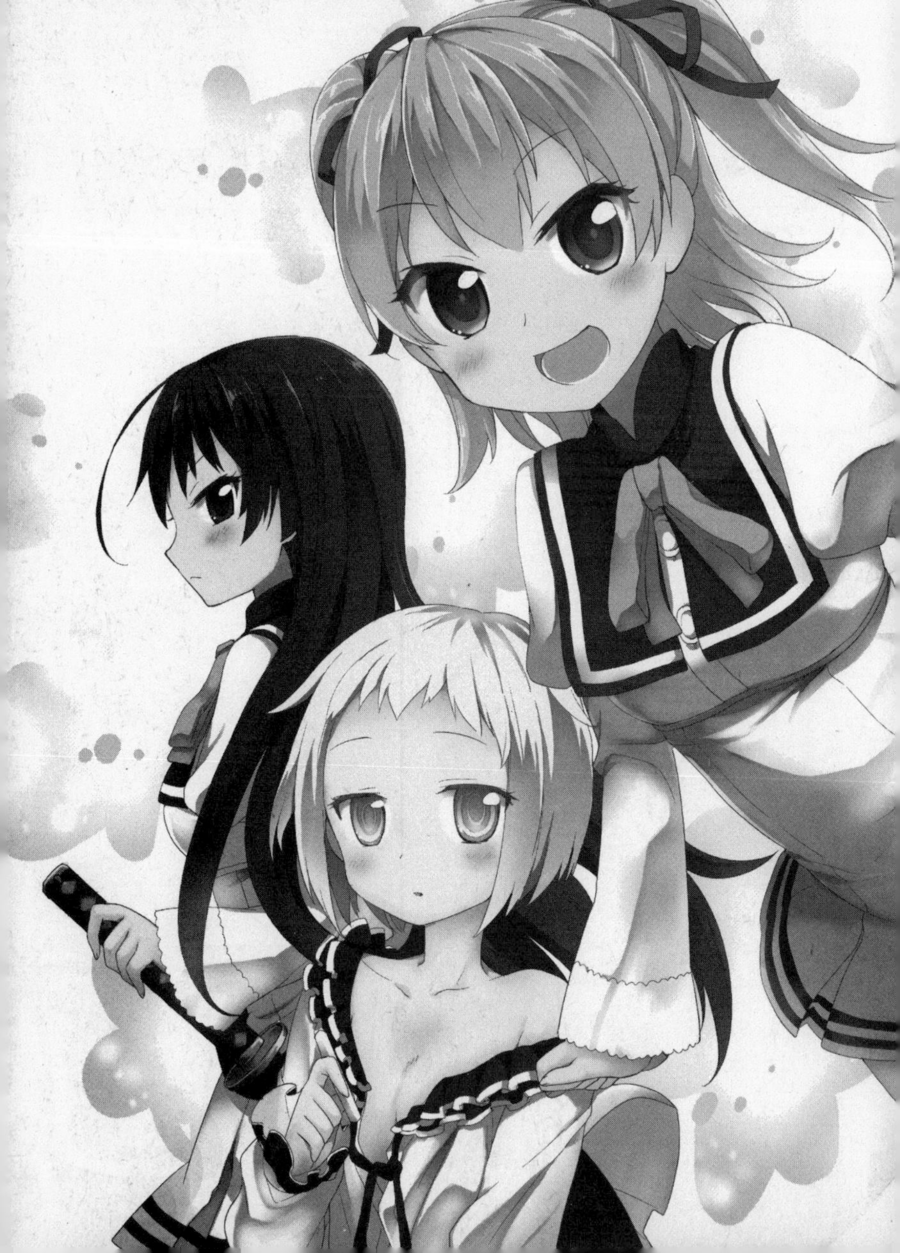

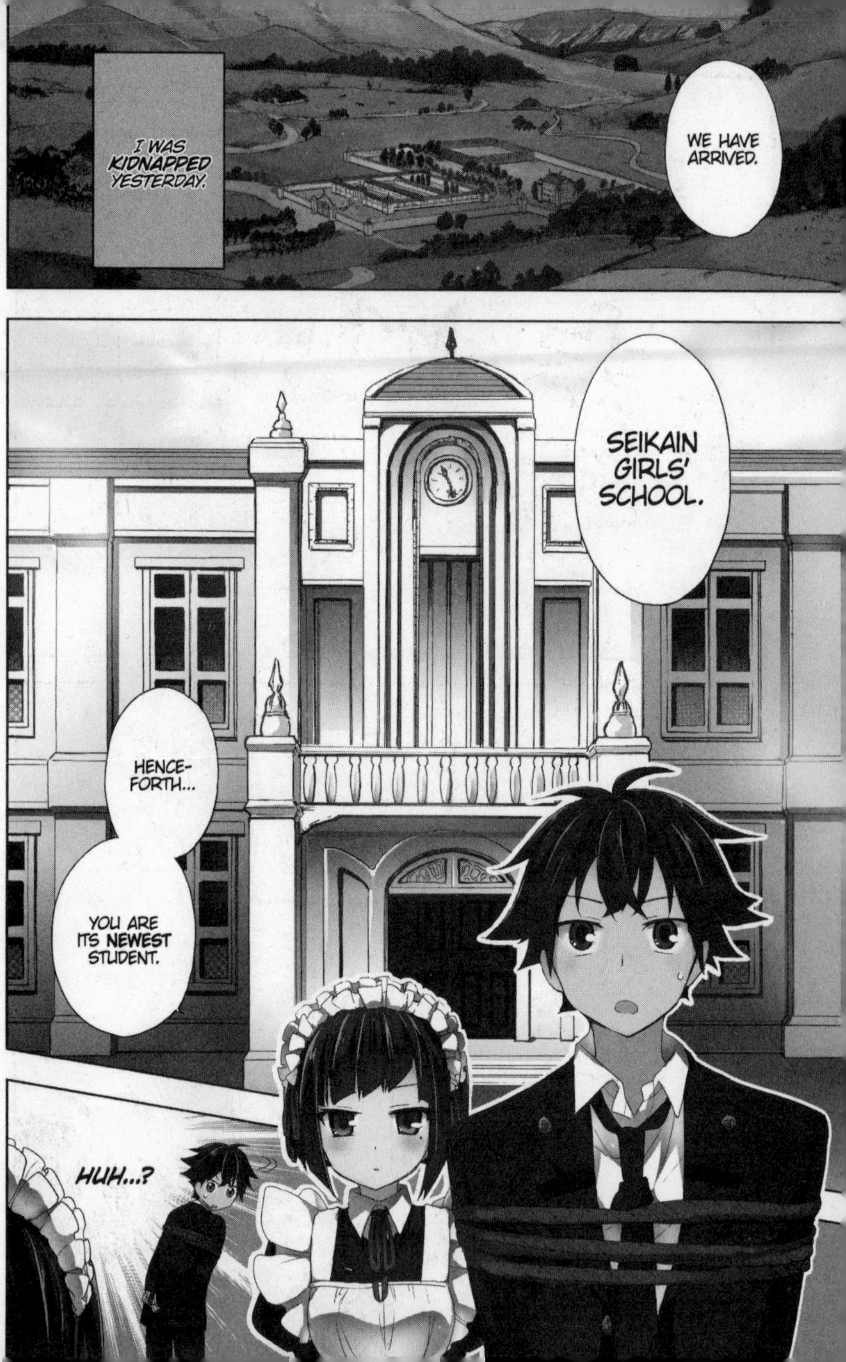
WE HAVE ARRIVED.
I WAS KIDNAPPED YESTERDAY.
SEIKAIN GIRLS' SCHOOL.
HENCE-FORTH...
YOU ARE ITS NEWEST STUDENT.
HUH...?

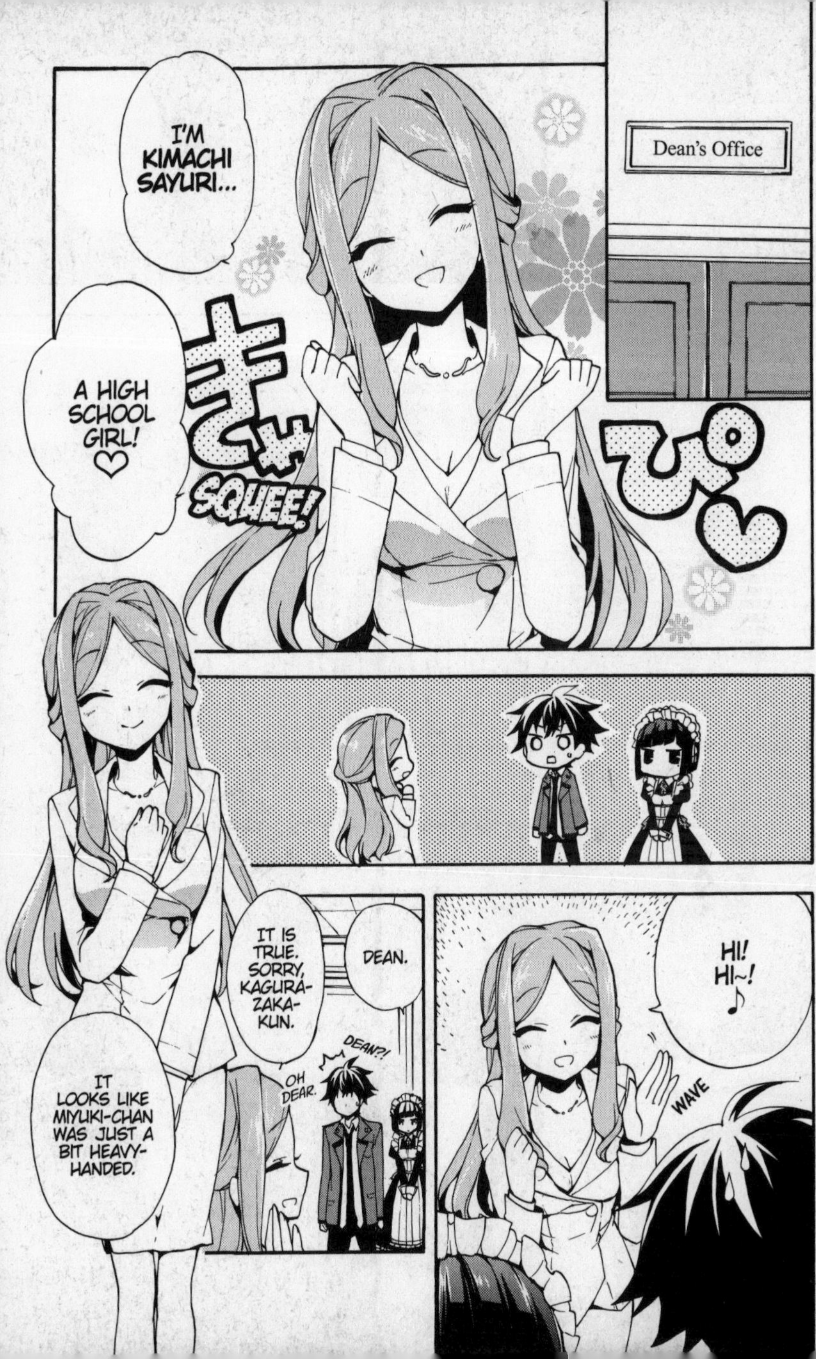
Dean's Office
I'M KIMACHI SAYURI...
A HIGH SCHOOL GIRL! ♡
きゅ
SQUEE!
ぴ
HI! HI~! ♪
WAVE
DEAN.
IT IS TRUE. SORRY, KAGURAZAKA-KUN.
DEAN?!
OH DEAR.
IT LOOKS LIKE MIYUKI-CHAN WAS JUST A BIT HEAVY-HANDED.

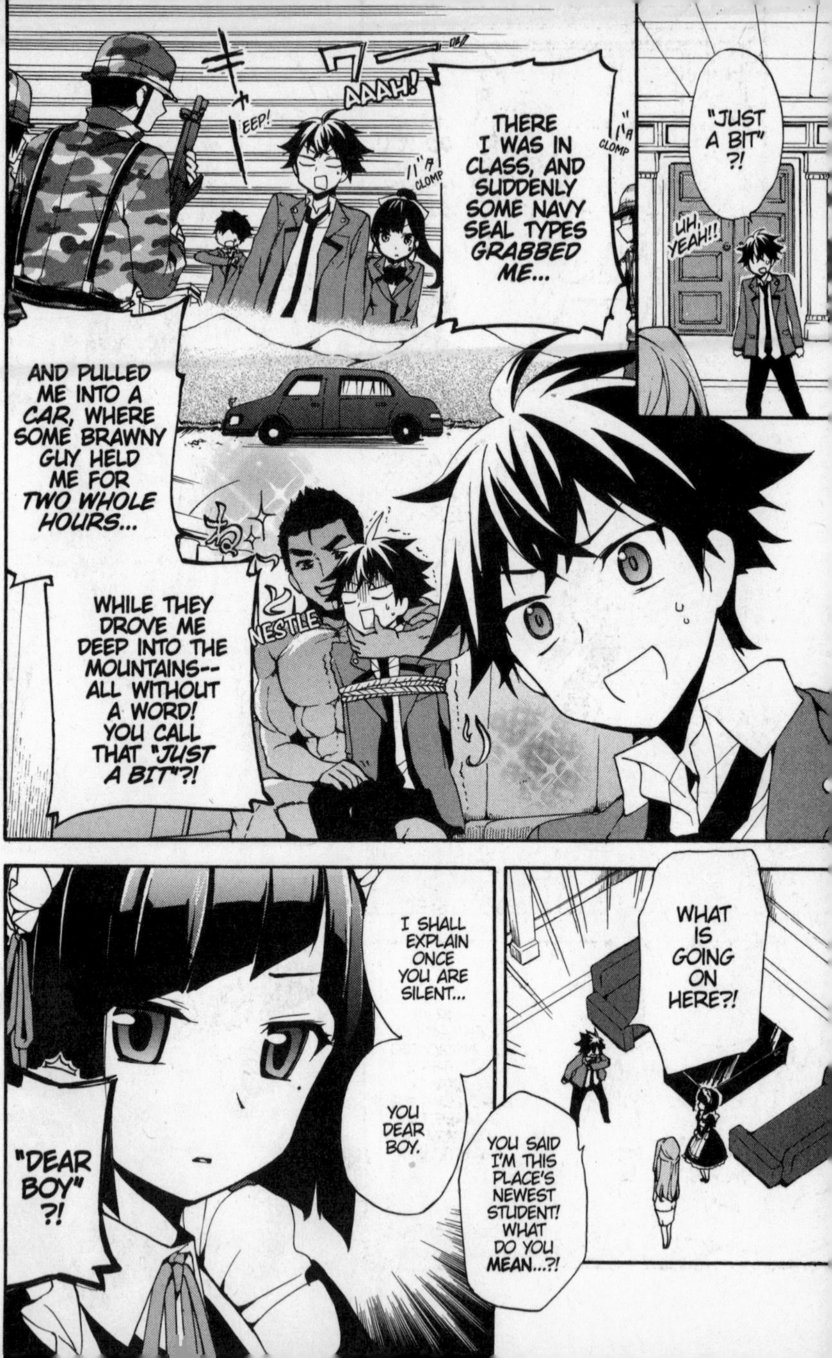
"JUST A BIT"?!
UH, YEAH!!
AAAH!
EEP!
CLOMP
CLOMP
THERE I WAS IN CLASS, AND SUDDENLY SOME NAVY SEAL TYPES GRABBED ME...
AND PULLED ME INTO A CAR, WHERE SOME BRAWNY GUY HELD ME FOR TWO WHOLE HOURS...
NESTLE
WHILE THEY DROVE ME DEEP INTO THE MOUNTAINS--ALL WITHOUT A WORD! YOU CALL THAT "JUST A BIT"?!
WHAT IS GOING ON HERE?!
YOU SAID I'M THIS PLACE'S NEWEST STUDENT! WHAT DO YOU MEAN...?!
I SHALL EXPLAIN ONCE YOU ARE SILENT...
YOU DEAR BOY.
"DEAR BOY"?!

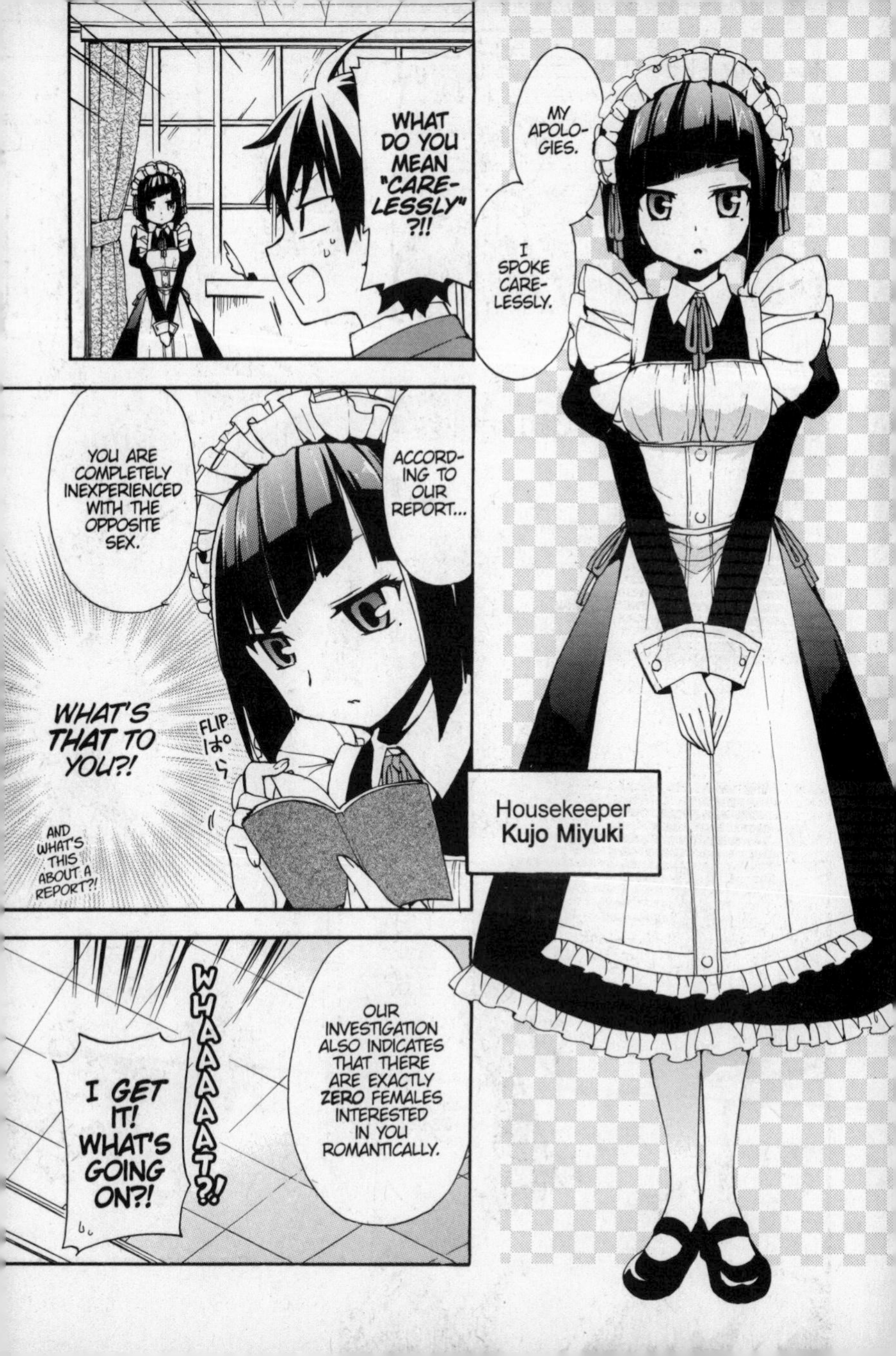
MY APOLOGIES.
I SPOKE CARELESSLY.
Housekeeper Kujo Miyuki
WHAT DO YOU MEAN "CARELESSLY"?!!
ACCORDING TO OUR REPORT...
YOU ARE COMPLETELY INEXPERIENCED WITH THE OPPOSITE SEX.
FLIP ぱら
WHAT'S THAT TO YOU?!
AND WHAT'S THIS ABOUT A REPORT?!
OUR INVESTIGATION ALSO INDICATES THAT THERE ARE EXACTLY ZERO FEMALES INTERESTED IN YOU ROMANTICALLY.
WHAAAAAT?!
I GET IT! WHAT'S GOING ON?!

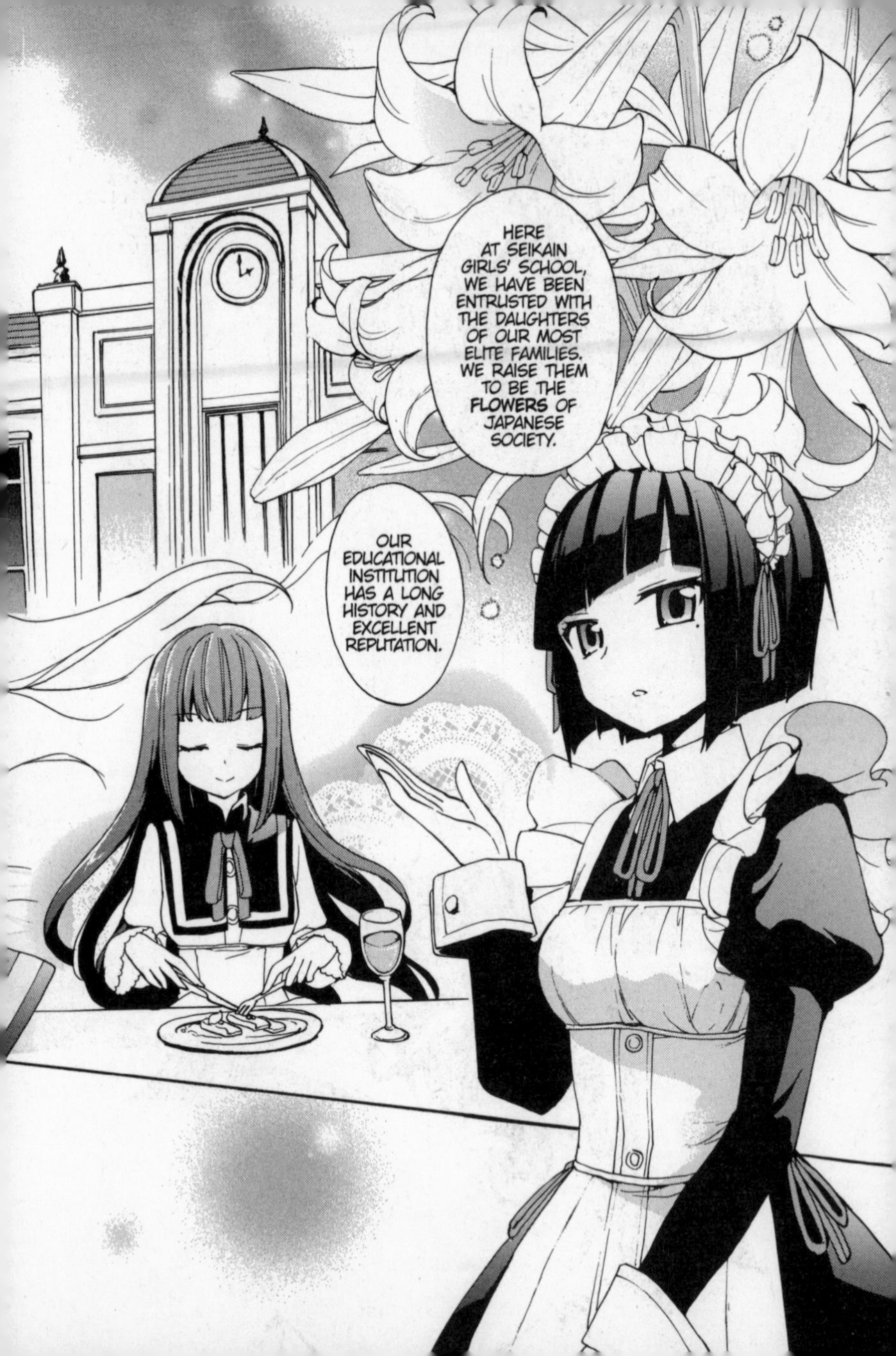
HERE AT SEIKAIN GIRLS' SCHOOL, WE HAVE BEEN ENTRUSTED WITH THE DAUGHTERS OF OUR MOST ELITE FAMILIES. WE RAISE THEM TO BE THE FLOWERS OF JAPANESE SOCIETY.
OUR EDUCATIONAL INSTITUTION HAS A LONG HISTORY AND EXCELLENT REPUTATION.

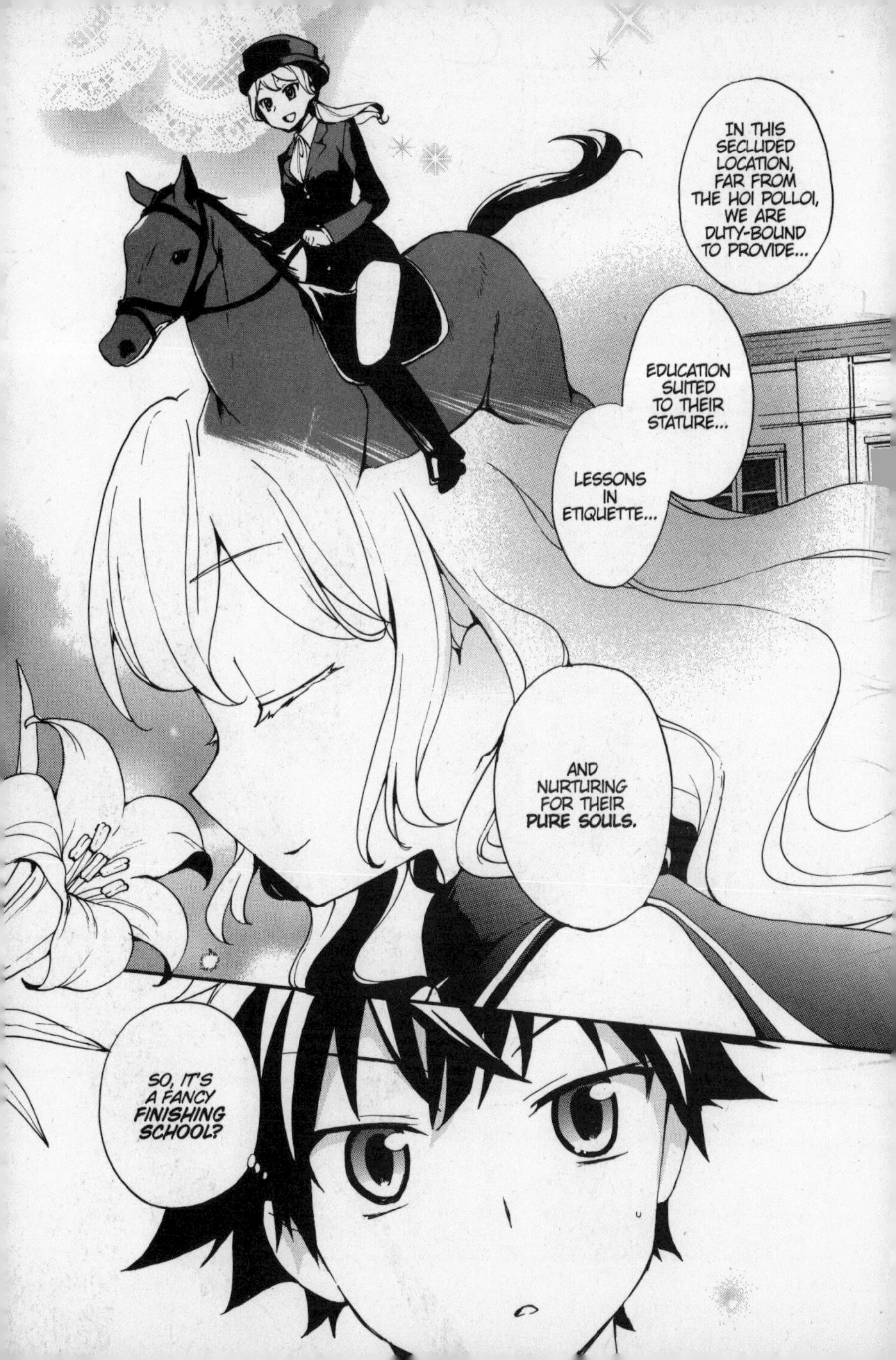
IN THIS SECLUDED LOCATION, FAR FROM THE HOI POLLOI, WE ARE DUTY-BOUND TO PROVIDE...
EDUCATION SUITED TO THEIR STATURE...
LESSONS IN ETIQUETTE...
AND NURTURING FOR THEIR **PURE SOULS.**
SO, IT'S A FANCY ***FINISHING SCHOOL?***

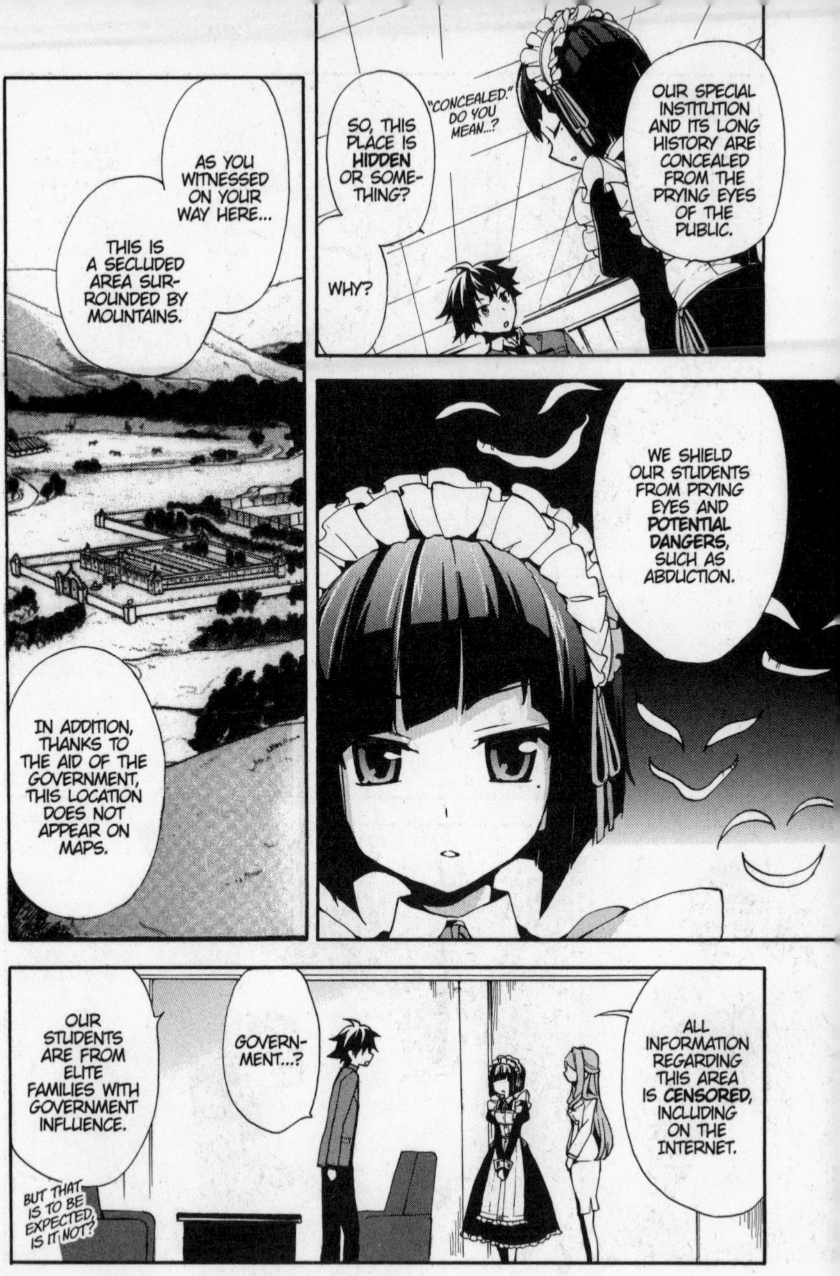
OUR SPECIAL INSTITUTION AND ITS LONG HISTORY ARE CONCEALED FROM THE PRYING EYES OF THE PUBLIC.
"CONCEALED." DO YOU MEAN...?
SO, THIS PLACE IS **HIDDEN** OR SOMETHING?
WHY?
WE SHIELD OUR STUDENTS FROM PRYING EYES AND **POTENTIAL DANGERS,** SUCH AS ABDUCTION.
AS YOU WITNESSED ON YOUR WAY HERE...
THIS IS A SECLUDED AREA SURROUNDED BY MOUNTAINS.
IN ADDITION, THANKS TO THE AID OF THE GOVERNMENT, THIS LOCATION DOES NOT APPEAR ON MAPS.
ALL INFORMATION REGARDING THIS AREA IS **CENSORED,** INCLUDING ON THE INTERNET.
GOVERNMENT...?
OUR STUDENTS ARE FROM ELITE FAMILIES WITH GOVERNMENT INFLUENCE.
BUT THAT IS TO BE EXPECTED, IS IT NOT?

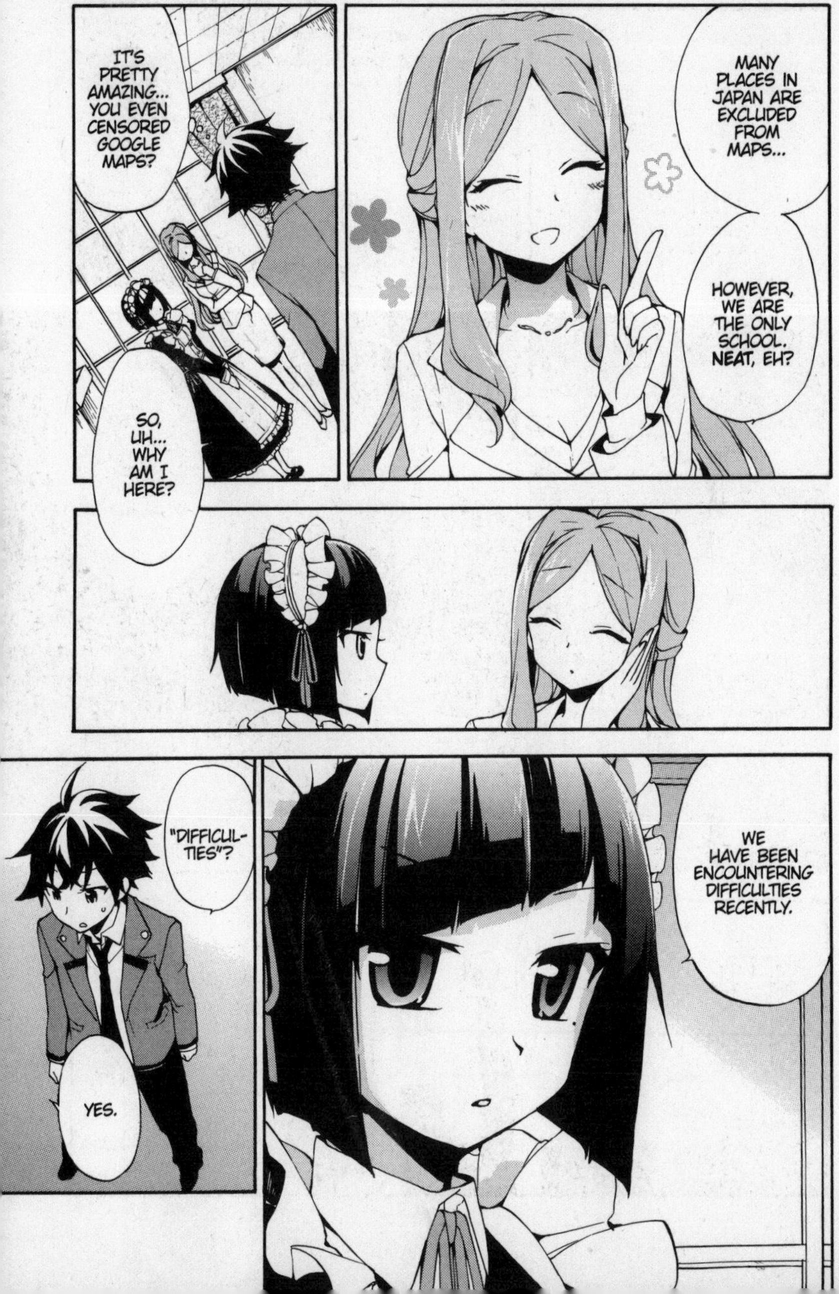
MANY PLACES IN JAPAN ARE EXCLUDED FROM MAPS...
HOWEVER, WE ARE THE ONLY SCHOOL. NEAT, EH?
IT'S PRETTY AMAZING... YOU EVEN CENSORED GOOGLE MAPS?
SO, UH... WHY AM I HERE?
WE HAVE BEEN ENCOUNTERING DIFFICULTIES RECENTLY.
"DIFFICUL-TIES"?
YES.

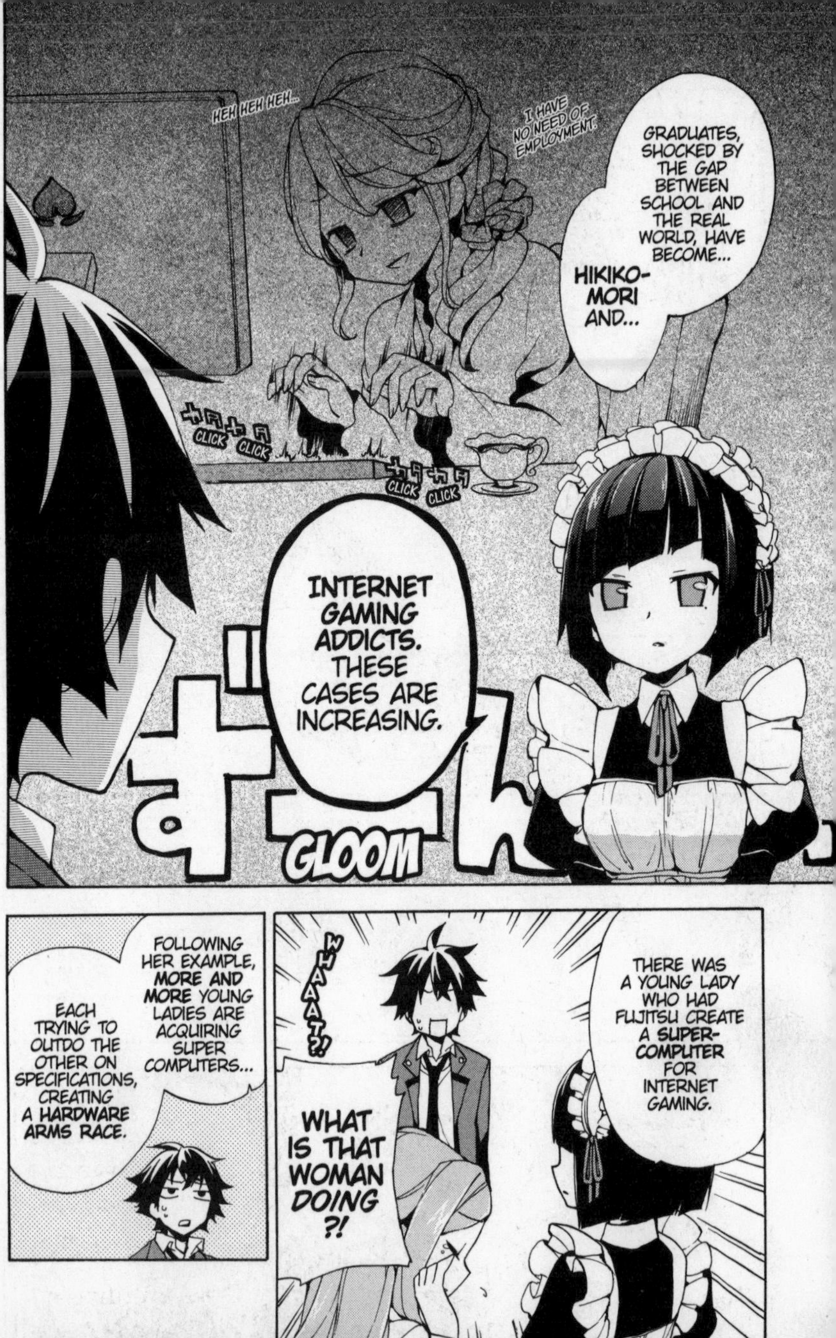
GRADUATES, SHOCKED BY THE GAP BETWEEN SCHOOL AND THE REAL WORLD, HAVE BECOME... HIKIKOMORI AND...
I HAVE NO NEED OF EMPLOYMENT.
HEH HEH HEH...
CLICK CLICK
CLICK CLICK
INTERNET GAMING ADDICTS. THESE CASES ARE INCREASING.
GLOOM
THERE WAS A YOUNG LADY WHO HAD FUJITSU CREATE A SUPER-COMPUTER FOR INTERNET GAMING.
WHAAAT?!
WHAT IS THAT WOMAN DOING?!
FOLLOWING HER EXAMPLE, MORE AND MORE YOUNG LADIES ARE ACQUIRING SUPER COMPUTERS...
EACH TRYING TO OUTDO THE OTHER ON SPECIFICATIONS, CREATING A HARDWARE ARMS RACE.

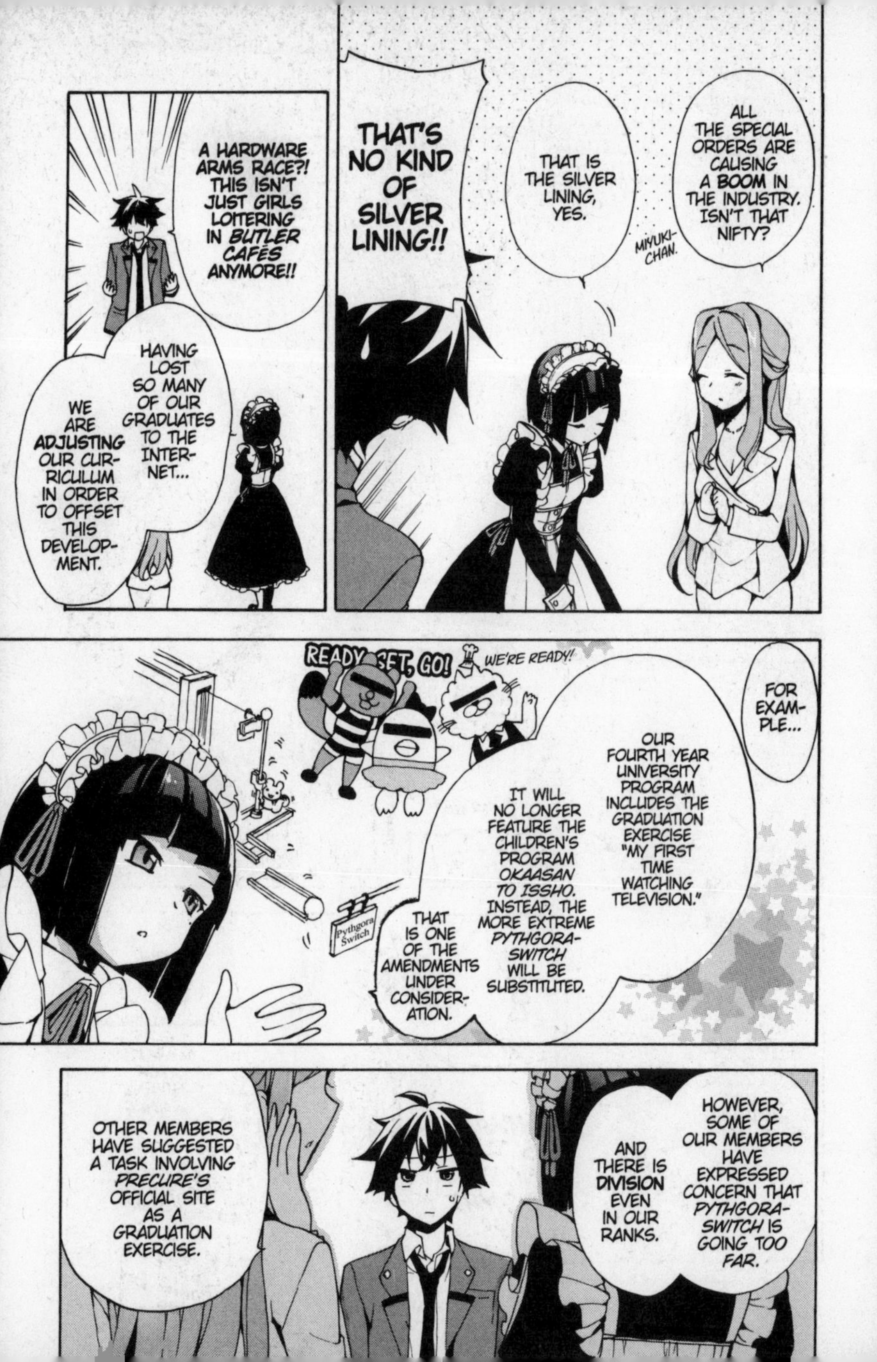
ALL THE SPECIAL ORDERS ARE CAUSING A BOOM IN THE INDUSTRY. ISN'T THAT NIFTY?
MIYUKI-CHAN.
THAT IS THE SILVER LINING, YES.
THAT'S NO KIND OF SILVER LINING!!
A HARDWARE ARMS RACE?! THIS ISN'T JUST GIRLS LOITERING IN *BUTLER CAFÉS* ANYMORE!!
HAVING LOST SO MANY OF OUR GRADUATES TO THE INTER-NET...
WE ARE **ADJUSTING** OUR CUR-RICULUM IN ORDER TO OFFSET THIS DEVELOP-MENT.
FOR EXAM-PLE...
OUR FOURTH YEAR UNIVERSITY PROGRAM INCLUDES THE GRADUATION EXERCISE "MY FIRST TIME WATCHING TELEVISION."
IT WILL NO LONGER FEATURE THE CHILDREN'S PROGRAM *OKAASAN TO ISSHO*. INSTEAD, THE MORE EXTREME *PYTHGORA-SWITCH* WILL BE SUBSTITUTED.
THAT IS ONE OF THE AMENDMENTS UNDER CONSIDER-ATION.
WE'RE READY!
READY SET, GO!
Pythgora Switch
HOWEVER, SOME OF OUR MEMBERS HAVE EXPRESSED CONCERN THAT *PYTHGORA-SWITCH* IS GOING TOO FAR.
AND THERE IS **DIVISION** EVEN IN OUR RANKS.
OTHER MEMBERS HAVE SUGGESTED A TASK INVOLVING *PRECURE'S* OFFICIAL SITE AS A GRADUATION EXERCISE.

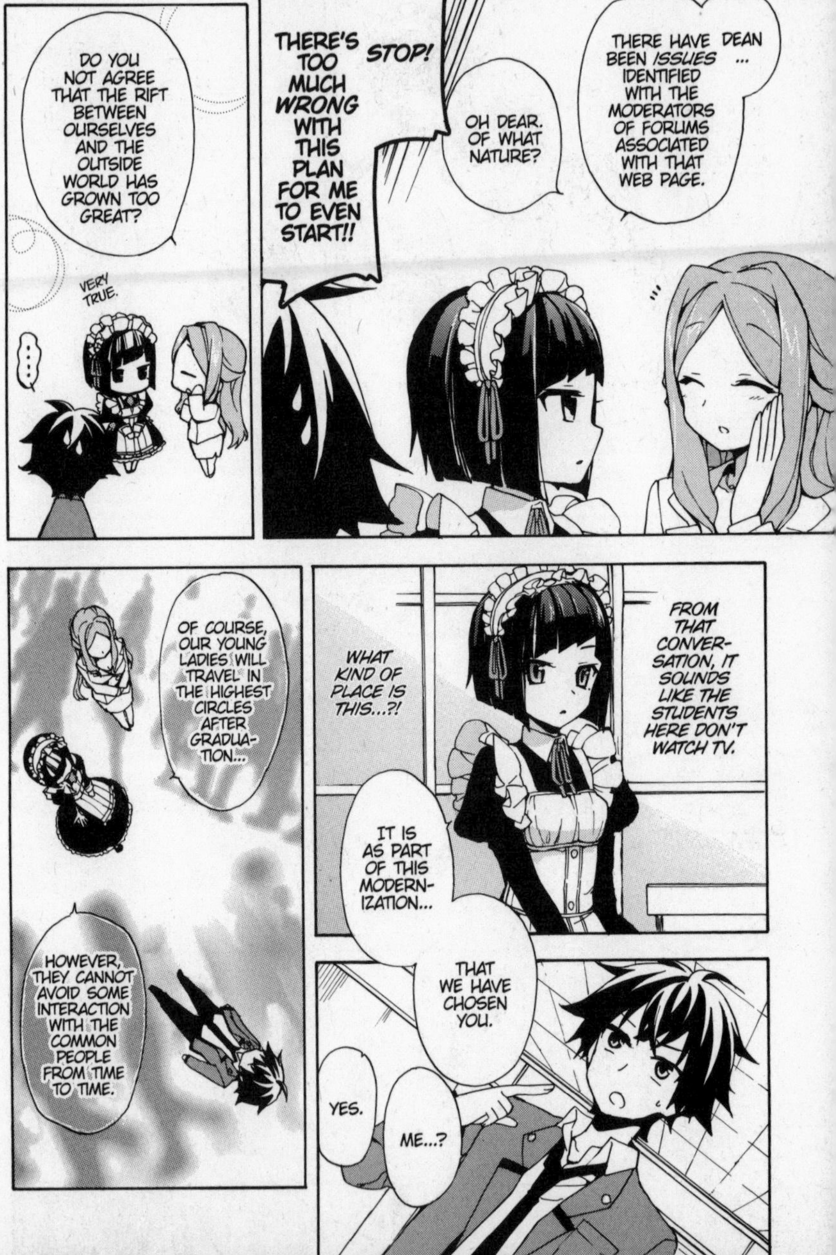
DEAN ...
THERE HAVE BEEN *ISSUES* IDENTIFIED WITH THE MODERATORS OF FORUMS ASSOCIATED WITH THAT WEB PAGE.
OH DEAR. OF WHAT NATURE?
STOP!
THERE'S TOO MUCH *WRONG* WITH THIS PLAN FOR ME TO EVEN START!!
DO YOU NOT AGREE THAT THE RIFT BETWEEN OURSELVES AND THE OUTSIDE WORLD HAS GROWN TOO GREAT?
VERY TRUE.
...
FROM THAT CONVERSATION, IT SOUNDS LIKE THE STUDENTS HERE DON'T WATCH TV.
WHAT KIND OF PLACE IS THIS...?!
OF COURSE, OUR YOUNG LADIES WILL TRAVEL IN THE HIGHEST CIRCLES AFTER GRADUATION...
HOWEVER, THEY CANNOT AVOID SOME INTERACTION WITH THE COMMON PEOPLE FROM TIME TO TIME.
IT IS AS PART OF THIS MODERNIZATION...
THAT WE HAVE CHOSEN YOU.
ME...?
YES.

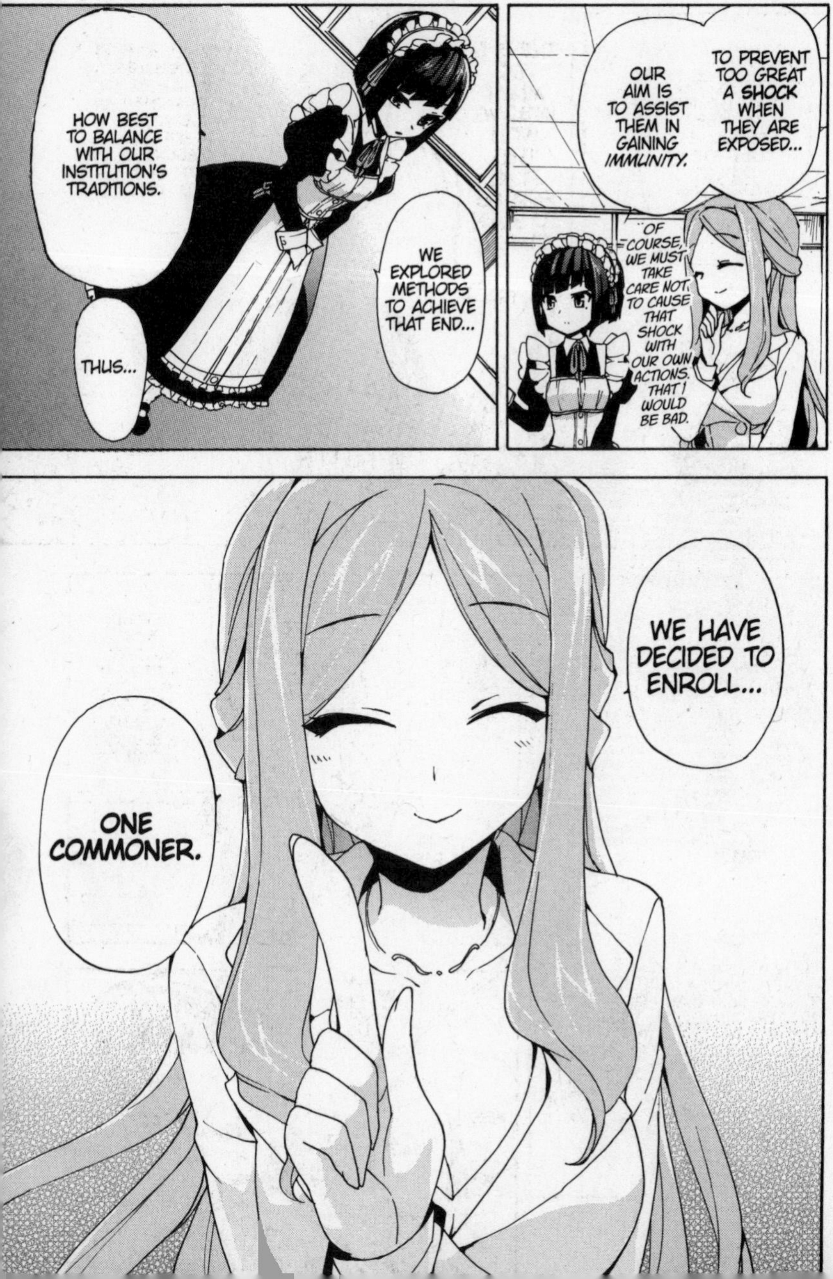

TO PREVENT TOO GREAT A SHOCK WHEN THEY ARE EXPOSED...
OUR AIM IS TO ASSIST THEM IN GAINING *IMMUNITY*.
OF COURSE, WE MUST TAKE CARE NOT TO CAUSE THAT SHOCK WITH OUR OWN ACTIONS. THAT WOULD BE BAD.
WE EXPLORED METHODS TO ACHIEVE THAT END...
HOW BEST TO BALANCE WITH OUR INSTITUTION'S TRADITIONS.
THUS...
WE HAVE DECIDED TO ENROLL...
ONE COMMONER.

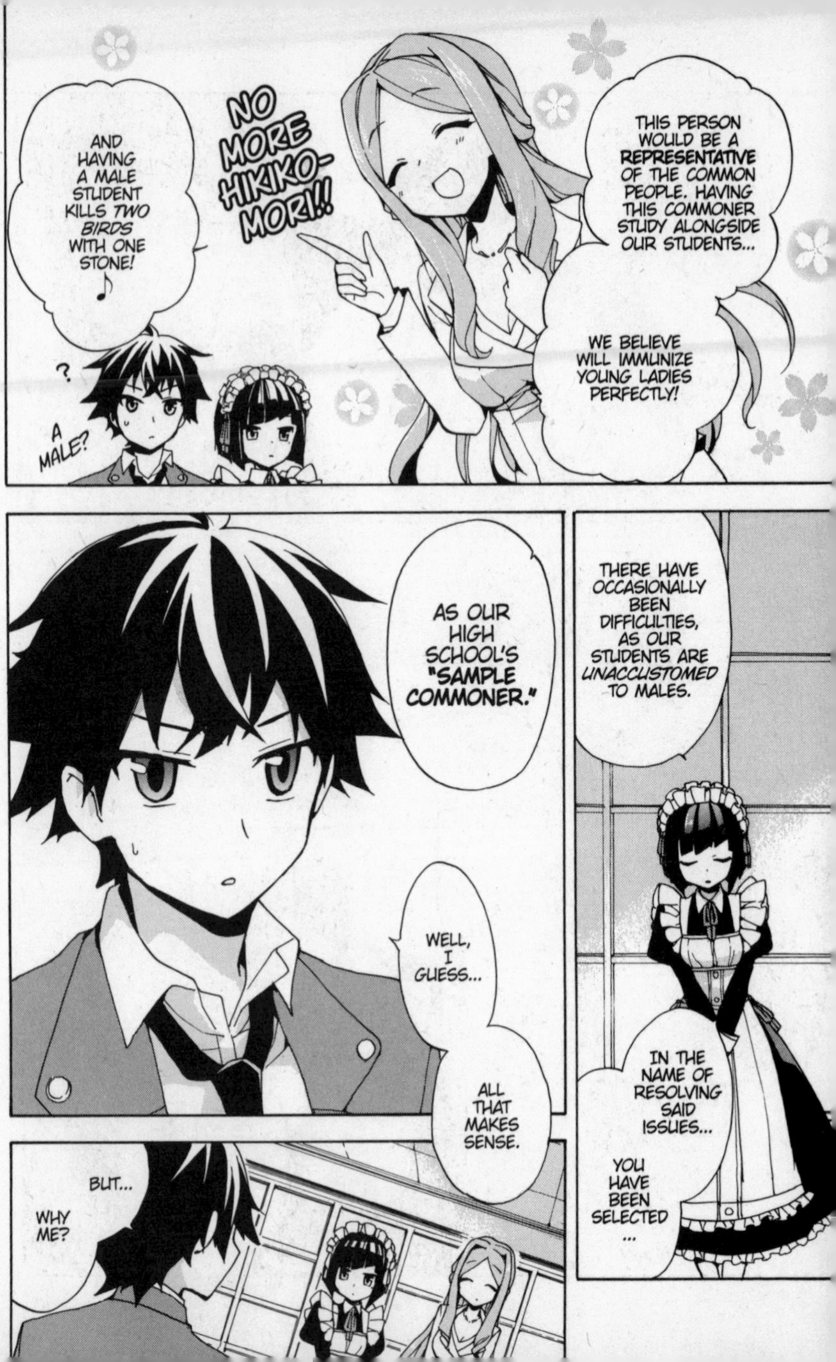
THIS PERSON WOULD BE A **REPRESENTATIVE** OF THE COMMON PEOPLE. HAVING THIS COMMONER STUDY ALONGSIDE OUR STUDENTS...
WE BELIEVE WILL IMMUNIZE YOUNG LADIES PERFECTLY!
NO MORE HIKIKOMORI!!
AND HAVING A MALE STUDENT KILLS *TWO BIRDS* WITH ONE STONE! ♪
?
A MALE?
THERE HAVE OCCASIONALLY BEEN DIFFICULTIES, AS OUR STUDENTS ARE *UNACCUSTOMED* TO MALES.
IN THE NAME OF RESOLVING SAID ISSUES...
YOU HAVE BEEN SELECTED ...
AS OUR HIGH SCHOOL'S **"SAMPLE COMMONER."**
WELL, I GUESS...
ALL THAT MAKES SENSE.
BUT...
WHY ME?

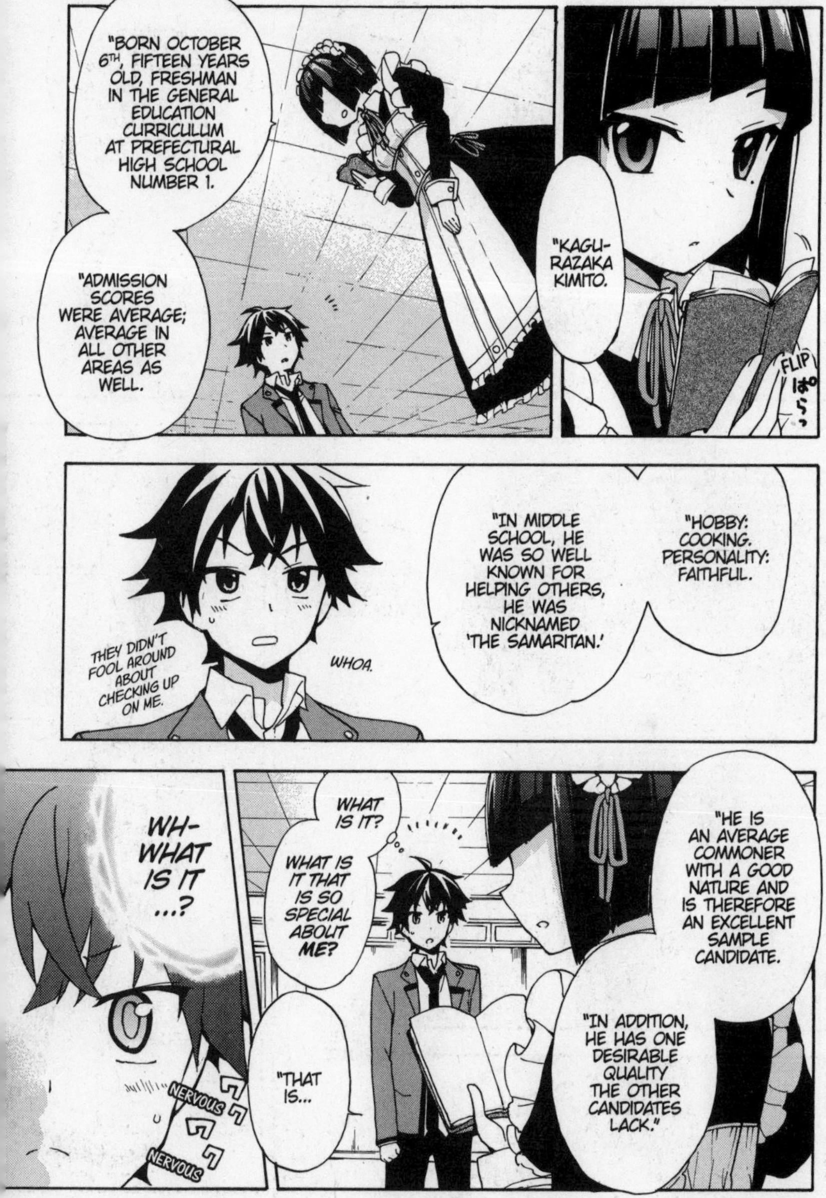
"KAGURAZAKA KIMITO.
FLIP
ぱらっ
"BORN OCTOBER 6TH, FIFTEEN YEARS OLD, FRESHMAN IN THE GENERAL EDUCATION CURRICULUM AT PREFECTURAL HIGH SCHOOL NUMBER 1.
"ADMISSION SCORES WERE AVERAGE; AVERAGE IN ALL OTHER AREAS AS WELL.
"HOBBY: COOKING. PERSONALITY: FAITHFUL.
"IN MIDDLE SCHOOL, HE WAS SO WELL KNOWN FOR HELPING OTHERS, HE WAS NICKNAMED 'THE SAMARITAN.'
WHOA.
THEY DIDN'T FOOL AROUND ABOUT CHECKING UP ON ME.
"HE IS AN AVERAGE COMMONER WITH A GOOD NATURE AND IS THEREFORE AN EXCELLENT SAMPLE CANDIDATE.
"IN ADDITION, HE HAS ONE DESIRABLE QUALITY THE OTHER CANDIDATES LACK."
WHAT IS IT?
WHAT IS IT THAT IS SO SPECIAL ABOUT ME?
"THAT IS...
WH-WHAT IS IT ...?
NERVOUS
NERVOUS

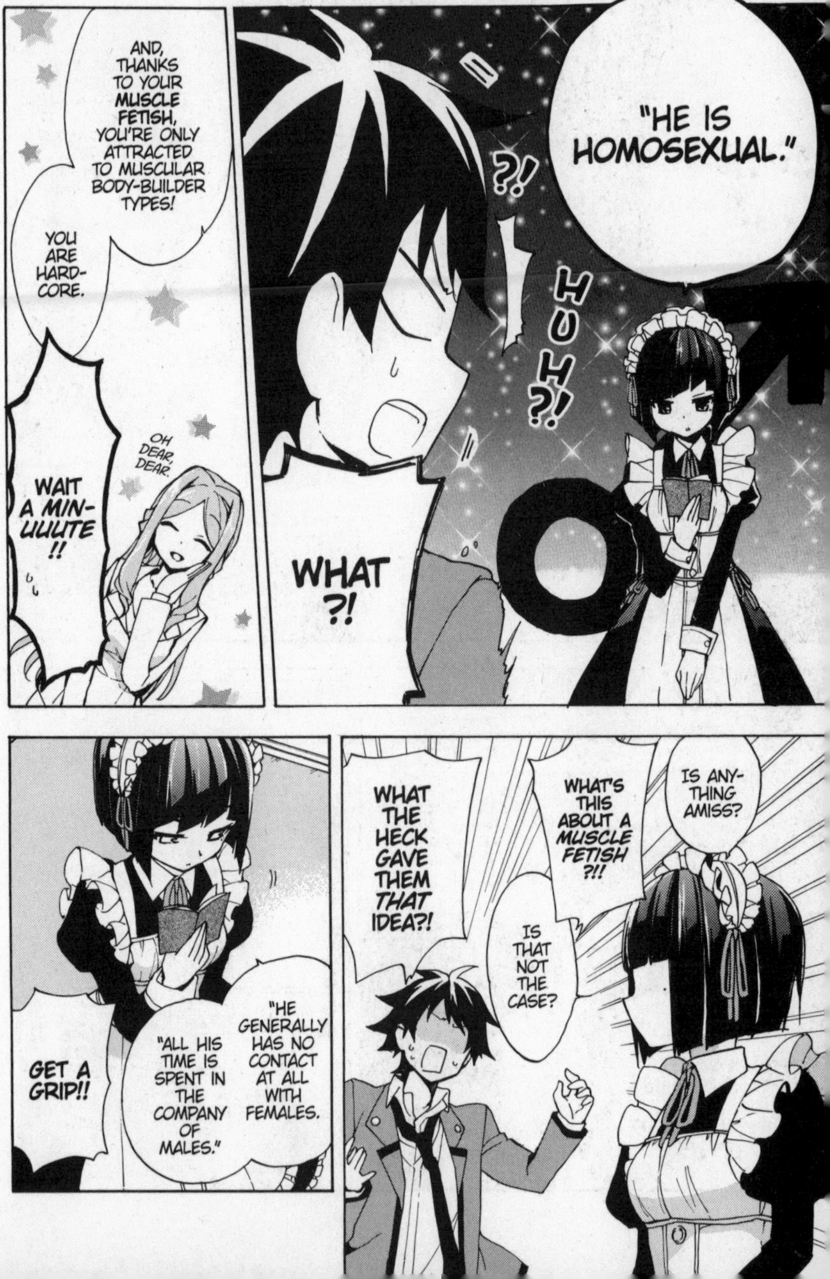

"HE IS HOMOSEXUAL."
HUH?!
?!
WHAT?!
AND, THANKS TO YOUR MUSCLE FETISH, YOU'RE ONLY ATTRACTED TO MUSCULAR BODY-BUILDER TYPES!
YOU ARE HARD-CORE.
OH DEAR, DEAR.
WAIT A MIN-UUUTE!!
IS ANY-THING AMISS?
WHAT'S THIS ABOUT A MUSCLE FETISH?!!
WHAT THE HECK GAVE THEM THAT IDEA?!
IS THAT NOT THE CASE?
"HE GENERALLY HAS NO CONTACT AT ALL WITH FEMALES.
"ALL HIS TIME IS SPENT IN THE COMPANY OF MALES."
GET A GRIP!!

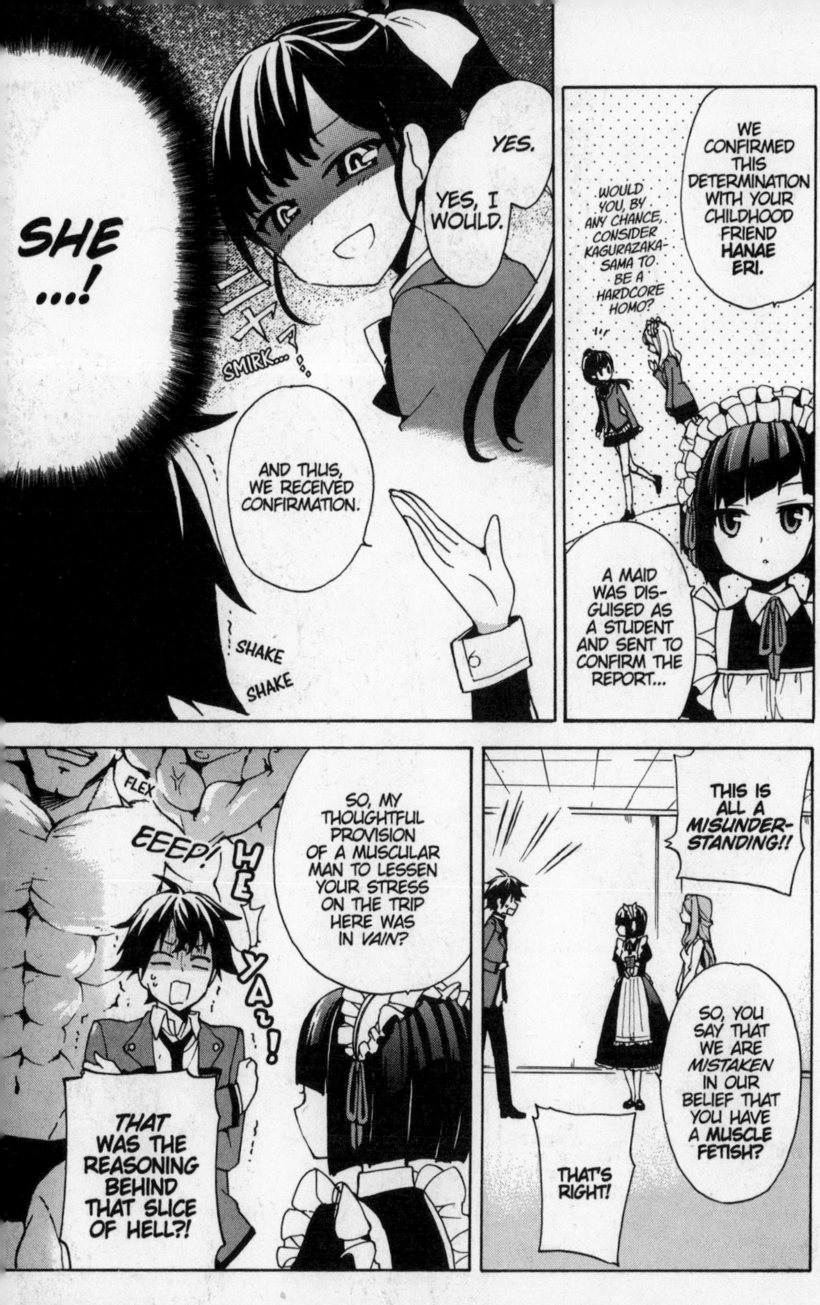
WE CONFIRMED THIS DETERMINATION WITH YOUR CHILDHOOD FRIEND HANAE ERI.
WOULD YOU, BY ANY CHANCE, CONSIDER KAGURAZAKA-SAMA TO BE A HARDCORE HOMO?
A MAID WAS DIS-GUISED AS A STUDENT AND SENT TO CONFIRM THE REPORT...
YES.
YES, I WOULD.
SMIRK...
SHE ...!
AND THUS, WE RECEIVED CONFIRMATION.
SHAKE
SHAKE
THIS IS ALL A MISUNDER-STANDING!!
SO, YOU SAY THAT WE ARE MISTAKEN IN OUR BELIEF THAT YOU HAVE A MUSCLE FETISH?
THAT'S RIGHT!
SO, MY THOUGHTFUL PROVISION OF A MUSCULAR MAN TO LESSEN YOUR STRESS ON THE TRIP HERE WAS IN VAIN?
FLEX
EEEP!
HEYA~!
THAT WAS THE REASONING BEHIND THAT SLICE OF HELL?!

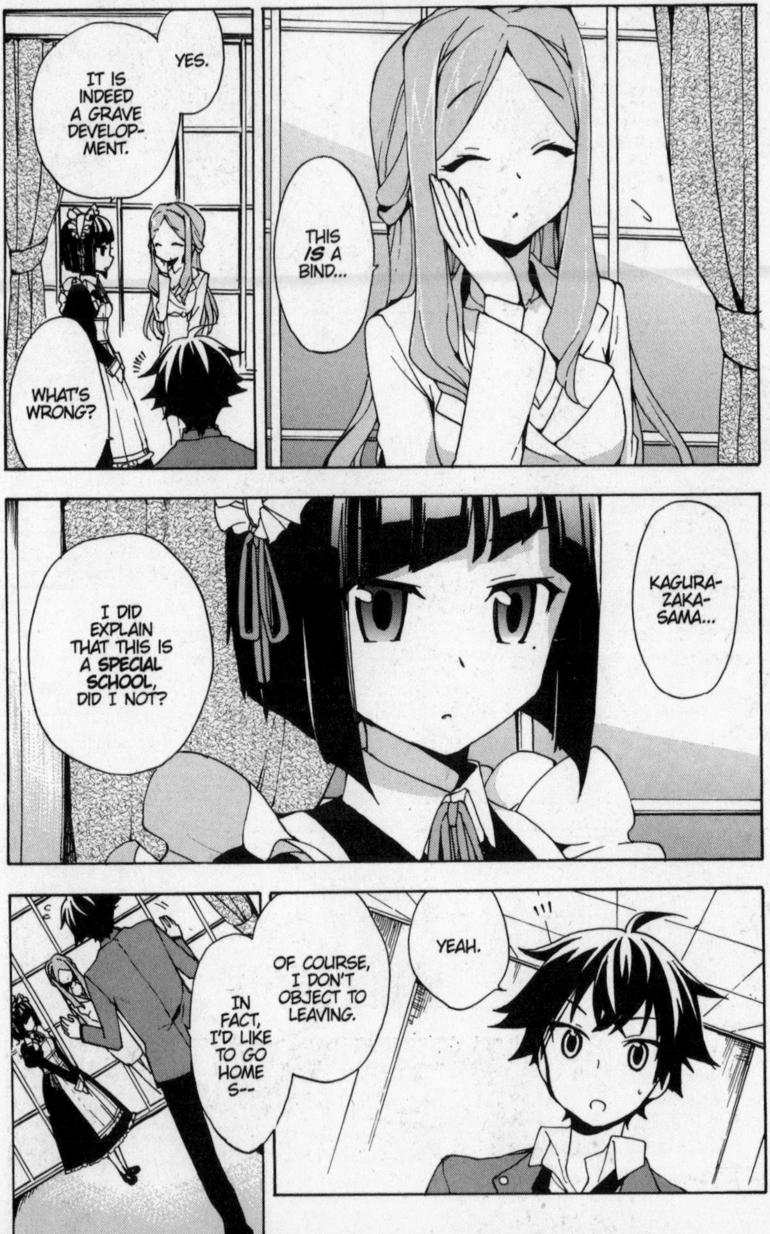
THIS *IS* A BIND...
YES.
IT IS INDEED A GRAVE DEVELOPMENT.
WHAT'S WRONG?
KAGURAZAKA-SAMA...
I DID EXPLAIN THAT THIS IS A SPECIAL SCHOOL, DID I NOT?
YEAH.
OF COURSE, I DON'T OBJECT TO LEAVING.
IN FACT, I'D LIKE TO GO HOME S--

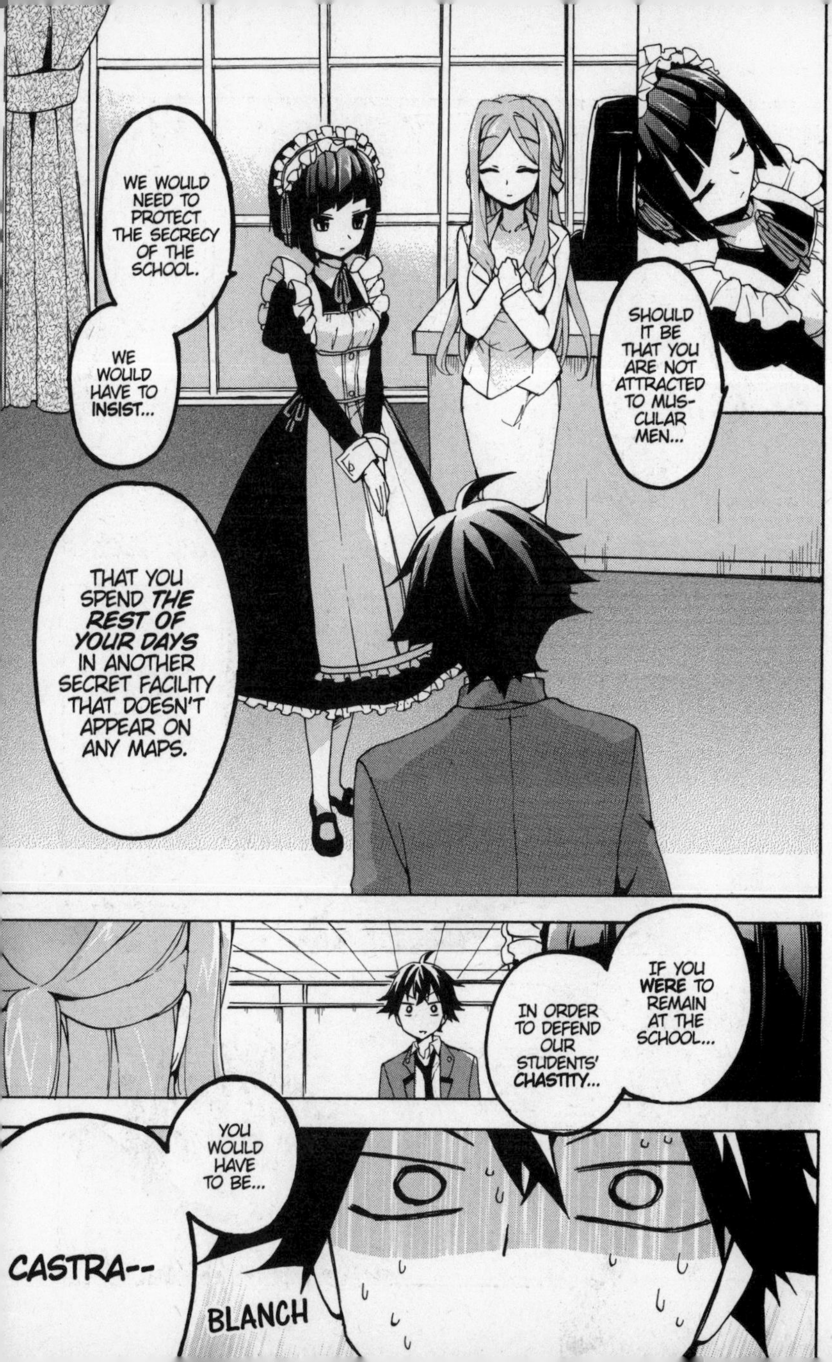
SHOULD IT BE THAT YOU ARE NOT ATTRACTED TO MUS-CULAR MEN...
WE WOULD NEED TO PROTECT THE SECRECY OF THE SCHOOL.
WE WOULD HAVE TO INSIST...
THAT YOU SPEND *THE REST OF YOUR DAYS* IN ANOTHER SECRET FACILITY THAT DOESN'T APPEAR ON ANY MAPS.
IF YOU **WERE** TO REMAIN AT THE SCHOOL...
IN ORDER TO DEFEND OUR STUDENTS' **CHASTITY**...
YOU WOULD HAVE TO BE...
CASTRA--
BLANCH

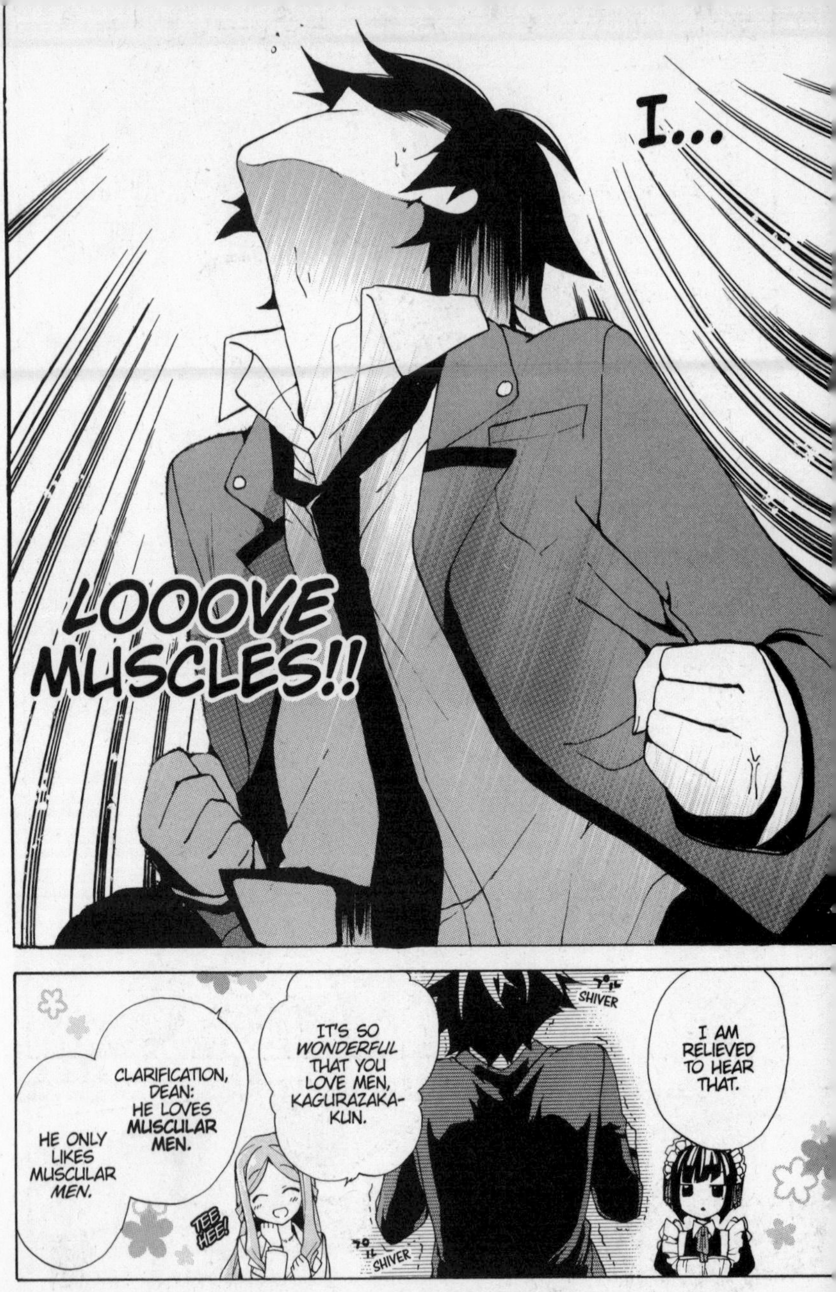
I...
LOOOVE MUSCLES!!
SHIVER
I AM RELIEVED TO HEAR THAT.
IT'S SO *WONDERFUL* THAT YOU LOVE MEN, KAGURAZAKA-KUN.
CLARIFICATION, DEAN: HE LOVES **MUSCULAR** MEN.
HE ONLY LIKES MUSCULAR *MEN*.
TEE HEE!
SHIVER

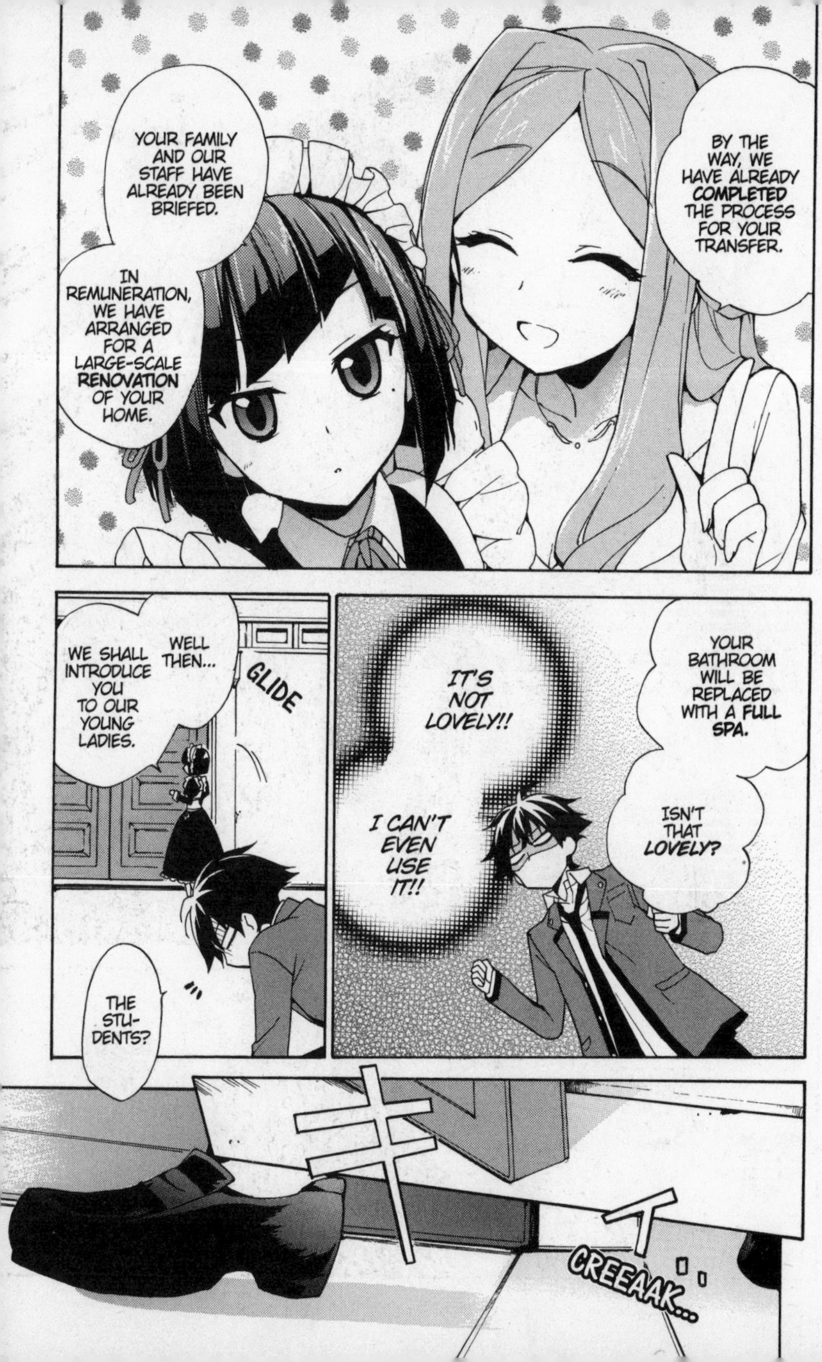
BY THE WAY, WE HAVE ALREADY **COMPLETED** THE PROCESS FOR YOUR TRANSFER.
YOUR FAMILY AND OUR STAFF HAVE ALREADY BEEN BRIEFED.
IN REMUNERATION, WE HAVE ARRANGED FOR A LARGE-SCALE **RENOVATION** OF YOUR HOME.
YOUR BATHROOM WILL BE REPLACED WITH A **FULL SPA.**
ISN'T THAT ***LOVELY?***
IT'S NOT LOVELY!!
I CAN'T EVEN USE IT!!
WELL THEN...
WE SHALL INTRODUCE YOU TO OUR YOUNG LADIES.
GLIDE
THE STU-DENTS?
CREEAAK...

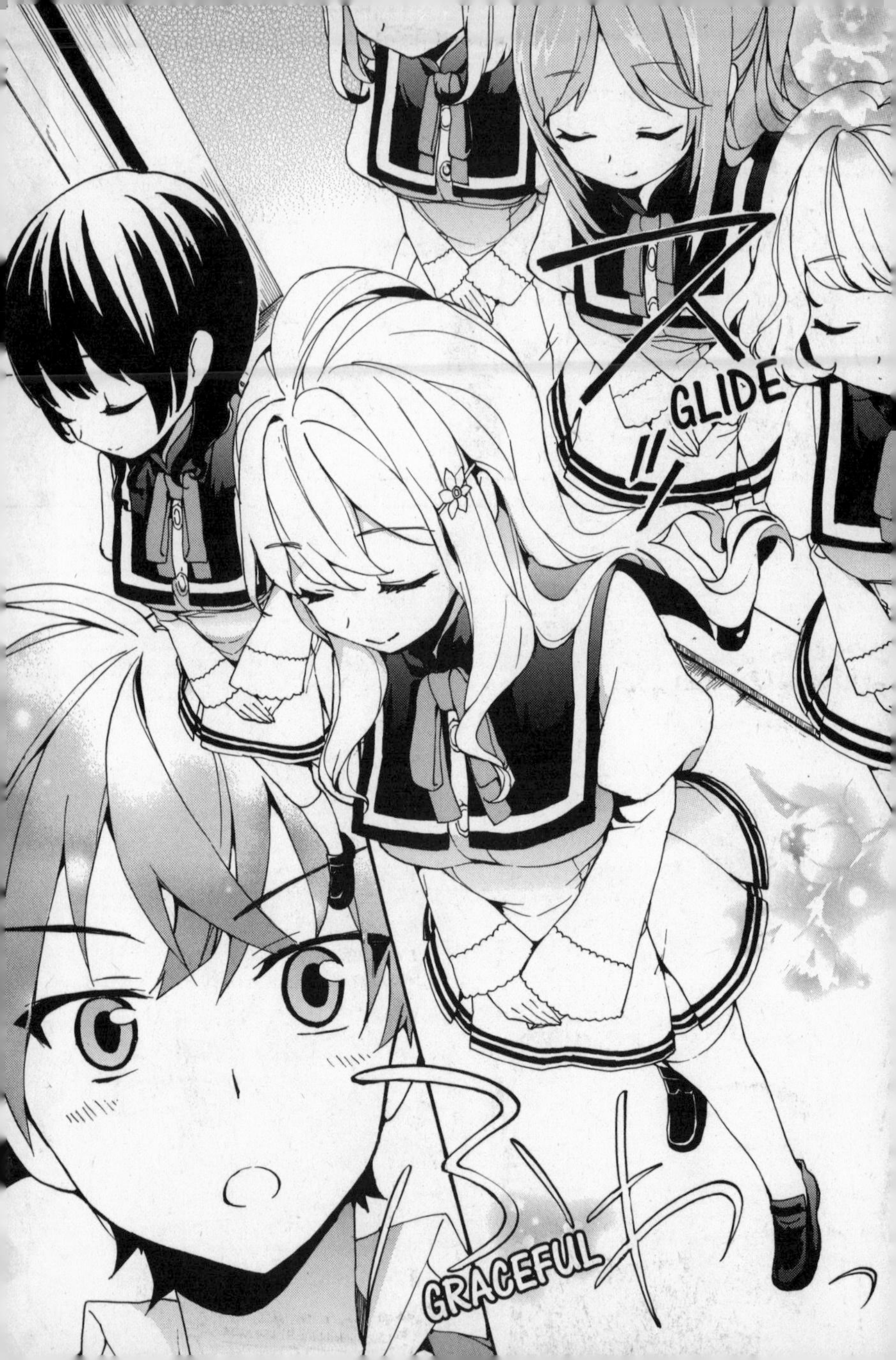
GLIDE
GRACEFUL

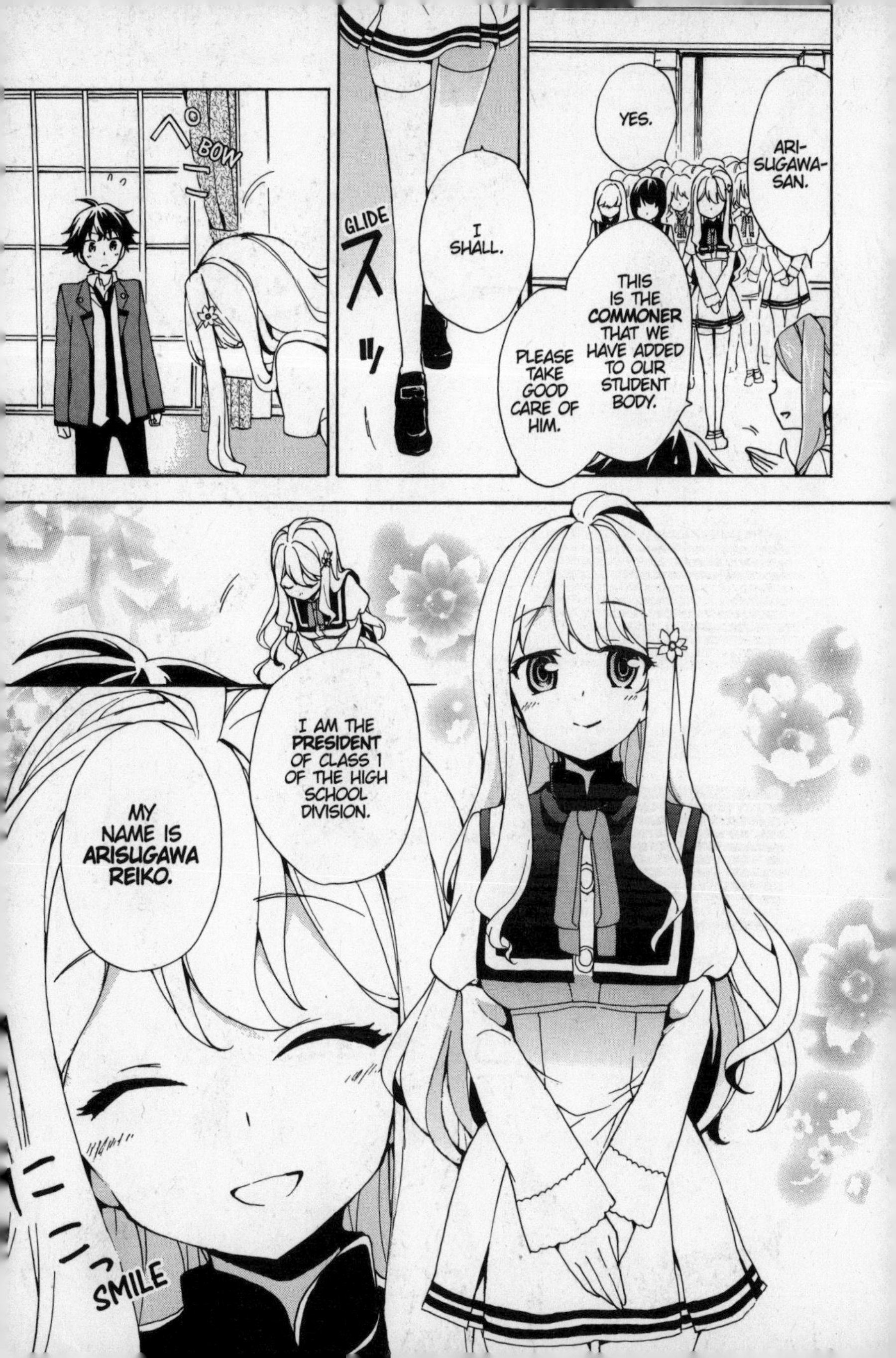
ARI-SUGAWA-SAN.
YES.
THIS IS THE COMMONER THAT WE HAVE ADDED TO OUR STUDENT BODY.
PLEASE TAKE GOOD CARE OF HIM.
I SHALL.
GLIDE
BOW
I AM THE PRESIDENT OF CLASS 1 OF THE HIGH SCHOOL DIVISION.
MY NAME IS ARISUGAWA REIKO.
SMILE

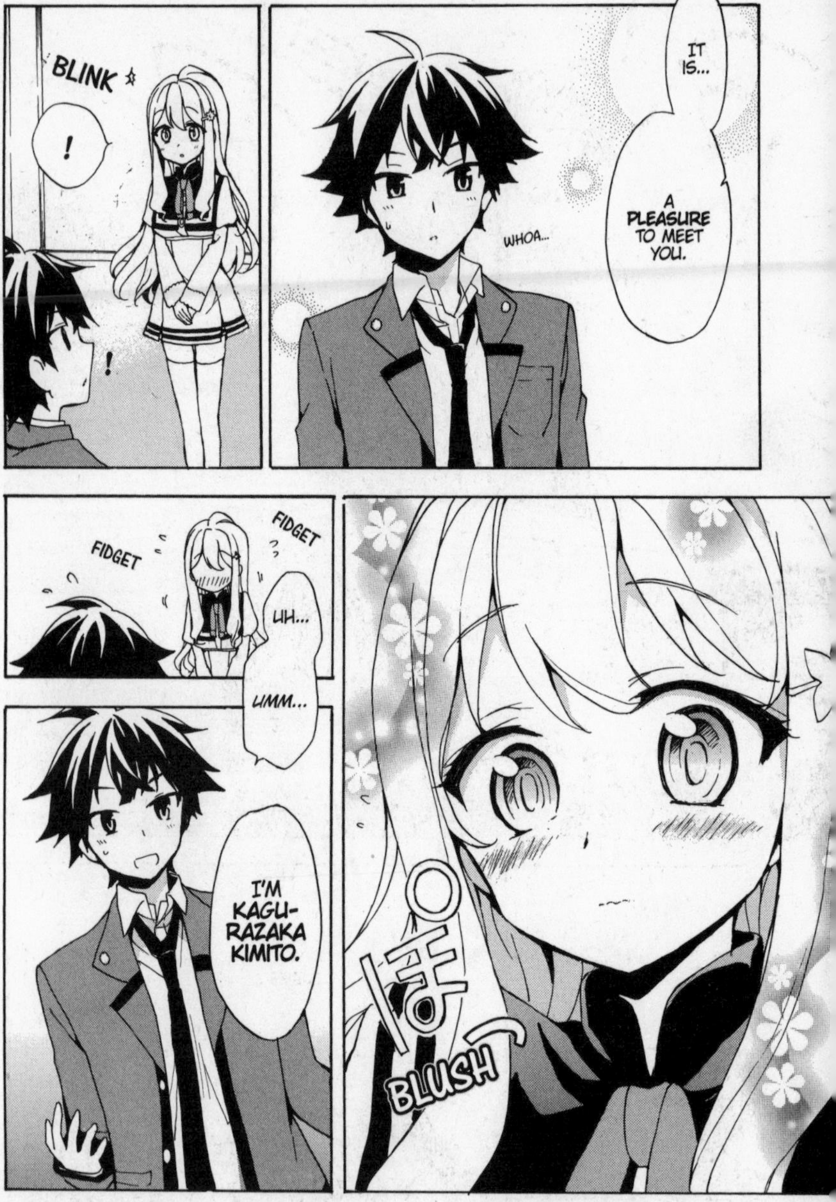
IT IS...
A PLEASURE TO MEET YOU.
WHOA...
BLINK
!
!
ぽっ
BLUSH
FIDGET
FIDGET
UH...
UMM...
I'M KAGURAZAKA KIMITO.

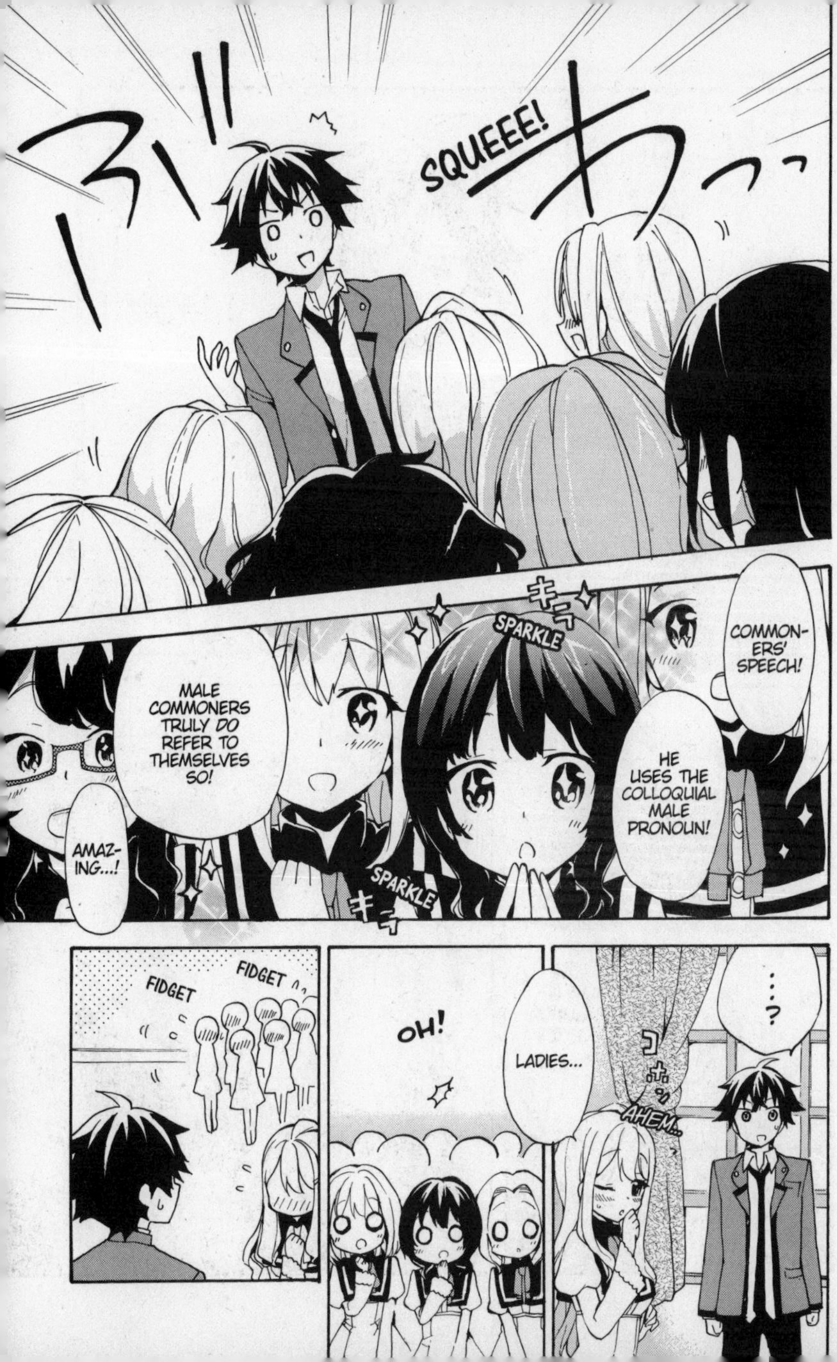
SQUEEE!
COMMONERS' SPEECH!
HE USES THE COLLOQUIAL MALE PRONOUN!
SPARKLE
SPARKLE
MALE COMMONERS TRULY *DO* REFER TO THEMSELVES SO!
AMAZING...!
...?
AHEM...
LADIES...
OH!
FIDGET
FIDGET

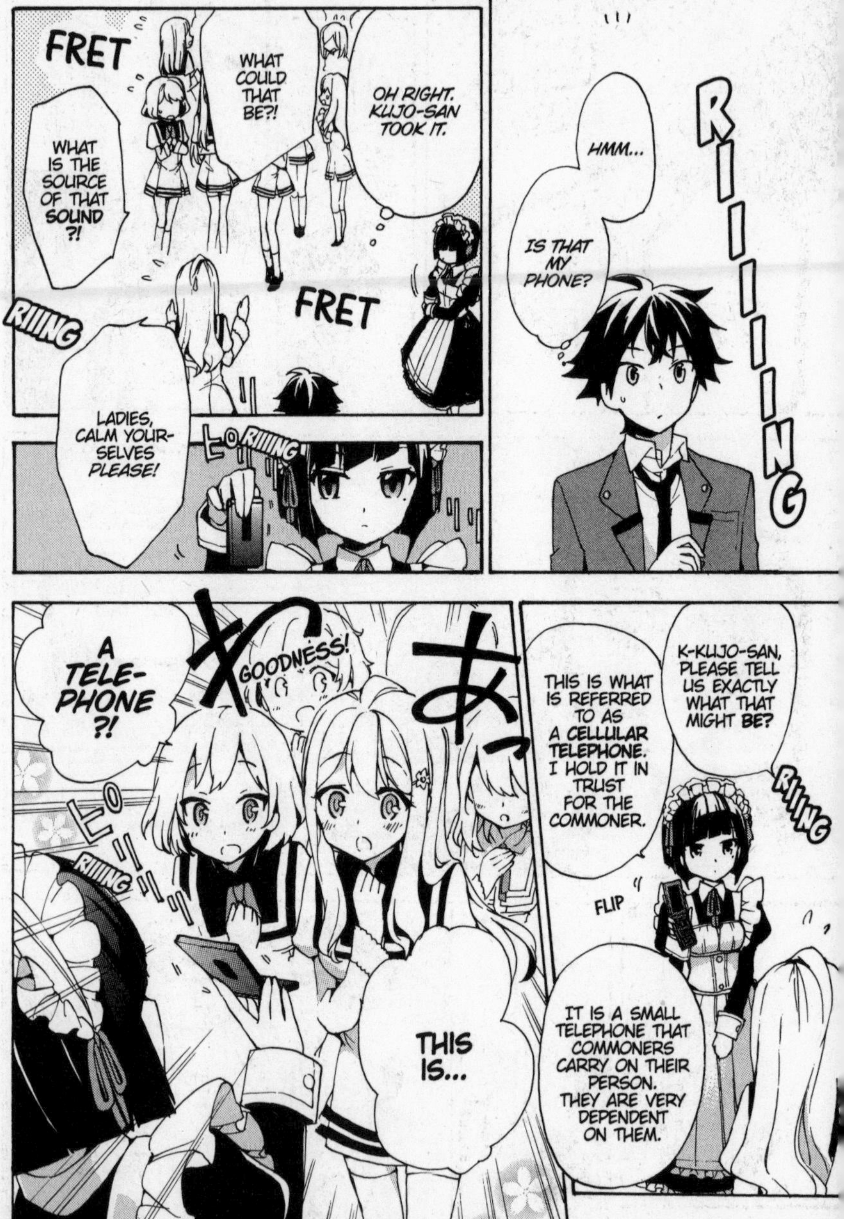

RIIIIIIING
HMM...
IS THAT MY PHONE?
OH RIGHT. KUJO-SAN TOOK IT.
WHAT COULD THAT BE?!
FRET
WHAT IS THE SOURCE OF THAT SOUND?!
FRET
RIIING
RIIING
LADIES, CALM YOURSELVES PLEASE!
K-KUJO-SAN, PLEASE TELL US EXACTLY WHAT THAT MIGHT BE?
RIIING
THIS IS WHAT IS REFERRED TO AS A CELLULAR TELEPHONE. I HOLD IT IN TRUST FOR THE COMMONER.
FLIP
IT IS A SMALL TELEPHONE THAT COMMONERS CARRY ON THEIR PERSON. THEY ARE VERY DEPENDENT ON THEM.
あっ
GOODNESS!
A TELEPHONE?!
RIIING
THIS IS...

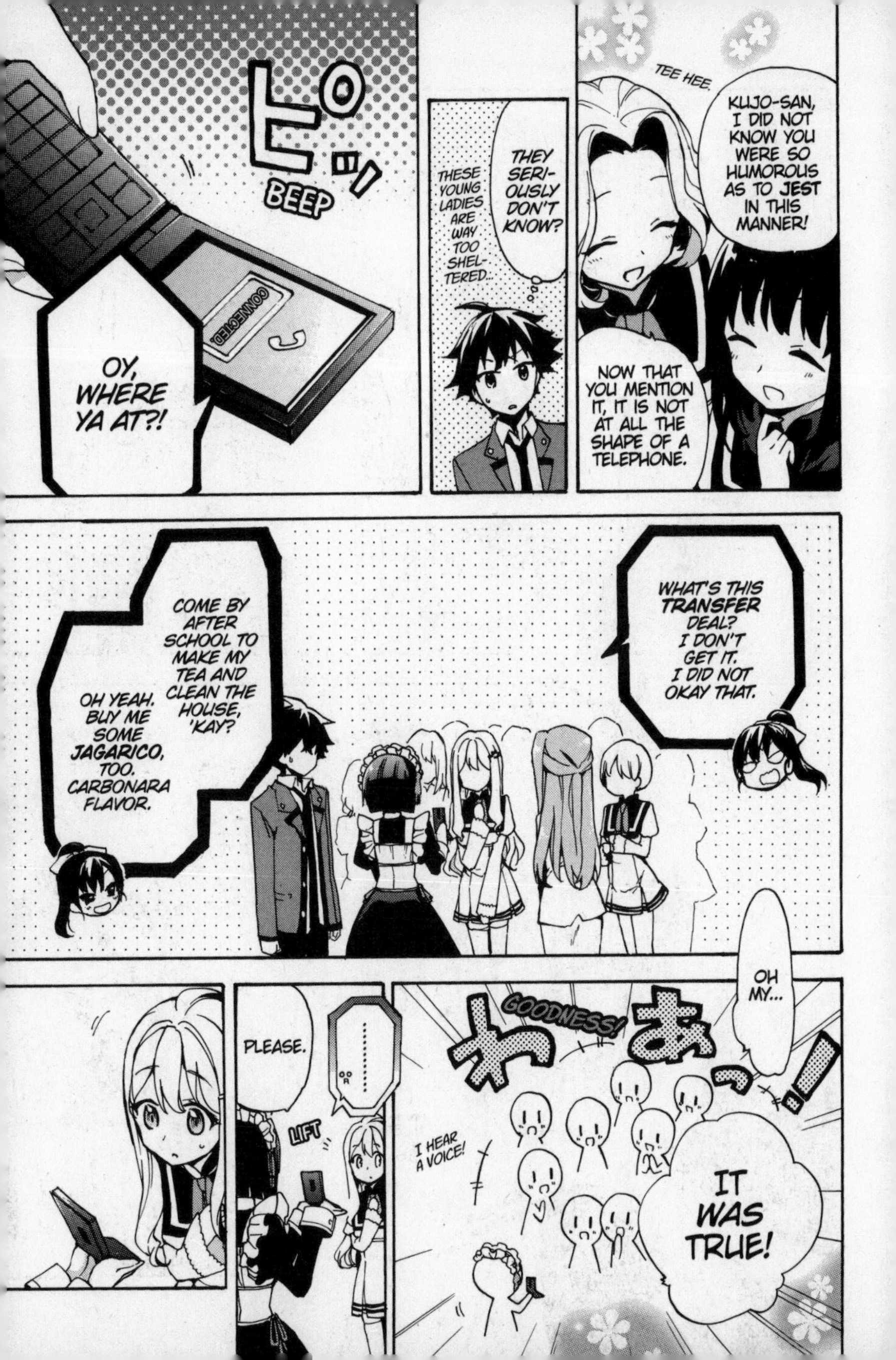
TEE HEE.
KUJO-SAN, I DID NOT KNOW YOU WERE SO HUMOROUS AS TO JEST IN THIS MANNER!
NOW THAT YOU MENTION IT, IT IS NOT AT ALL THE SHAPE OF A TELEPHONE.
THEY SERI-OUSLY DON'T KNOW?
THESE YOUNG LADIES ARE WAY TOO SHEL-TERED...
BEEP
CONNECTED
OY, WHERE YA AT?!
WHAT'S THIS TRANSFER DEAL? I DON'T GET IT. I DID NOT OKAY THAT.
COME BY AFTER SCHOOL TO MAKE MY TEA AND CLEAN THE HOUSE, 'KAY?
OH YEAH. BUY ME SOME JAGARICO, TOO. CARBONARA FLAVOR.
OH MY...
GOODNESS!
IT WAS TRUE!
I HEAR A VOICE!
......
PLEASE.
LIFT

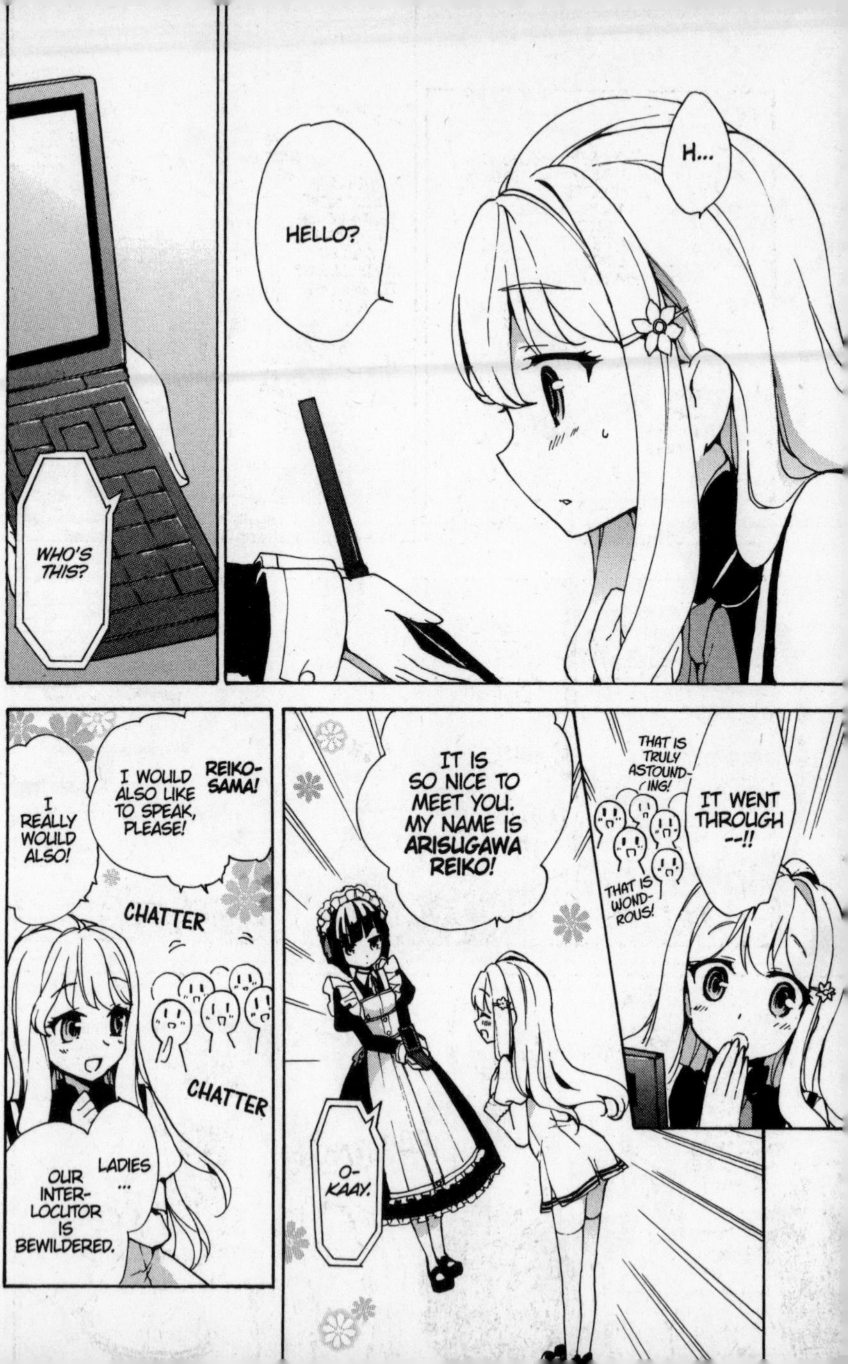
H...
HELLO?
WHO'S THIS?
IT WENT THROUGH--!!
THAT IS TRULY ASTOUNDING!
THAT IS WONDROUS!
IT IS SO NICE TO MEET YOU. MY NAME IS ARISUGAWA REIKO!
O-KAAY.
REIKO-SAMA!
I WOULD ALSO LIKE TO SPEAK, PLEASE!
I REALLY WOULD ALSO!
CHATTER
CHATTER
LADIES...
OUR INTERLOCUTOR IS BEWILDERED.

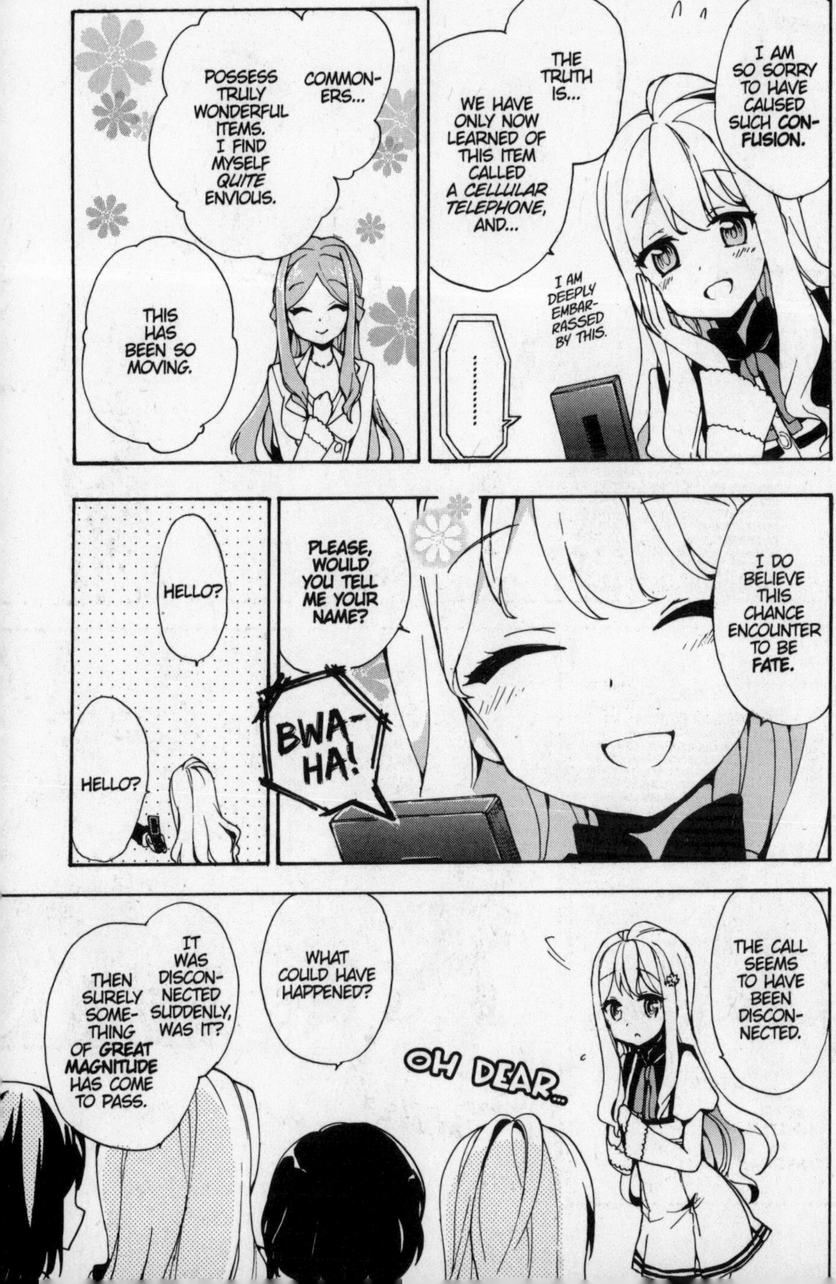
I AM SO SORRY TO HAVE CAUSED SUCH CONFUSION.
THE TRUTH IS...
WE HAVE ONLY NOW LEARNED OF THIS ITEM CALLED A CELLULAR TELEPHONE, AND...
I AM DEEPLY EMBARRASSED BY THIS.
......
COMMONERS...
POSSESS TRULY WONDERFUL ITEMS. I FIND MYSELF QUITE ENVIOUS.
THIS HAS BEEN SO MOVING.
I DO BELIEVE THIS CHANCE ENCOUNTER TO BE FATE.
PLEASE, WOULD YOU TELL ME YOUR NAME?
BWA-HA!
HELLO?
HELLO?
THE CALL SEEMS TO HAVE BEEN DISCONNECTED.
OH DEAR...
WHAT COULD HAVE HAPPENED?
IT WAS DISCONNECTED SUDDENLY, WAS IT?
THEN SURELY SOMETHING OF GREAT MAGNITUDE HAS COME TO PASS.

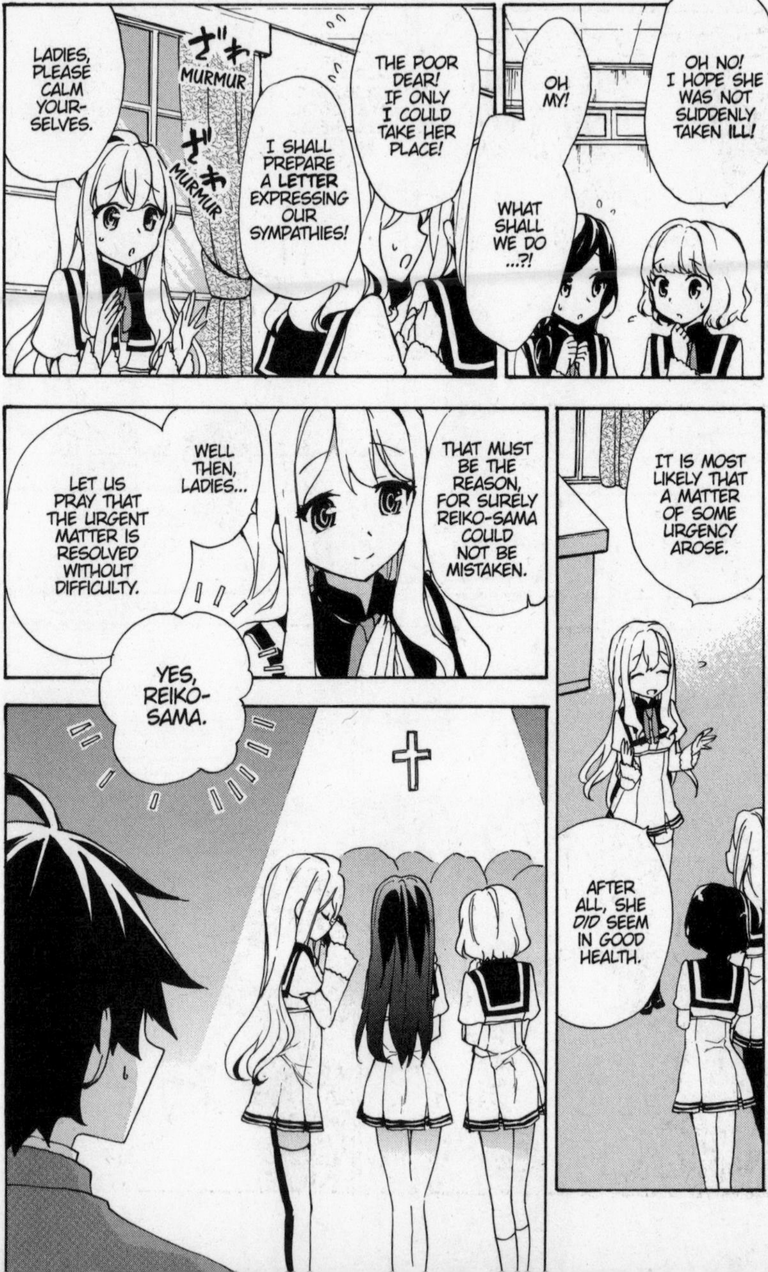
OH NO! I HOPE SHE WAS NOT SUDDENLY TAKEN ILL!
OH MY!
WHAT SHALL WE DO ...?!
THE POOR DEAR! IF ONLY I COULD TAKE HER PLACE!
I SHALL PREPARE A LETTER EXPRESSING OUR SYMPATHIES!
ざわ MURMUR
ざわ MURMUR
LADIES, PLEASE CALM YOUR-SELVES.
IT IS MOST LIKELY THAT A MATTER OF SOME URGENCY AROSE.
AFTER ALL, SHE DID SEEM IN GOOD HEALTH.
THAT MUST BE THE REASON, FOR SURELY REIKO-SAMA COULD NOT BE MISTAKEN.
WELL THEN, LADIES...
LET US PRAY THAT THE URGENT MATTER IS RESOLVED WITHOUT DIFFICULTY.
YES, REIKO-SAMA.

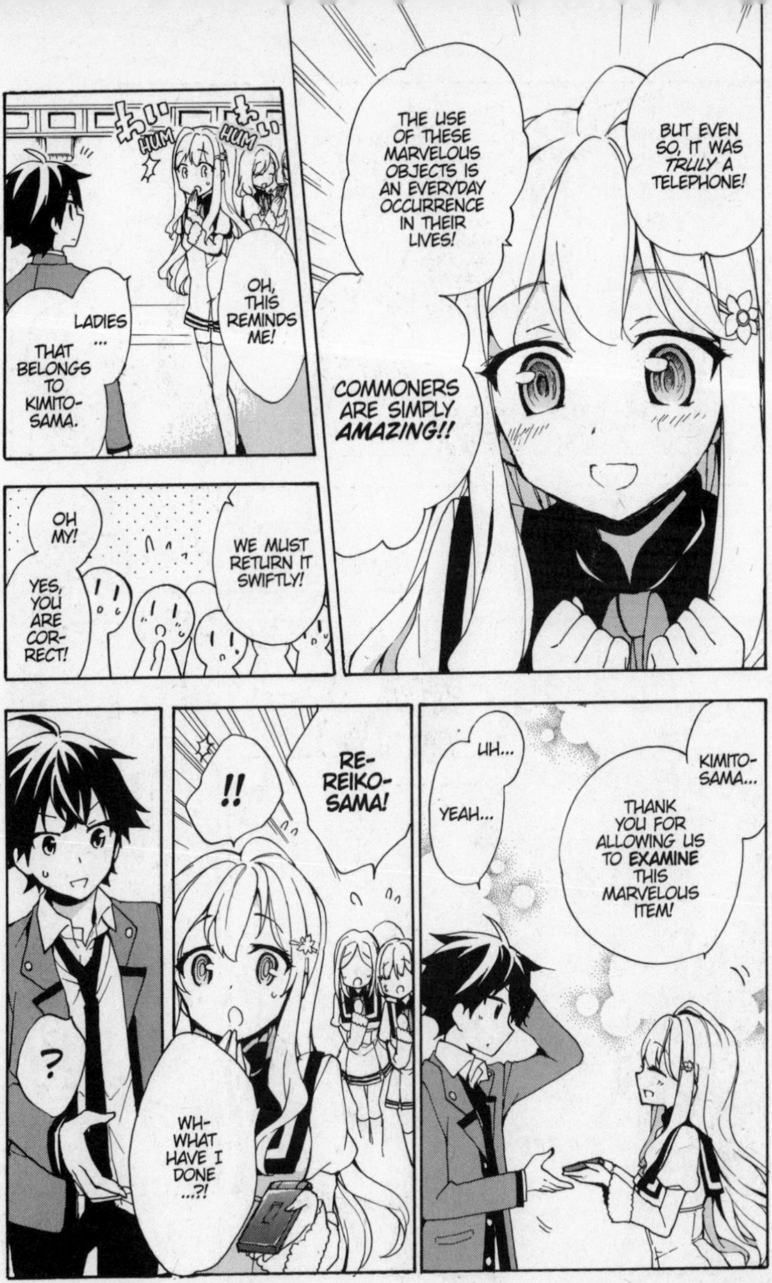
BUT EVEN SO, IT WAS *TRULY* A TELEPHONE!
THE USE OF THESE MARVELOUS OBJECTS IS AN EVERYDAY OCCURRENCE IN THEIR LIVES!
COMMONERS ARE SIMPLY ***AMAZING!!***
HUM
HUM
OH, THIS REMINDS ME!
LADIES ...
THAT BELONGS TO KIMITO-SAMA.
WE MUST RETURN IT SWIFTLY!
OH MY!
YES, YOU ARE COR-RECT!
KIMITO-SAMA...
THANK YOU FOR ALLOWING US TO **EXAMINE** THIS MARVELOUS ITEM!
UH...
YEAH...
RE-REIKO-SAMA!
!!
WH-WHAT HAVE I DONE ...?!
?

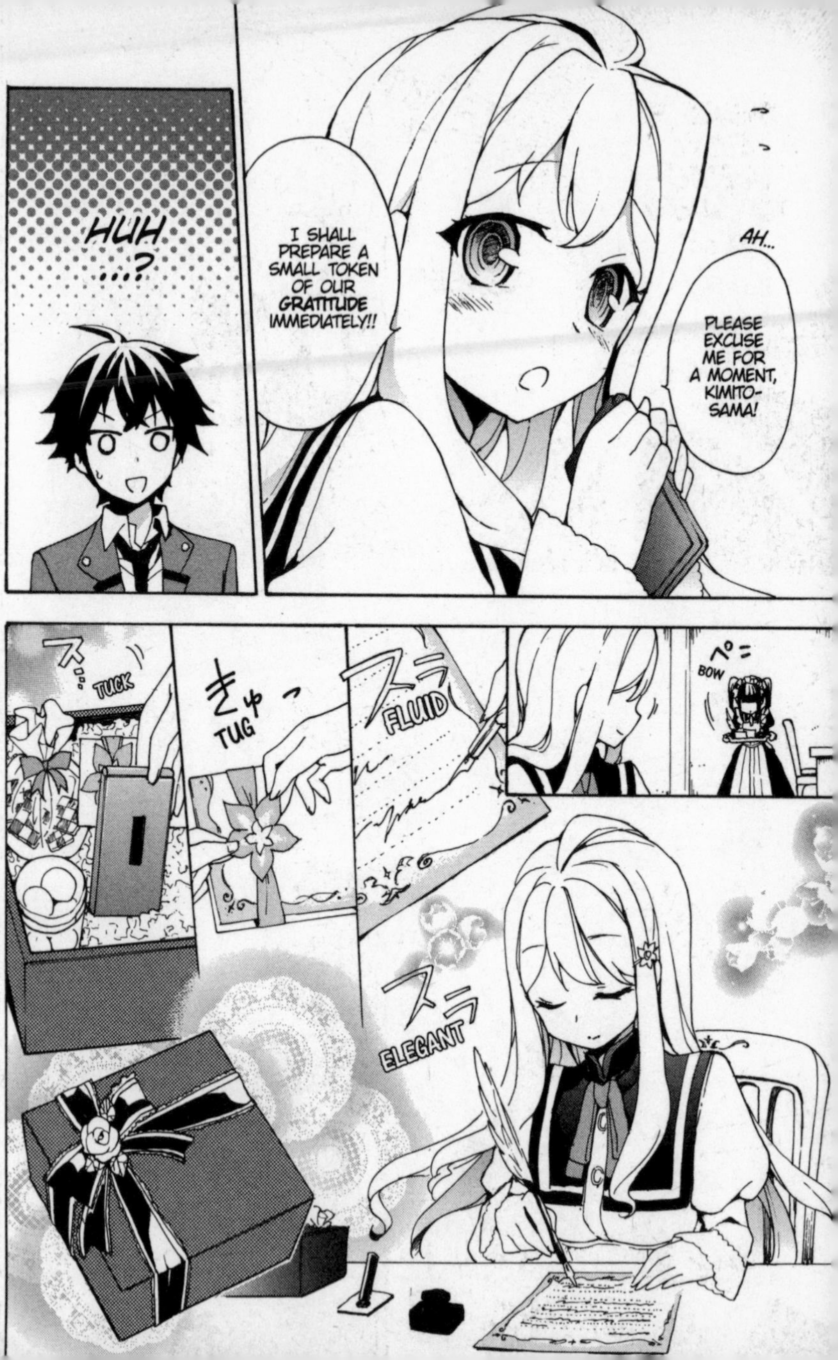
AH...
PLEASE EXCUSE ME FOR A MOMENT, KIMITO-SAMA!
I SHALL PREPARE A SMALL TOKEN OF OUR GRATITUDE IMMEDIATELY!!
HUH ...?
ぺ
BOW
スラ
FLUID
きゅっ
TUG
ス
TUCK
スラ
ELEGANT

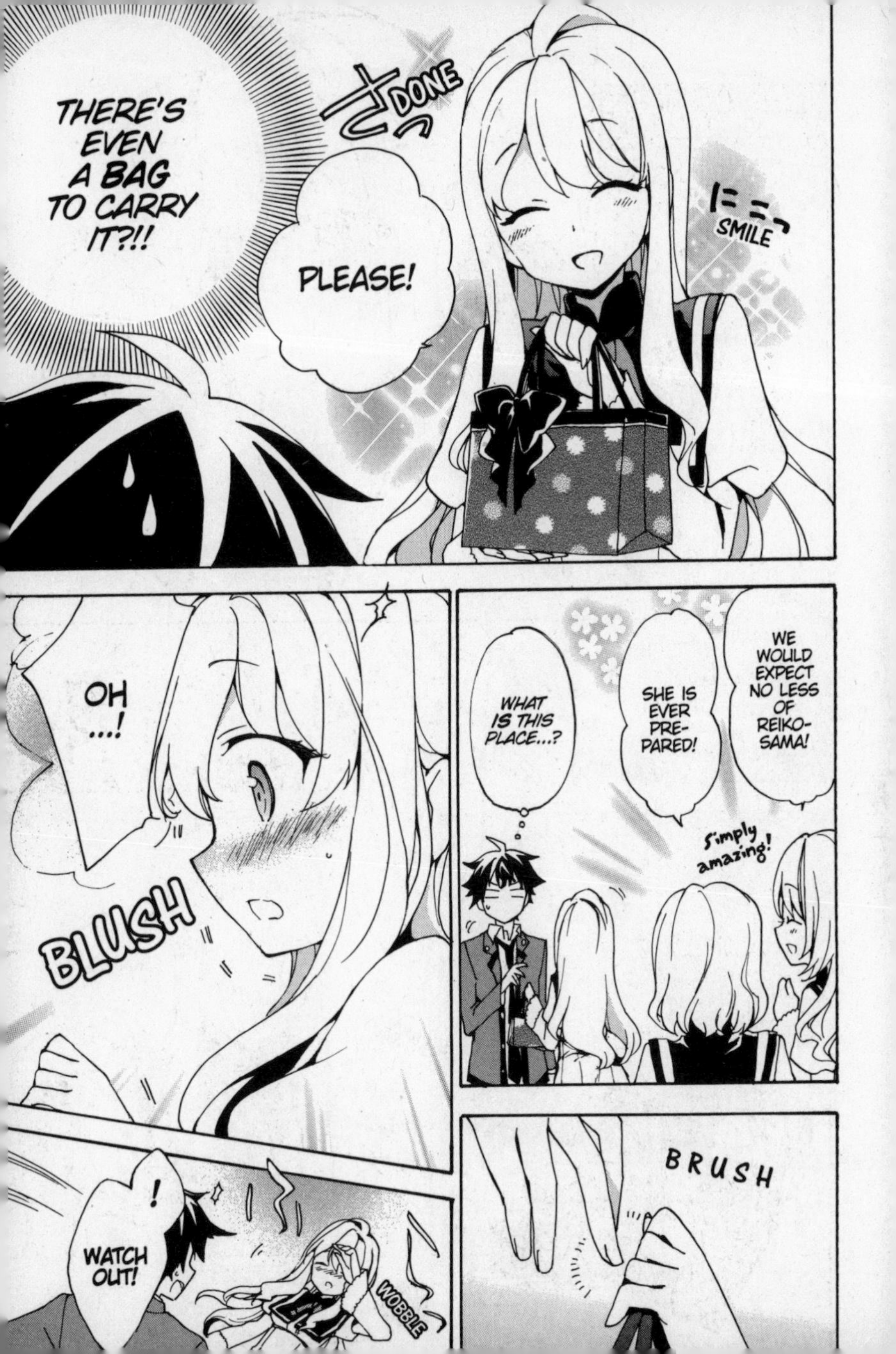
さっ
DONE
にこっ
SMILE
PLEASE!
THERE'S EVEN A BAG TO CARRY IT?!!
WE WOULD EXPECT NO LESS OF REIKO-SAMA!
SHE IS EVER PRE-PARED!
WHAT IS THIS PLACE...?
Simply amazing!
OH ...!
BLUSH
BRUSH
!
WATCH OUT!
WOBBLE

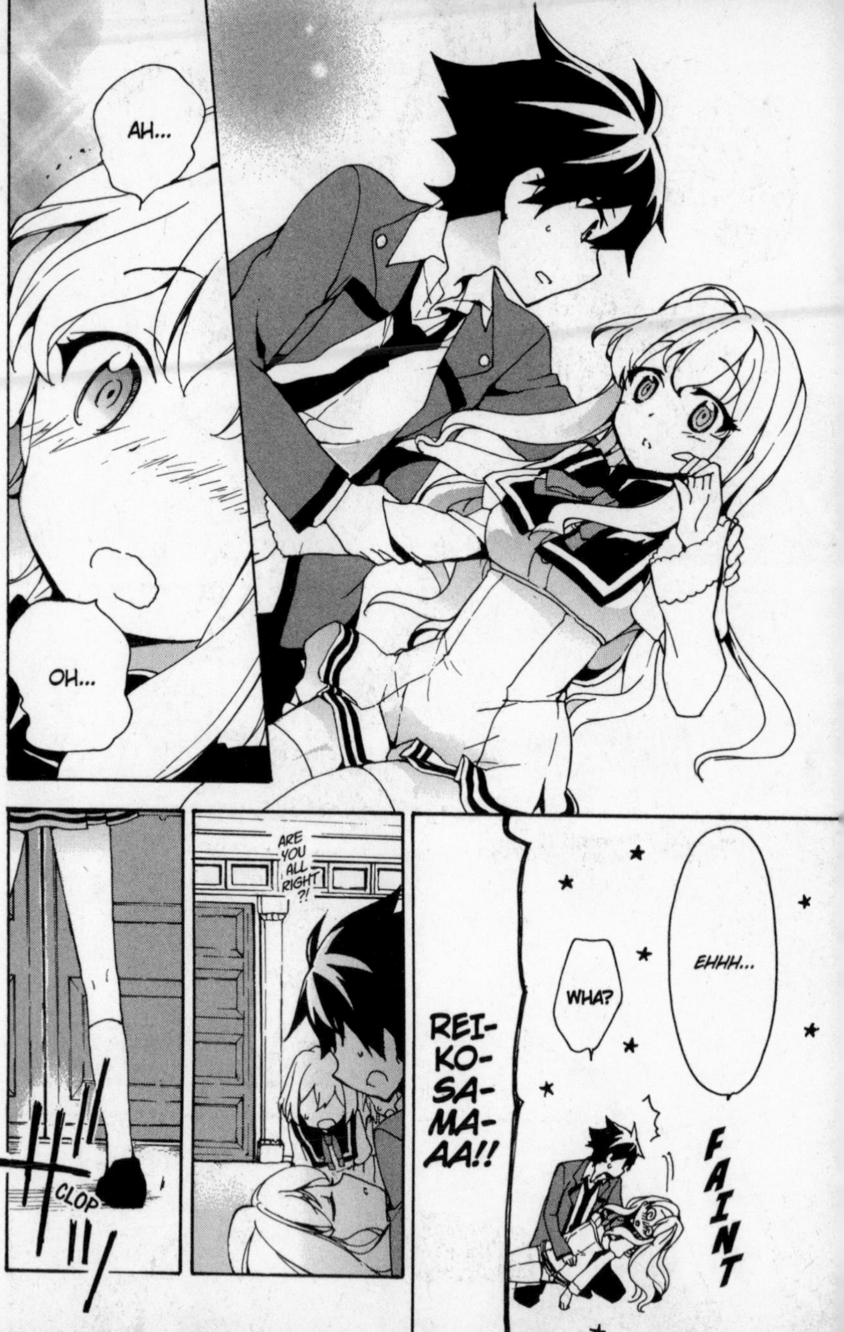
AH...
OH...
EHHH...
WHA?
REI-KO-SA-MA-AA!!
FAINT
ARE YOU ALL RIGHT?!
CLOP

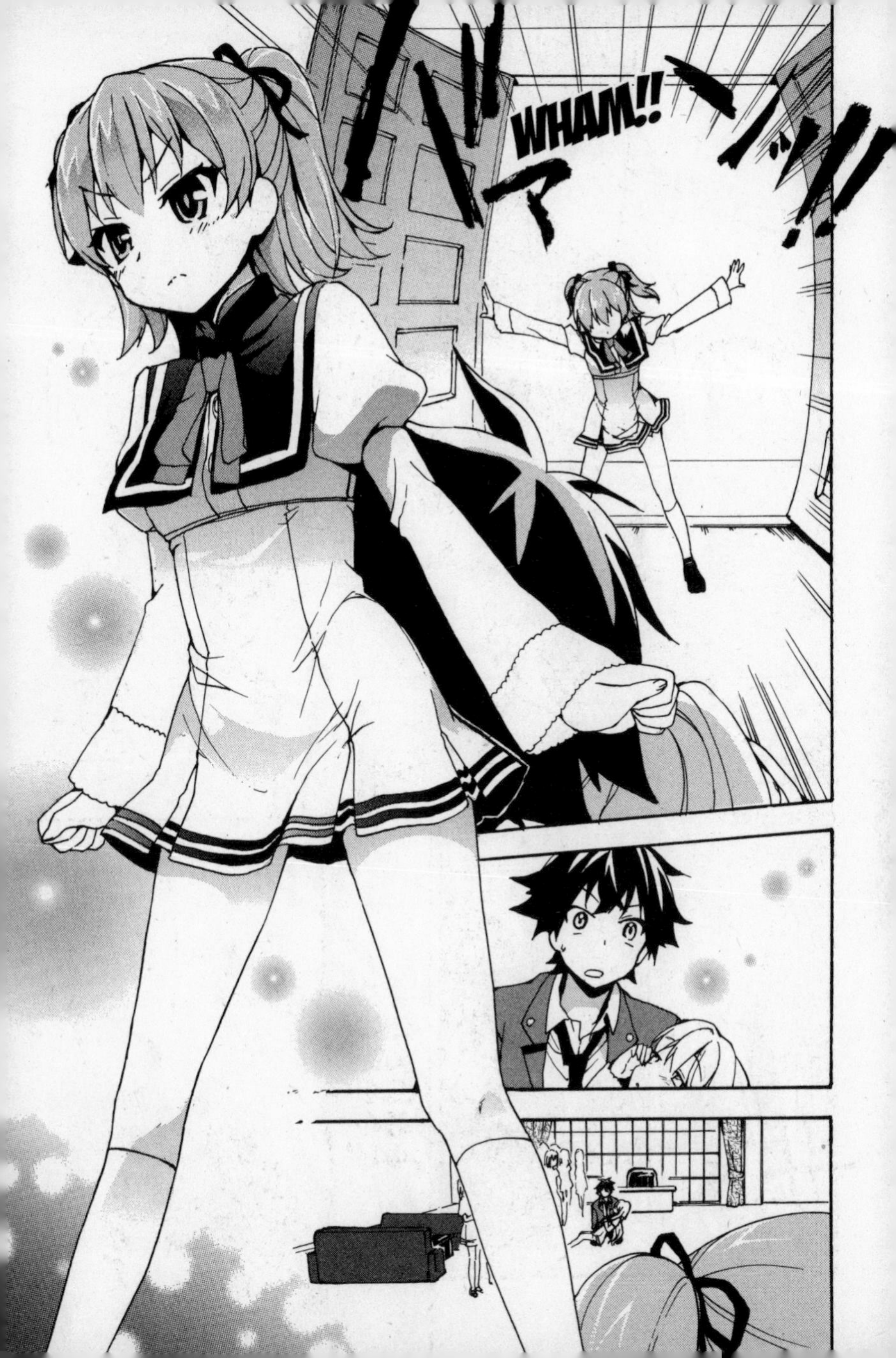
WHAM!!

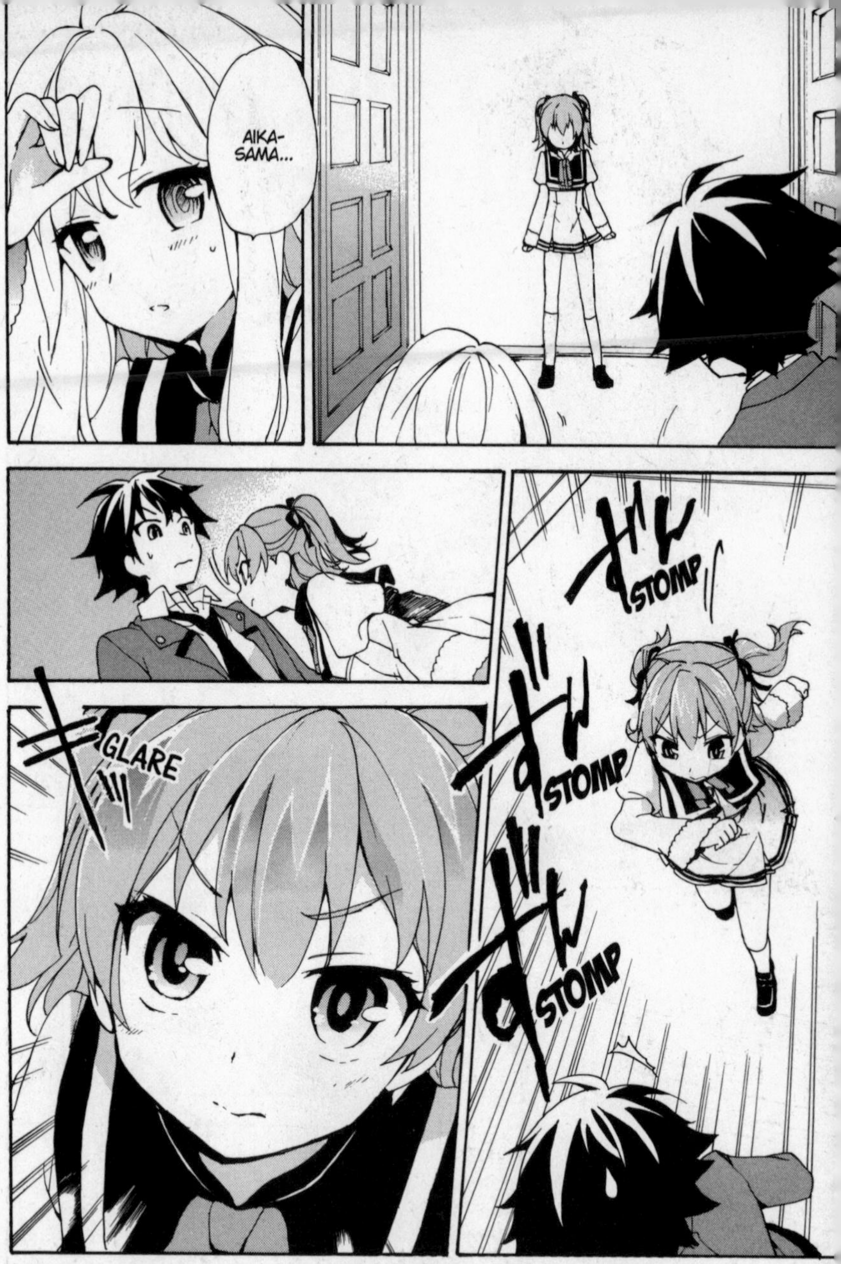
AIKA-SAMA...
STOMP
STOMP
STOMP
GLARE

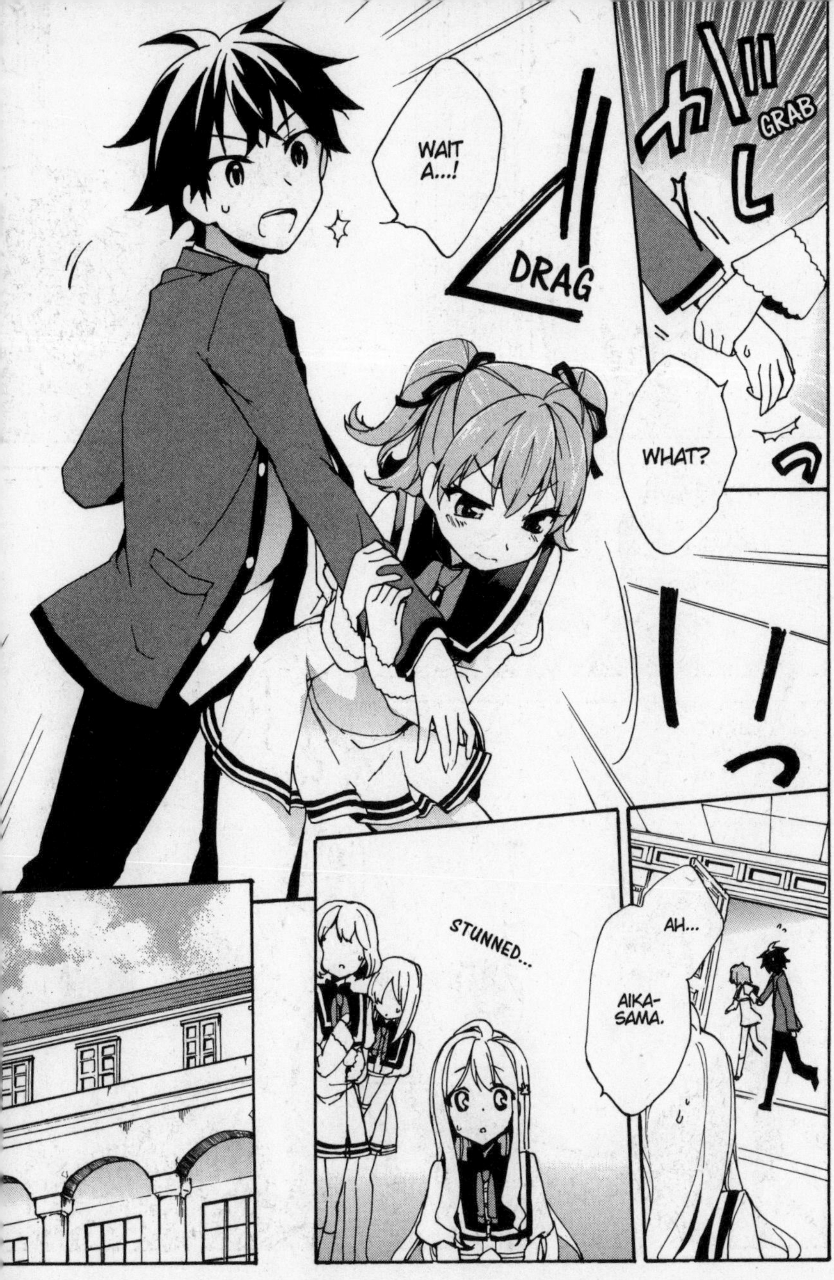
GRAB
WAIT A...!
DRAG
WHAT?
AH... AIKA-SAMA.
STUNNED...

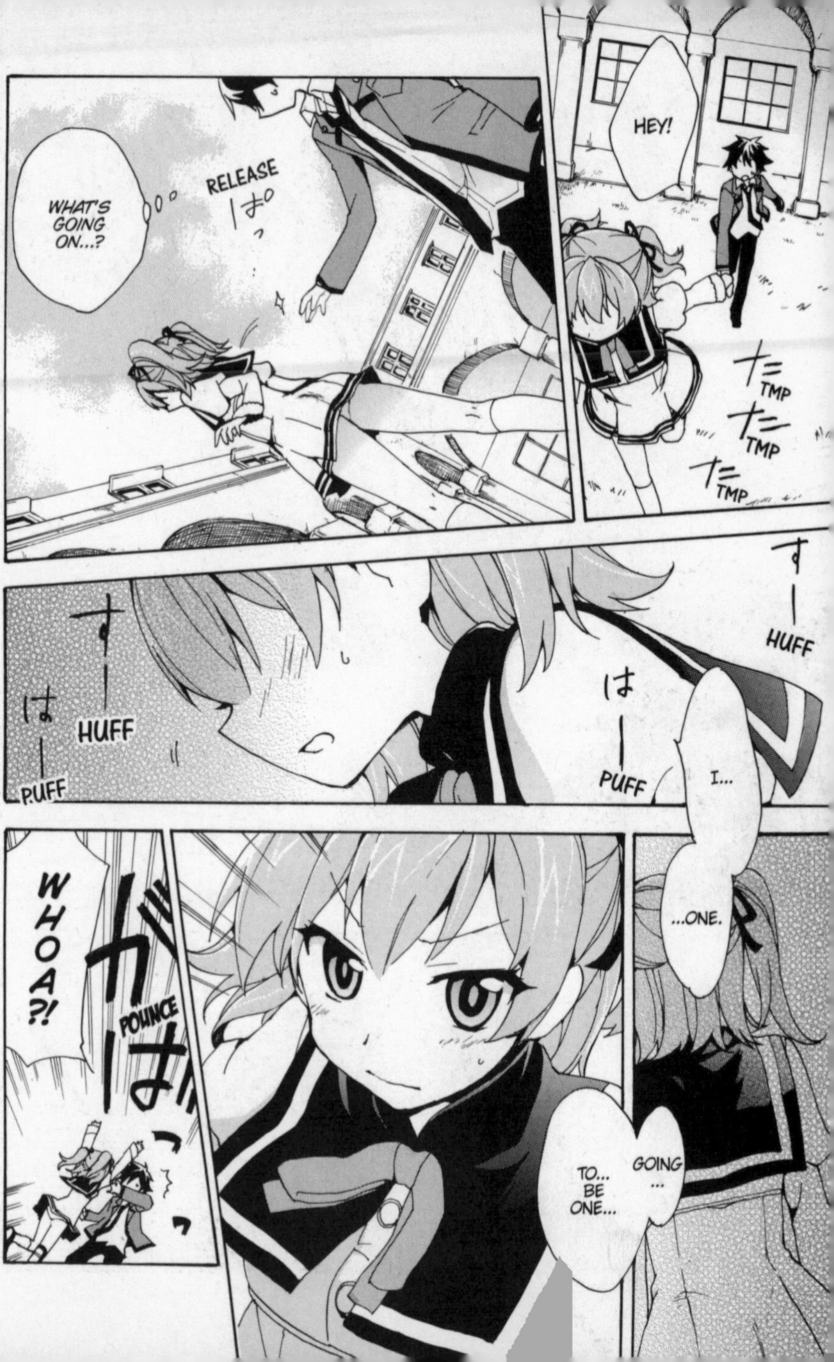
HEY!
TMP
TMP
TMP
WHAT'S GOING ON...?
ぱっ
RELEASE
すー
HUFF
はー
PUFF
すー
HUFF
はー
PUFF
I...
...ONE.
GOING...
TO... BE ONE...
WHOA?!
がばっ
POUNCE

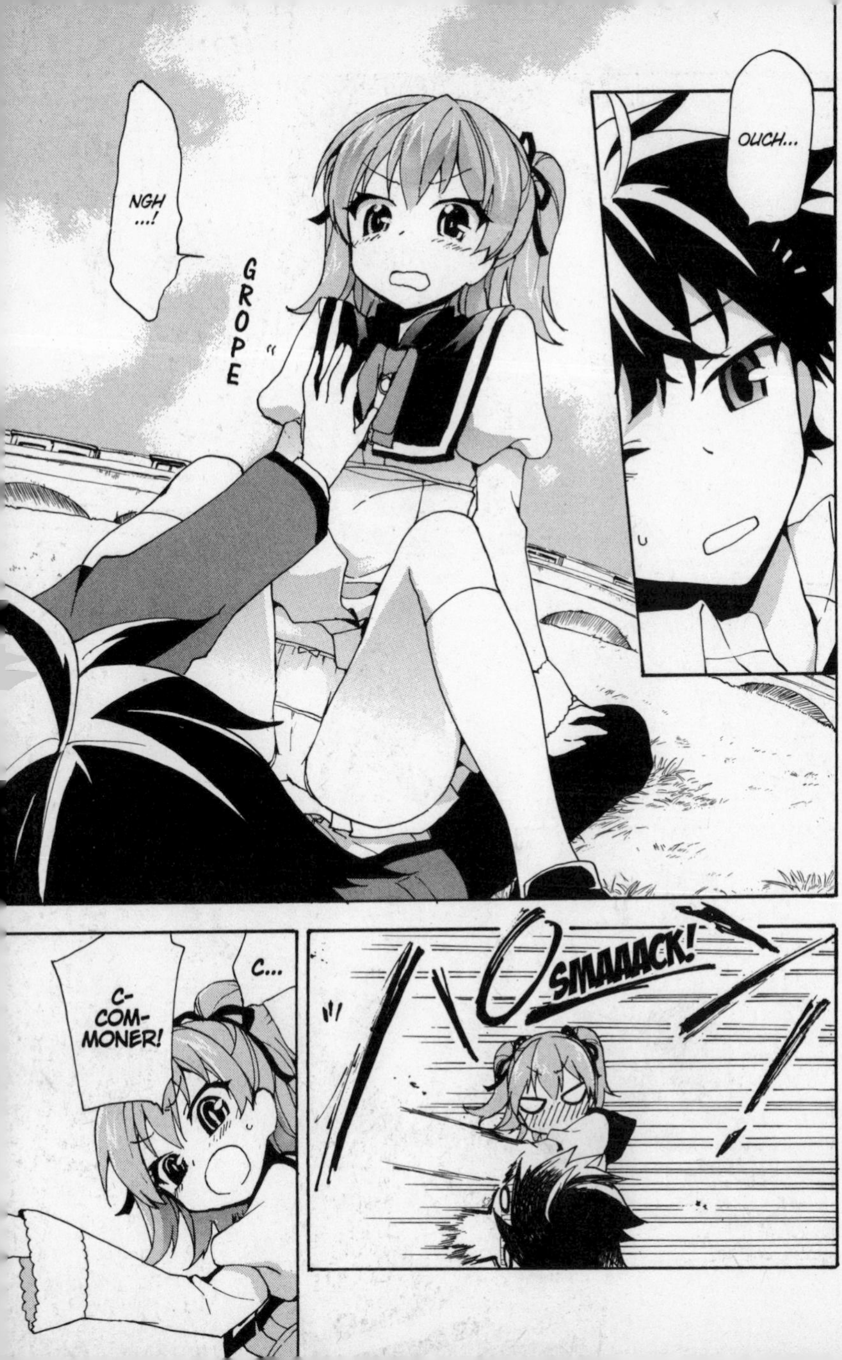
OUCH...
NGH ...!
GROPE
SMAAACK!
C...
C-COMMONER!

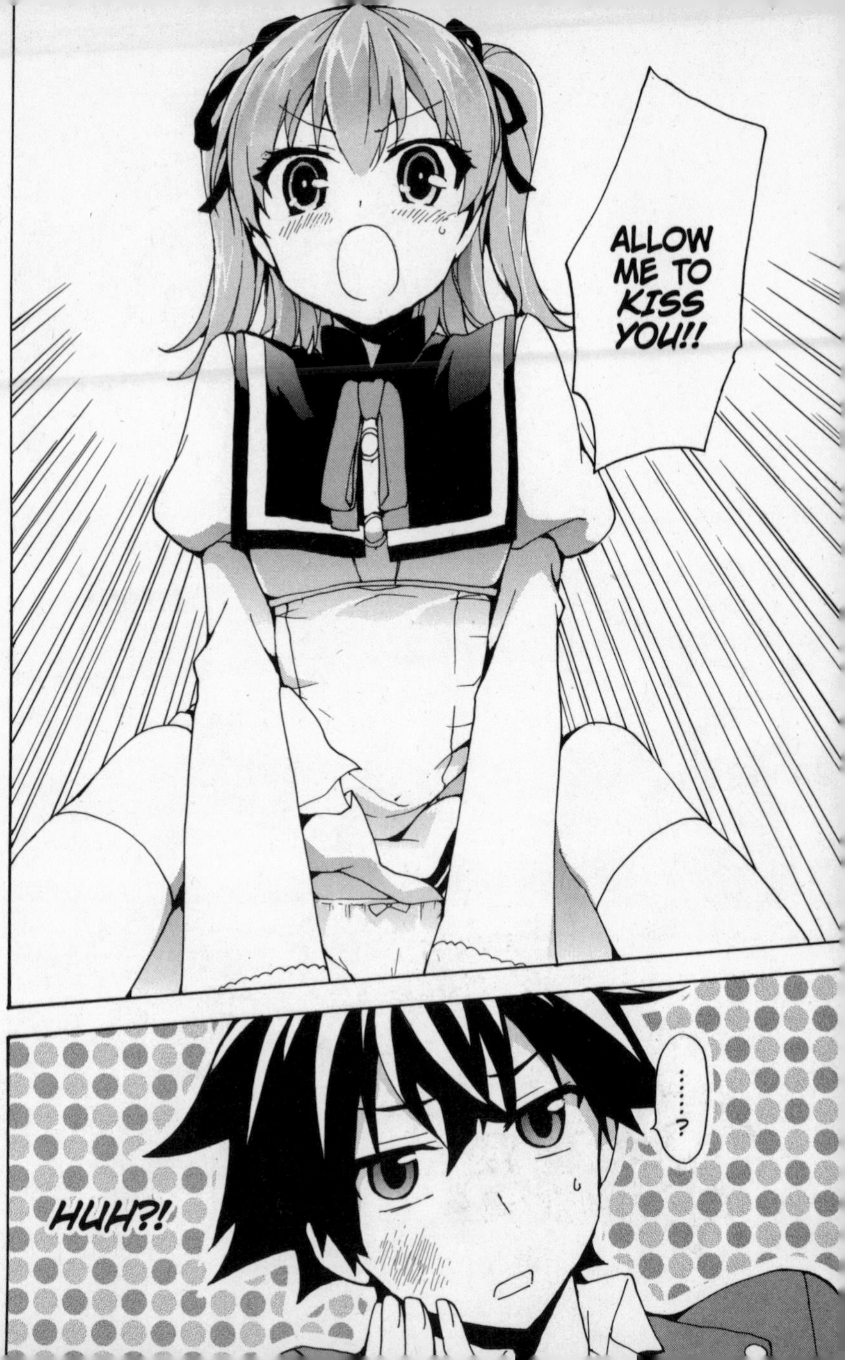
ALLOW ME TO KISS YOU!!
......?
HUH?!

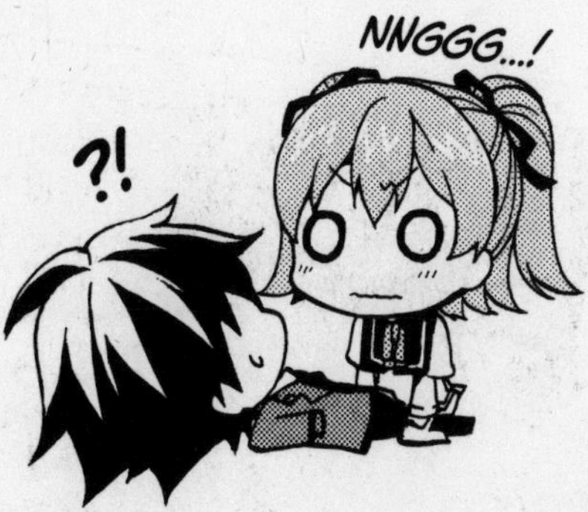
NNGGG...!
?!

SHOMIN SAMPLE

SAMPLE ①

I Was Abducted by an Elite All-Girls
School as a Sample Commoner

Chapter 2
Allow Me to Kiss You

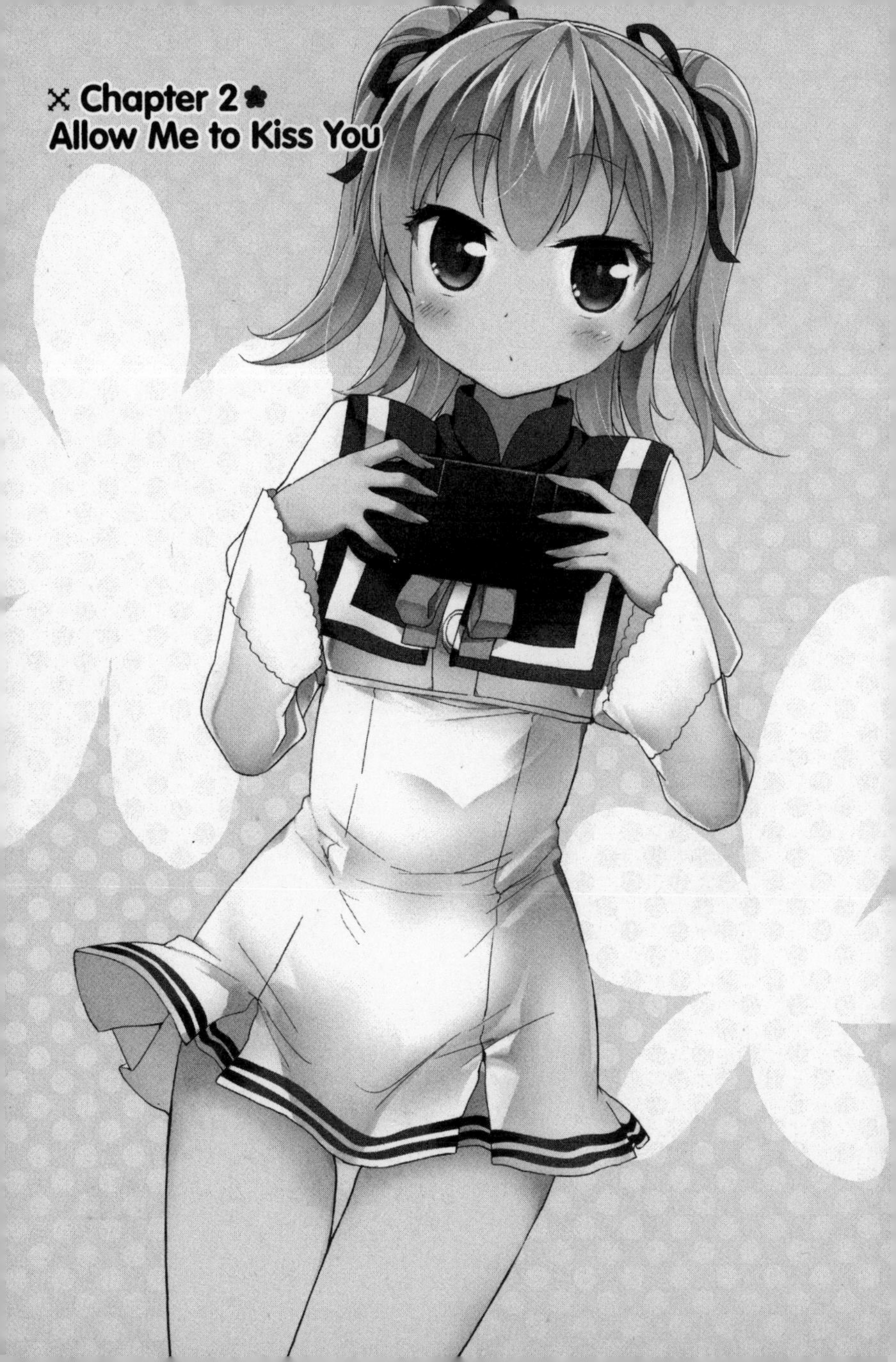

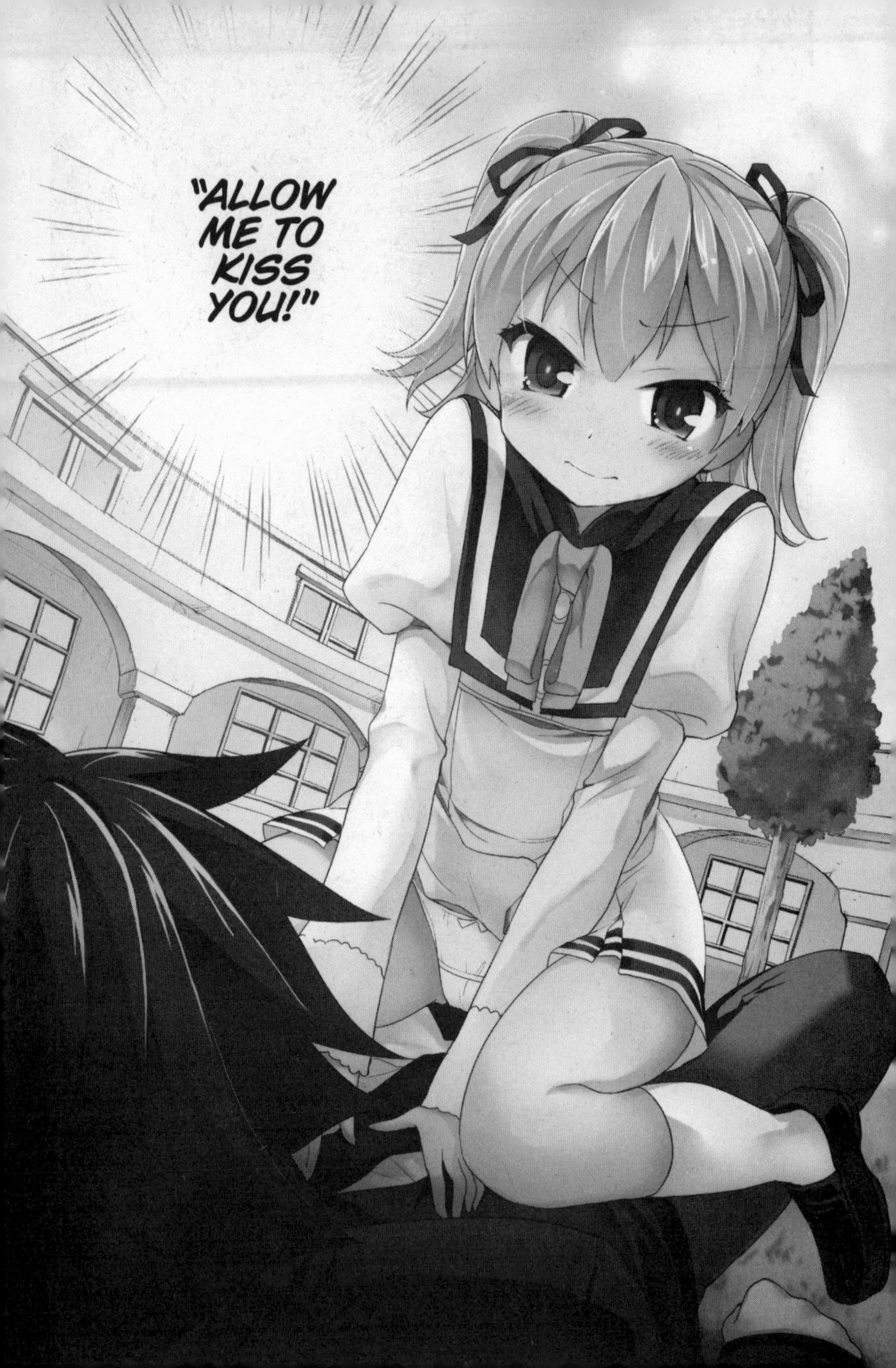
"ALLOW ME TO KISS YOU!"

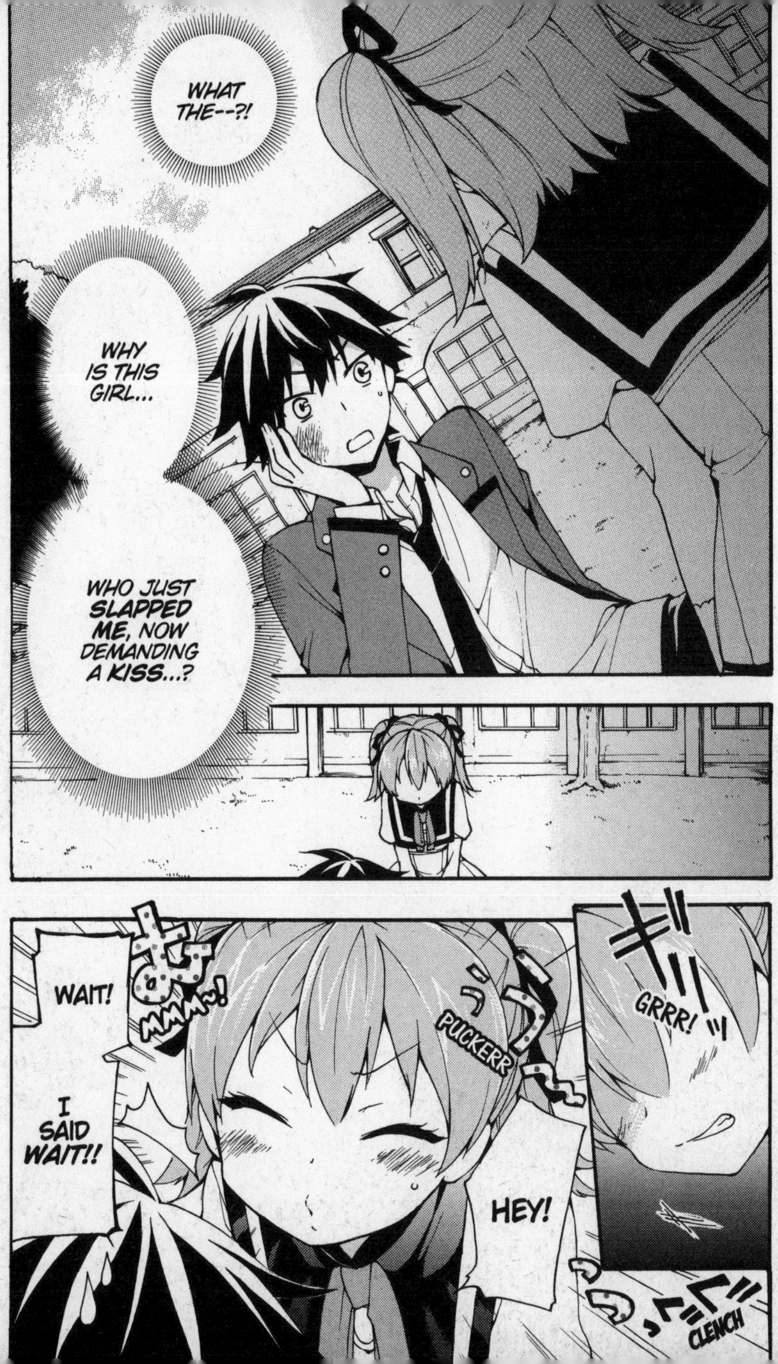
WHAT THE--?!
WHY IS THIS GIRL...
WHO JUST SLAPPED ME, NOW DEMANDING A KISS...?
GRRR!
CLENCH
HEY!
PUCKERR
MMM~!
WAIT!
I SAID WAIT!!

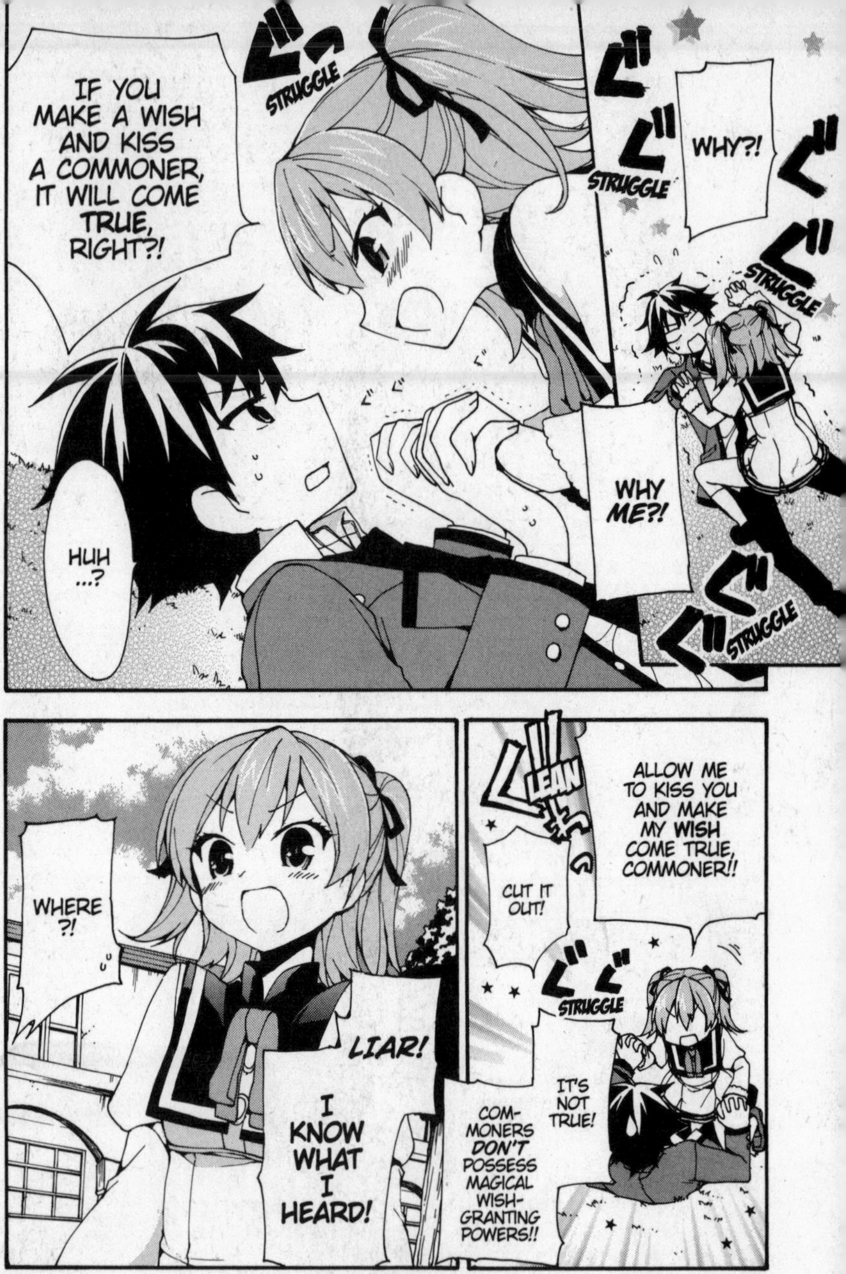
STRUGGLE
WHY?!
STRUGGLE
STRUGGLE
WHY ME?!
STRUGGLE
IF YOU MAKE A WISH AND KISS A COMMONER, IT WILL COME TRUE, RIGHT?!
HUH ...?
LEAN
ALLOW ME TO KISS YOU AND MAKE MY WISH COME TRUE, COMMONER!!
CUT IT OUT!
STRUGGLE
IT'S NOT TRUE!
COMMONERS DON'T POSSESS MAGICAL WISH-GRANTING POWERS!!
WHERE ?!
LIAR!
I KNOW WHAT I HEARD!

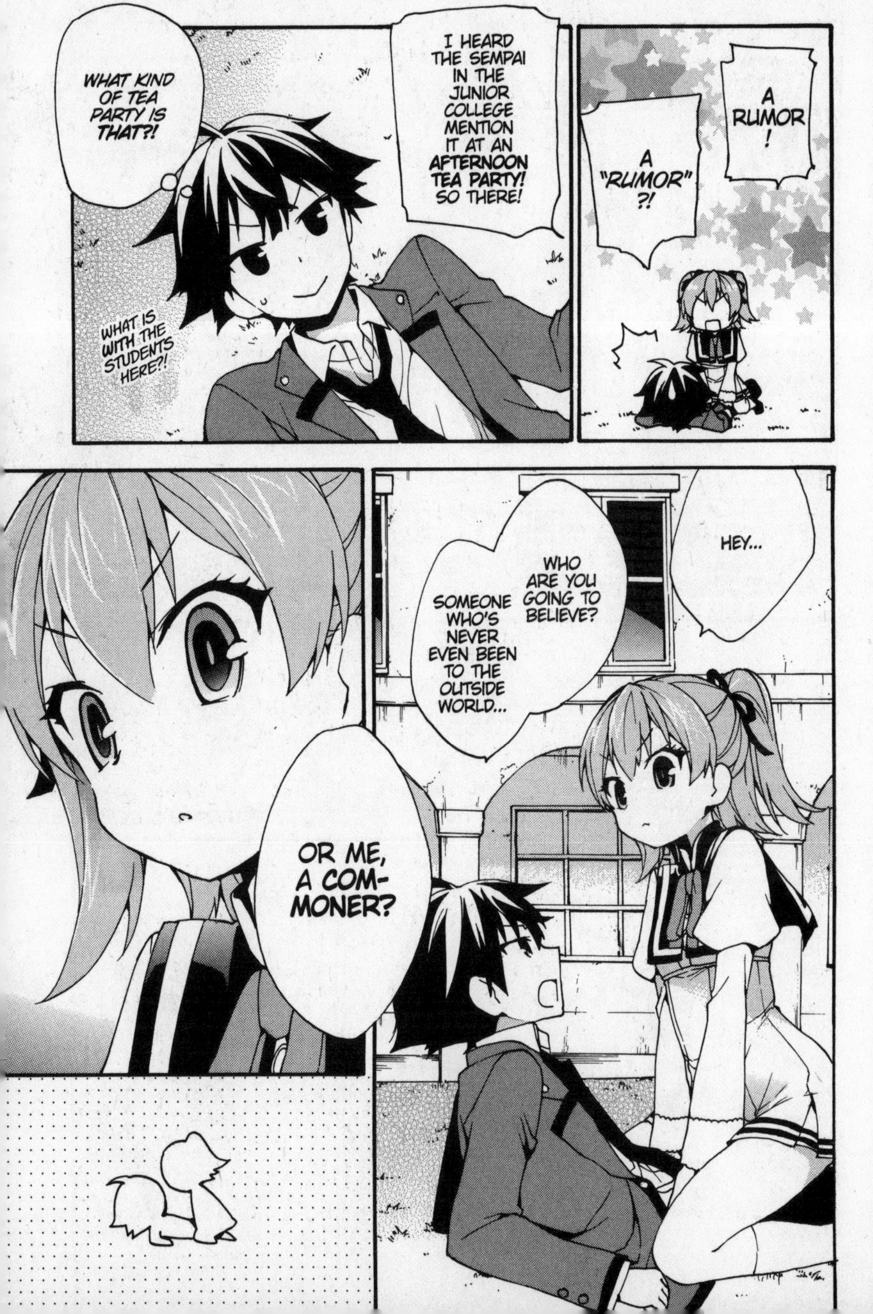
A RUMOR!
A "RUMOR"?!
I HEARD THE SEMPAI IN THE JUNIOR COLLEGE MENTION IT AT AN AFTERNOON TEA PARTY! SO THERE!
WHAT KIND OF TEA PARTY IS THAT?!
WHAT IS WITH THE STUDENTS HERE?!
HEY...
WHO ARE YOU GOING TO BELIEVE?
SOMEONE WHO'S NEVER EVEN BEEN TO THE OUTSIDE WORLD...
OR ME, A COM-MONER?

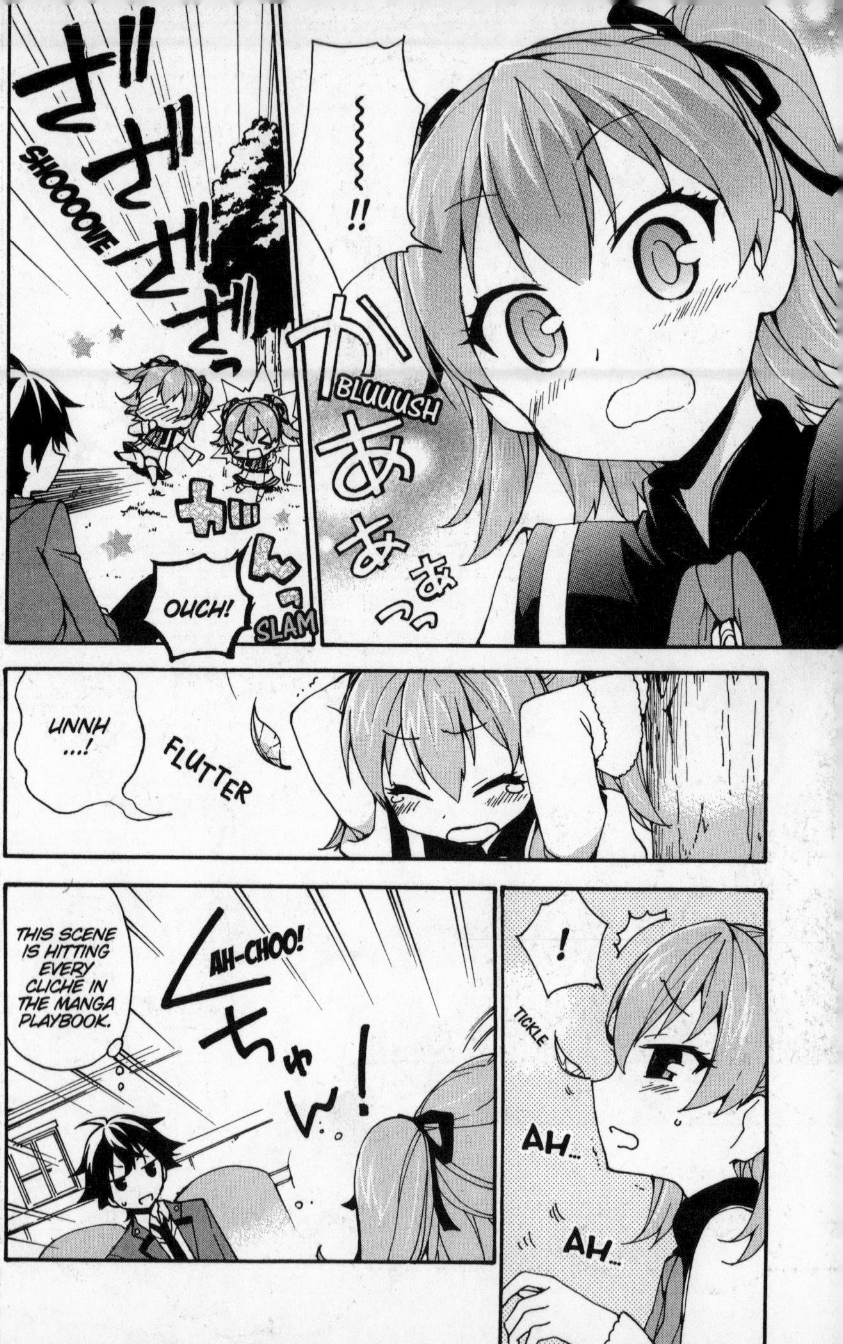

かぁあぁっ
BLUUUSH
ざざざざっ
SHOOOOVE
がんっ
SLAM
OUCH!
UNNH ...!
FLUTTER
!
TICKLE
AH...
AH...
くちゅん!
AH-CHOO!
THIS SCENE IS HITTING EVERY CLICHE IN THE MANGA PLAYBOOK.

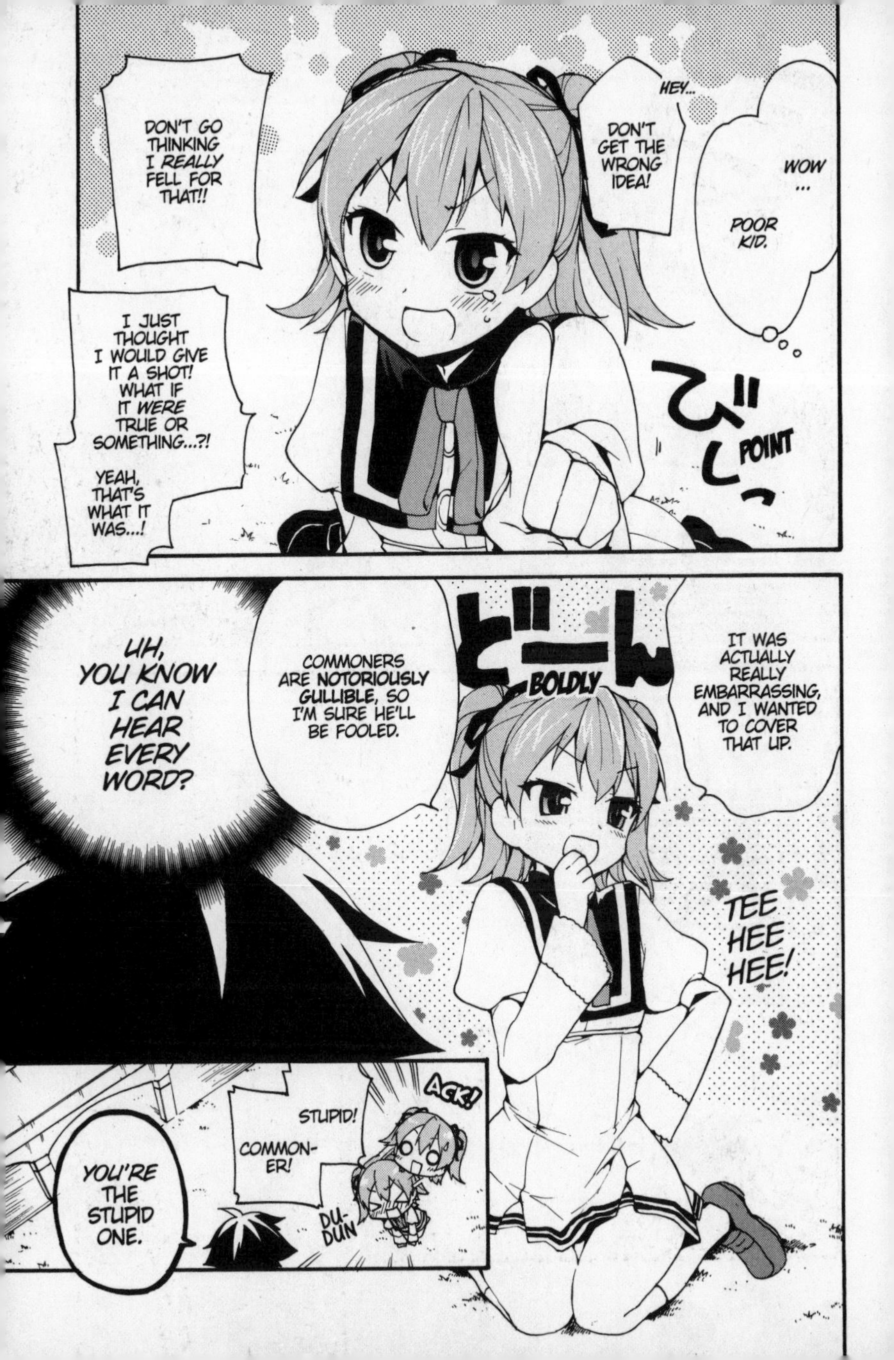
WOW... POOR KID.
HEY...
DON'T GET THE WRONG IDEA!
ぴしっ
POINT
DON'T GO THINKING I REALLY FELL FOR THAT!!
I JUST THOUGHT I WOULD GIVE IT A SHOT! WHAT IF IT WERE TRUE OR SOMETHING...?!
YEAH, THAT'S WHAT IT WAS...!
IT WAS ACTUALLY REALLY EMBARRASSING, AND I WANTED TO COVER THAT UP.
どーん
BOLDLY
COMMONERS ARE NOTORIOUSLY GULLIBLE, SO I'M SURE HE'LL BE FOOLED.
TEE HEE HEE!
UH, YOU KNOW I CAN HEAR EVERY WORD?
ACK!
STUPID!
COMMON-ER!
DU-DUN
YOU'RE THE STUPID ONE.

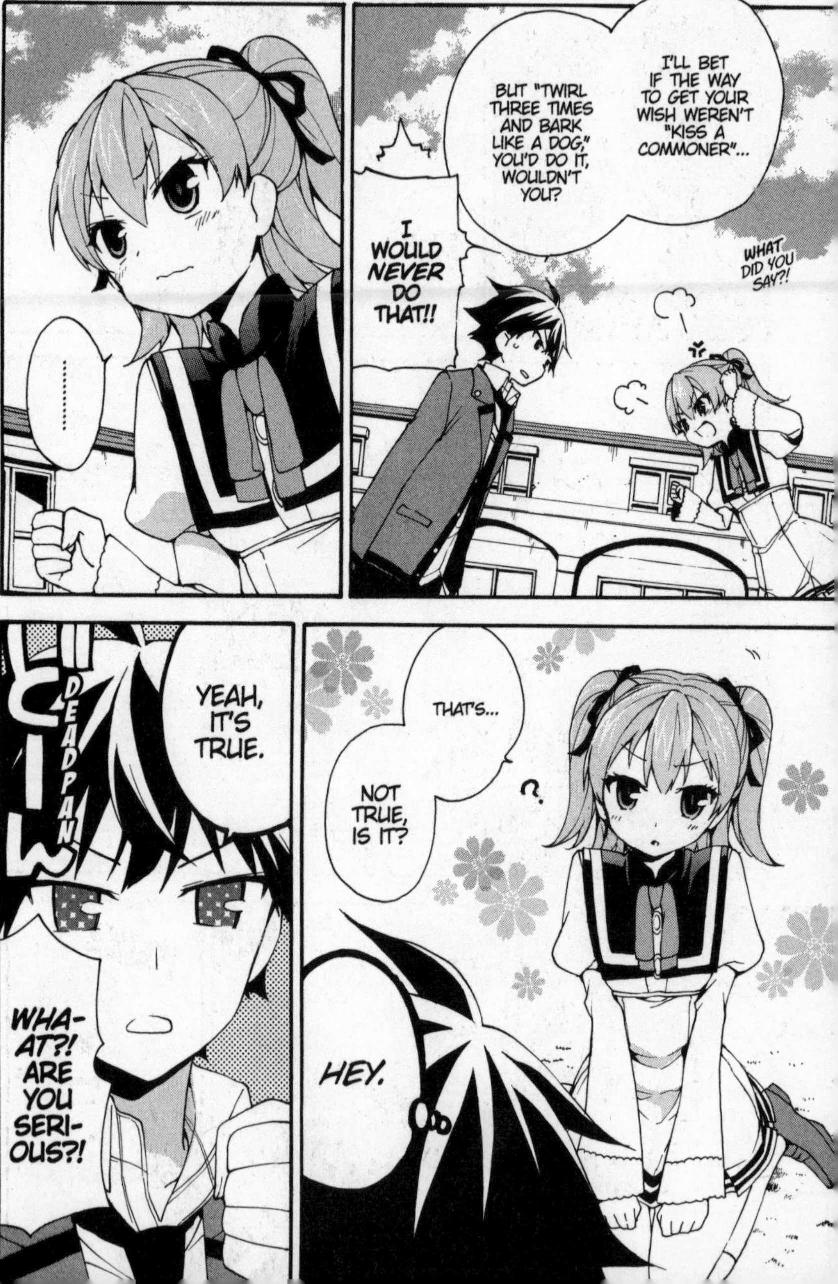
I'LL BET IF THE WAY TO GET YOUR WISH WEREN'T "KISS A COMMONER"...
BUT "TWIRL THREE TIMES AND BARK LIKE A DOG," YOU'D DO IT, WOULDN'T YOU?
WHAT DID YOU SAY?!
I WOULD *NEVER* DO THAT!!
......
THAT'S...
NOT TRUE, IS IT?
HEY.
YEAH, IT'S TRUE.
DEADPAN
WHA-AT?! ARE YOU SERI-OUS?!

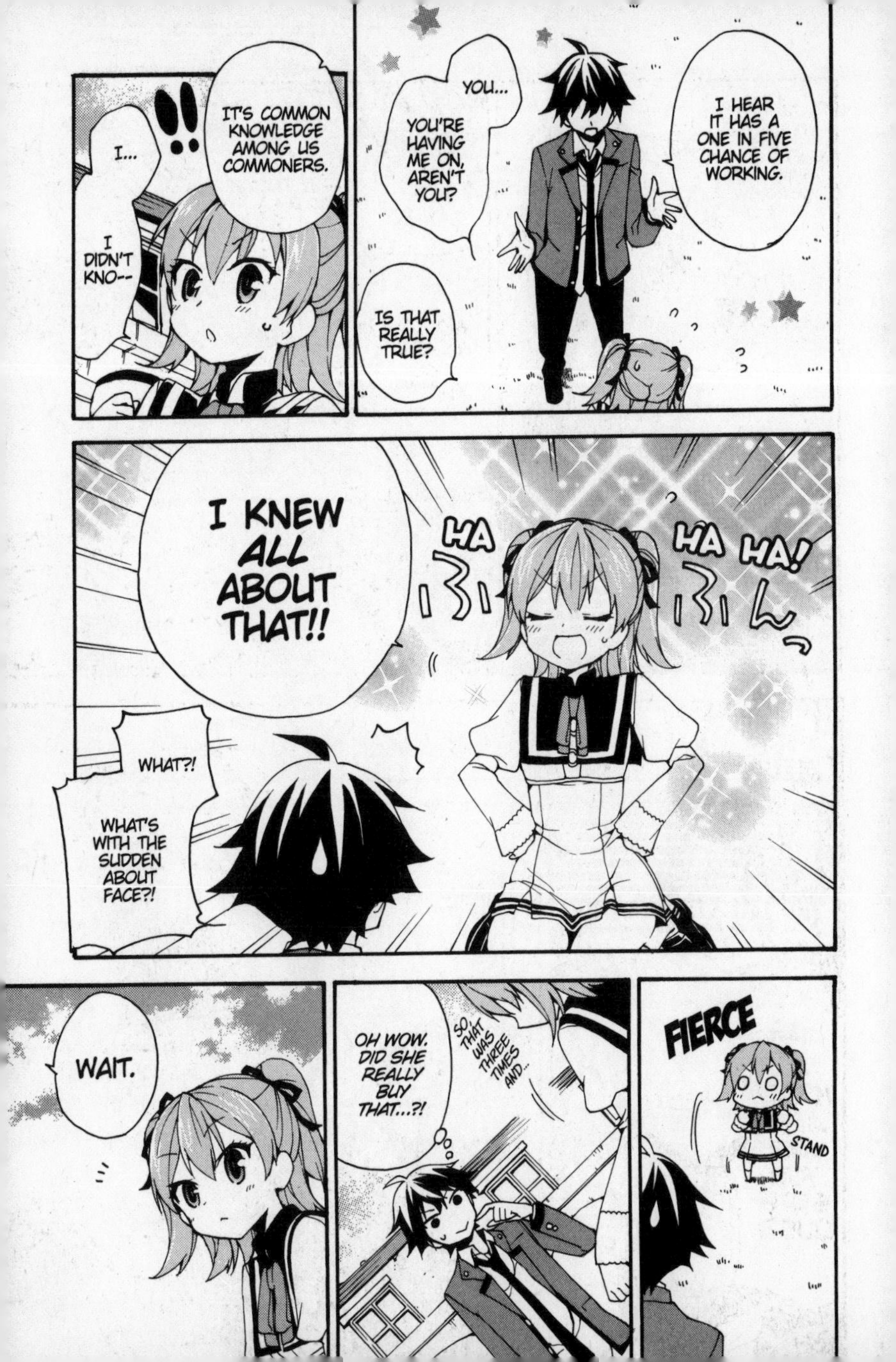

I HEAR IT HAS A ONE IN FIVE CHANCE OF WORKING.
YOU...
YOU'RE HAVING ME ON, AREN'T YOU?
IS THAT REALLY TRUE?
IT'S COMMON KNOWLEDGE AMONG US COMMONERS.
!!
I...
I DIDN'T KNO--
HA HA!
ふん
HA
ふ
I KNEW ALL ABOUT THAT!!
WHAT?!
WHAT'S WITH THE SUDDEN ABOUT FACE?!
FIERCE
STAND
SO, THAT WAS THREE TIMES AND...
OH WOW. DID SHE REALLY BUY THAT...?!
WAIT.

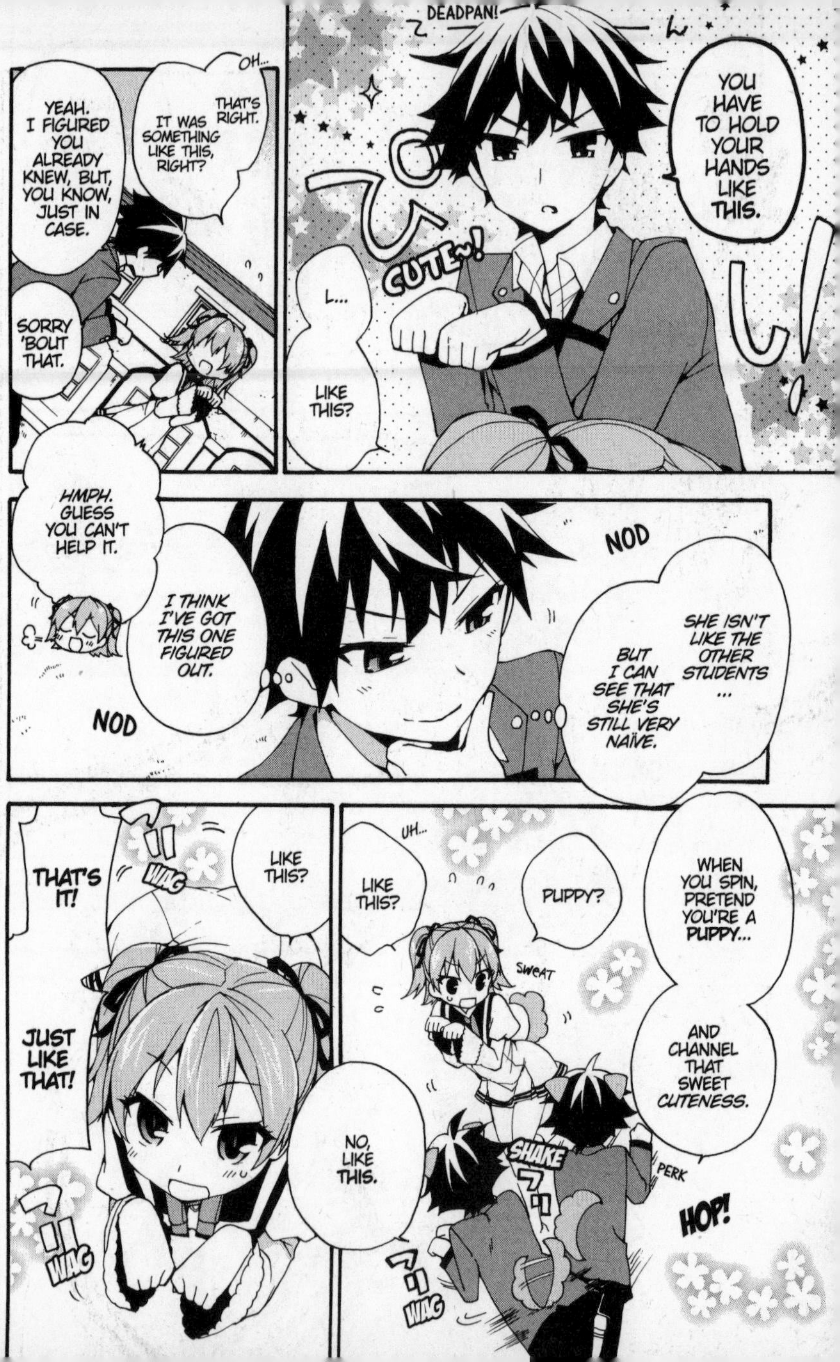
DEADPAN!
YOU HAVE TO HOLD YOUR HANDS LIKE THIS.
CUTE~!
L... LIKE THIS?
OH... THAT'S RIGHT. IT WAS SOMETHING LIKE THIS, RIGHT?
YEAH. I FIGURED YOU ALREADY KNEW, BUT, YOU KNOW, JUST IN CASE.
SORRY 'BOUT THAT.
NOD
SHE ISN'T LIKE THE OTHER STUDENTS... BUT I CAN SEE THAT SHE'S STILL VERY NAÏVE.
I THINK I'VE GOT THIS ONE FIGURED OUT.
NOD
HMPH. GUESS YOU CAN'T HELP IT.
WHEN YOU SPIN, PRETEND YOU'RE A PUPPY...
AND CHANNEL THAT SWEET CUTENESS.
PUPPY?
UH... LIKE THIS?
SWEAT
PERK
HOP!
SHAKE
NO, LIKE THIS.
WAG
LIKE THIS?
WAG
THAT'S IT!
JUST LIKE THAT!
WAG

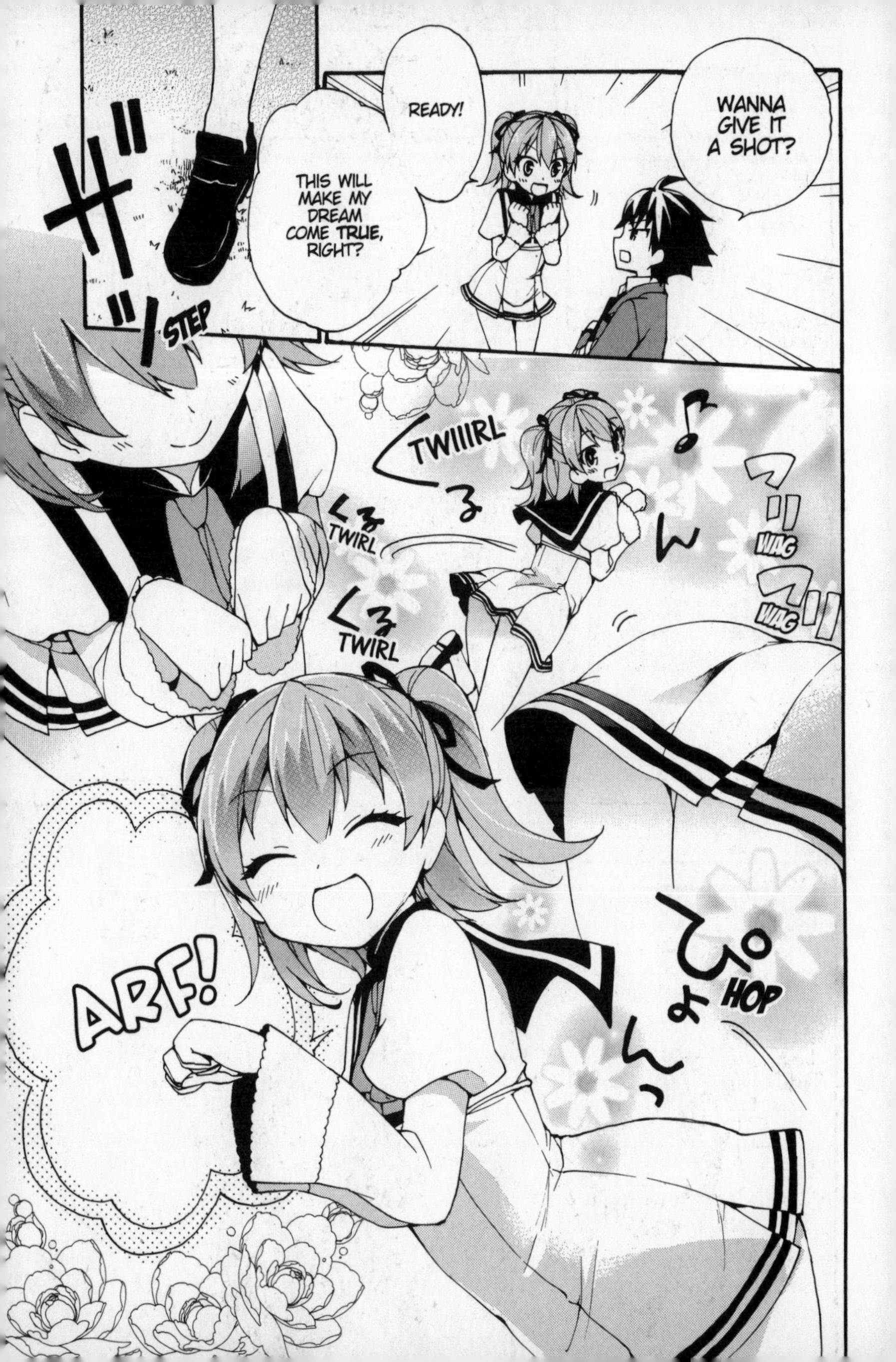
WANNA GIVE IT A SHOT?
READY!
THIS WILL MAKE MY DREAM COME TRUE, RIGHT?
STEP
TWIIIRL
TWIRL
TWIRL
WAG
WAG
HOP
ARF!

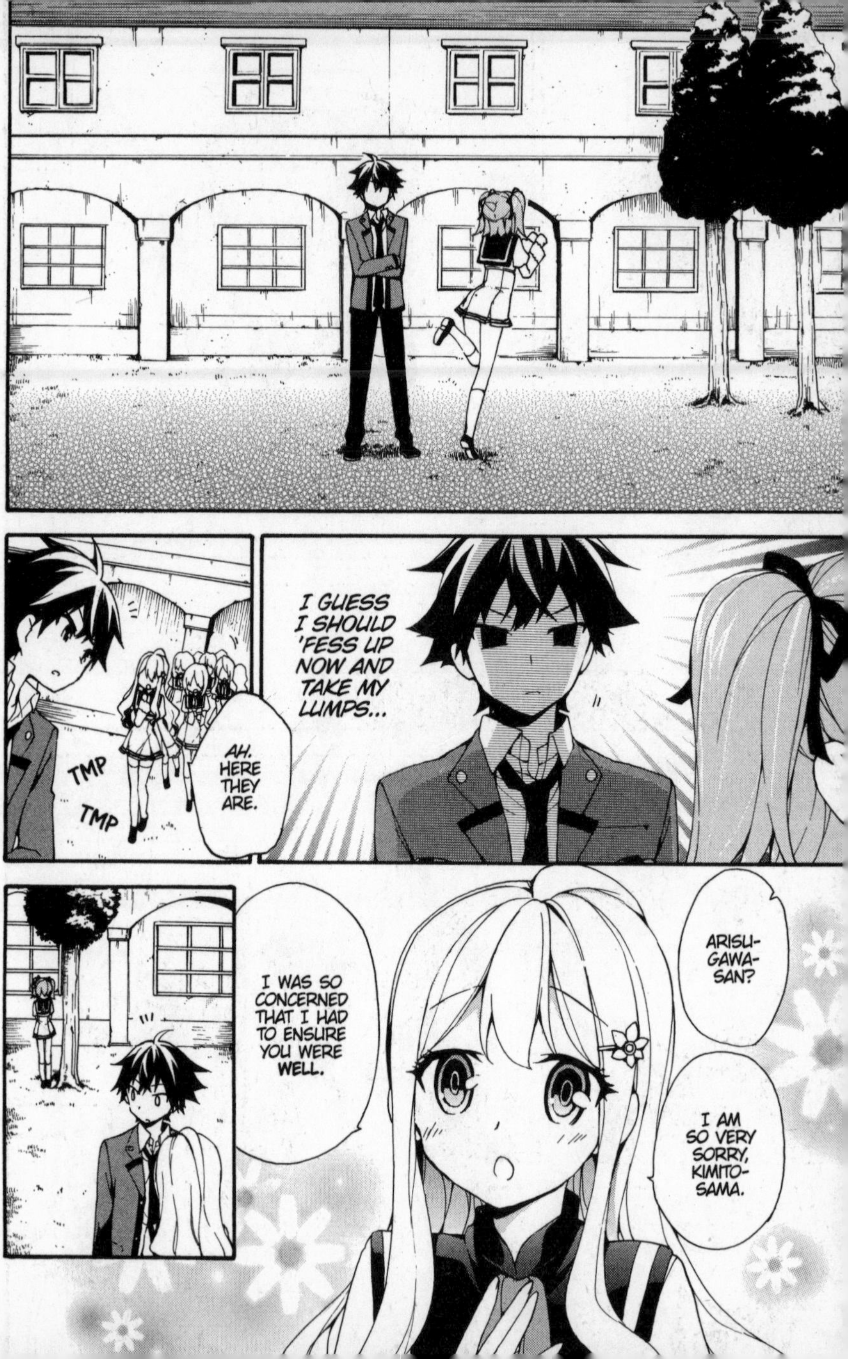
I GUESS I SHOULD 'FESS UP NOW AND TAKE MY LUMPS...
AH. HERE THEY ARE.
TMP
TMP
ARISU-GAWA-SAN?
I AM SO VERY SORRY, KIMITO-SAMA.
I WAS SO CONCERNED THAT I HAD TO ENSURE YOU WERE WELL.

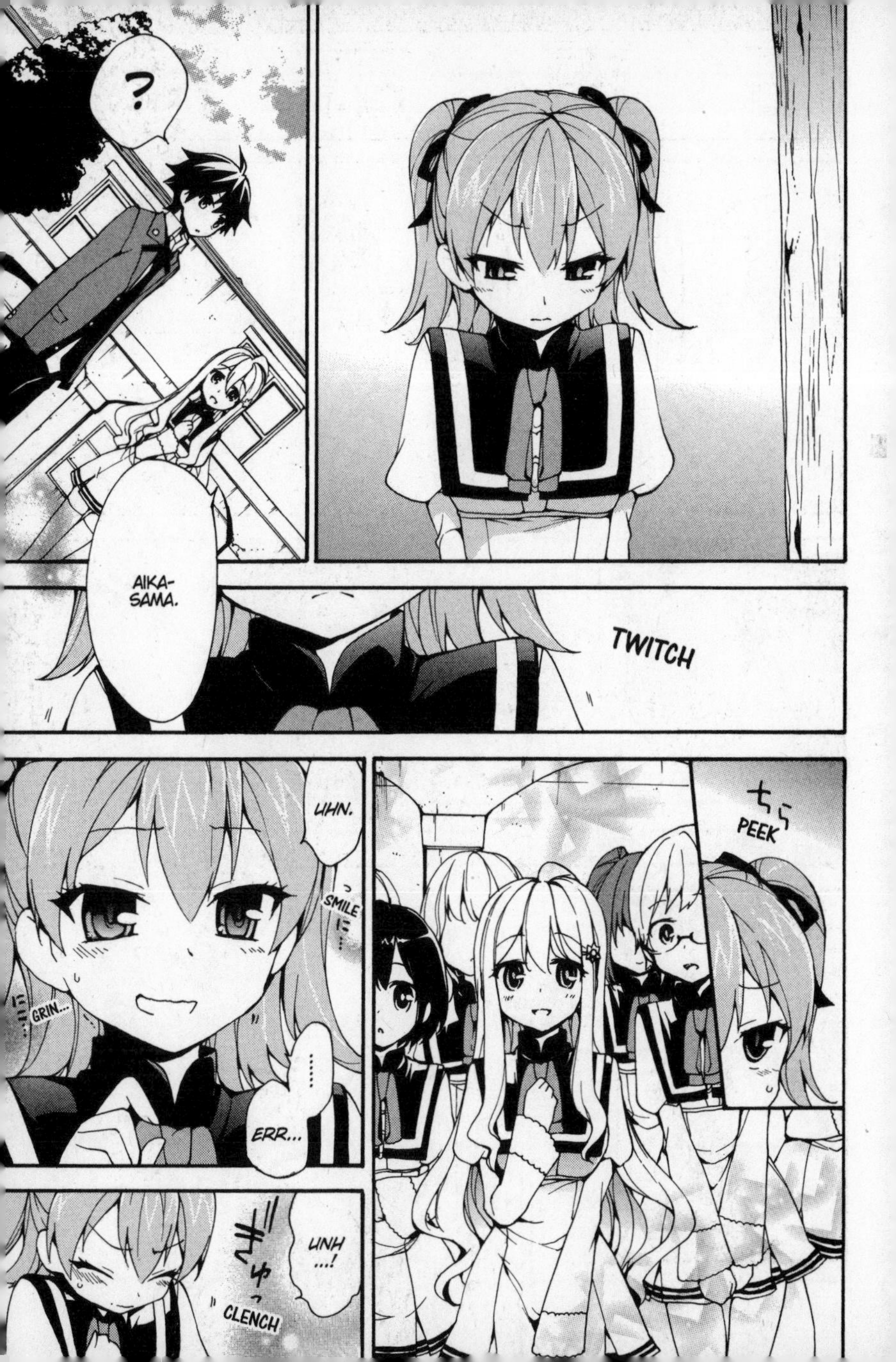

?
AIKA-SAMA.
TWITCH
ちら
PEEK
UHN.
SMILE
GRIN...
......
ERR...
UNH ...!
CLENCH

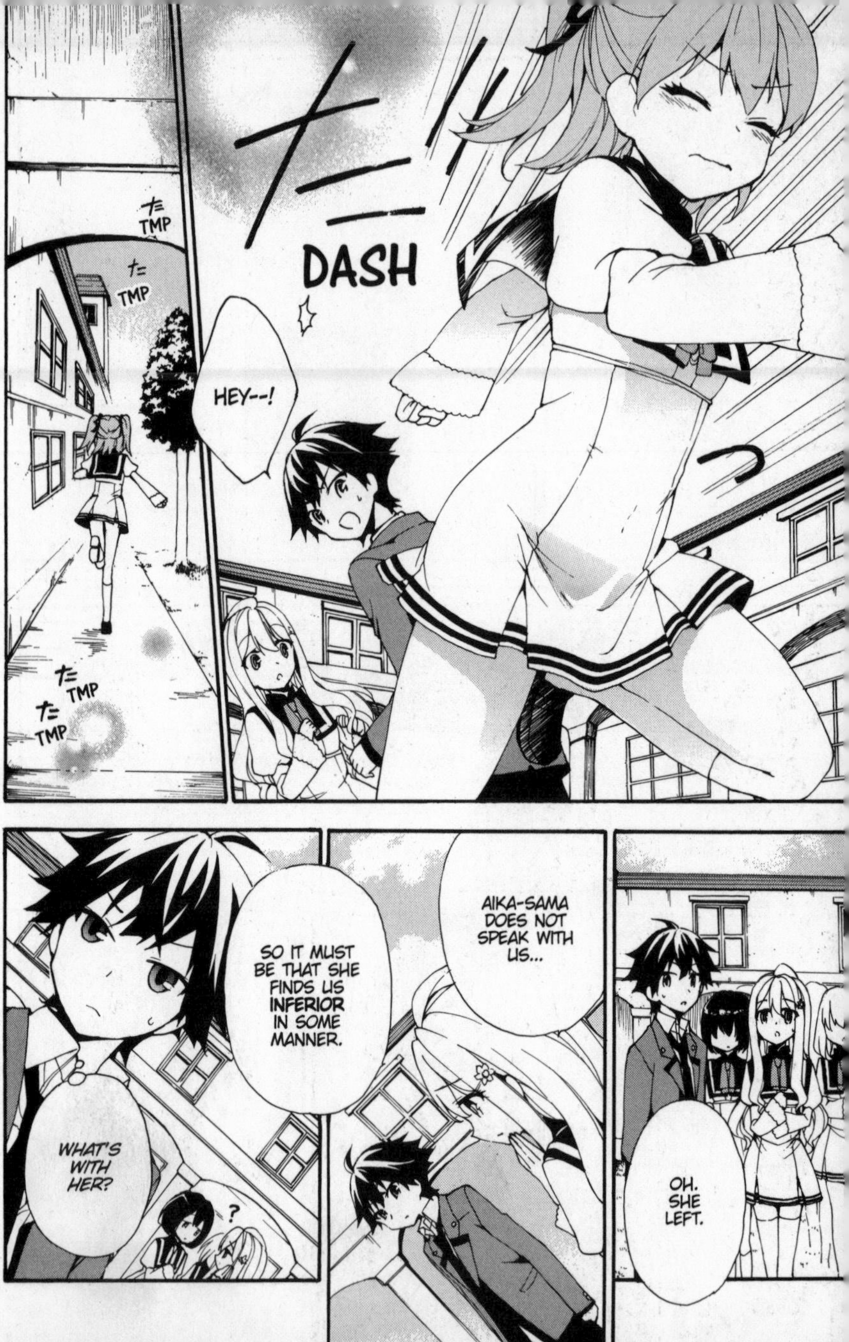
DASH
HEY--!
た TMP
た TMP
た TMP
た TMP
OH. SHE LEFT.
AIKA-SAMA DOES NOT SPEAK WITH US...
SO IT MUST BE THAT SHE FINDS US INFERIOR IN SOME MANNER.
WHAT'S WITH HER?
?

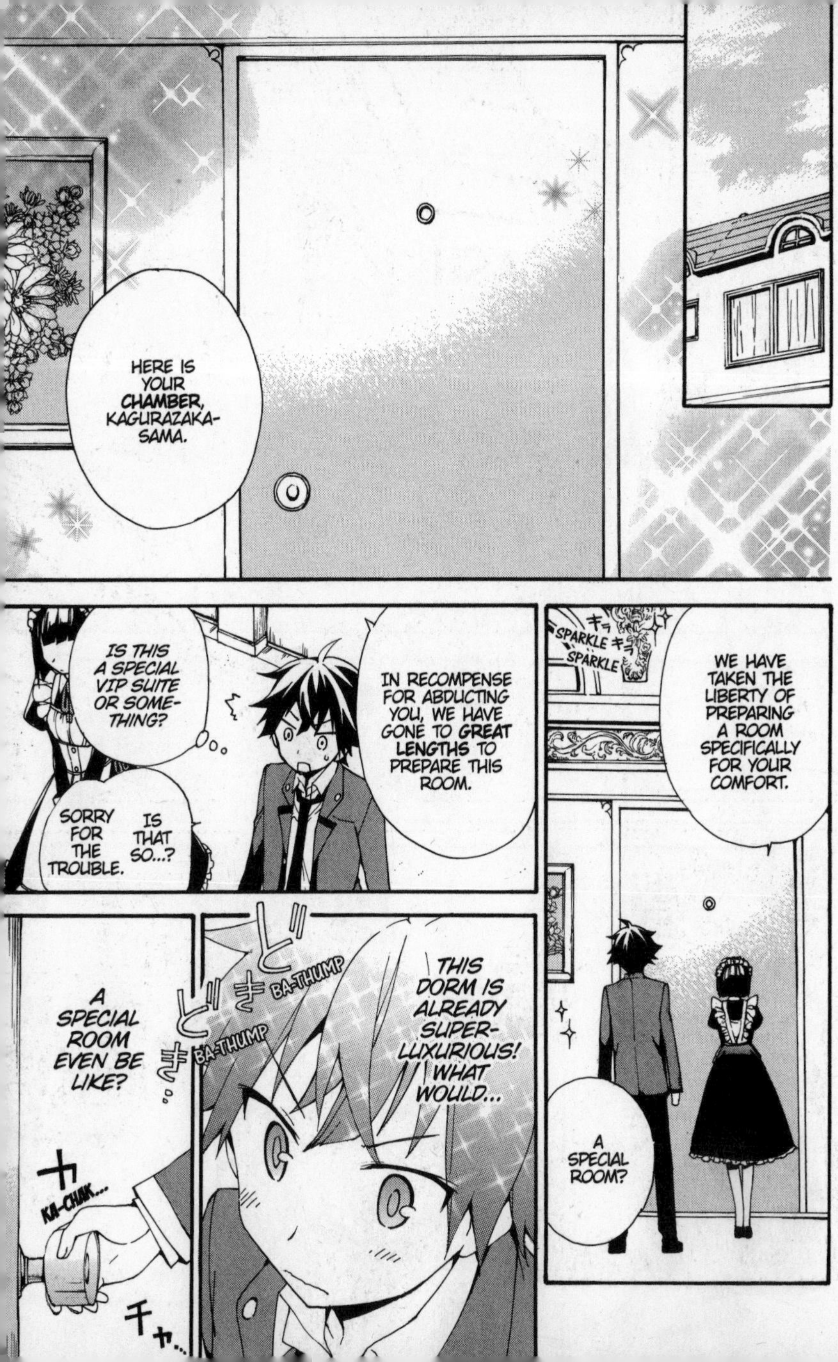
HERE IS YOUR CHAMBER, KAGURAZAKA-SAMA.
SPARKLE SPARKLE
WE HAVE TAKEN THE LIBERTY OF PREPARING A ROOM SPECIFICALLY FOR YOUR COMFORT.
A SPECIAL ROOM?
IN RECOMPENSE FOR ABDUCTING YOU, WE HAVE GONE TO GREAT LENGTHS TO PREPARE THIS ROOM.
IS THIS A SPECIAL VIP SUITE OR SOME-THING?
IS THAT SO...?
SORRY FOR THE TROUBLE.
BA-THUMP
BA-THUMP
THIS DORM IS ALREADY SUPER-LUXURIOUS! WHAT WOULD...
A SPECIAL ROOM EVEN BE LIKE?
KA-CHAK...

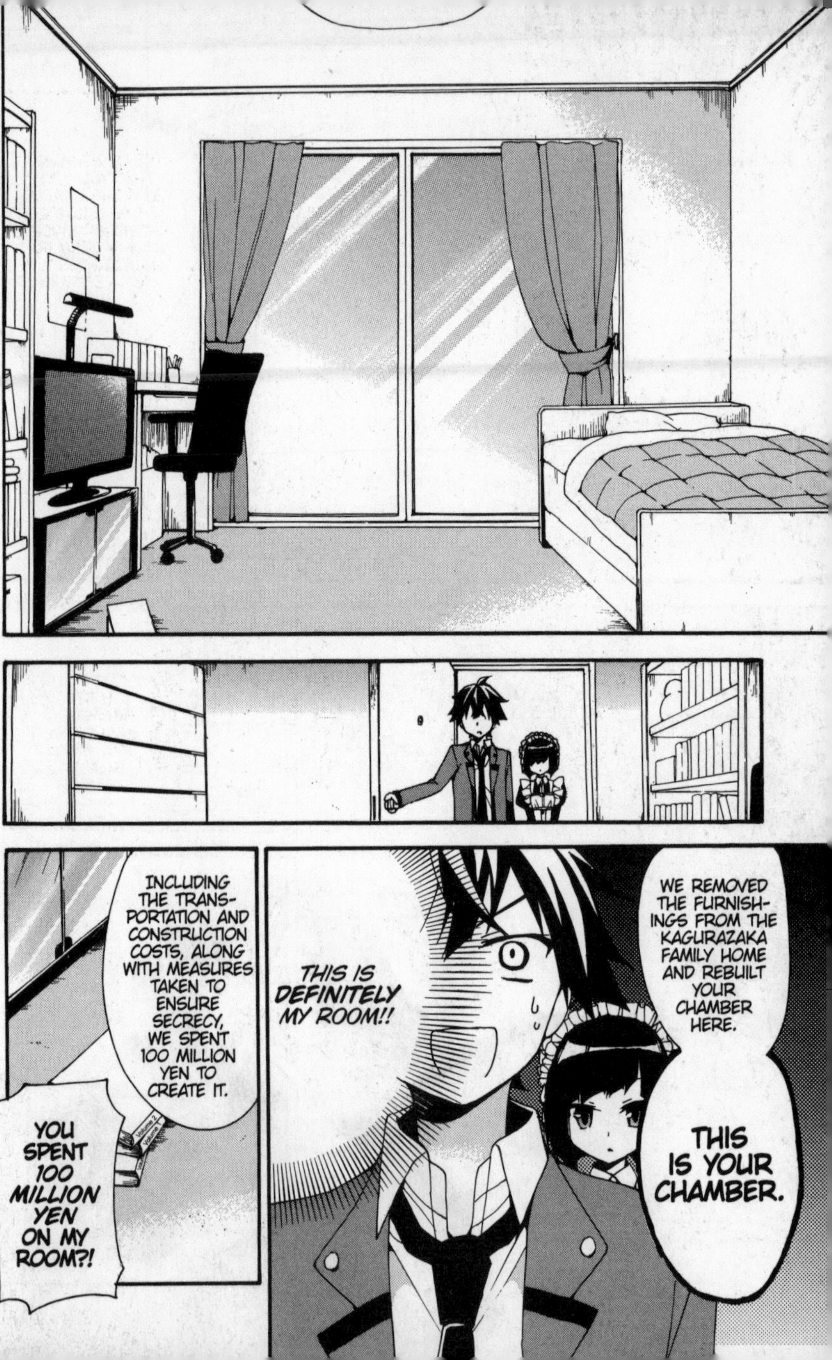
WE REMOVED THE FURNISHINGS FROM THE KAGURAZAKA FAMILY HOME AND REBUILT YOUR CHAMBER HERE.
THIS IS YOUR CHAMBER.
THIS IS DEFINITELY MY ROOM!!
INCLUDING THE TRANSPORTATION AND CONSTRUCTION COSTS, ALONG WITH MEASURES TAKEN TO ENSURE SECRECY, WE SPENT 100 MILLION YEN TO CREATE IT.
YOU SPENT 100 MILLION YEN ON MY ROOM?!

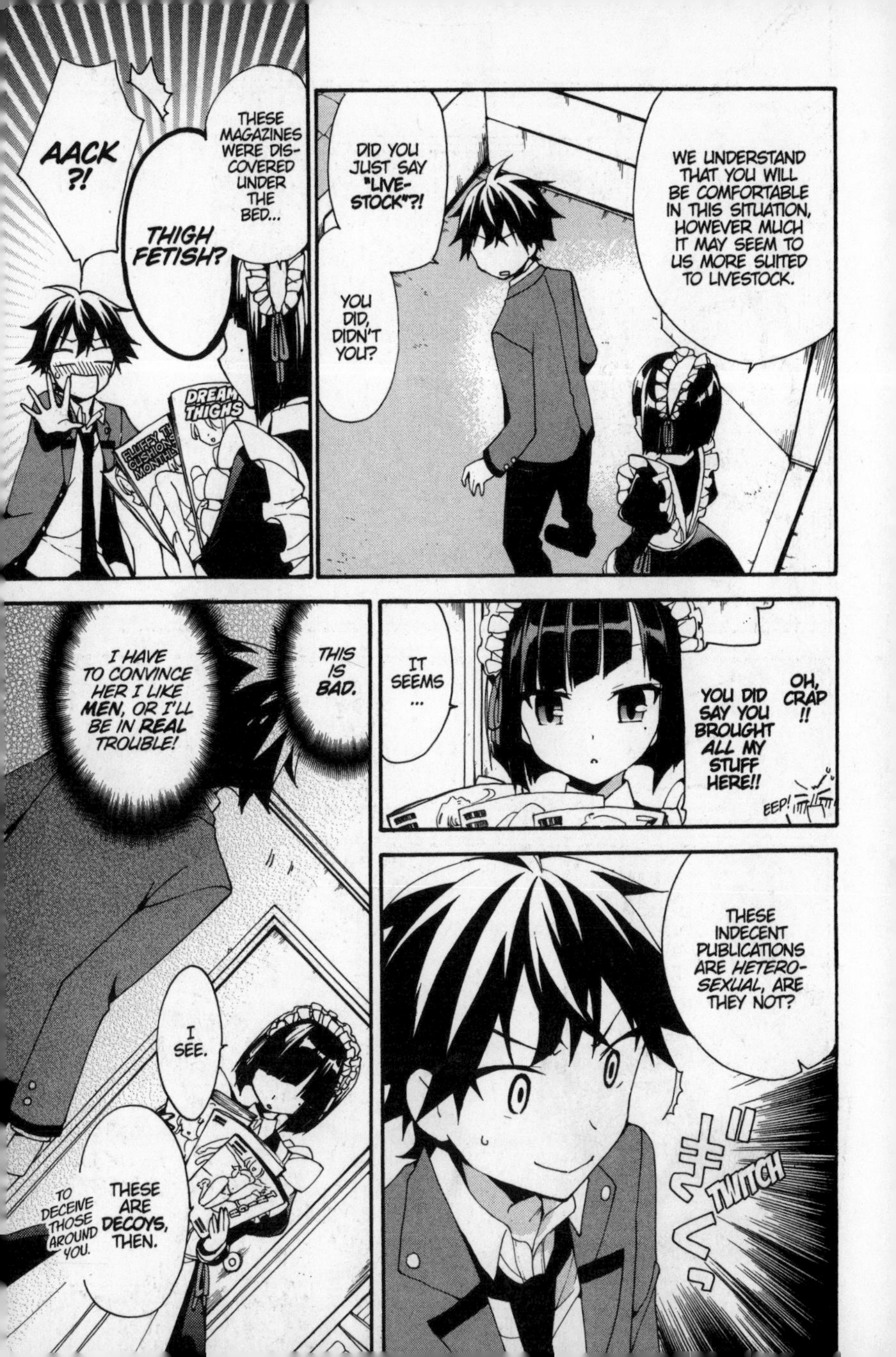
WE UNDERSTAND THAT YOU WILL BE COMFORTABLE IN THIS SITUATION, HOWEVER MUCH IT MAY SEEM TO US MORE SUITED TO LIVESTOCK.
DID YOU JUST SAY "LIVE-STOCK"?!
YOU DID, DIDN'T YOU?
THESE MAGAZINES WERE DIS-COVERED UNDER THE BED...
THIGH FETISH?
AACK ?!
DREAM THIGHS
OH, CRAP!!
YOU DID SAY YOU BROUGHT ALL MY STUFF HERE!!
IT SEEMS ...
EEP!
THESE INDECENT PUBLICATIONS ARE HETERO-SEXUAL, ARE THEY NOT?
TWITCH
THIS IS BAD.
I HAVE TO CONVINCE HER I LIKE MEN, OR I'LL BE IN REAL TROUBLE!
I SEE.
THESE ARE DECOYS, THEN.
TO DECEIVE THOSE AROUND YOU.

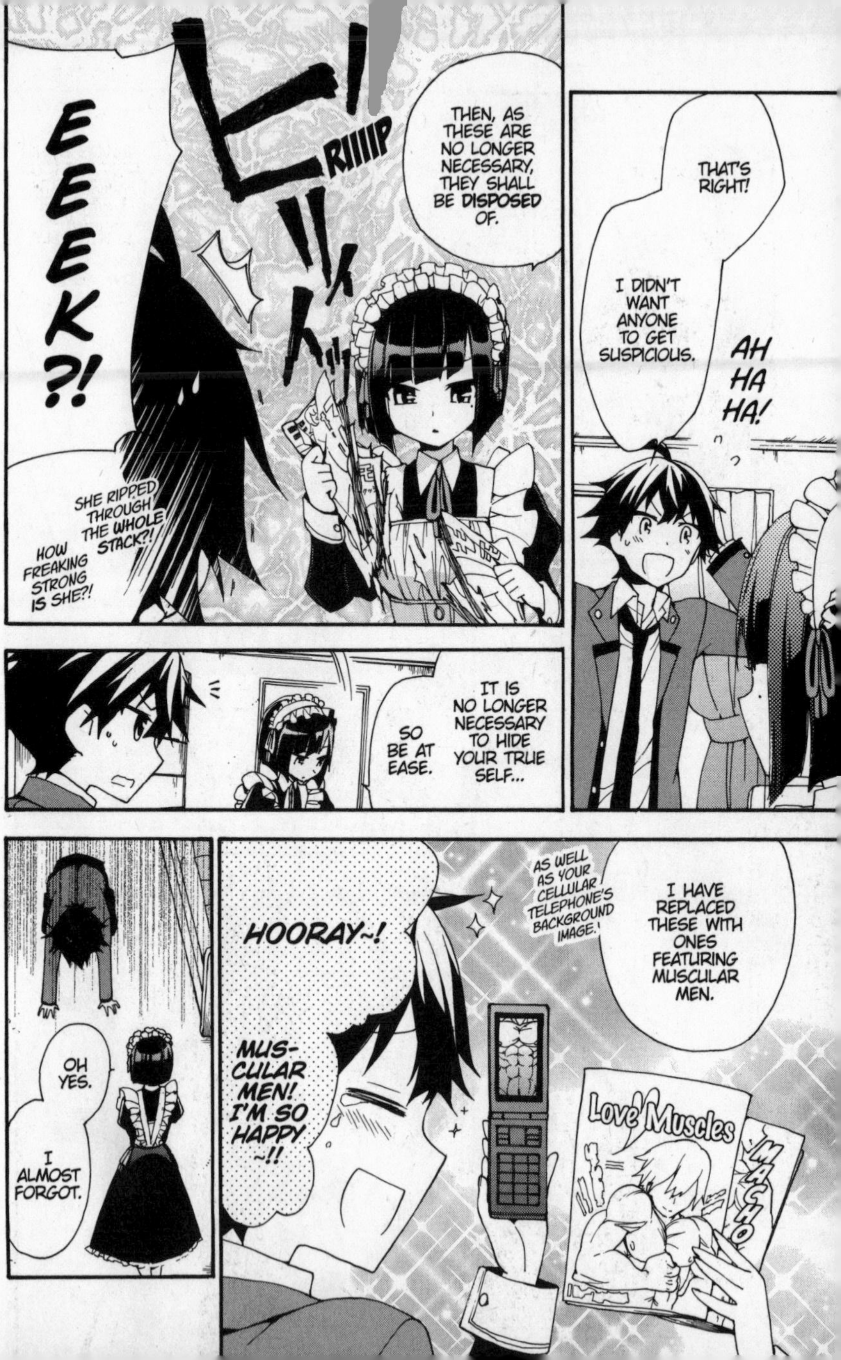
THAT'S RIGHT!
I DIDN'T WANT ANYONE TO GET SUSPICIOUS.
AH HA HA!
THEN, AS THESE ARE NO LONGER NECESSARY, THEY SHALL BE DISPOSED OF.
RIIIIP
EEEEK?!
SHE RIPPED THROUGH THE WHOLE STACK?!
HOW FREAKING STRONG IS SHE?!
IT IS NO LONGER NECESSARY TO HIDE YOUR TRUE SELF...
SO BE AT EASE.
I HAVE REPLACED THESE WITH ONES FEATURING MUSCULAR MEN.
AS WELL AS YOUR CELLULAR TELEPHONE'S BACKGROUND IMAGE.
HOORAY~!
MUS-CULAR MEN! I'M SO HAPPY ~!!
Love Muscles
MACHO
OH YES.
I ALMOST FORGOT.

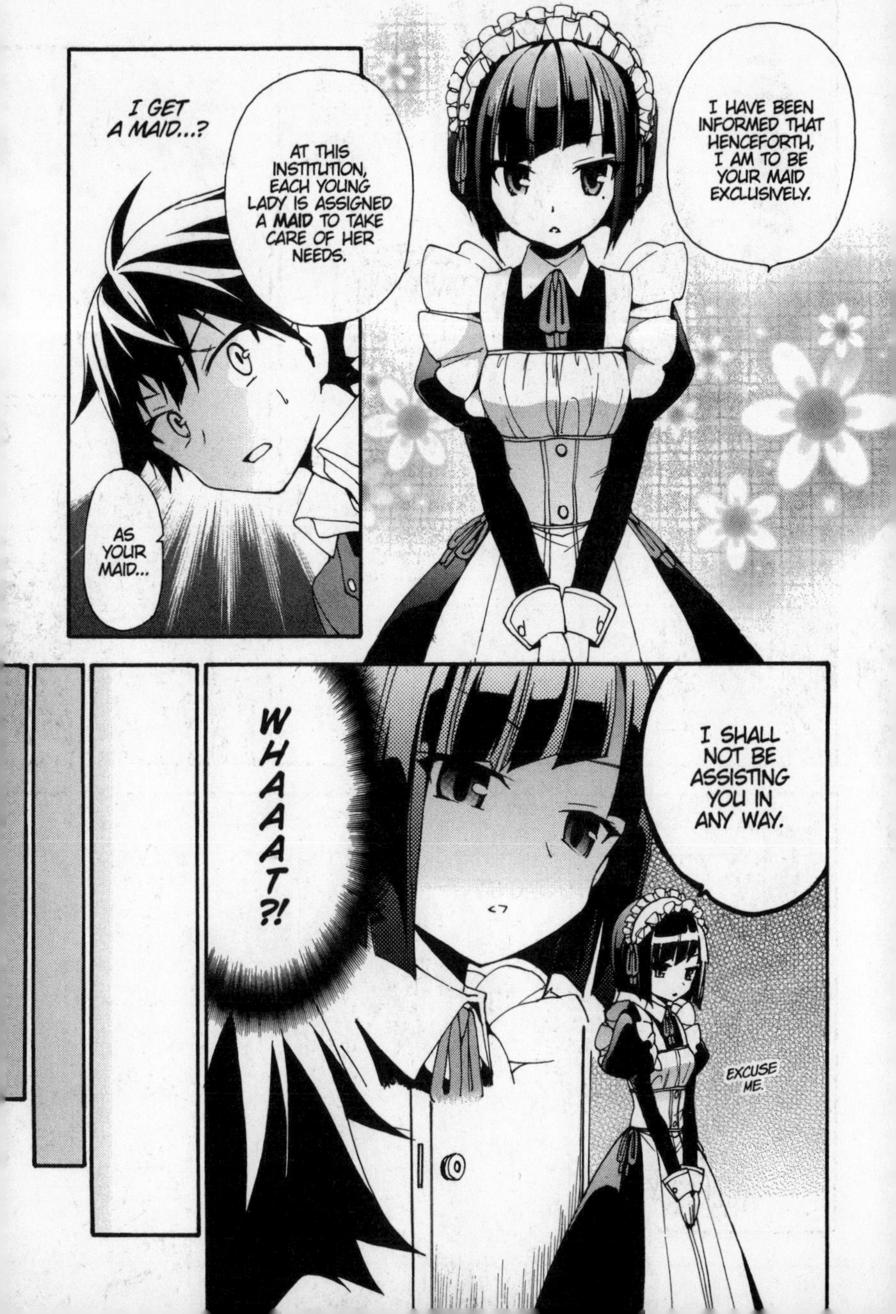
I HAVE BEEN INFORMED THAT HENCEFORTH, I AM TO BE YOUR MAID EXCLUSIVELY.
AT THIS INSTITUTION, EACH YOUNG LADY IS ASSIGNED A MAID TO TAKE CARE OF HER NEEDS.
I GET A MAID...?
AS YOUR MAID...
I SHALL NOT BE ASSISTING YOU IN ANY WAY.
EXCUSE ME.
WHAAAAT?!

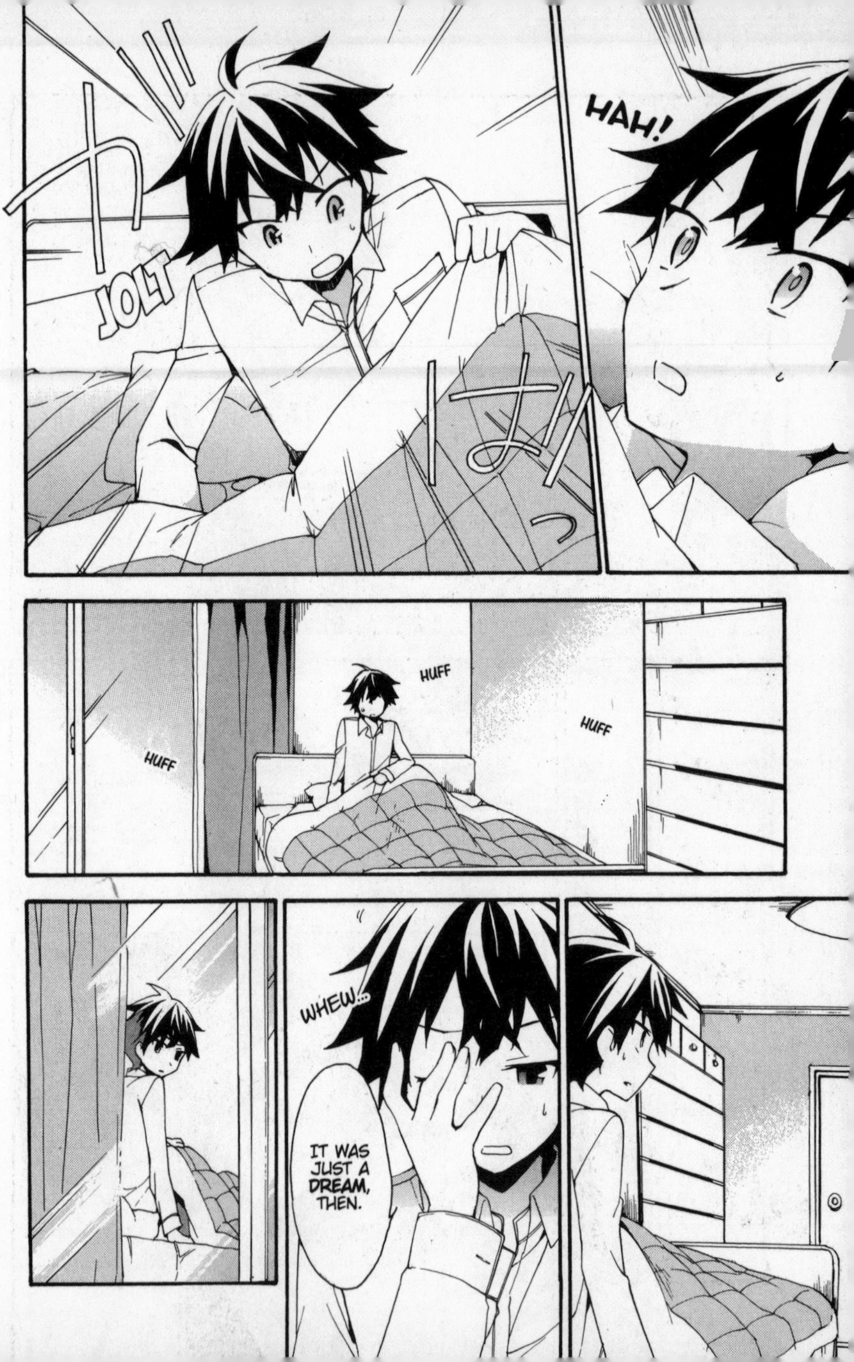
HAH!
はっ
JOLT
HUFF
HUFF
HUFF
WHEW...
IT WAS JUST A DREAM, THEN.

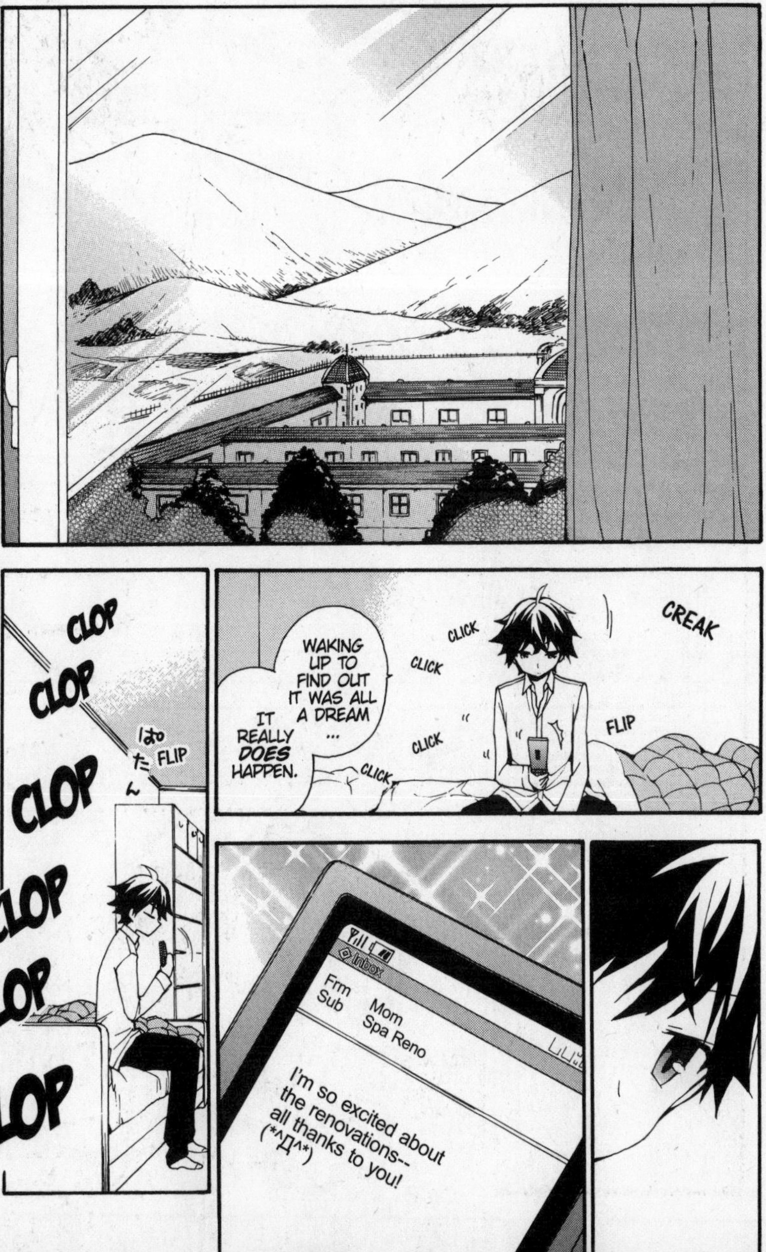
CREAK
CLICK
WAKING UP TO FIND OUT IT WAS ALL A DREAM ...
CLICK
FLIP
IT REALLY DOES HAPPEN.
CLICK
CLICK
Inbox
Frm Mom
Sub Spa Reno
I'm so excited about the renovations-- all thanks to you! (*^Д^*)
CLOP
CLOP
ぱたん FLIP
CLOP
CLOP
CLOP
CLOP

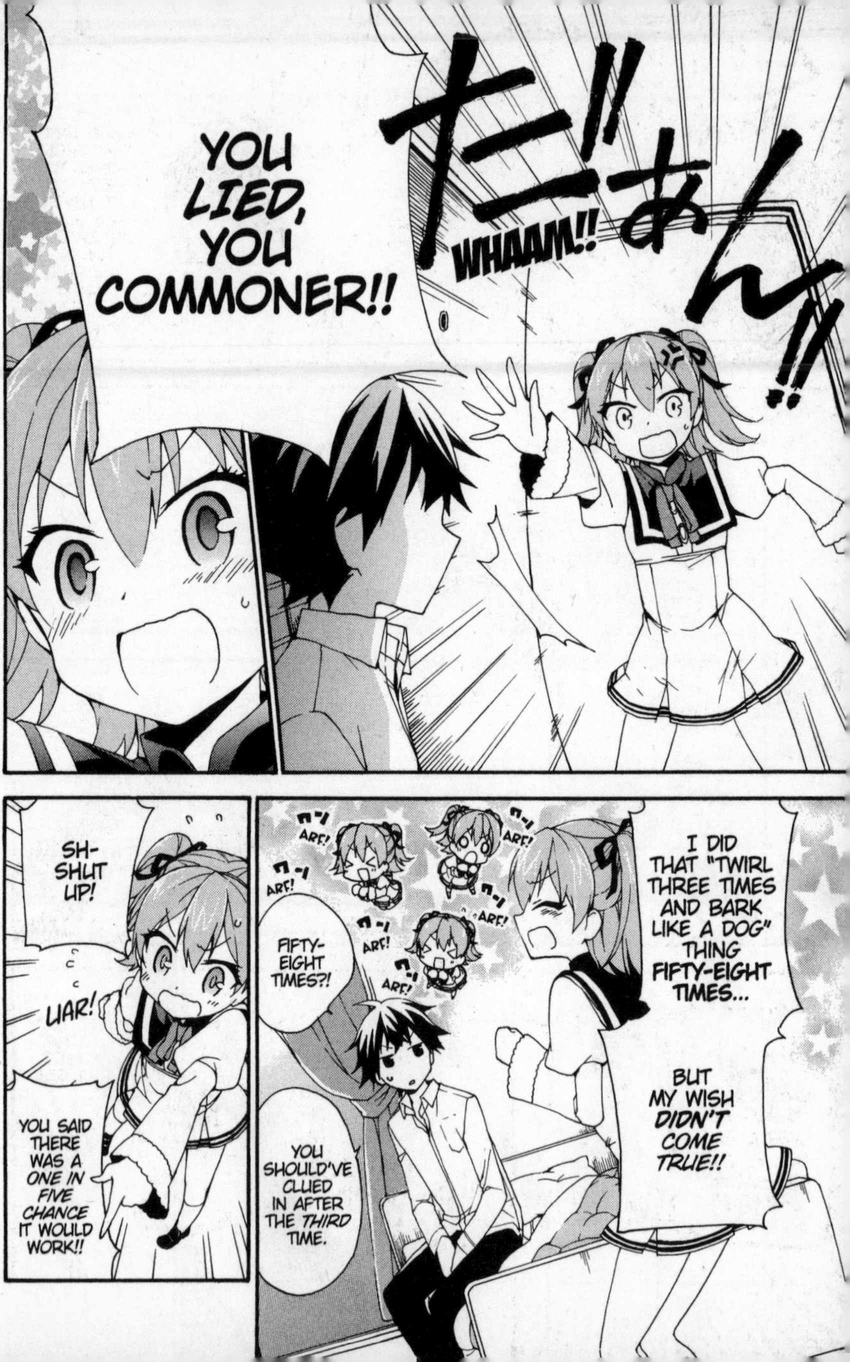
だあん!!
WHAAM!!
YOU LIED, YOU COMMONER!!
I DID THAT "TWIRL THREE TIMES AND BARK LIKE A DOG" THING FIFTY-EIGHT TIMES...
BUT MY WISH DIDN'T COME TRUE!!
ARF!
ARF!
ARF!
ARF!
ARF!
ARF!
FIFTY-EIGHT TIMES?!
YOU SHOULD'VE CLUED IN AFTER THE THIRD TIME.
SH-SHUT UP!
LIAR!
YOU SAID THERE WAS A ONE IN FIVE CHANCE IT WOULD WORK!!

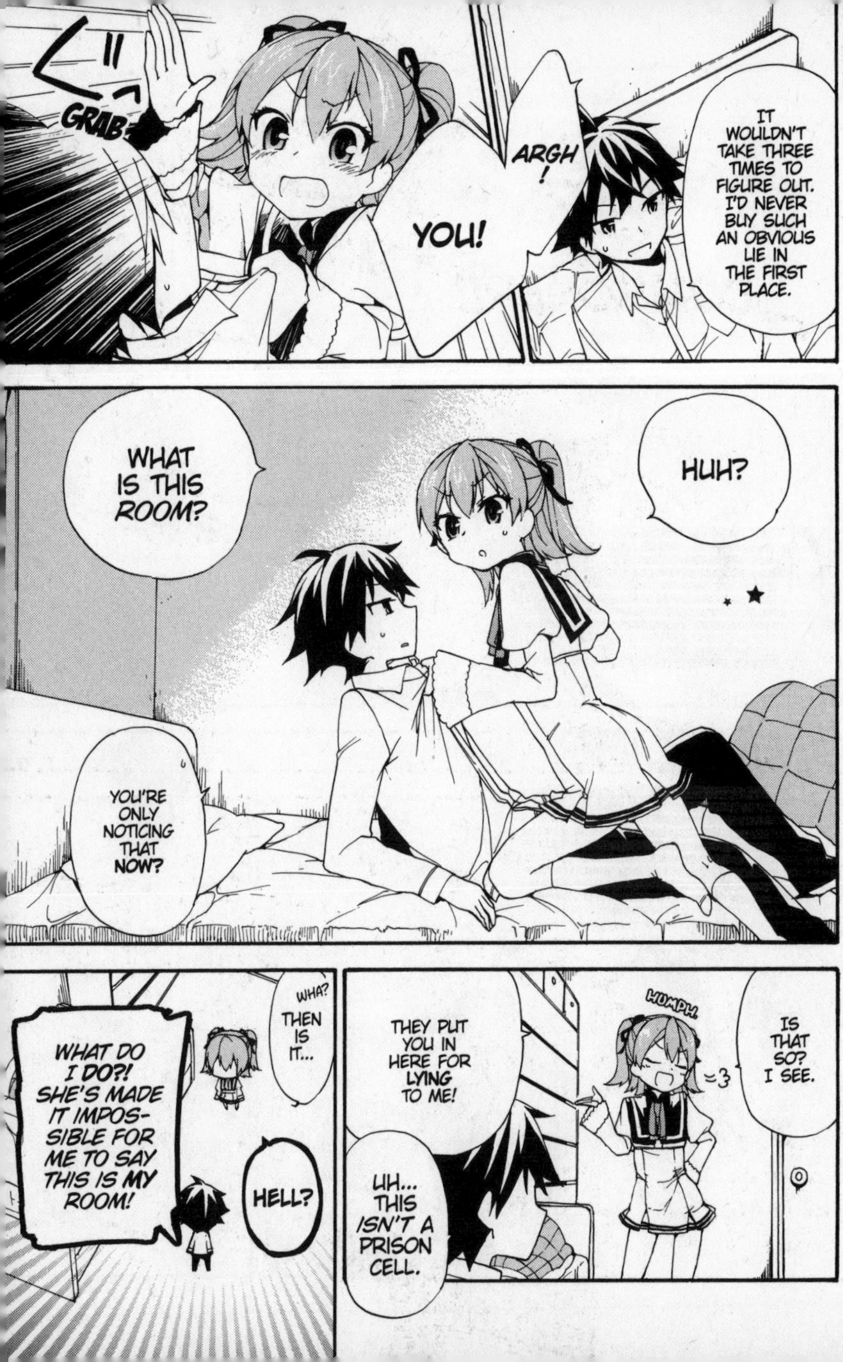
IT WOULDN'T TAKE THREE TIMES TO FIGURE OUT. I'D NEVER BUY SUCH AN OBVIOUS LIE IN THE FIRST PLACE.
ARGH!
YOU!
GRAB
HUH?
WHAT IS THIS ROOM?
YOU'RE ONLY NOTICING THAT NOW?
HUMPH.
IS THAT SO? I SEE.
THEY PUT YOU IN HERE FOR LYING TO ME!
UH... THIS ISN'T A PRISON CELL.
WHA? THEN IS IT...
HELL?
WHAT DO I DO?! SHE'S MADE IT IMPOSSIBLE FOR ME TO SAY THIS IS MY ROOM!

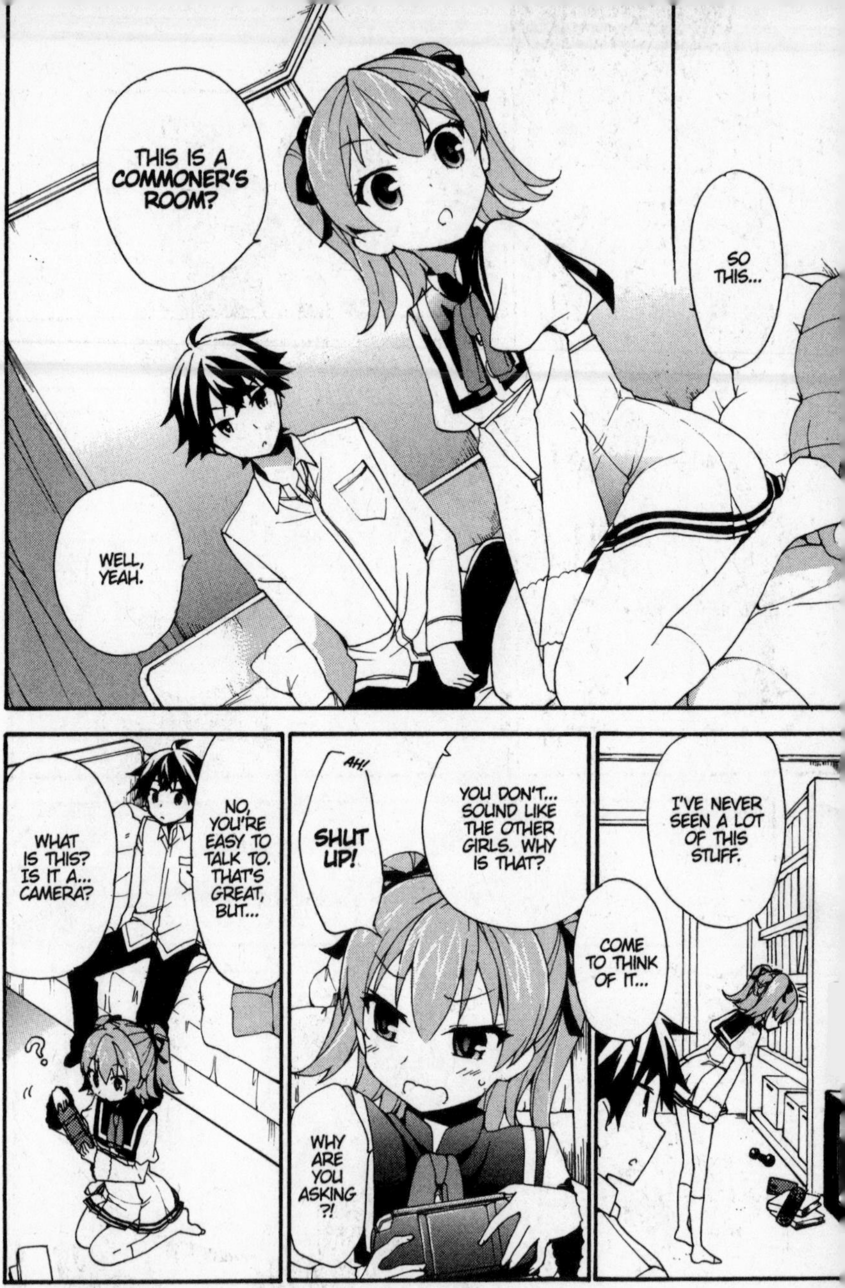
SO THIS...
THIS IS A COMMONER'S ROOM?
WELL, YEAH.
I'VE NEVER SEEN A LOT OF THIS STUFF.
COME TO THINK OF IT...
YOU DON'T... SOUND LIKE THE OTHER GIRLS. WHY IS THAT?
AH!
SHUT UP!
WHY ARE YOU ASKING?!
NO, YOU'RE EASY TO TALK TO. THAT'S GREAT, BUT...
WHAT IS THIS? IS IT A... CAMERA?

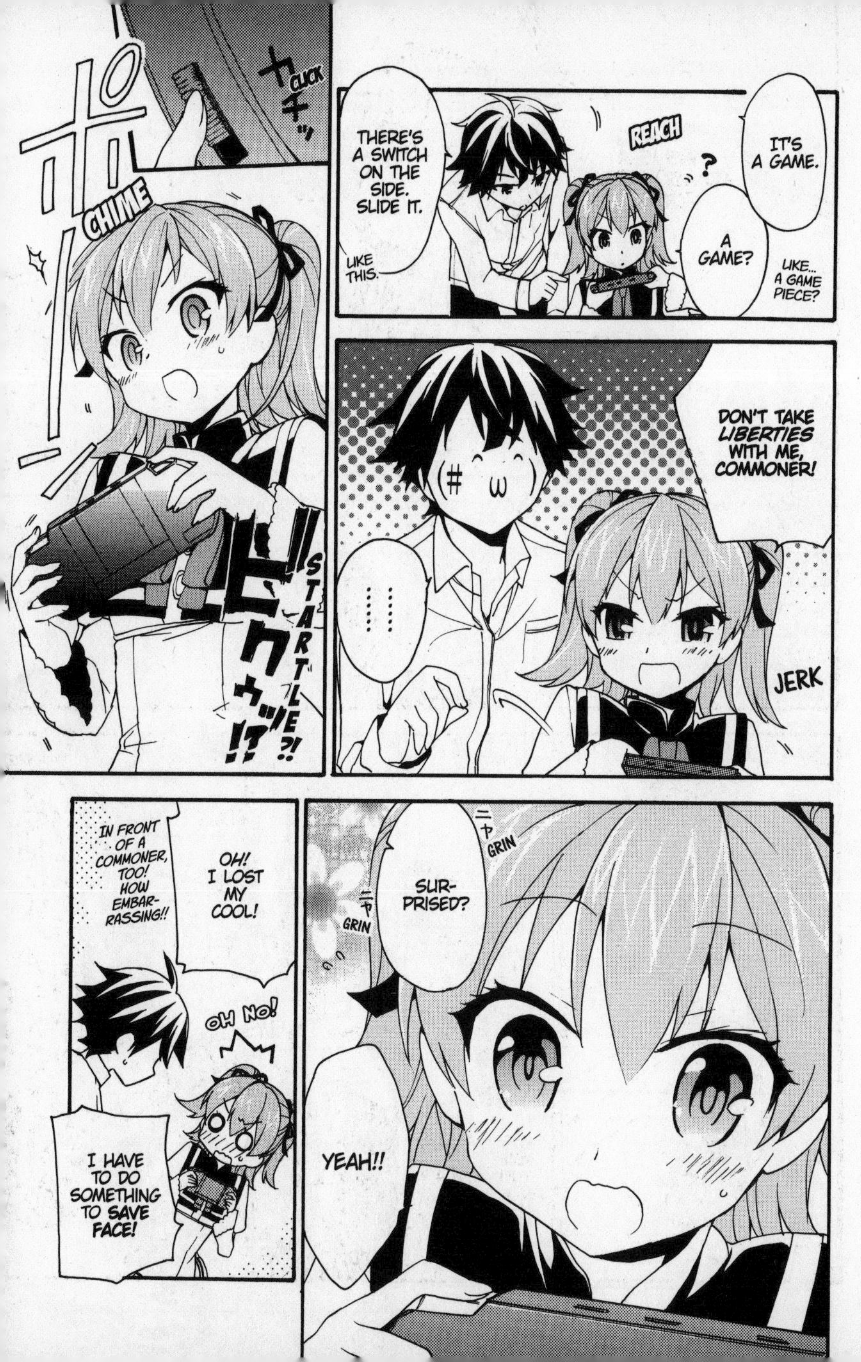
IT'S A GAME.
A GAME?
LIKE... A GAME PIECE?
?
REACH
THERE'S A SWITCH ON THE SIDE. SLIDE IT.
LIKE THIS.
CLICK
CHIME
STARTLE?!
DON'T TAKE LIBERTIES WITH ME, COMMONER!
JERK
......
GRIN
SUR-PRISED?
GRIN
YEAH!!
OH! I LOST MY COOL!
IN FRONT OF A COMMONER, TOO! HOW EMBAR-RASSING!!
OH NO!
I HAVE TO DO SOMETHING TO SAVE FACE!

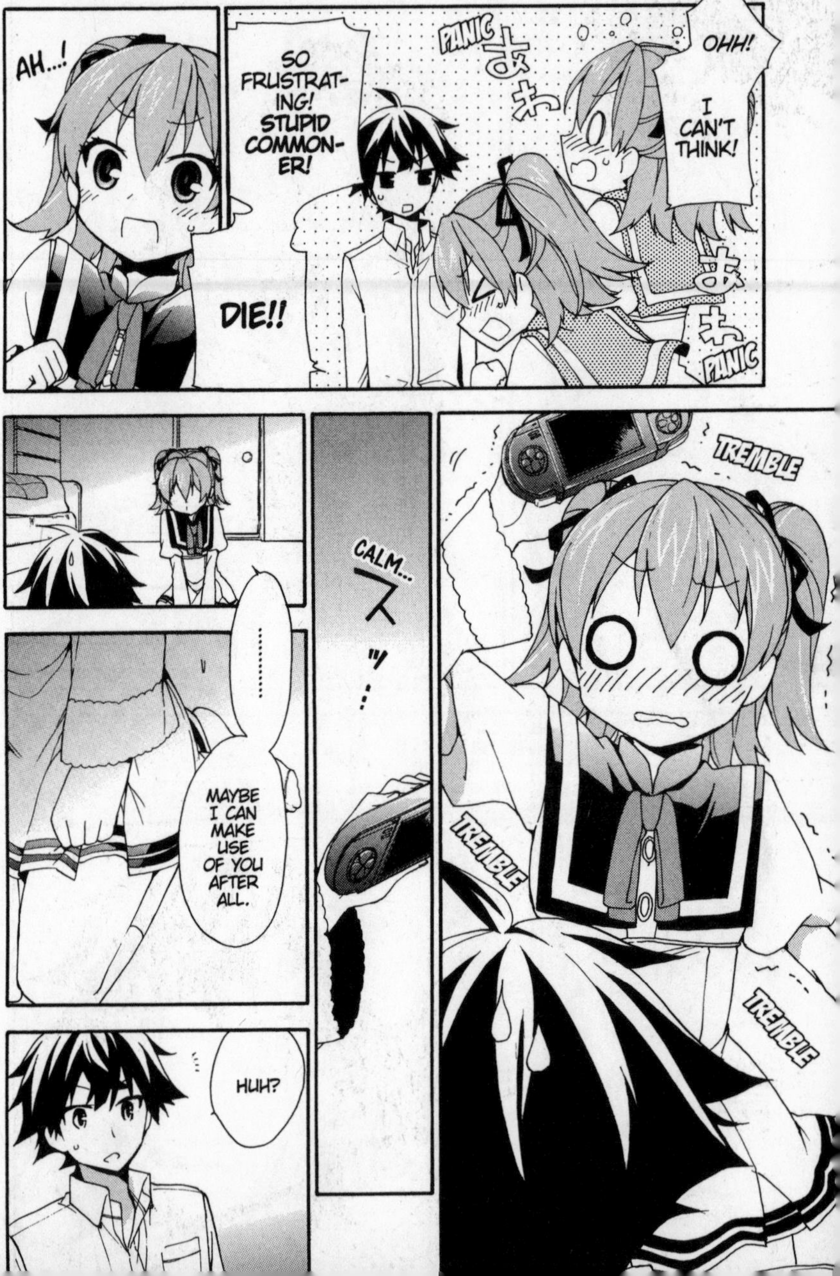
OHH!
I CAN'T THINK!
PANIC あわ
SO FRUSTRATING! STUPID COMMONER!
あわ PANIC
DIE!!
AH...!
TREMBLE
TREMBLE
TREMBLE
CALM... スッ
......
MAYBE I CAN MAKE USE OF YOU AFTER ALL.
HUH?

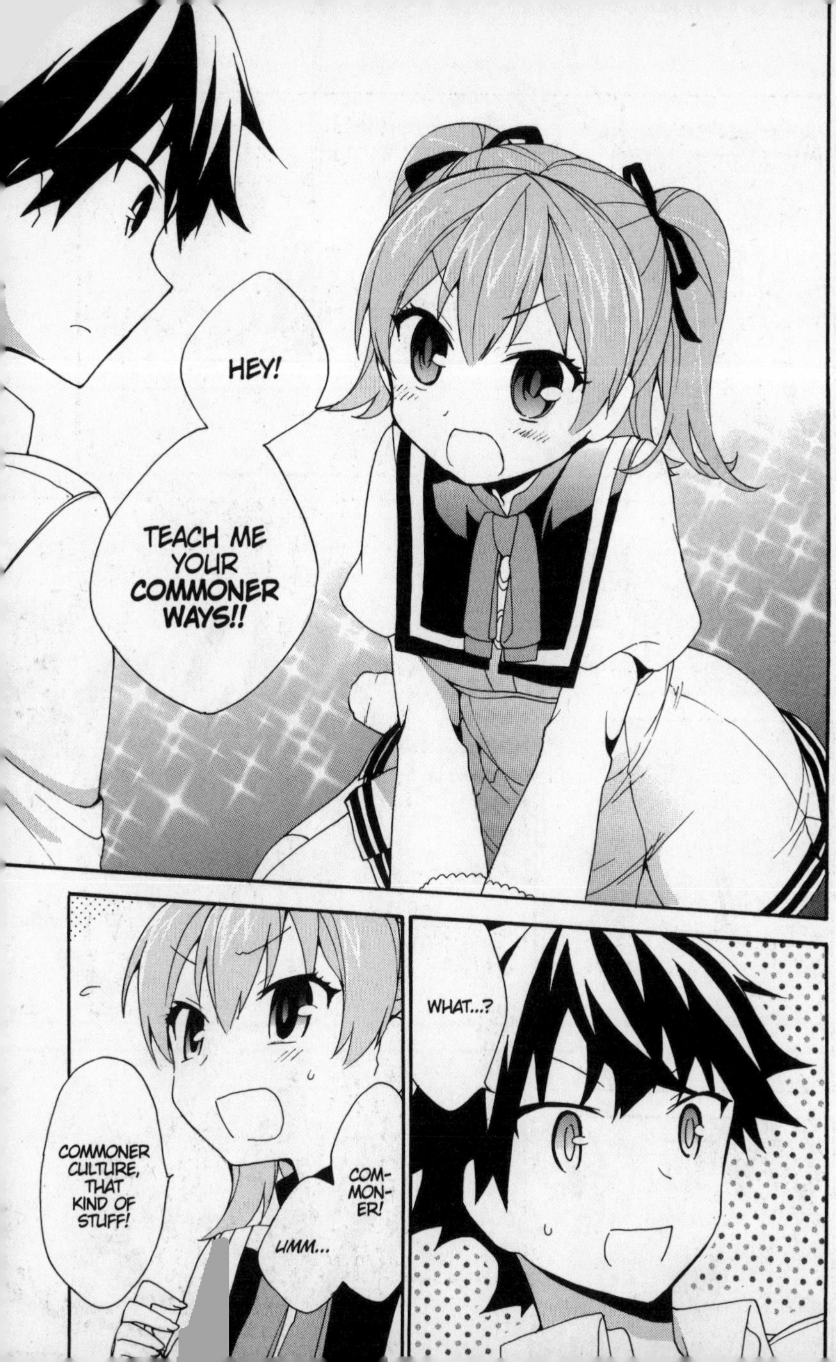
HEY!
TEACH ME YOUR COMMONER WAYS!!
WHAT...?
COM-MON-ER!
UMM...
COMMONER CULTURE, THAT KIND OF STUFF!

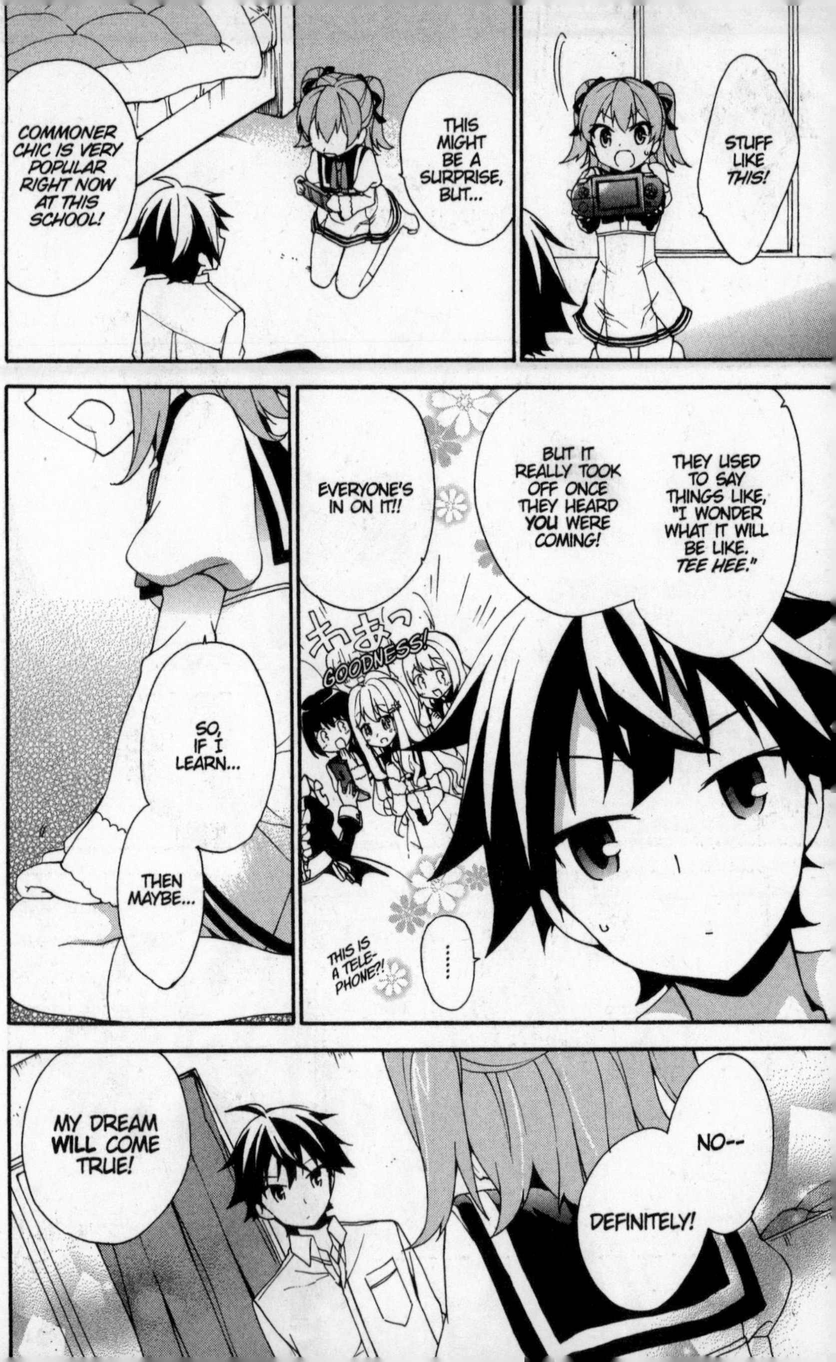
STUFF LIKE THIS!
THIS MIGHT BE A SURPRISE, BUT...
COMMONER CHIC IS VERY POPULAR RIGHT NOW AT THIS SCHOOL!
THEY USED TO SAY THINGS LIKE, "I WONDER WHAT IT WILL BE LIKE. TEE HEE."
BUT IT REALLY TOOK OFF ONCE THEY HEARD YOU WERE COMING!
EVERYONE'S IN ON IT!!
わぁっ
GOODNESS!
THIS IS A TELE-PHONE?!
......
SO, IF I LEARN...
THEN MAYBE...
NO--
DEFINITELY!
MY DREAM WILL COME TRUE!

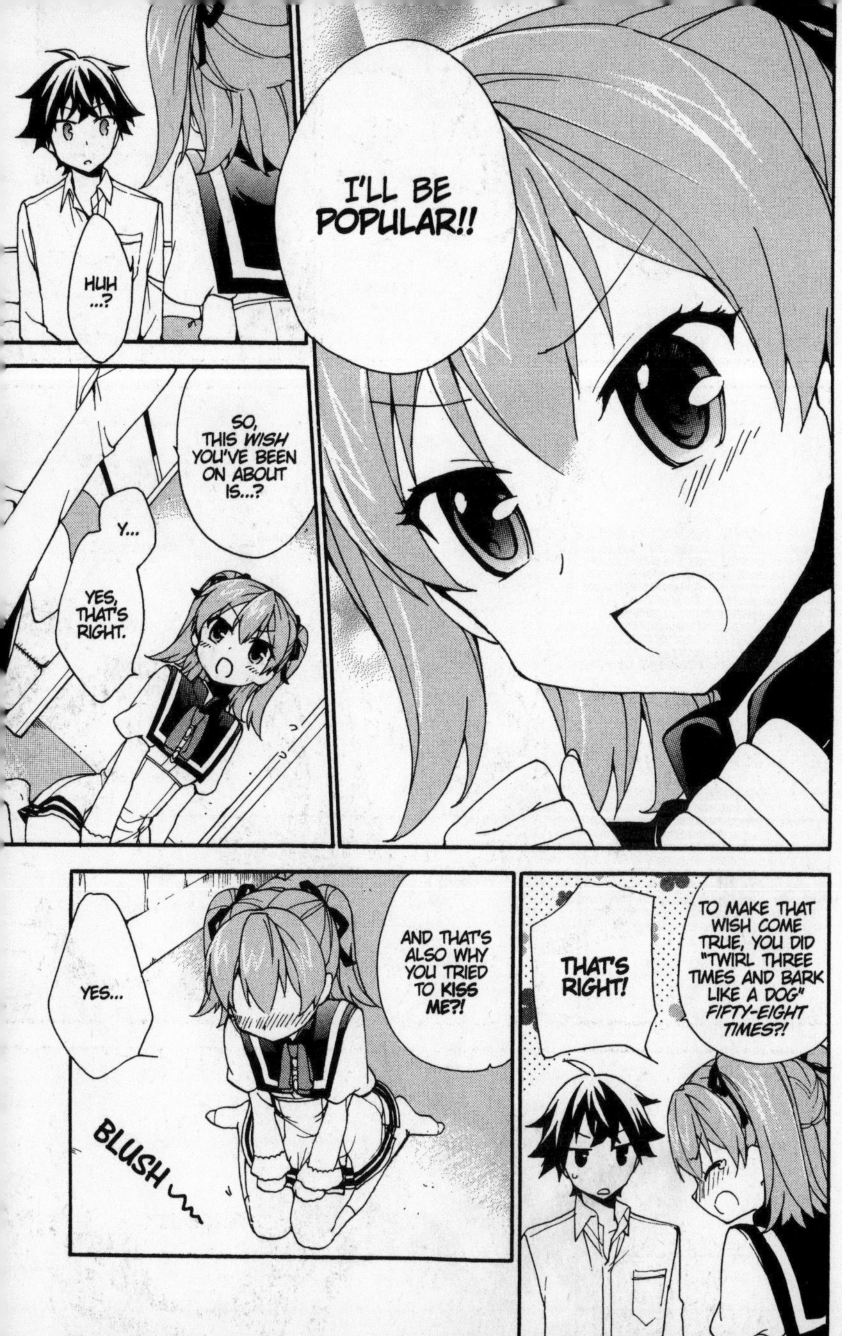
I'LL BE POPULAR!!
HUH ...?
SO, THIS *WISH* YOU'VE BEEN ON ABOUT IS...?
Y...
YES, THAT'S RIGHT.
TO MAKE THAT WISH COME TRUE, YOU DID "TWIRL THREE TIMES AND BARK LIKE A DOG" *FIFTY-EIGHT TIMES?!*
THAT'S RIGHT!
AND THAT'S ALSO WHY YOU TRIED TO KISS *ME?!*
YES...
BLUSH~

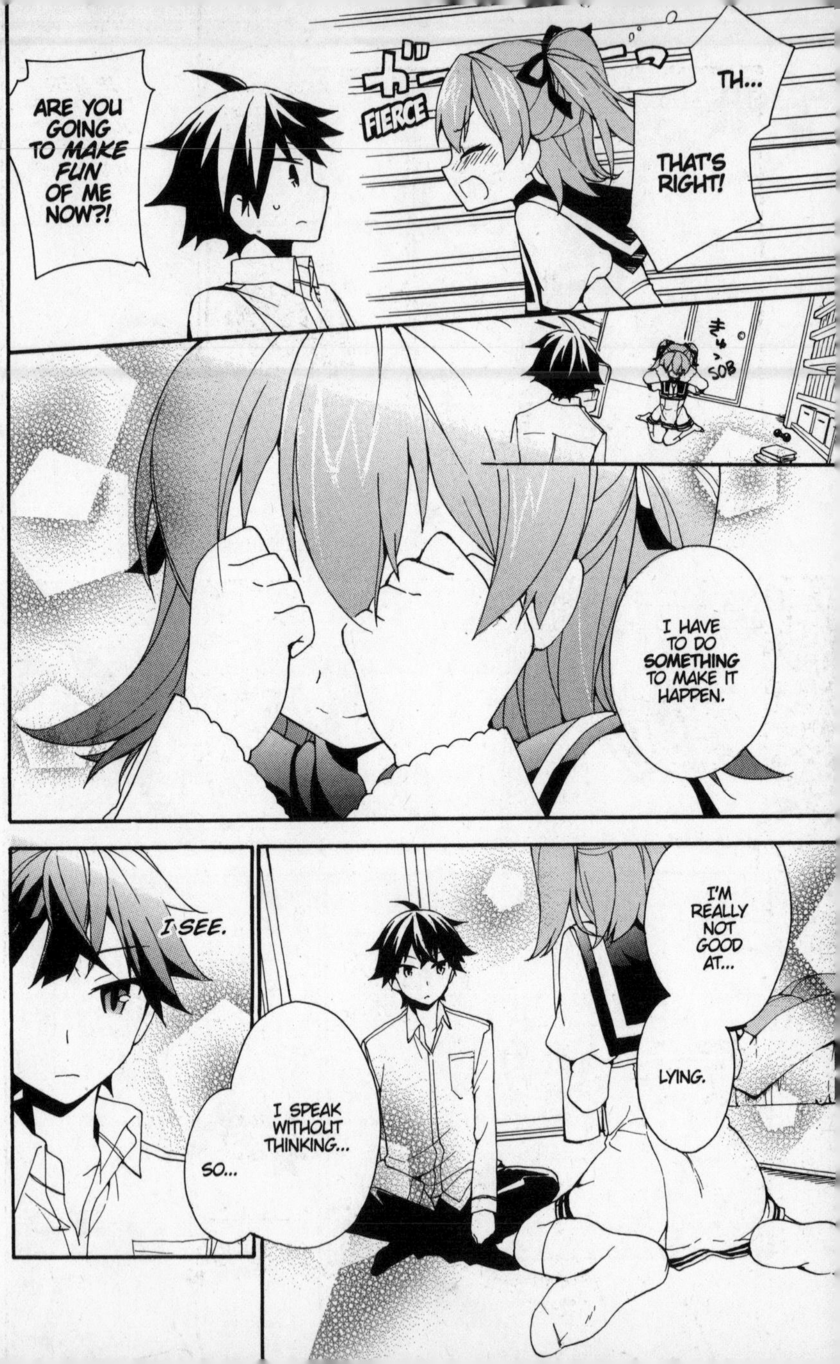
TH...
THAT'S RIGHT!
FIERCE
ARE YOU GOING TO MAKE FUN OF ME NOW?!
SOB
I HAVE TO DO SOMETHING TO MAKE IT HAPPEN.
I'M REALLY NOT GOOD AT...
LYING.
I SPEAK WITHOUT THINKING...
SO...
I SEE.

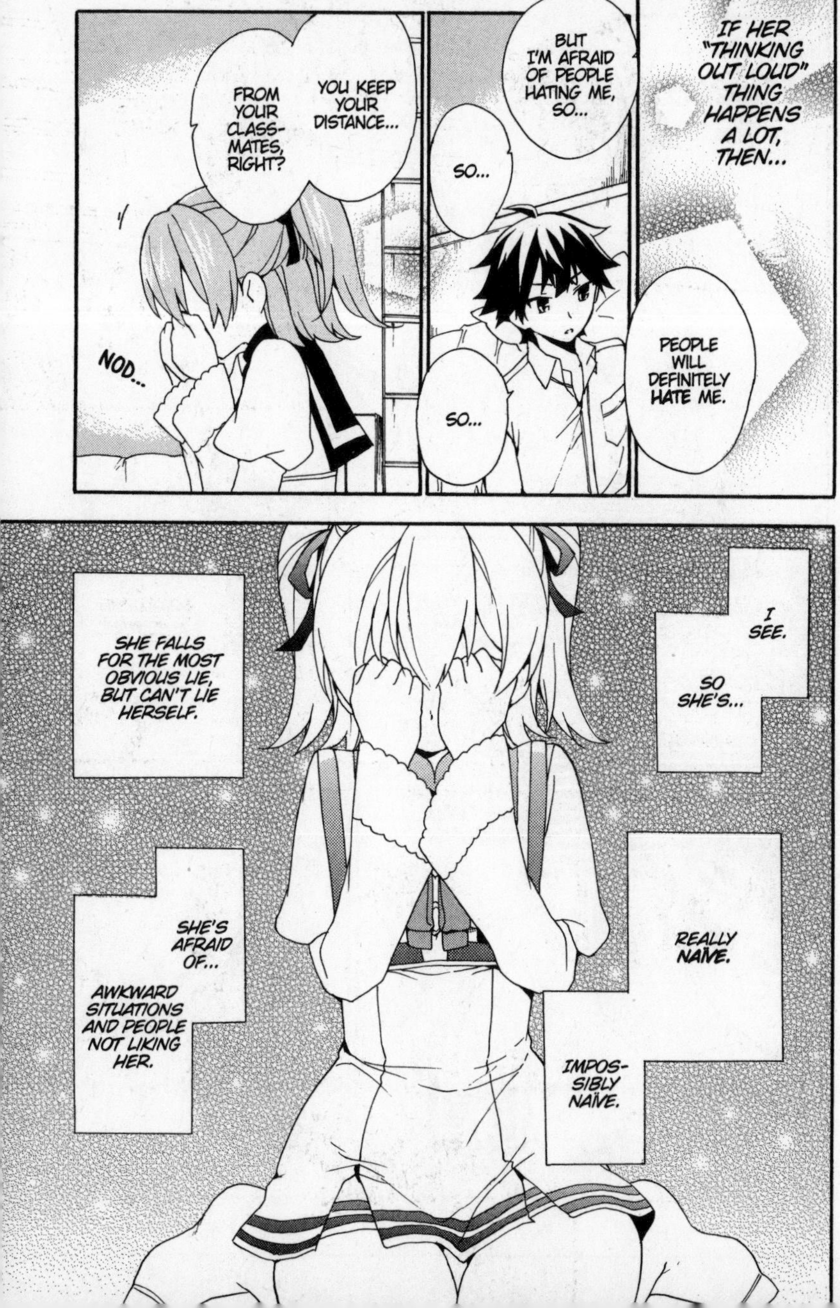
IF HER "THINKING OUT LOUD" THING HAPPENS A LOT, THEN...
PEOPLE WILL DEFINITELY HATE ME.
BUT I'M AFRAID OF PEOPLE HATING ME, SO...
SO...
SO...
YOU KEEP YOUR DISTANCE...
FROM YOUR CLASSMATES, RIGHT?
NOD...
I SEE.
SO SHE'S...
REALLY NAÏVE.
IMPOSSIBLY NAÏVE.
SHE FALLS FOR THE MOST OBVIOUS LIE, BUT CAN'T LIE HERSELF.
SHE'S AFRAID OF...
AWKWARD SITUATIONS AND PEOPLE NOT LIKING HER.

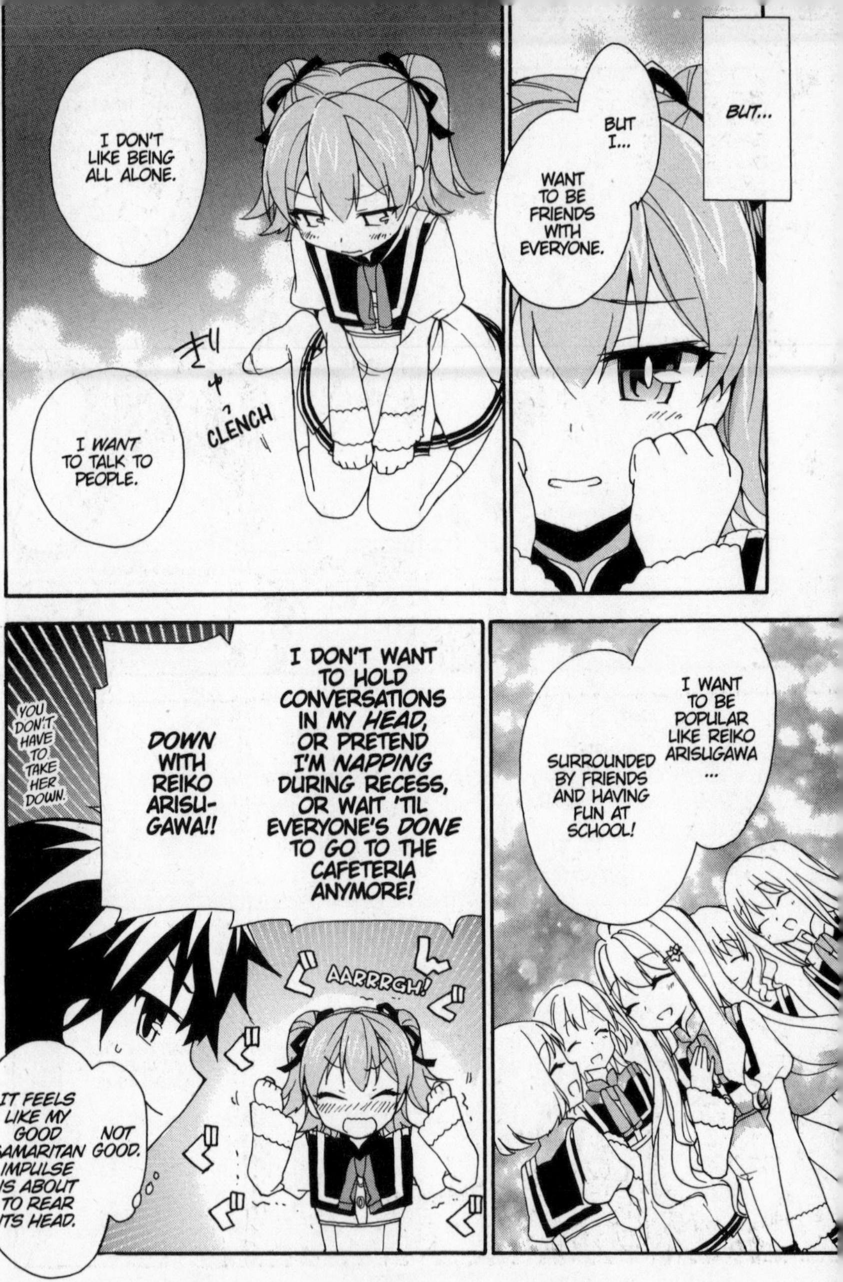
BUT...
BUT I...
WANT TO BE FRIENDS WITH EVERYONE.
I DON'T LIKE BEING ALL ALONE.
I *WANT* TO TALK TO PEOPLE.
CLENCH
I WANT TO BE POPULAR LIKE REIKO ARISUGAWA...
SURROUNDED BY FRIENDS AND HAVING FUN AT SCHOOL!
I DON'T WANT TO HOLD CONVERSATIONS IN MY *HEAD*, OR PRETEND I'M *NAPPING* DURING RECESS, OR WAIT 'TIL EVERYONE'S *DONE* TO GO TO THE CAFETERIA ANYMORE!
DOWN WITH REIKO ARISU-GAWA!!
YOU DON'T HAVE TO TAKE HER DOWN.
AARRRGH!
NOT GOOD.
IT FEELS LIKE MY GOOD SAMARITAN IMPULSE IS ABOUT TO REAR ITS HEAD.

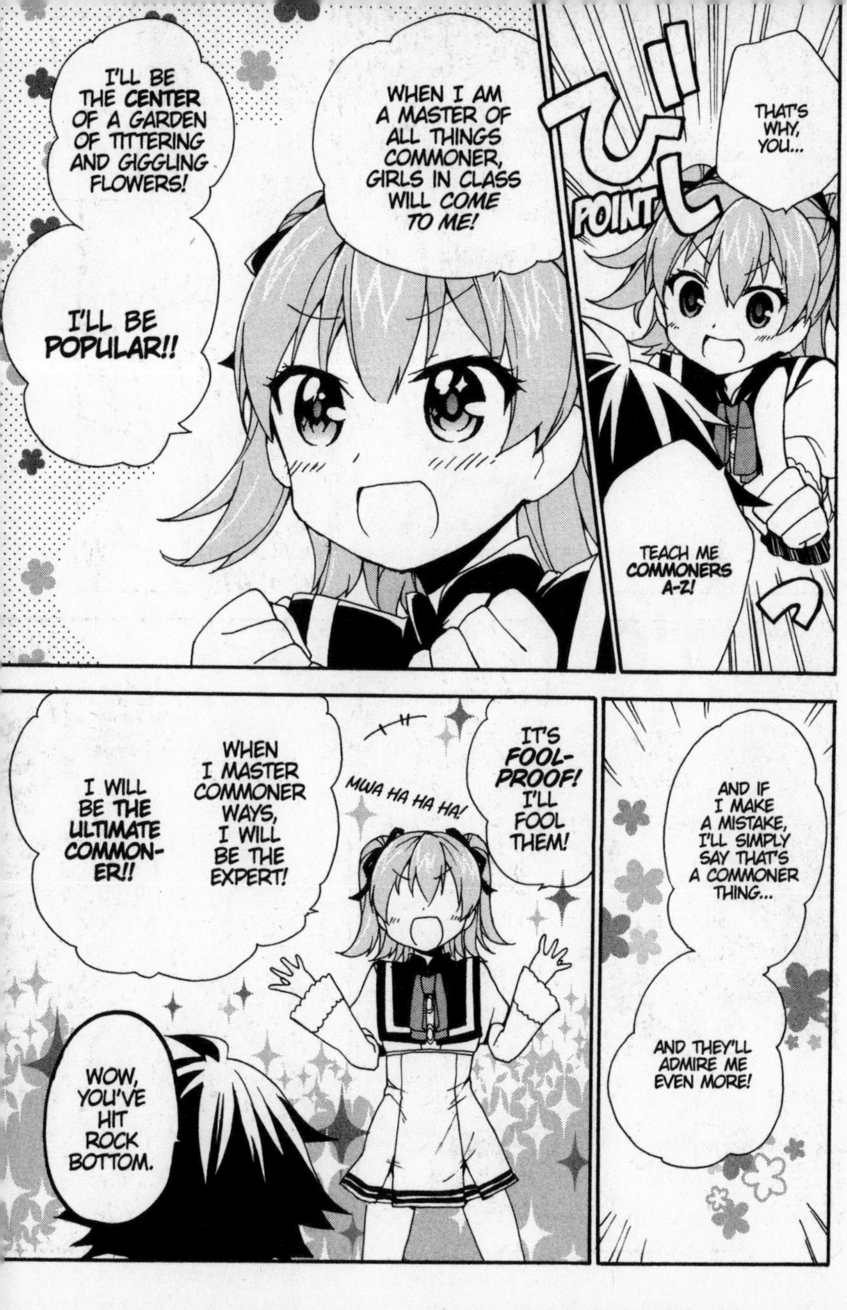

ひし
POINT
THAT'S WHY, YOU...
TEACH ME COMMONERS A-Z!
WHEN I AM A MASTER OF ALL THINGS COMMONER, GIRLS IN CLASS WILL COME TO ME!
I'LL BE THE CENTER OF A GARDEN OF TITTERING AND GIGGLING FLOWERS!
I'LL BE POPULAR!!
AND IF I MAKE A MISTAKE, I'LL SIMPLY SAY THAT'S A COMMONER THING...
AND THEY'LL ADMIRE ME EVEN MORE!
IT'S FOOL-PROOF! I'LL FOOL THEM!
MWA HA HA HA!
WHEN I MASTER COMMONER WAYS, I WILL BE THE EXPERT!
I WILL BE THE ULTIMATE COMMON-ER!!
WOW, YOU'VE HIT ROCK BOTTOM.

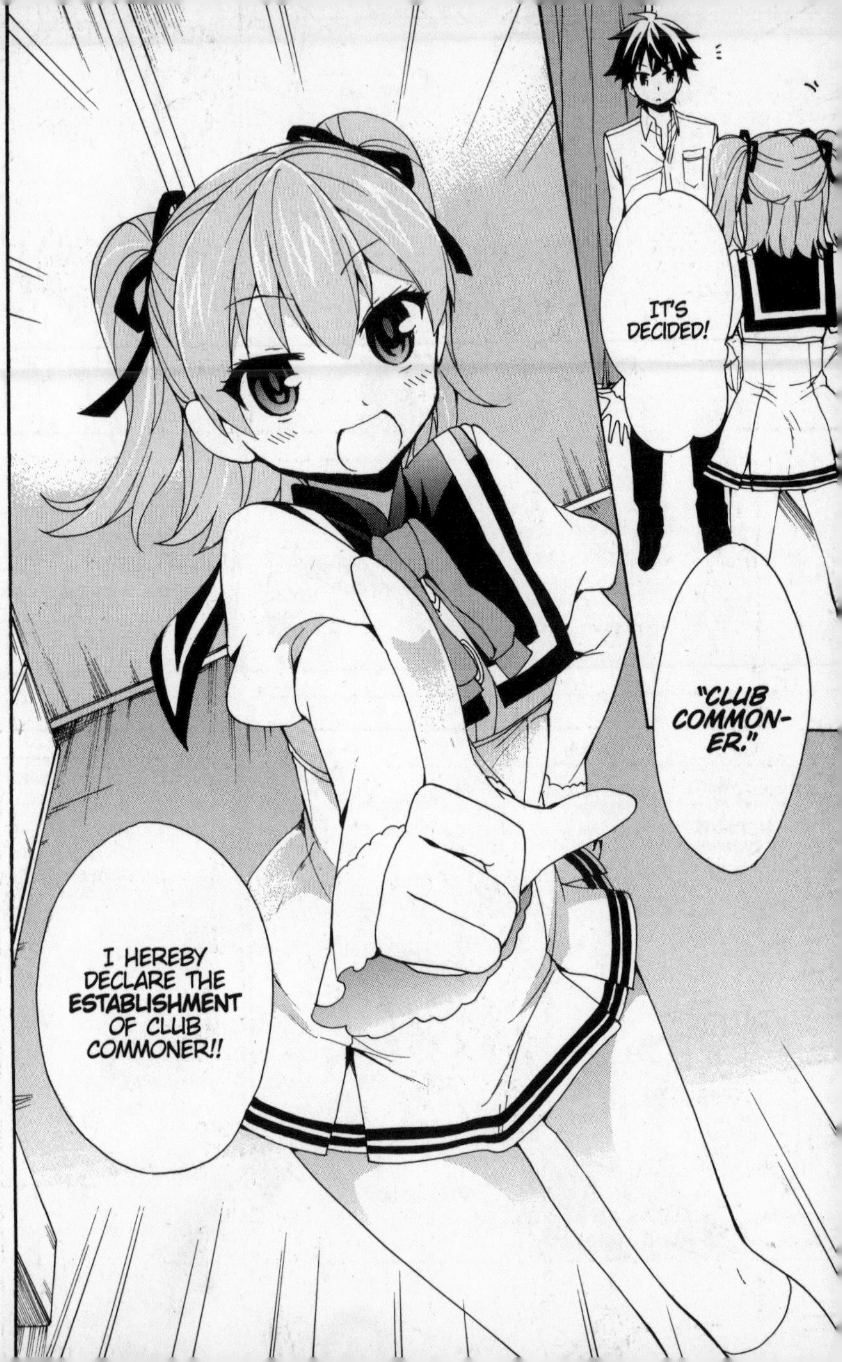
IT'S DECIDED!
"CLUB COMMON-ER."
I HEREBY DECLARE THE ESTABLISHMENT OF CLUB COMMONER!!

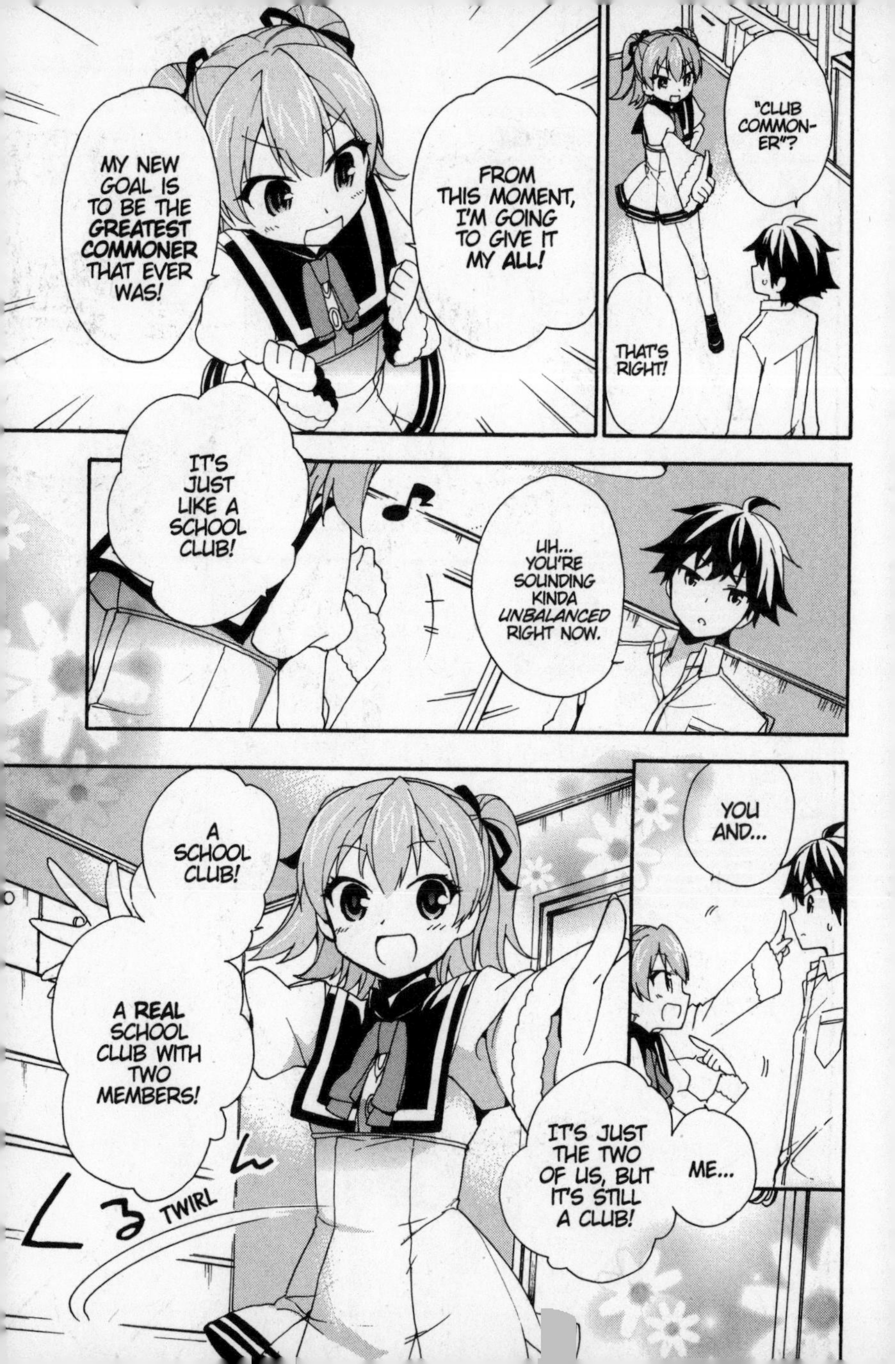

"CLUB COMMONER"?
THAT'S RIGHT!
FROM THIS MOMENT, I'M GOING TO GIVE IT MY ALL!
MY NEW GOAL IS TO BE THE GREATEST COMMONER THAT EVER WAS!
IT'S JUST LIKE A SCHOOL CLUB!
UH... YOU'RE SOUNDING KINDA *UNBALANCED* RIGHT NOW.
YOU AND...
ME...
IT'S JUST THE TWO OF US, BUT IT'S STILL A CLUB!
A SCHOOL CLUB!
A REAL SCHOOL CLUB WITH TWO MEMBERS!
TWIRL

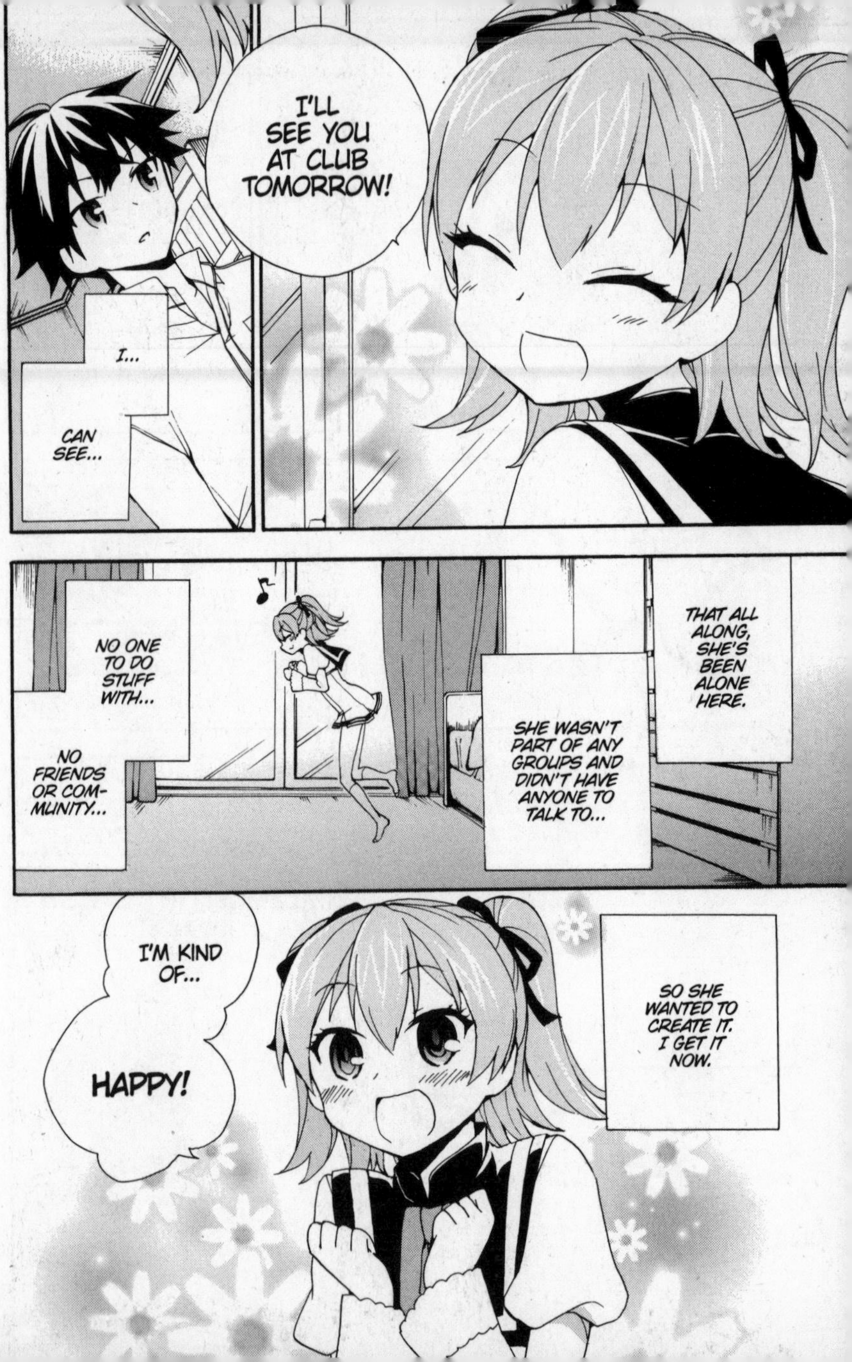
I'LL SEE YOU AT CLUB TOMORROW!
I... CAN SEE...
THAT ALL ALONG, SHE'S BEEN ALONE HERE.
SHE WASN'T PART OF ANY GROUPS AND DIDN'T HAVE ANYONE TO TALK TO...
NO ONE TO DO STUFF WITH...
NO FRIENDS OR COM-MUNITY...
SO SHE WANTED TO CREATE IT. I GET IT NOW.
I'M KIND OF... HAPPY!

Chapter 3 ✿ Maiden with a Pure Heart

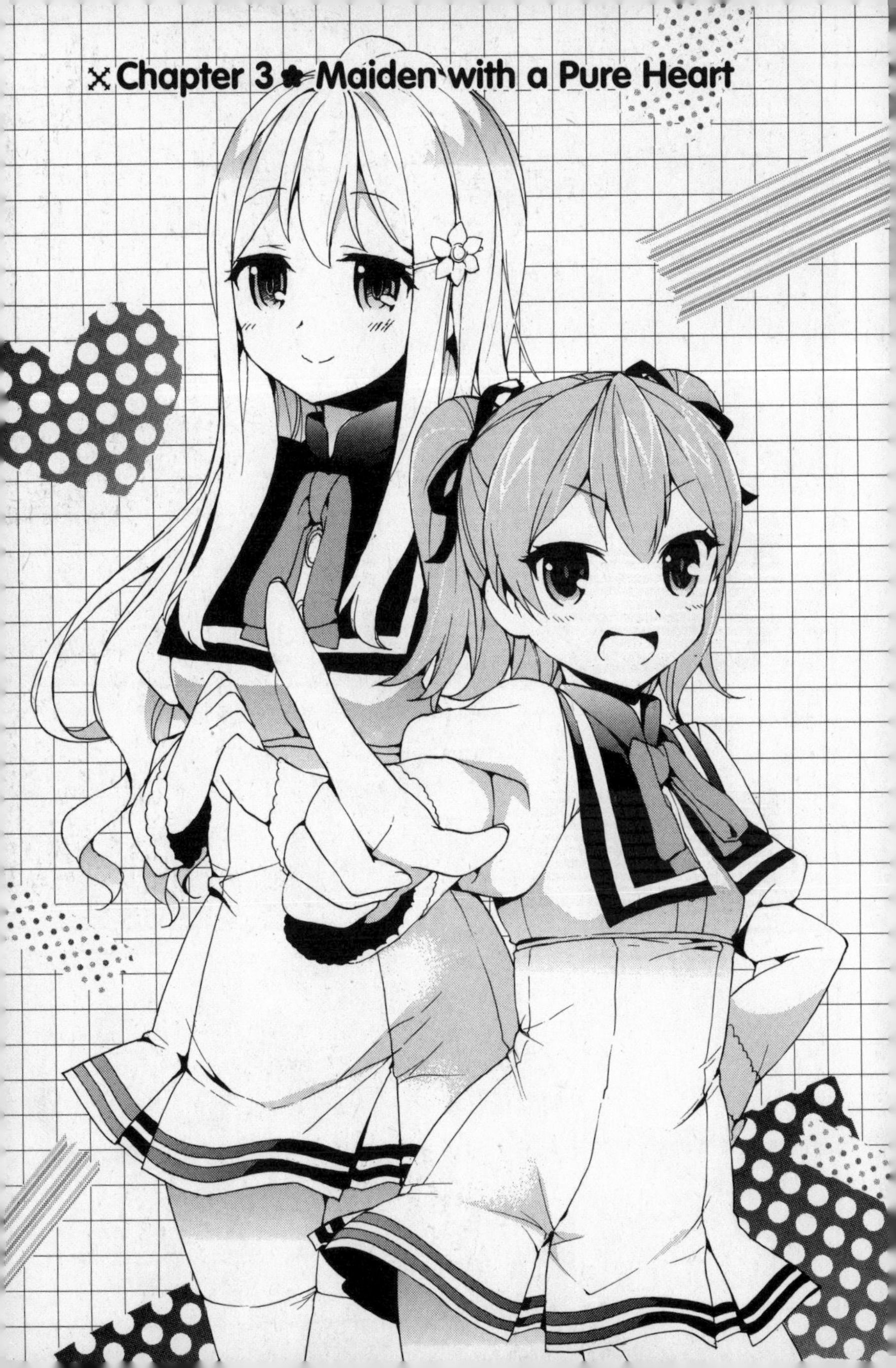

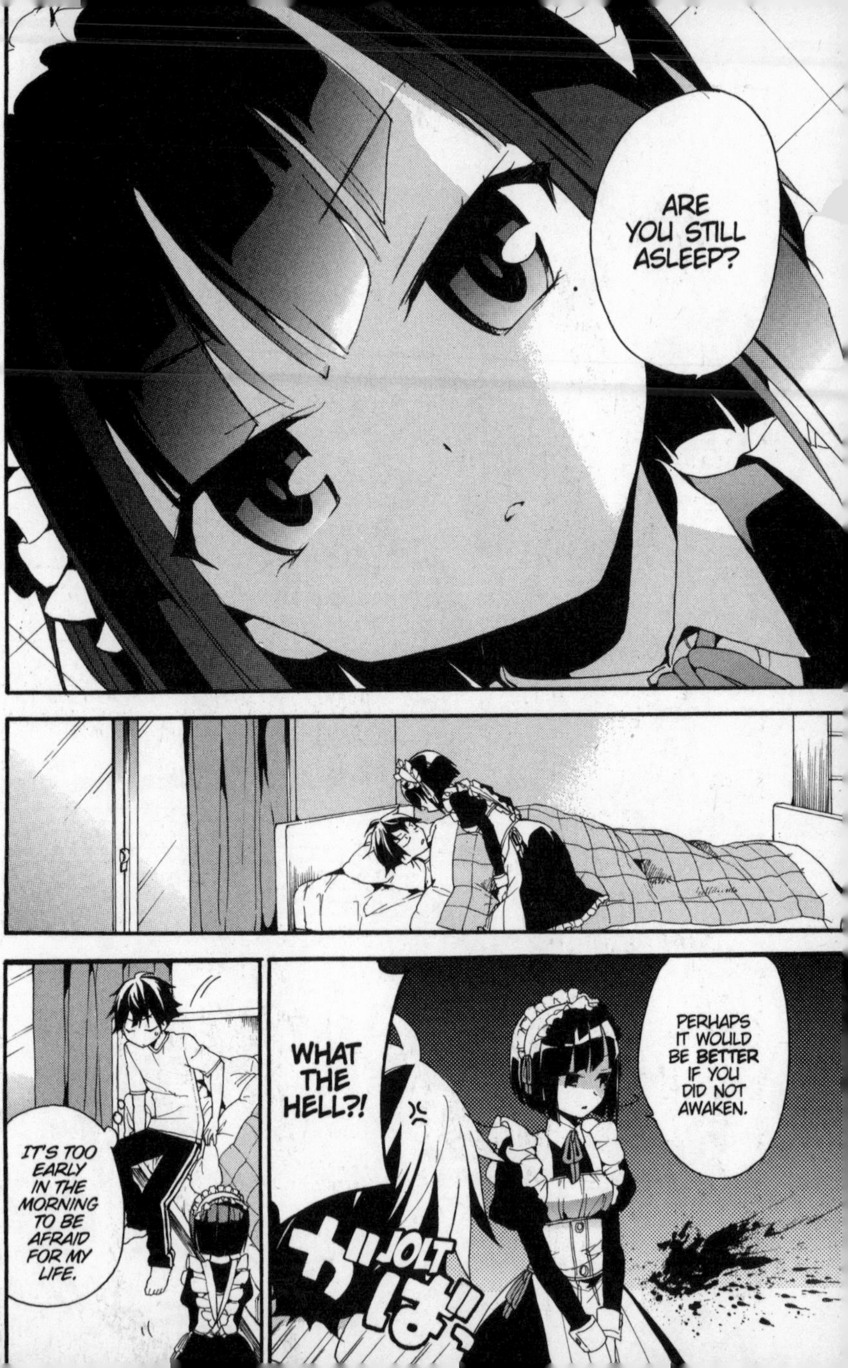
ARE YOU STILL ASLEEP?
PERHAPS IT WOULD BE BETTER IF YOU DID NOT AWAKEN.
WHAT THE HELL?!
JOLT
IT'S TOO EARLY IN THE MORNING TO BE AFRAID FOR MY LIFE.

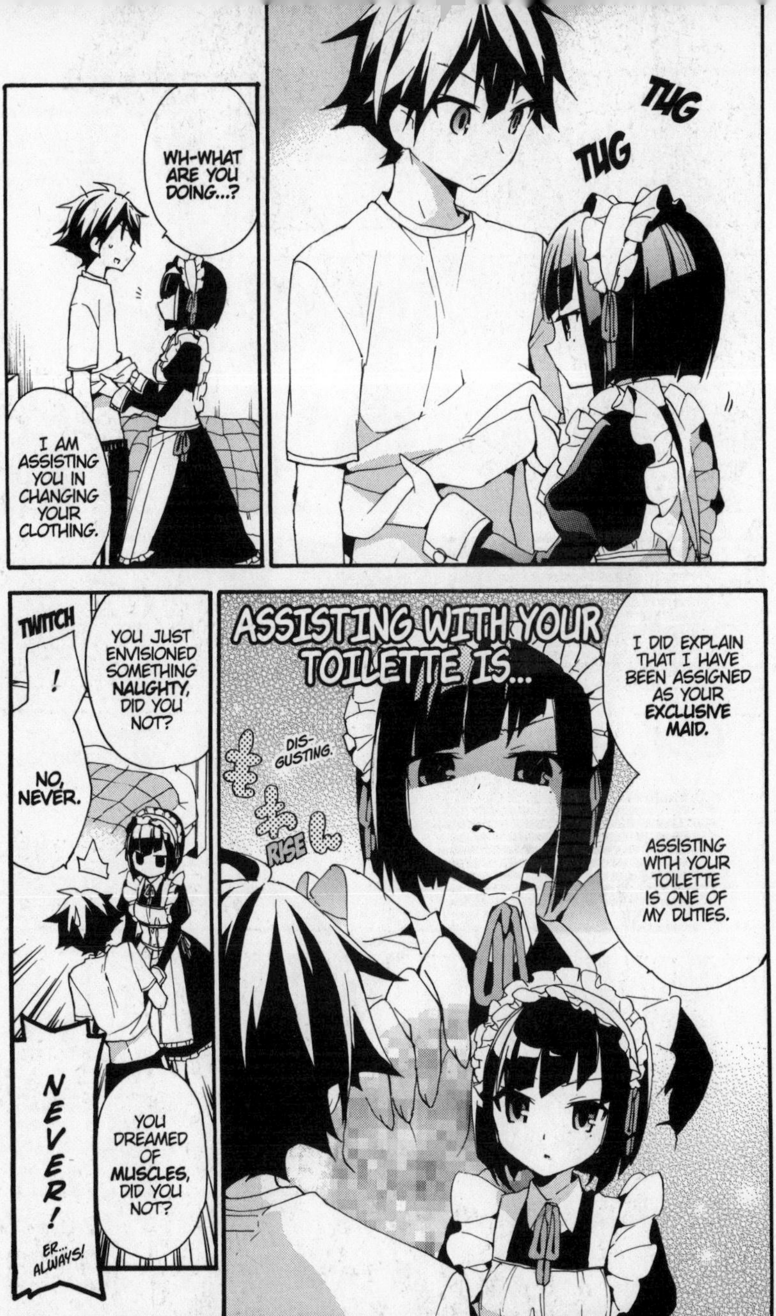
TUG
TUG
WH-WHAT ARE YOU DOING...?
I AM ASSISTING YOU IN CHANGING YOUR CLOTHING.
I DID EXPLAIN THAT I HAVE BEEN ASSIGNED AS YOUR EXCLUSIVE MAID.
ASSISTING WITH YOUR TOILETTE IS ONE OF MY DUTIES.
ASSISTING WITH YOUR TOILETTE IS...
DIS-GUSTING.
RISE
YOU JUST ENVISIONED SOMETHING NAUGHTY, DID YOU NOT?
TWITCH
!
NO, NEVER.
YOU DREAMED OF MUSCLES, DID YOU NOT?
NEVER!
ER... ALWAYS!

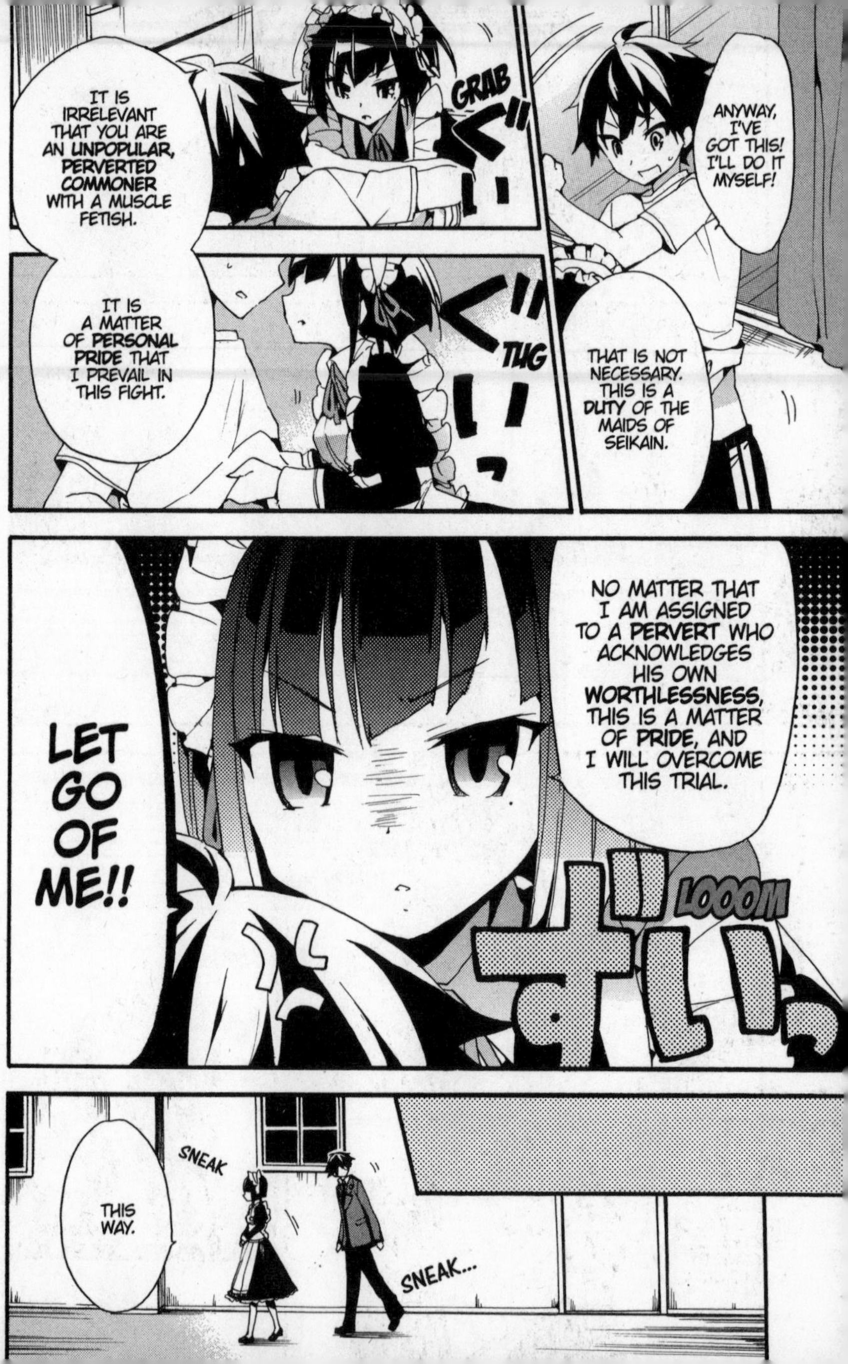
ANYWAY, I'VE GOT THIS! I'LL DO IT MYSELF!
THAT IS NOT NECESSARY. THIS IS A DUTY OF THE MAIDS OF SEIKAIN.
GRAB
IT IS IRRELEVANT THAT YOU ARE AN UNPOPULAR, PERVERTED COMMONER WITH A MUSCLE FETISH.
TUG
IT IS A MATTER OF PERSONAL PRIDE THAT I PREVAIL IN THIS FIGHT.
NO MATTER THAT I AM ASSIGNED TO A PERVERT WHO ACKNOWLEDGES HIS OWN WORTHLESSNESS, THIS IS A MATTER OF PRIDE, AND I WILL OVERCOME THIS TRIAL.
LOOOM
LET GO OF ME!!
SNEAK
THIS WAY.
SNEAK...

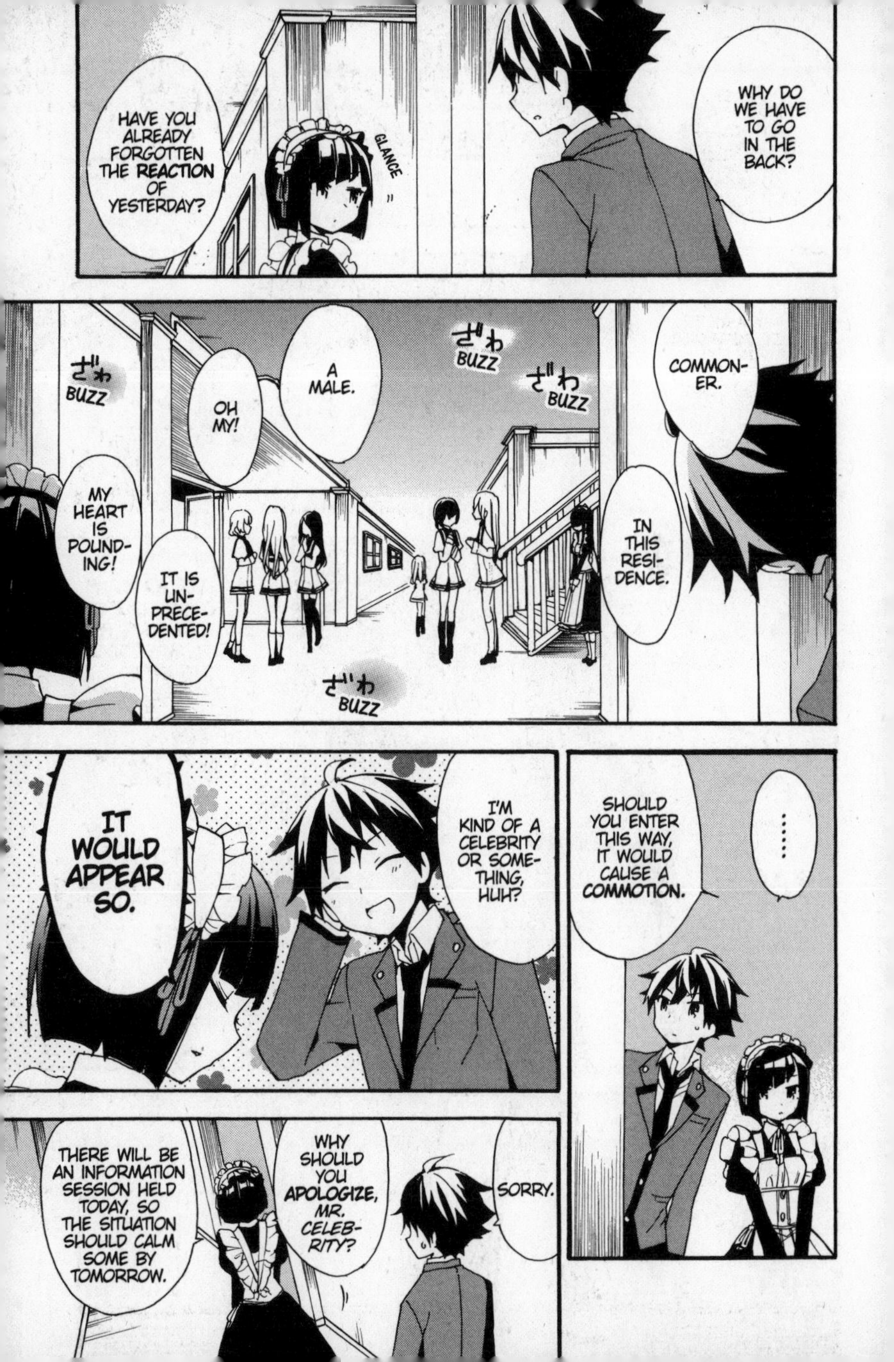
WHY DO WE HAVE TO GO IN THE BACK?
GLANCE
HAVE YOU ALREADY FORGOTTEN THE REACTION OF YESTERDAY?
COMMONER.
IN THIS RESIDENCE.
ざわ BUZZ
ざわ BUZZ
A MALE.
OH MY!
ざわ BUZZ
MY HEART IS POUNDING!
IT IS UNPRECEDENTED!
ざわ BUZZ
……
SHOULD YOU ENTER THIS WAY, IT WOULD CAUSE A COMMOTION.
I'M KIND OF A CELEBRITY OR SOMETHING, HUH?
IT WOULD APPEAR SO.
SORRY.
WHY SHOULD YOU APOLOGIZE, MR. CELEBRITY?
THERE WILL BE AN INFORMATION SESSION HELD TODAY, SO THE SITUATION SHOULD CALM SOME BY TOMORROW.

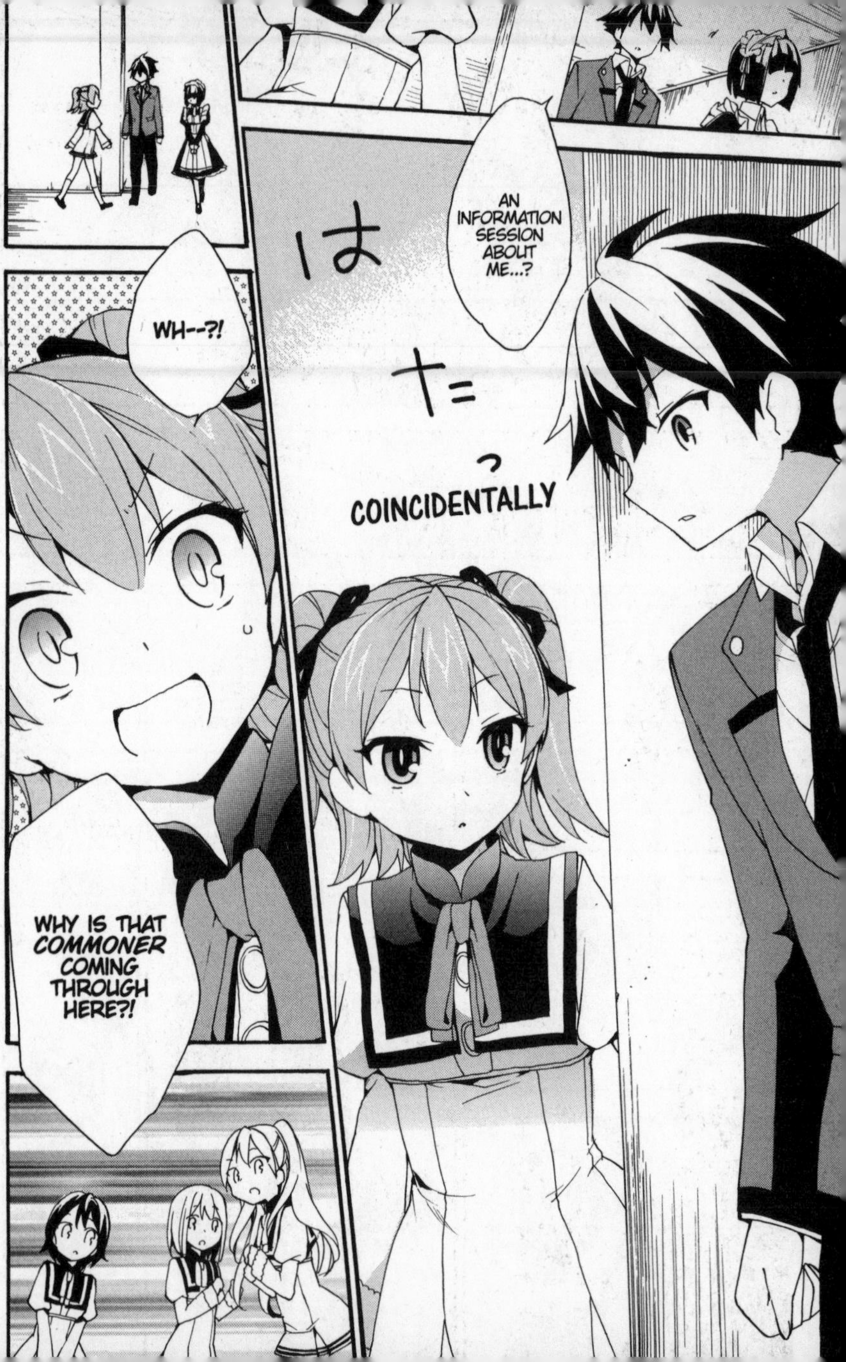
AN INFORMATION SESSION ABOUT ME...?
はたっ
COINCIDENTALLY
WH--?!
WHY IS THAT COMMONER COMING THROUGH HERE?!

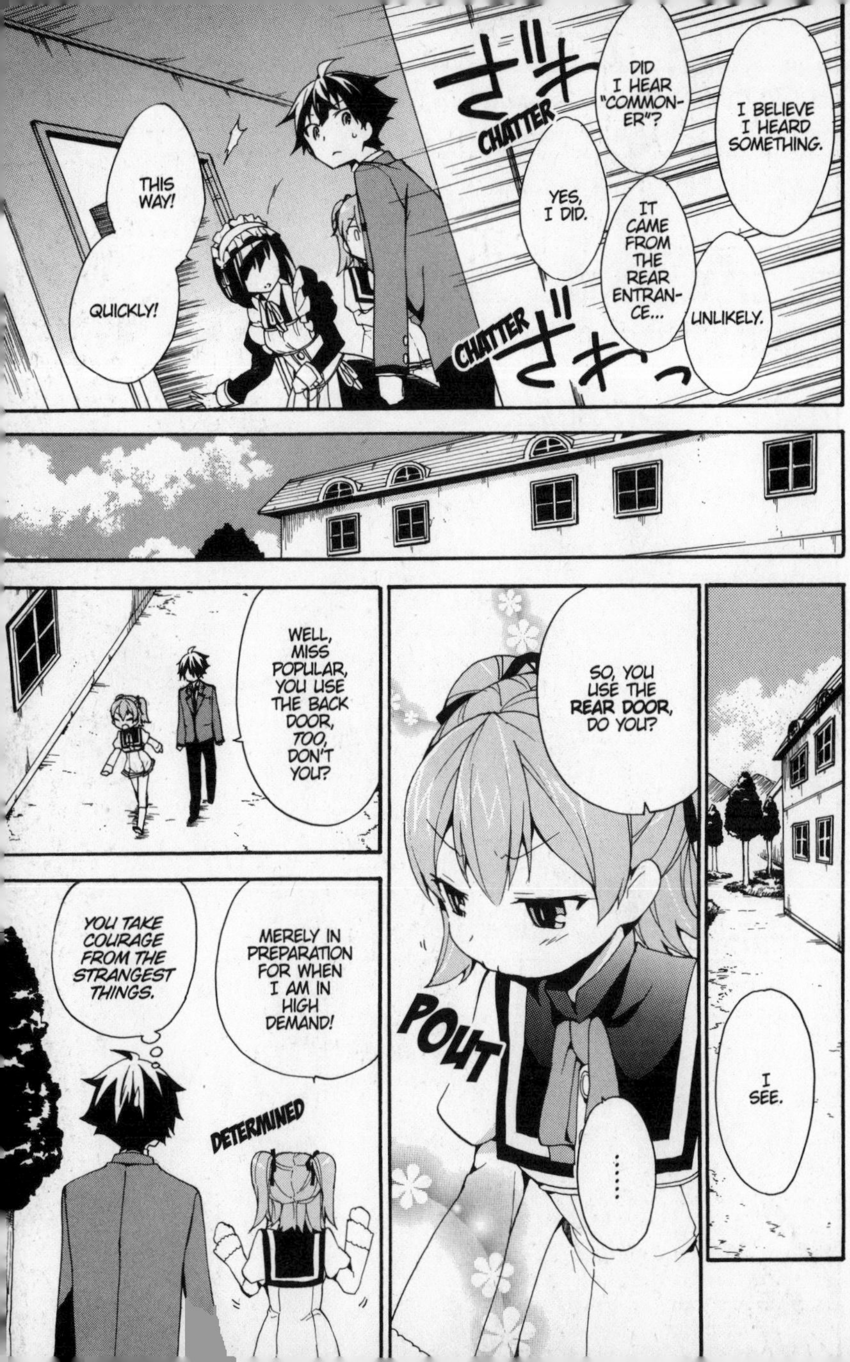

I BELIEVE I HEARD SOMETHING.
DID I HEAR "COMMONER"?
CHATTER
UNLIKELY.
IT CAME FROM THE REAR ENTRANCE...
YES, I DID.
CHATTER
THIS WAY!
QUICKLY!
SO, YOU USE THE REAR DOOR, DO YOU?
I SEE.
POUT
......
WELL, MISS POPULAR, YOU USE THE BACK DOOR, TOO, DON'T YOU?
MERELY IN PREPARATION FOR WHEN I AM IN HIGH DEMAND!
YOU TAKE COURAGE FROM THE STRANGEST THINGS.
DETERMINED

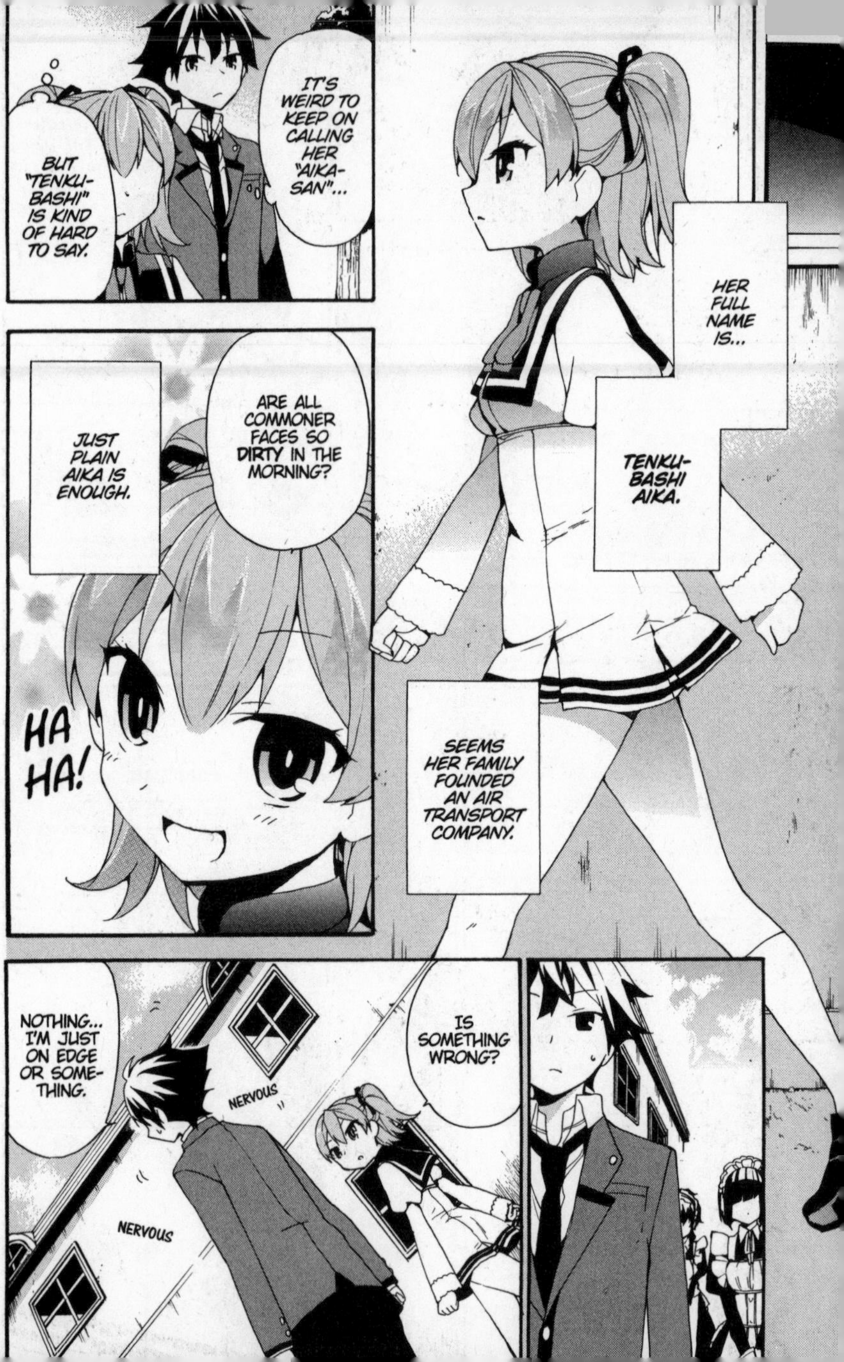
HER FULL NAME IS...
TENKU-BASHI AIKA.
SEEMS HER FAMILY FOUNDED AN AIR TRANSPORT COMPANY.
IT'S WEIRD TO KEEP ON CALLING HER "AIKA-SAN"...
BUT "TENKU-BASHI" IS KIND OF HARD TO SAY.
ARE ALL COMMONER FACES SO DIRTY IN THE MORNING?
JUST PLAIN AIKA IS ENOUGH.
HA HA!
IS SOMETHING WRONG?
NERVOUS
NOTHING... I'M JUST ON EDGE OR SOME-THING.
NERVOUS

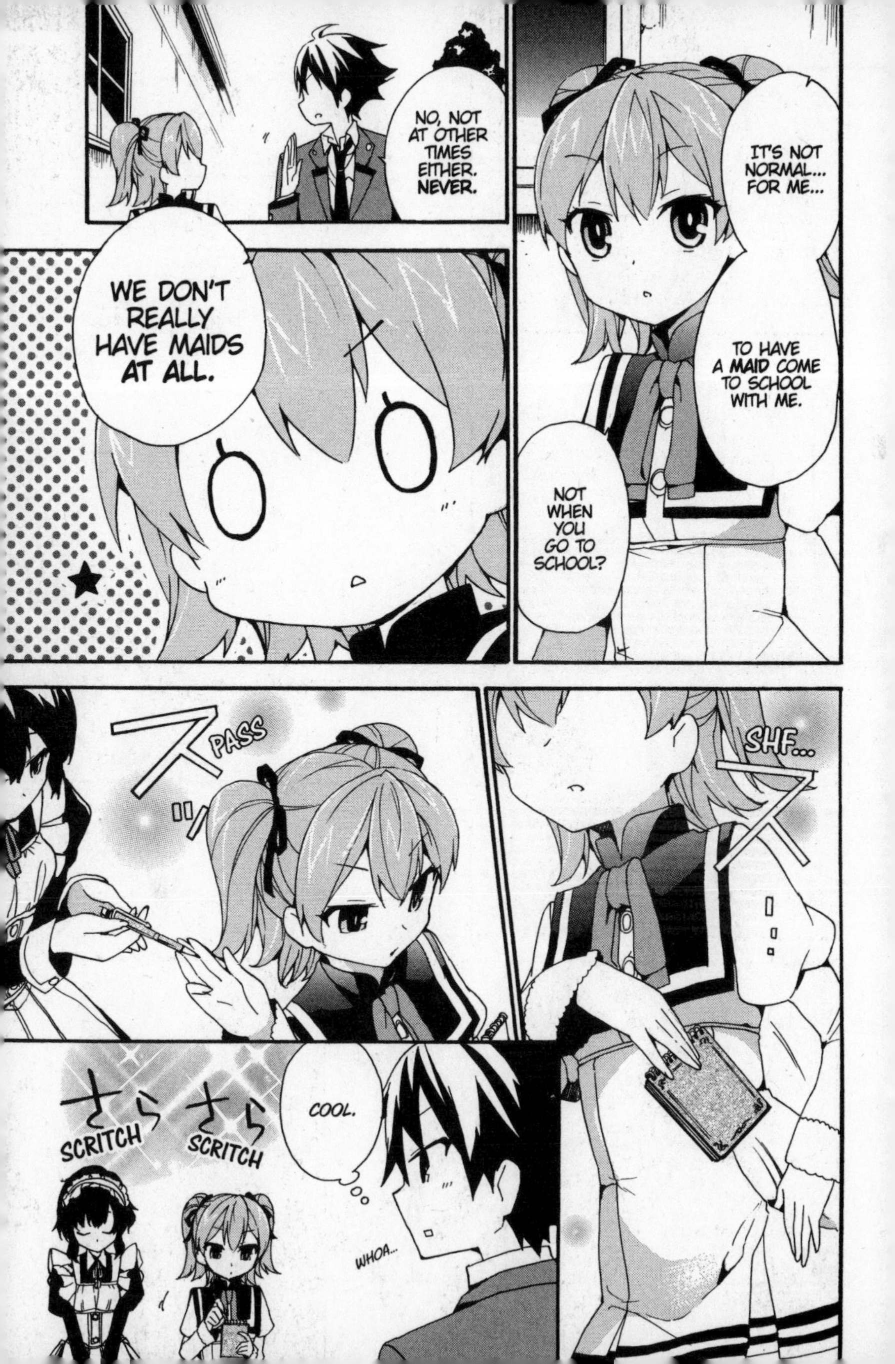
IT'S NOT NORMAL... FOR ME...
TO HAVE A MAID COME TO SCHOOL WITH ME.
NOT WHEN YOU GO TO SCHOOL?
NO, NOT AT OTHER TIMES EITHER. NEVER.
WE DON'T REALLY HAVE MAIDS AT ALL.
SHF...
PASS
COOL.
WHOA...
さら SCRITCH
さら SCRITCH

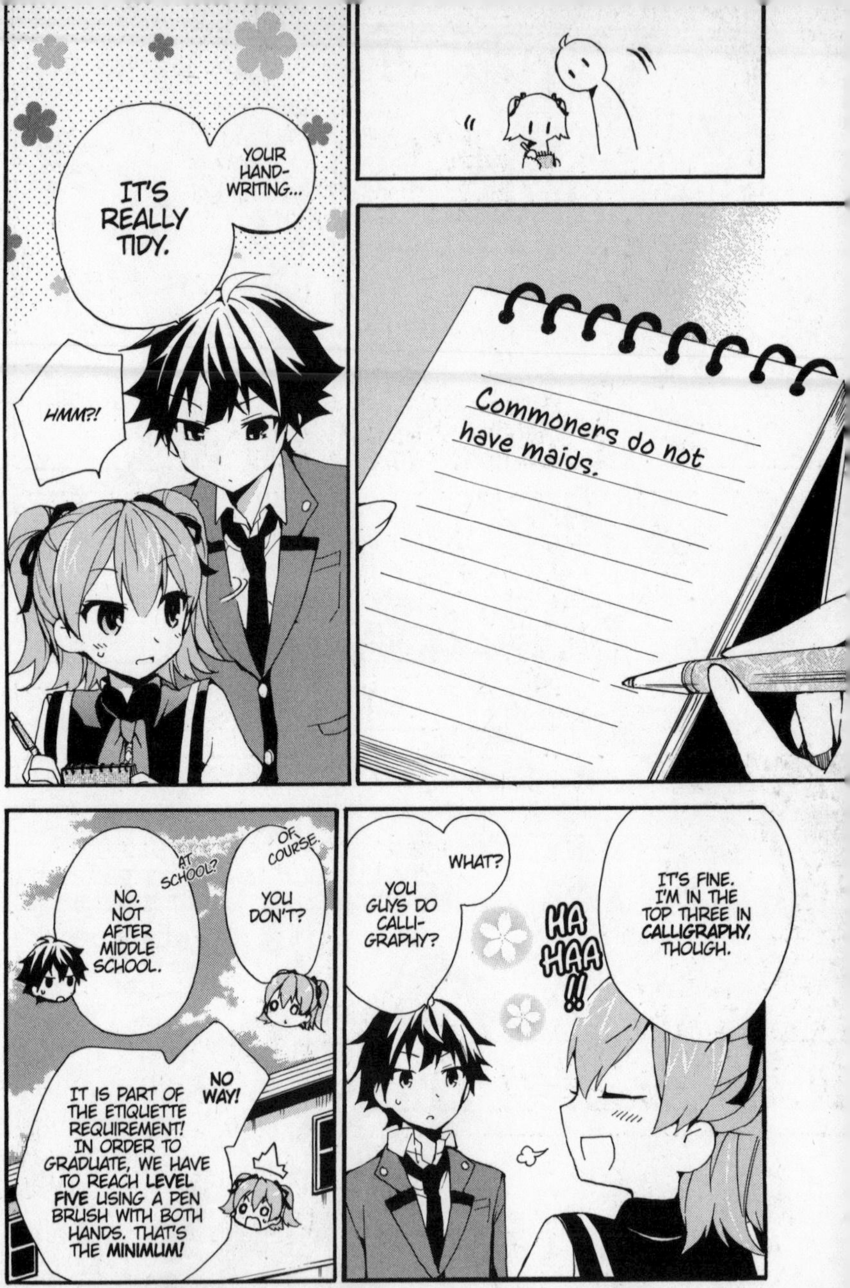
Commoners do not have maids.
YOUR HAND-WRITING...
IT'S REALLY TIDY.
HMM?!
IT'S FINE. I'M IN THE TOP THREE IN CALLIGRAPHY, THOUGH.
HA HAA!!
WHAT?
YOU GUYS DO CALLI-GRAPHY?
OF COURSE.
YOU DON'T?
AT SCHOOL?
NO. NOT AFTER MIDDLE SCHOOL.
NO WAY!
IT IS PART OF THE ETIQUETTE REQUIREMENT! IN ORDER TO GRADUATE, WE HAVE TO REACH LEVEL FIVE USING A PEN BRUSH WITH BOTH HANDS. THAT'S THE MINIMUM!

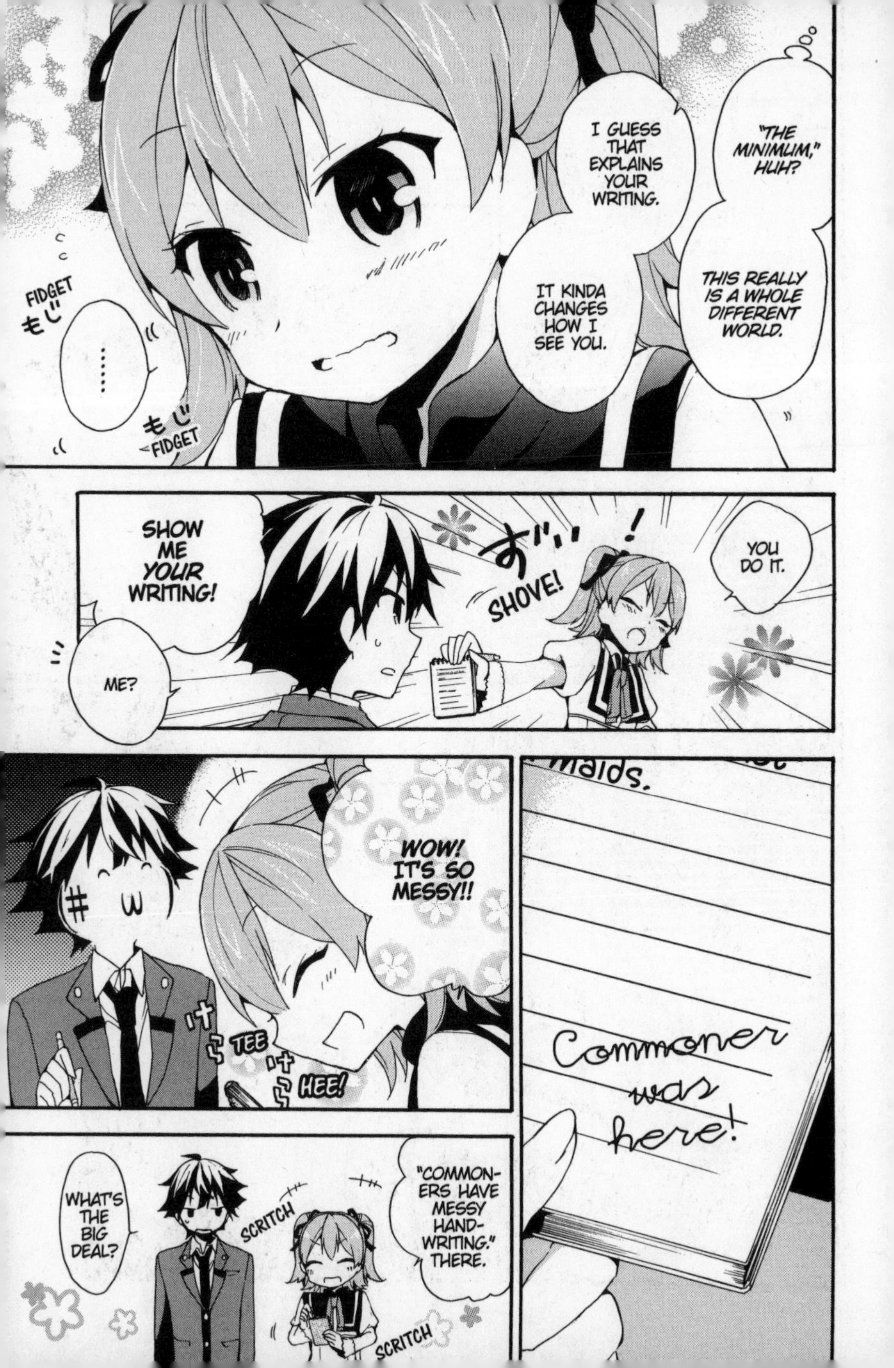
"THE MINIMUM," HUH?
THIS REALLY IS A WHOLE DIFFERENT WORLD.
I GUESS THAT EXPLAINS YOUR WRITING.
IT KINDA CHANGES HOW I SEE YOU.
......
FIDGET もじ
もじ FIDGET
YOU DO IT.
!
SHOVE!
SHOW ME YOUR WRITING!
ME?
maids.
Commoner was here!
WOW! IT'S SO MESSY!!
TEE
HEE!
"COMMONERS HAVE MESSY HANDWRITING." THERE.
SCRITCH
SCRITCH
WHAT'S THE BIG DEAL?

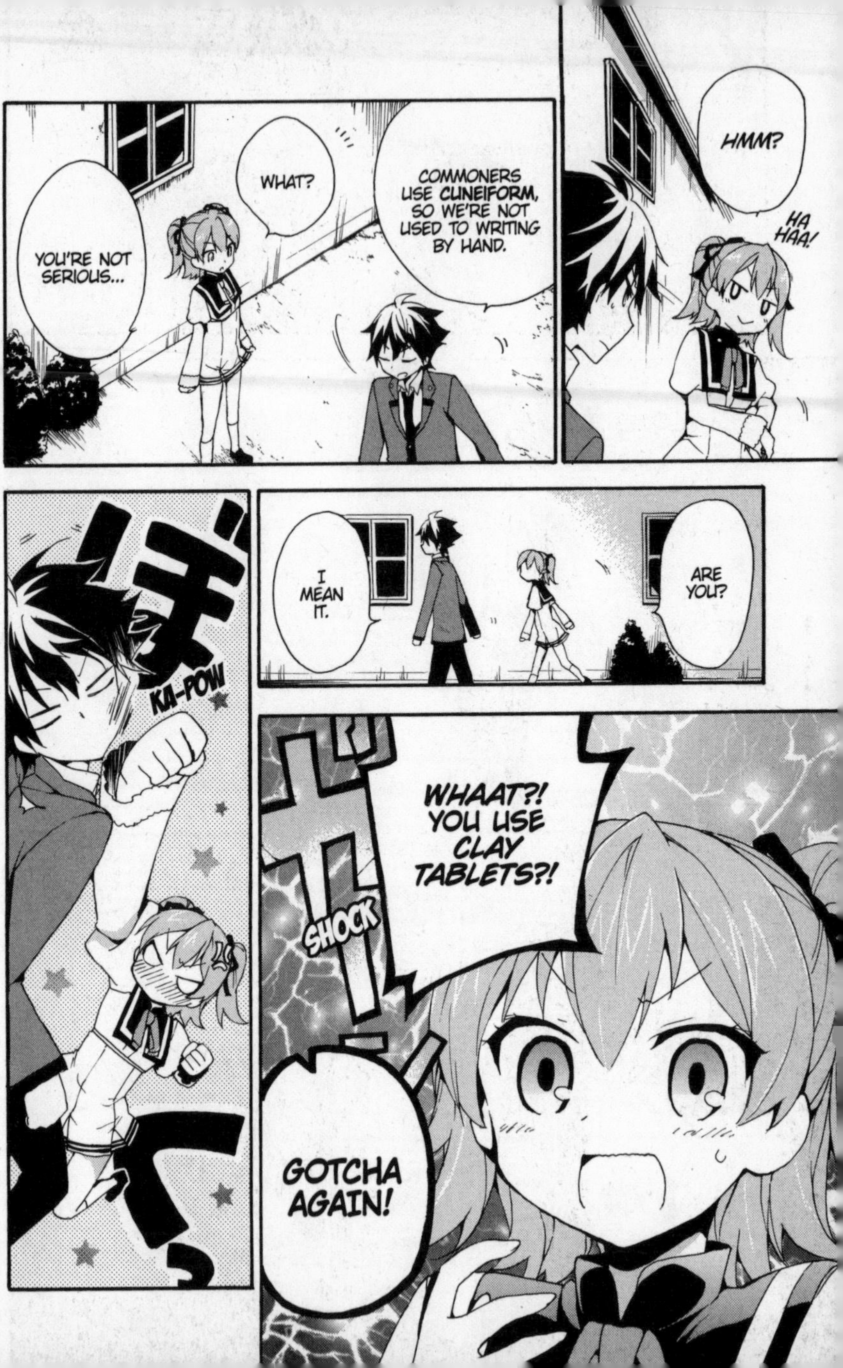
HMM?
HA HAA!
COMMONERS USE CUNEIFORM, SO WE'RE NOT USED TO WRITING BY HAND.
WHAT?
YOU'RE NOT SERIOUS...
ARE YOU?
I MEAN IT.
WHAAT?! YOU USE CLAY TABLETS?!
SHOCK
GOTCHA AGAIN!
KA-POW

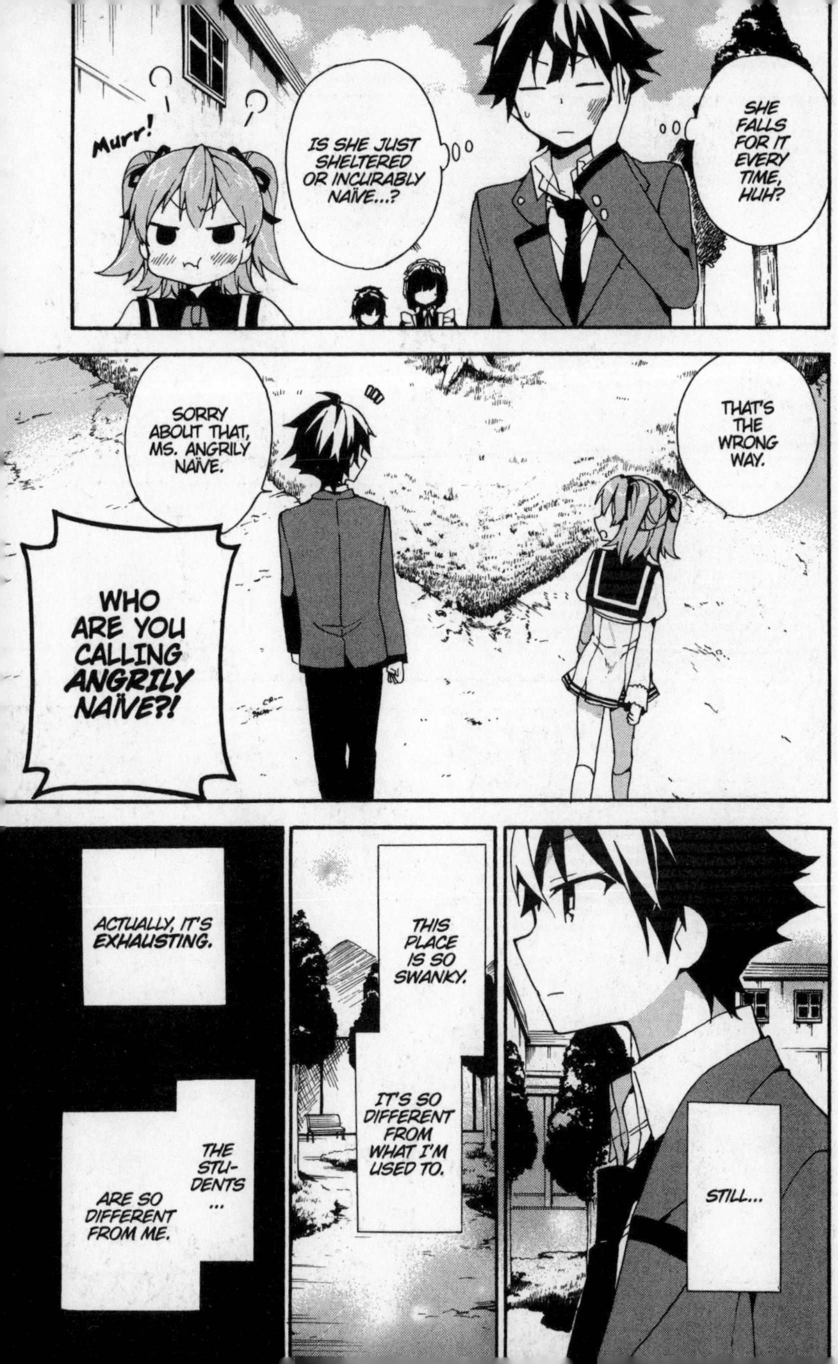
SHE FALLS FOR IT EVERY TIME, HUH?
IS SHE JUST SHELTERED OR INCURABLY NAÏVE...?
Murr!
THAT'S THE WRONG WAY.
SORRY ABOUT THAT, MS. ANGRILY NAÏVE.
WHO ARE YOU CALLING ANGRILY NAÏVE?!
STILL...
THIS PLACE IS SO SWANKY.
IT'S SO DIFFERENT FROM WHAT I'M USED TO.
ACTUALLY, IT'S EXHAUSTING.
THE STUDENTS...
ARE SO DIFFERENT FROM ME.

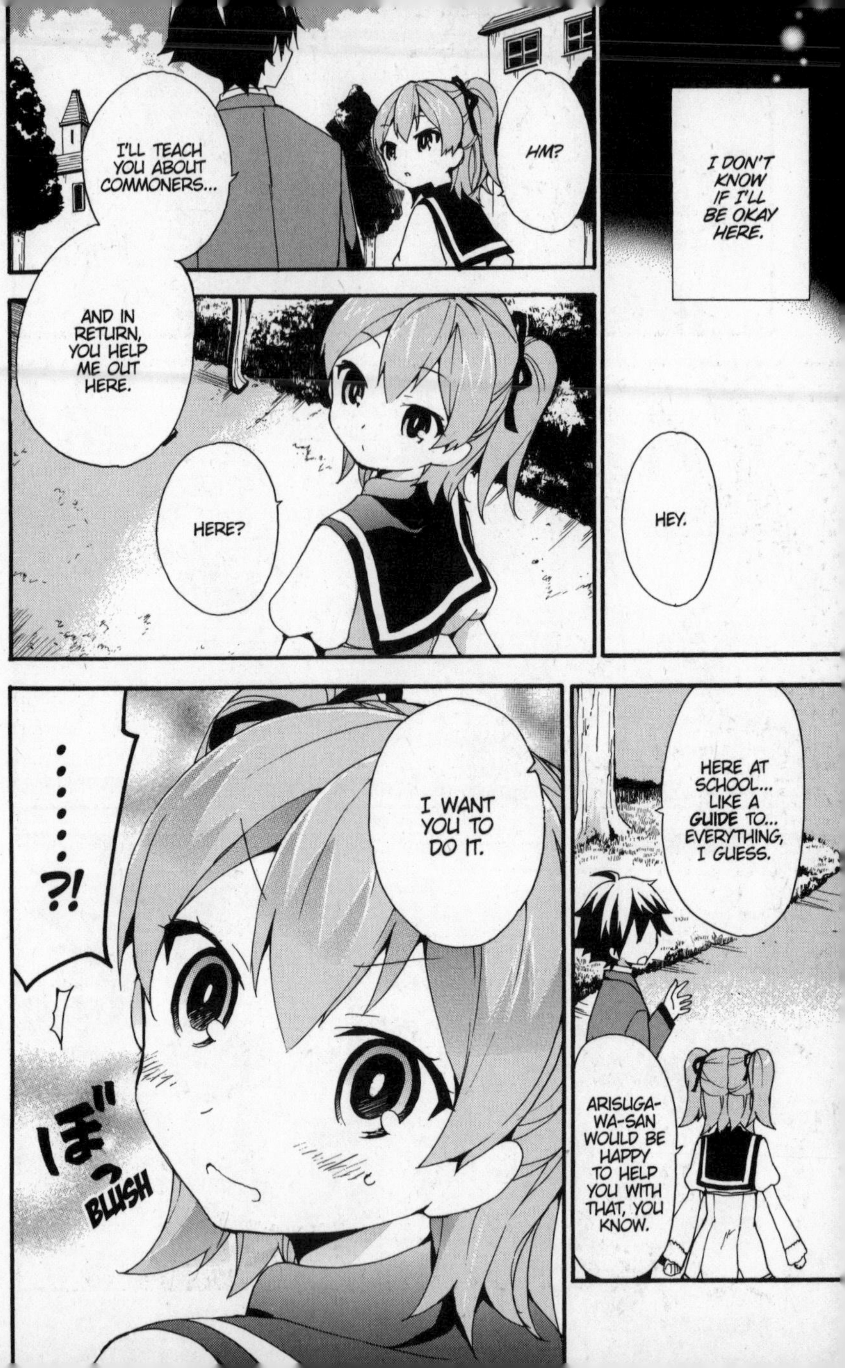
I DON'T KNOW IF I'LL BE OKAY HERE.
HEY.
HM?
I'LL TEACH YOU ABOUT COMMONERS...
AND IN RETURN, YOU HELP ME OUT HERE.
HERE?
HERE AT SCHOOL... LIKE A GUIDE TO... EVERYTHING, I GUESS.
ARISUGA-WA-SAN WOULD BE HAPPY TO HELP YOU WITH THAT, YOU KNOW.
I WANT YOU TO DO IT.
......?!
ぼっ
BLUSH

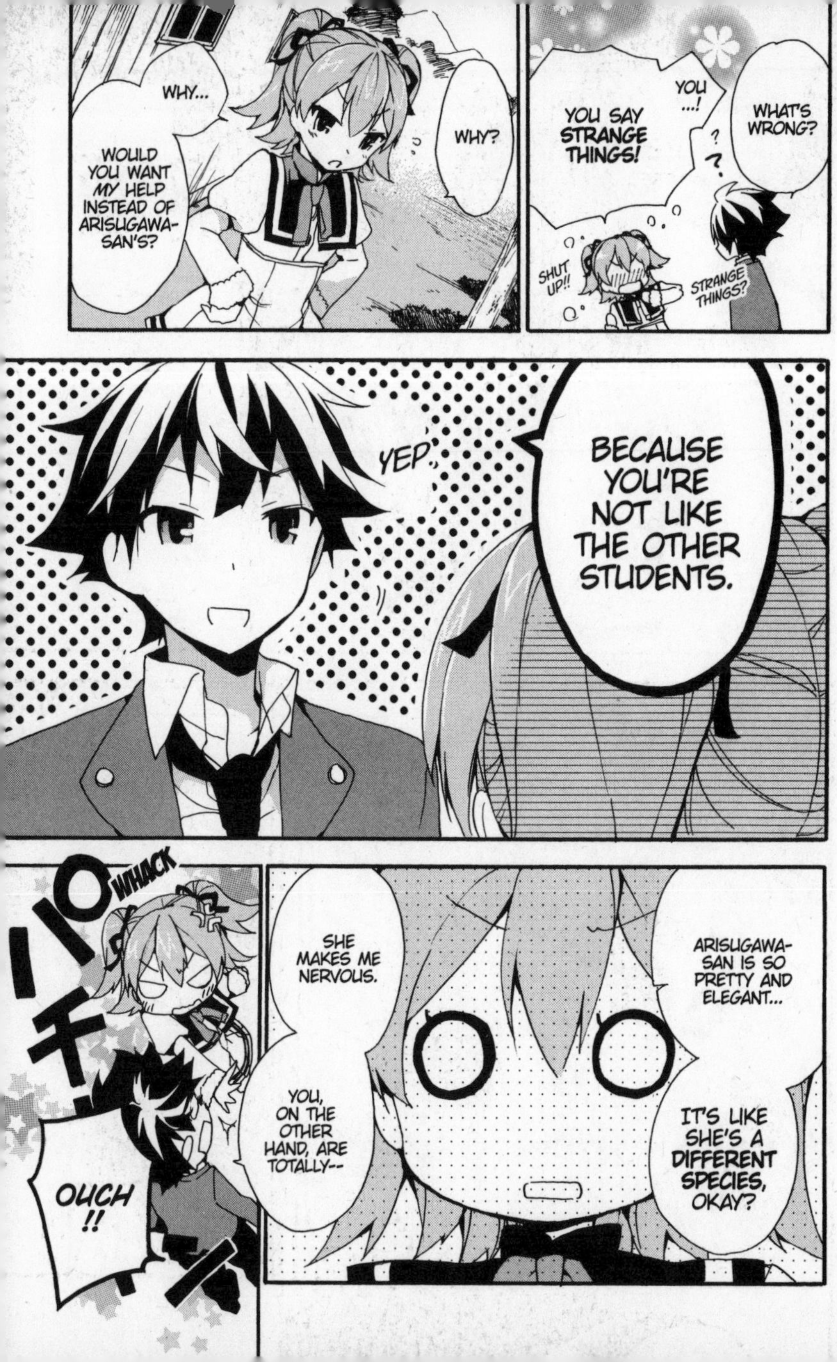
WHAT'S WRONG?
YOU ...!
YOU SAY STRANGE THINGS!
STRANGE THINGS?
SHUT UP!!
WHY?
WHY...
WOULD YOU WANT MY HELP INSTEAD OF ARISUGAWA-SAN'S?
BECAUSE YOU'RE NOT LIKE THE OTHER STUDENTS.
YEP.
ARISUGAWA-SAN IS SO PRETTY AND ELEGANT...
IT'S LIKE SHE'S A DIFFERENT SPECIES, OKAY?
SHE MAKES ME NERVOUS.
YOU, ON THE OTHER HAND, ARE TOTALLY--
WHACK
OUCH!!

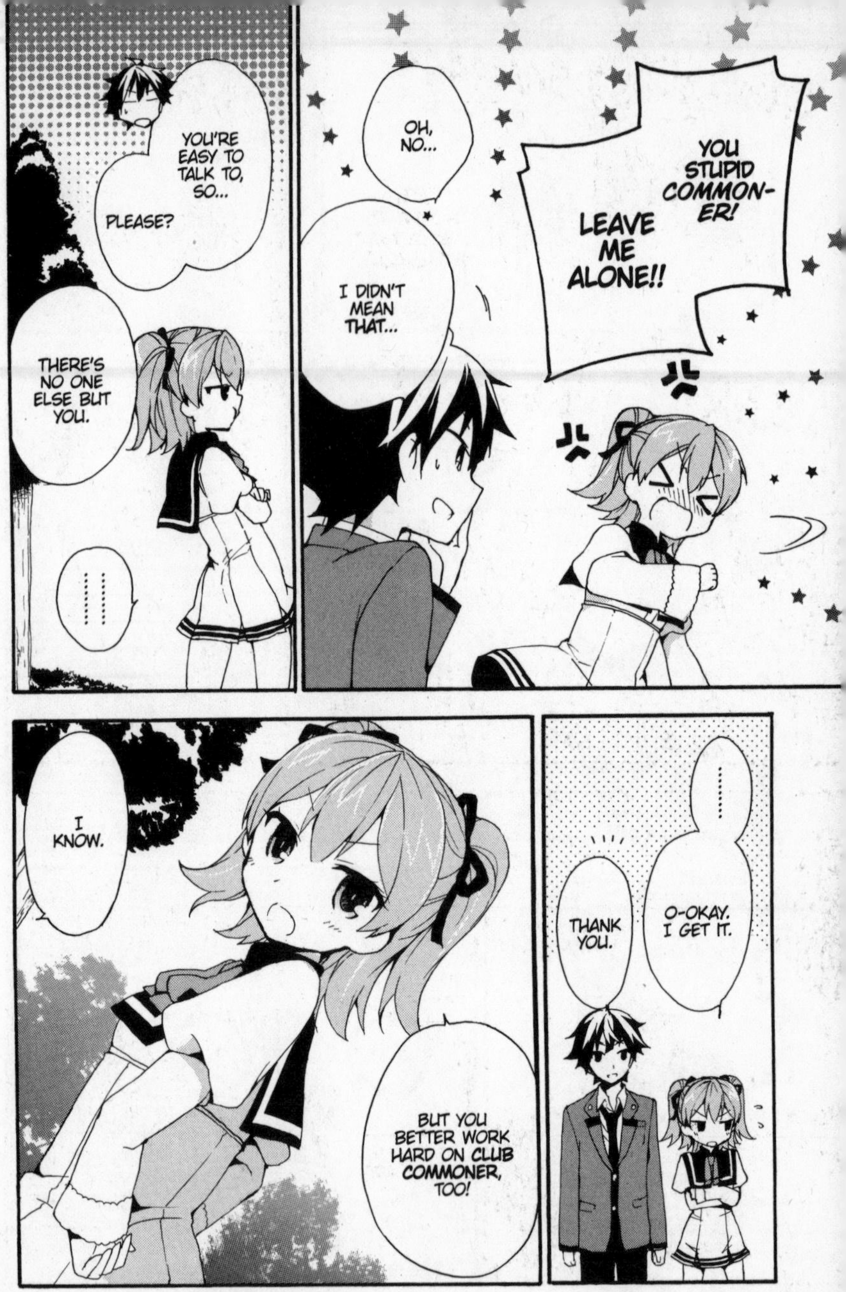
YOU STUPID COMMONER-ER!
LEAVE ME ALONE!!
OH, NO...
I DIDN'T MEAN THAT...
YOU'RE EASY TO TALK TO, SO...
PLEASE?
THERE'S NO ONE ELSE BUT YOU.
......
......
O-OKAY. I GET IT.
THANK YOU.
I KNOW.
BUT YOU BETTER WORK HARD ON CLUB COMMONER, TOO!

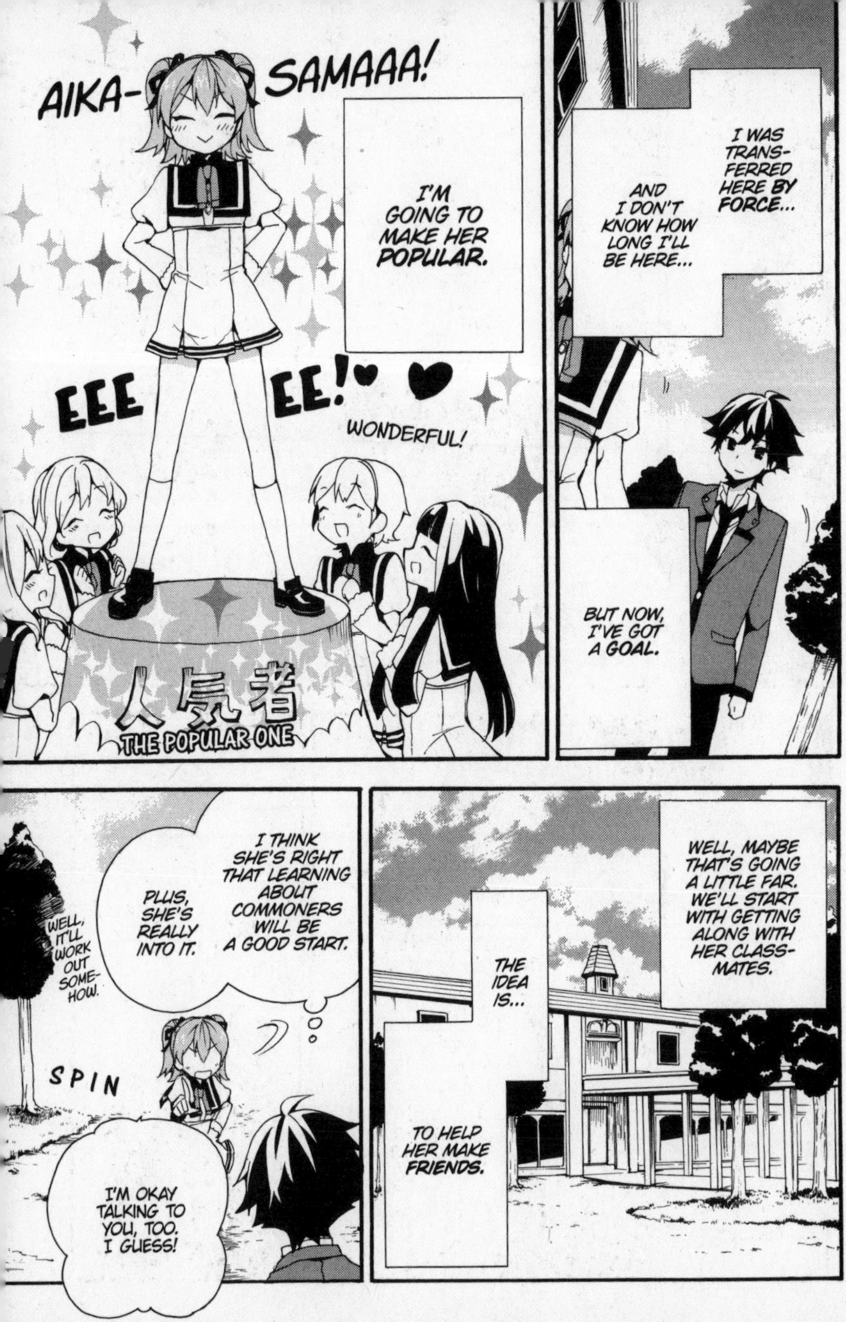
I WAS TRANSFERRED HERE BY FORCE...
AND I DON'T KNOW HOW LONG I'LL BE HERE...
BUT NOW, I'VE GOT A GOAL.
I'M GOING TO MAKE HER POPULAR.
AIKA-SAMAAA!
EEE EE!
WONDERFUL!
人気者
THE POPULAR ONE
WELL, MAYBE THAT'S GOING A LITTLE FAR. WE'LL START WITH GETTING ALONG WITH HER CLASSMATES.
THE IDEA IS...
TO HELP HER MAKE FRIENDS.
I THINK SHE'S RIGHT THAT LEARNING ABOUT COMMONERS WILL BE A GOOD START.
PLUS, SHE'S REALLY INTO IT.
WELL, IT'LL WORK OUT SOMEHOW.
SPIN
I'M OKAY TALKING TO YOU, TOO. I GUESS!

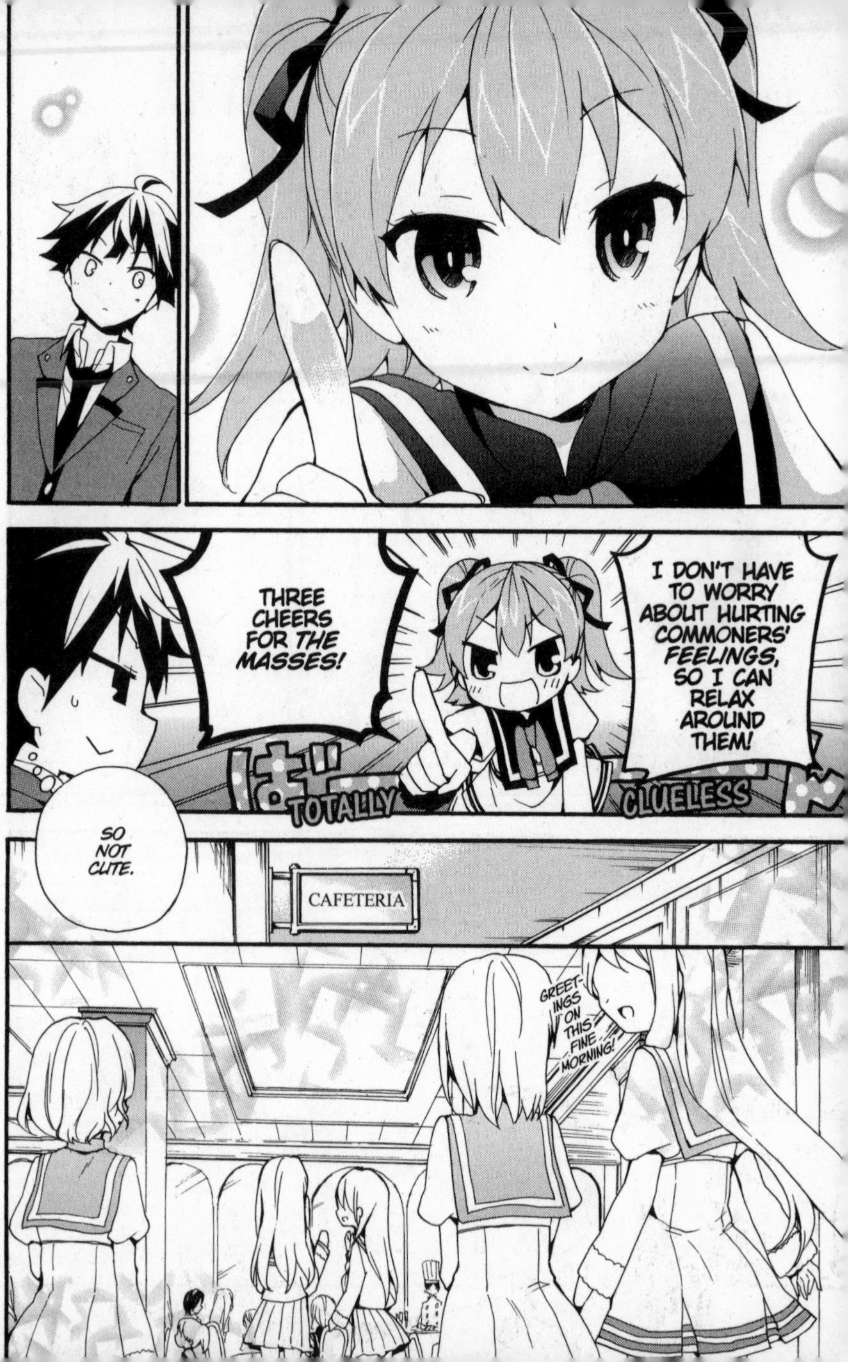
I DON'T HAVE TO WORRY ABOUT HURTING COMMONERS' FEELINGS, SO I CAN RELAX AROUND THEM!
THREE CHEERS FOR THE MASSES!
TOTALLY CLUELESS
SO NOT CUTE.
CAFETERIA
GREETINGS ON THIS FINE MORNING!

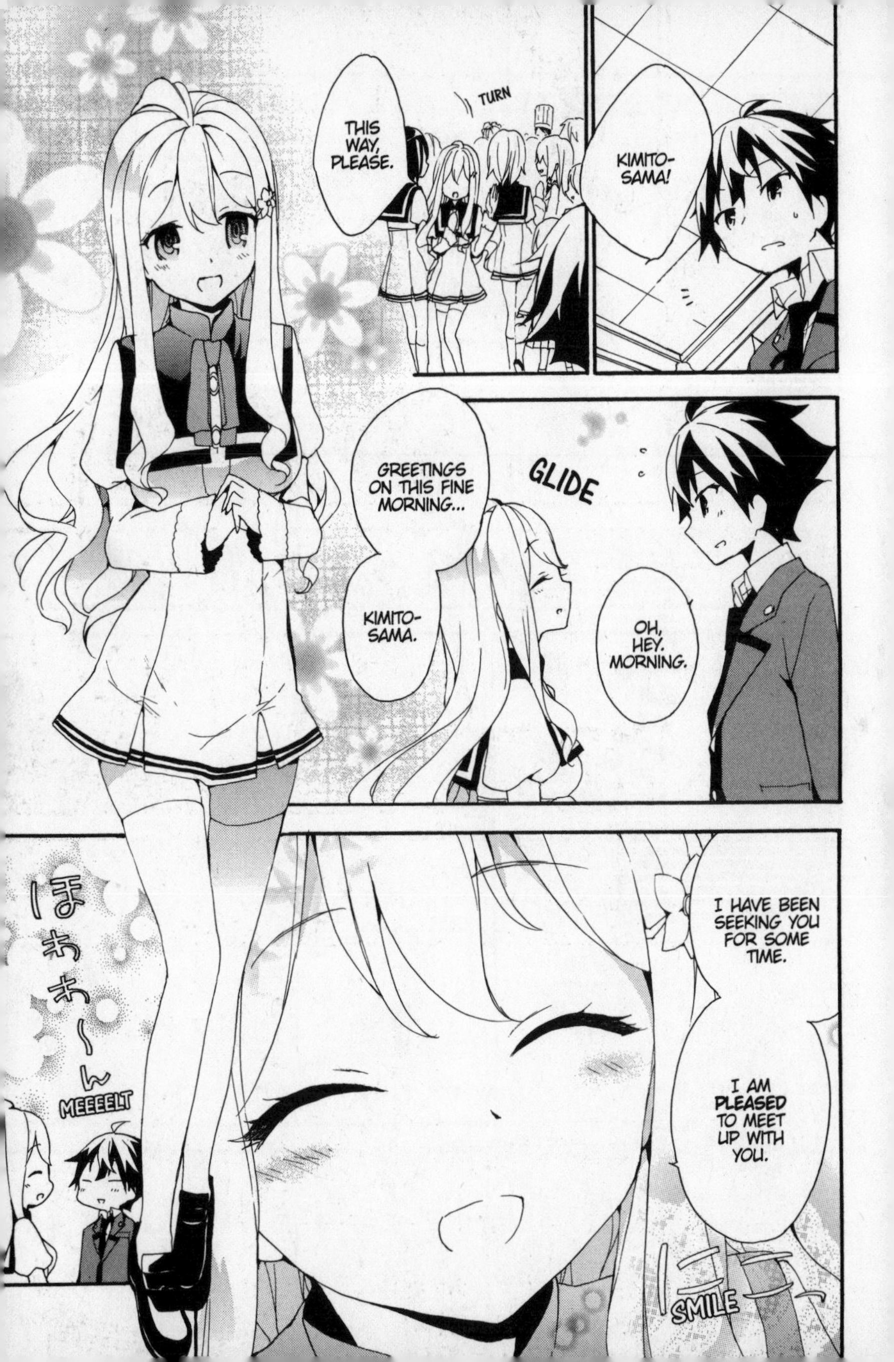
KIMITO-SAMA!
TURN
THIS WAY, PLEASE.
GREETINGS ON THIS FINE MORNING...
KIMITO-SAMA.
GLIDE
OH, HEY. MORNING.
I HAVE BEEN SEEKING YOU FOR SOME TIME.
I AM PLEASED TO MEET UP WITH YOU.
SMILE
ほぁ〜ん
MEEEELT

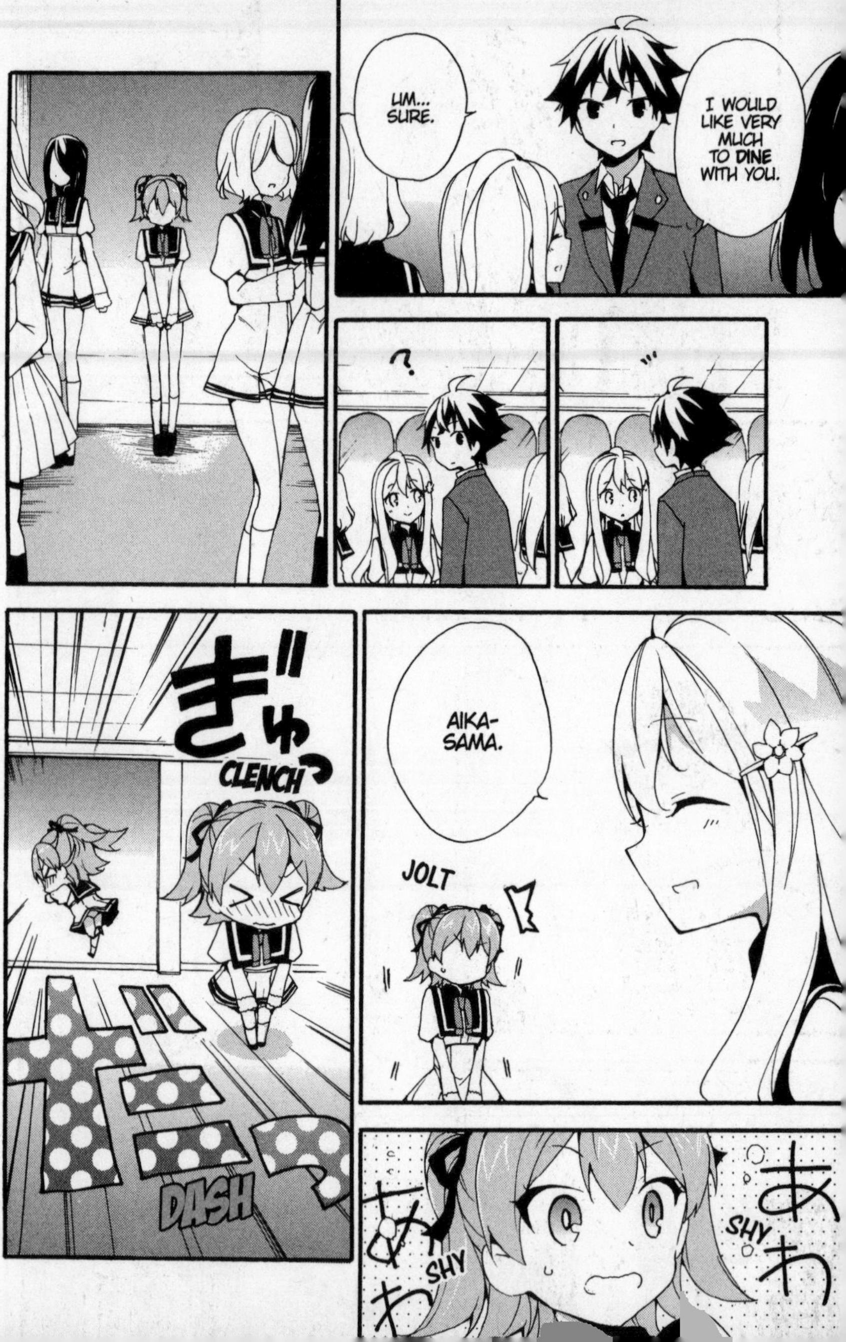

I WOULD LIKE VERY MUCH TO DINE WITH YOU.
UM... SURE.
?
AIKA-SAMA.
JOLT
あわ
SHY
SHY
ぎゅっ
CLENCH
DASH

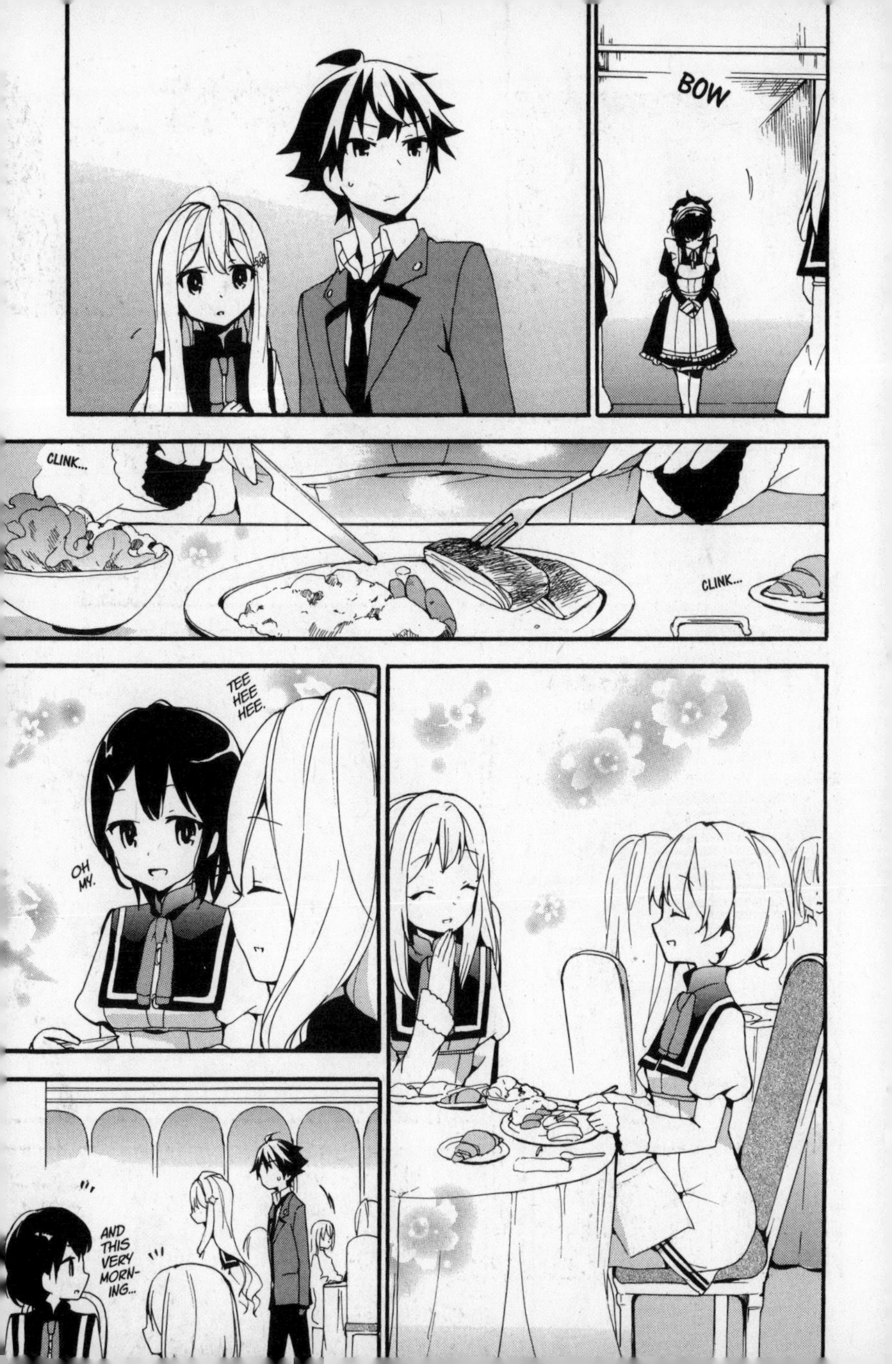
BOW
CLINK...
CLINK...
TEE HEE HEE.
OH MY.
AND THIS VERY MORNING...

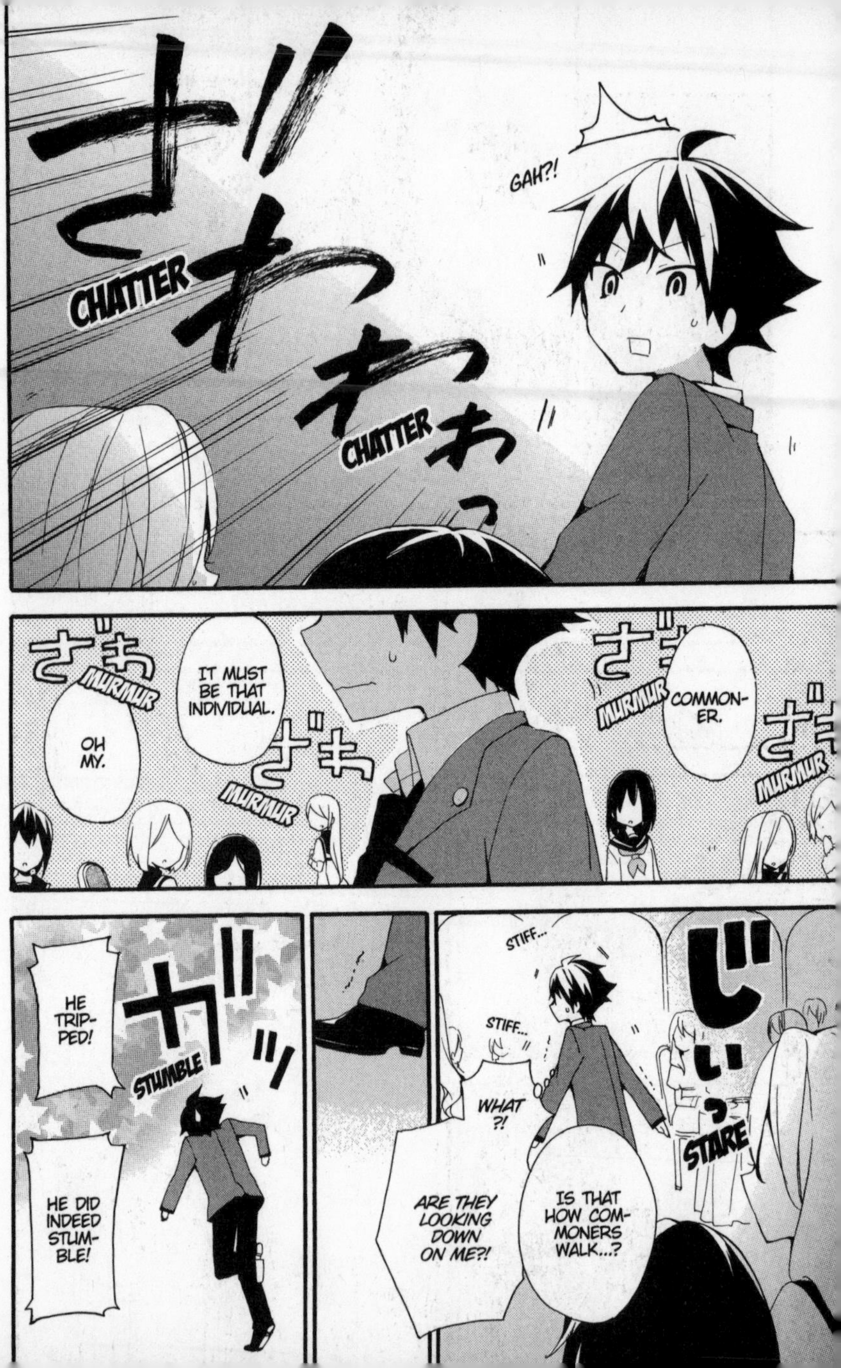

GAH?!
CHATTER
CHATTER
COMMON-
ER.
MURMUR
MURMUR
IT MUST
BE THAT
INDIVIDUAL.
MURMUR
OH
MY.
MURMUR
STARE
STIFF...
STIFF...
WHAT
?!
IS THAT
HOW COM-
MONERS
WALK...?
ARE THEY
LOOKING
DOWN
ON ME?!
HE
TRIP-
PED!
STUMBLE
HE DID
INDEED
STUM-
BLE!

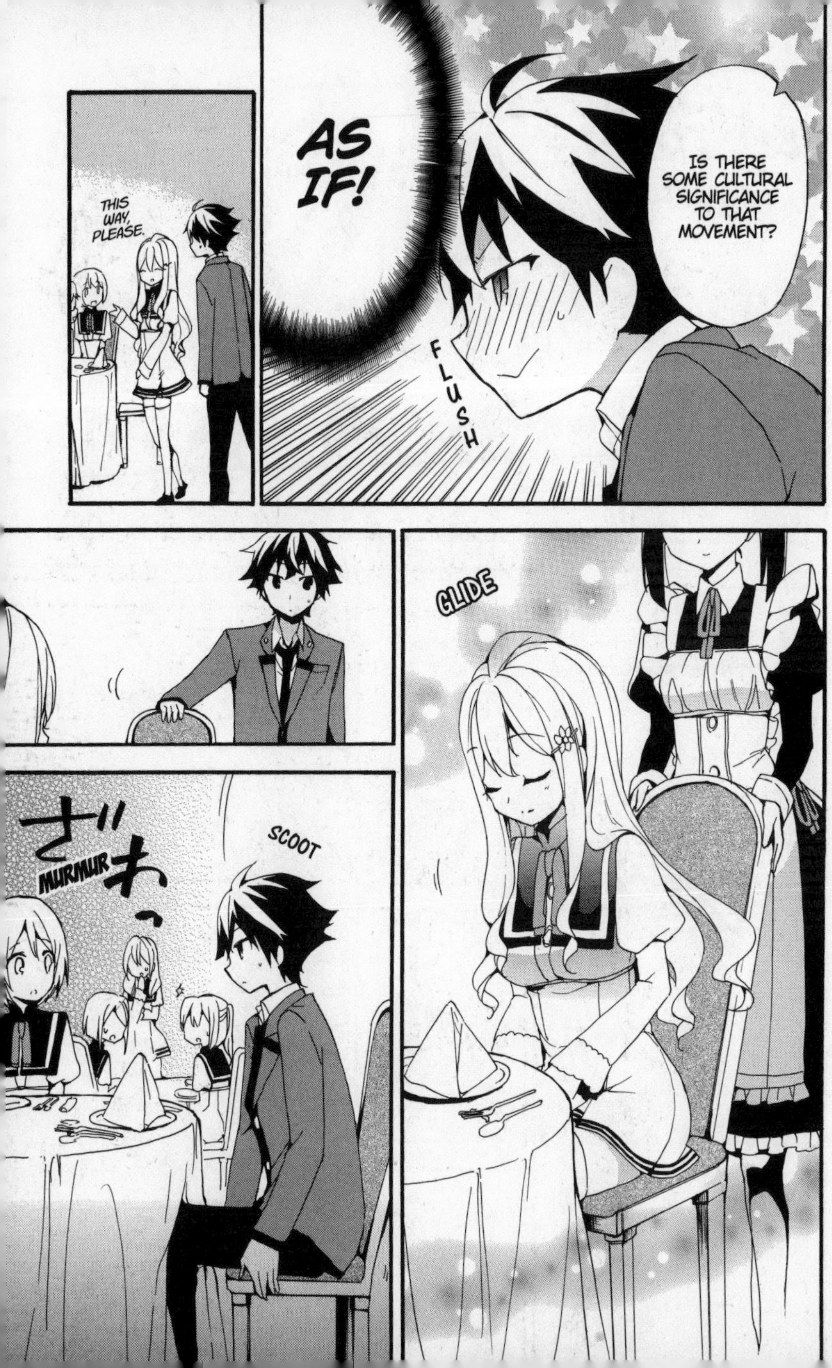
IS THERE SOME CULTURAL SIGNIFICANCE TO THAT MOVEMENT?
FLUSH
AS IF!
THIS WAY, PLEASE.
GLIDE
SCOOT
ざわっ
MURMUR

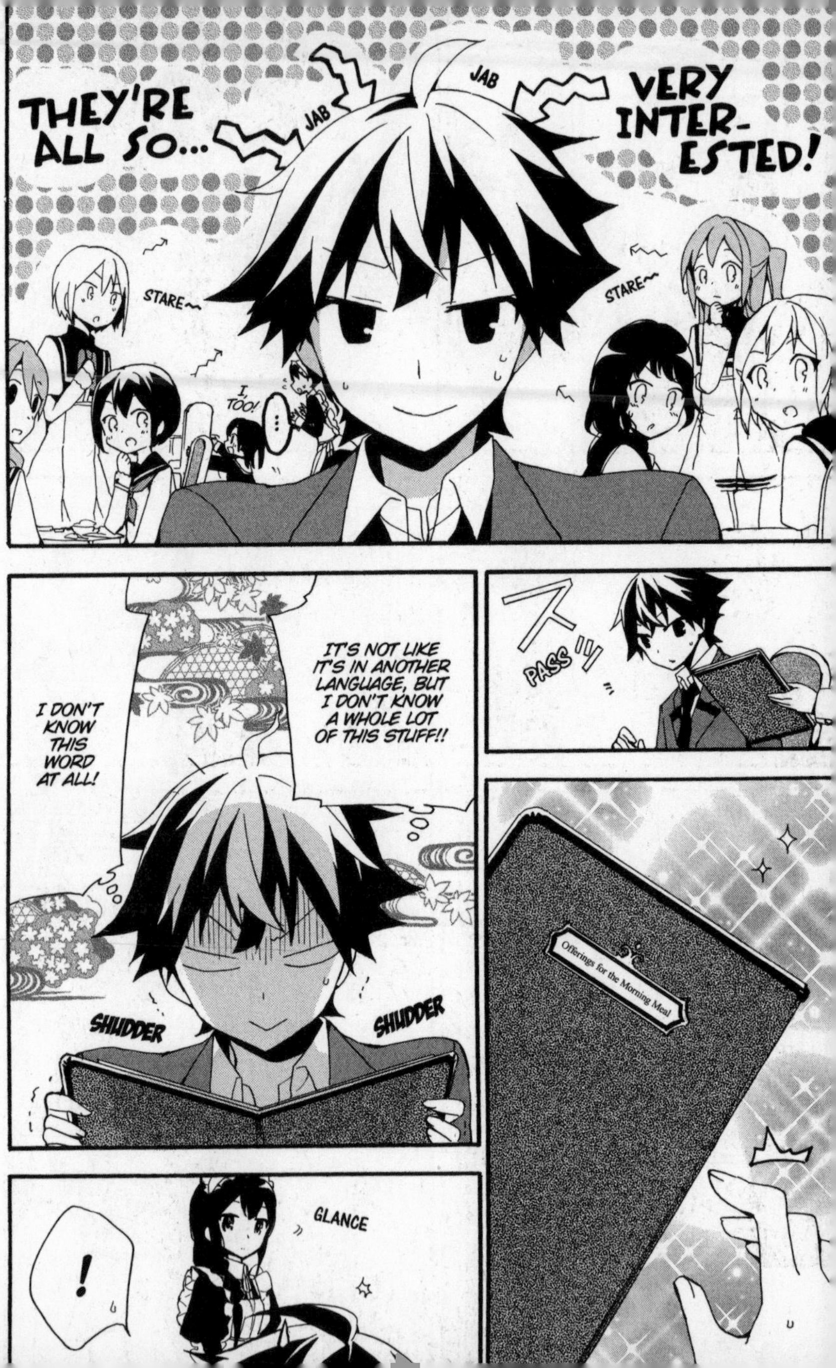
THEY'RE ALL SO...
VERY INTER-ESTED!
JAB
JAB
STARE~
STARE~
I, TOO!
...
PASS
Offerings for the Morning Meal
IT'S NOT LIKE IT'S IN ANOTHER LANGUAGE, BUT I DON'T KNOW A WHOLE LOT OF THIS STUFF!!
I DON'T KNOW THIS WORD AT ALL!
SHUDDER
SHUDDER
GLANCE
!

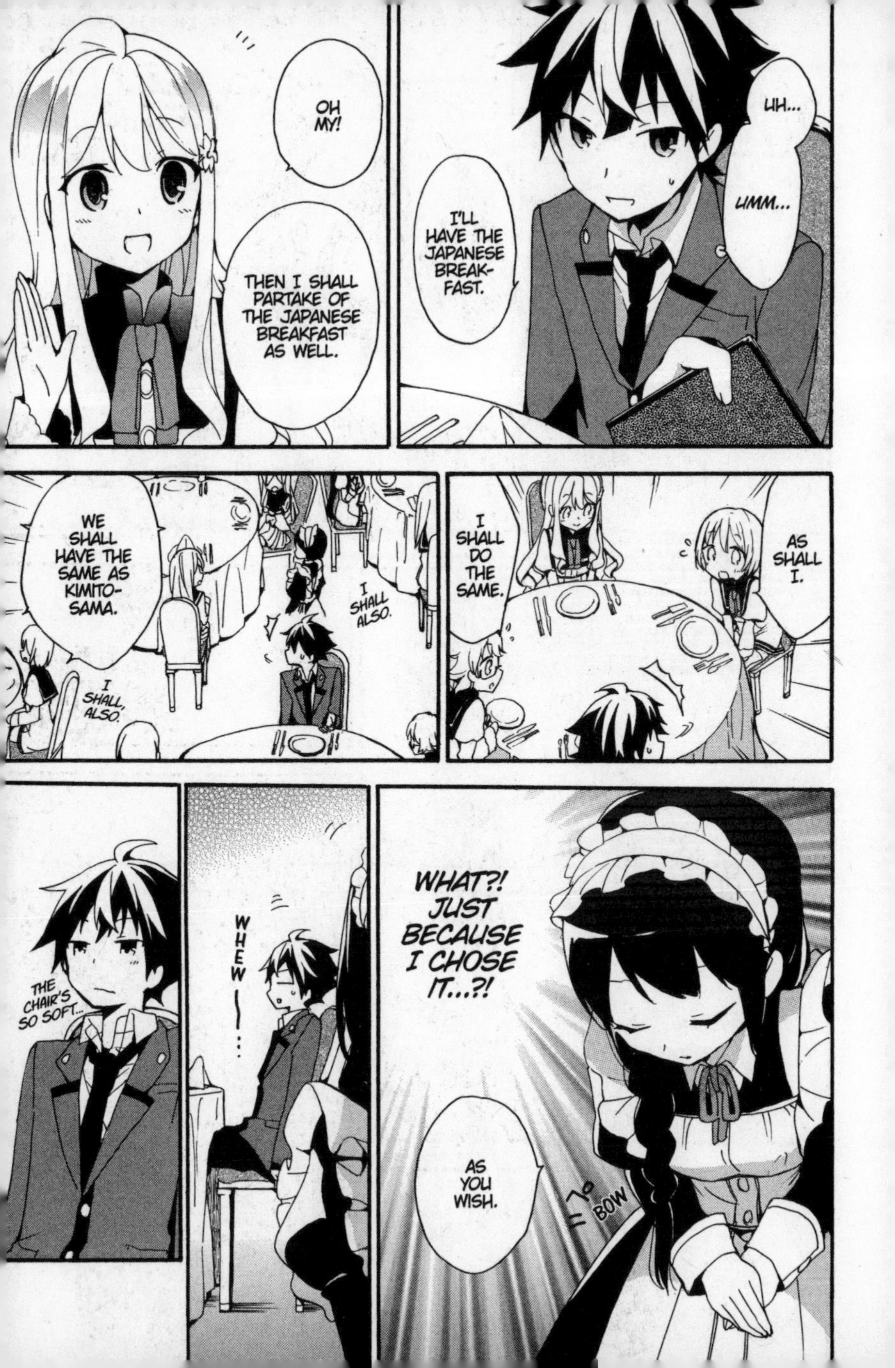
UH...
UMM...
I'LL HAVE THE JAPANESE BREAK-FAST.
OH MY!
THEN I SHALL PARTAKE OF THE JAPANESE BREAKFAST AS WELL.
AS SHALL I.
I SHALL DO THE SAME.
WE SHALL HAVE THE SAME AS KIMITO-SAMA.
I SHALL ALSO.
I SHALL, ALSO.
WHAT?! JUST BECAUSE I CHOSE IT...?!
AS YOU WISH.
BOW
WHEW...
THE CHAIR'S SO SOFT...

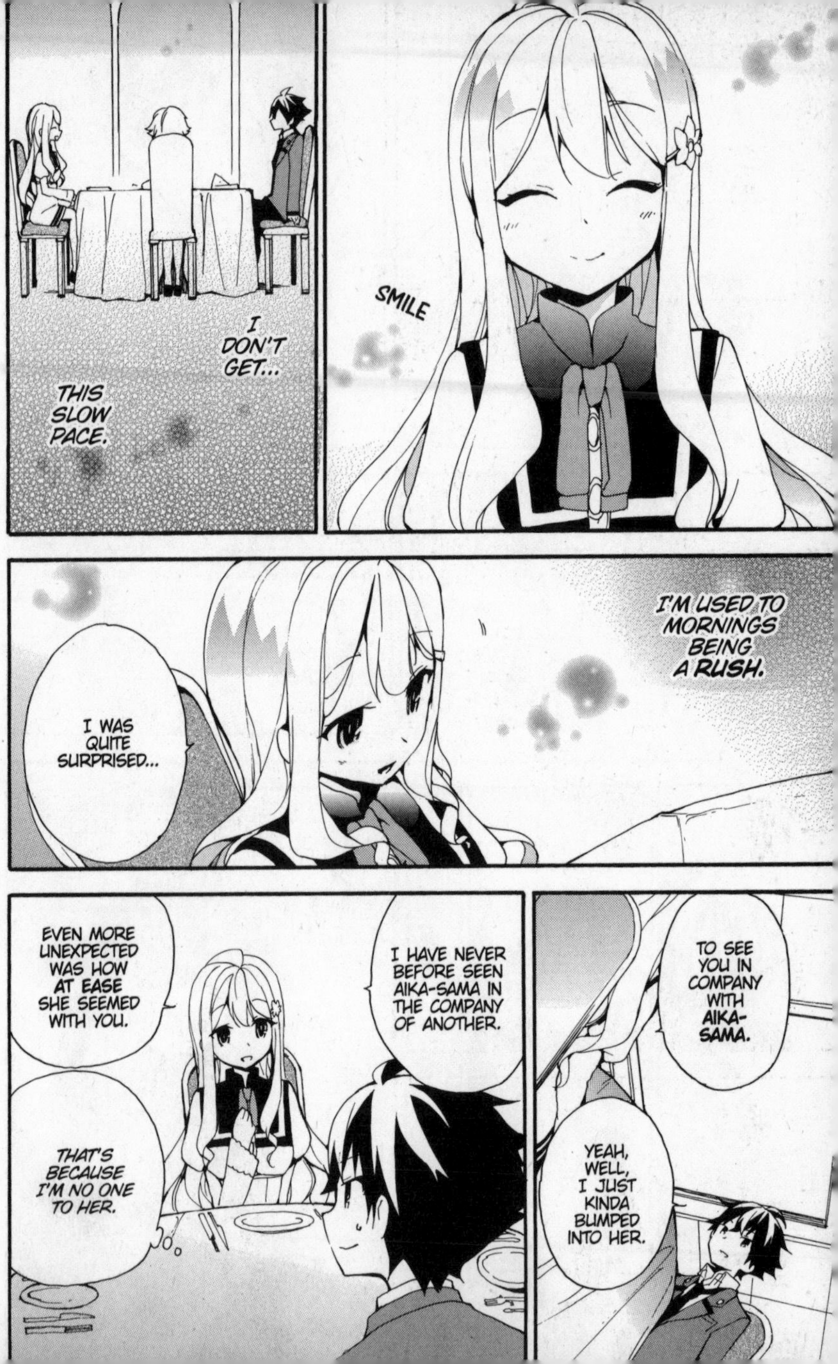
SMILE
I DON'T GET...
THIS SLOW PACE.
I'M USED TO MORNINGS BEING A RUSH.
I WAS QUITE SURPRISED...
TO SEE YOU IN COMPANY WITH AIKA-SAMA.
YEAH, WELL, I JUST KINDA BUMPED INTO HER.
I HAVE NEVER BEFORE SEEN AIKA-SAMA IN THE COMPANY OF ANOTHER.
EVEN MORE UNEXPECTED WAS HOW AT EASE SHE SEEMED WITH YOU.
THAT'S BECAUSE I'M NO ONE TO HER.

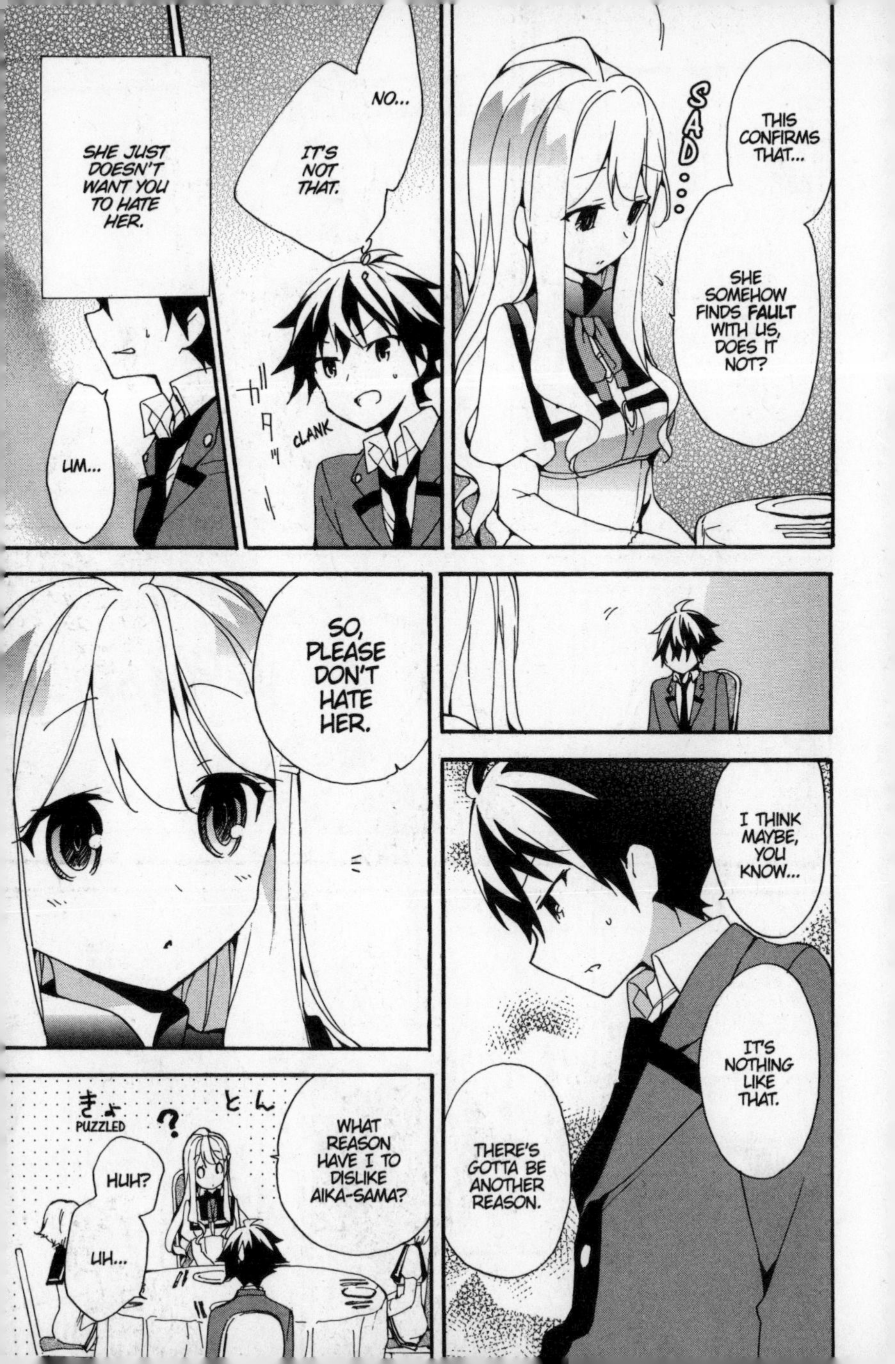

SAD...
THIS CONFIRMS THAT...
SHE SOMEHOW FINDS FAULT WITH US, DOES IT NOT?
NO...
IT'S NOT THAT.
ガタッ
CLANK
SHE JUST DOESN'T WANT YOU TO HATE HER.
UM...
SO, PLEASE DON'T HATE HER.
I THINK MAYBE, YOU KNOW...
IT'S NOTHING LIKE THAT.
THERE'S GOTTA BE ANOTHER REASON.
WHAT REASON HAVE I TO DISLIKE AIKA-SAMA?
きょとん
PUZZLED
HUH?
UH...

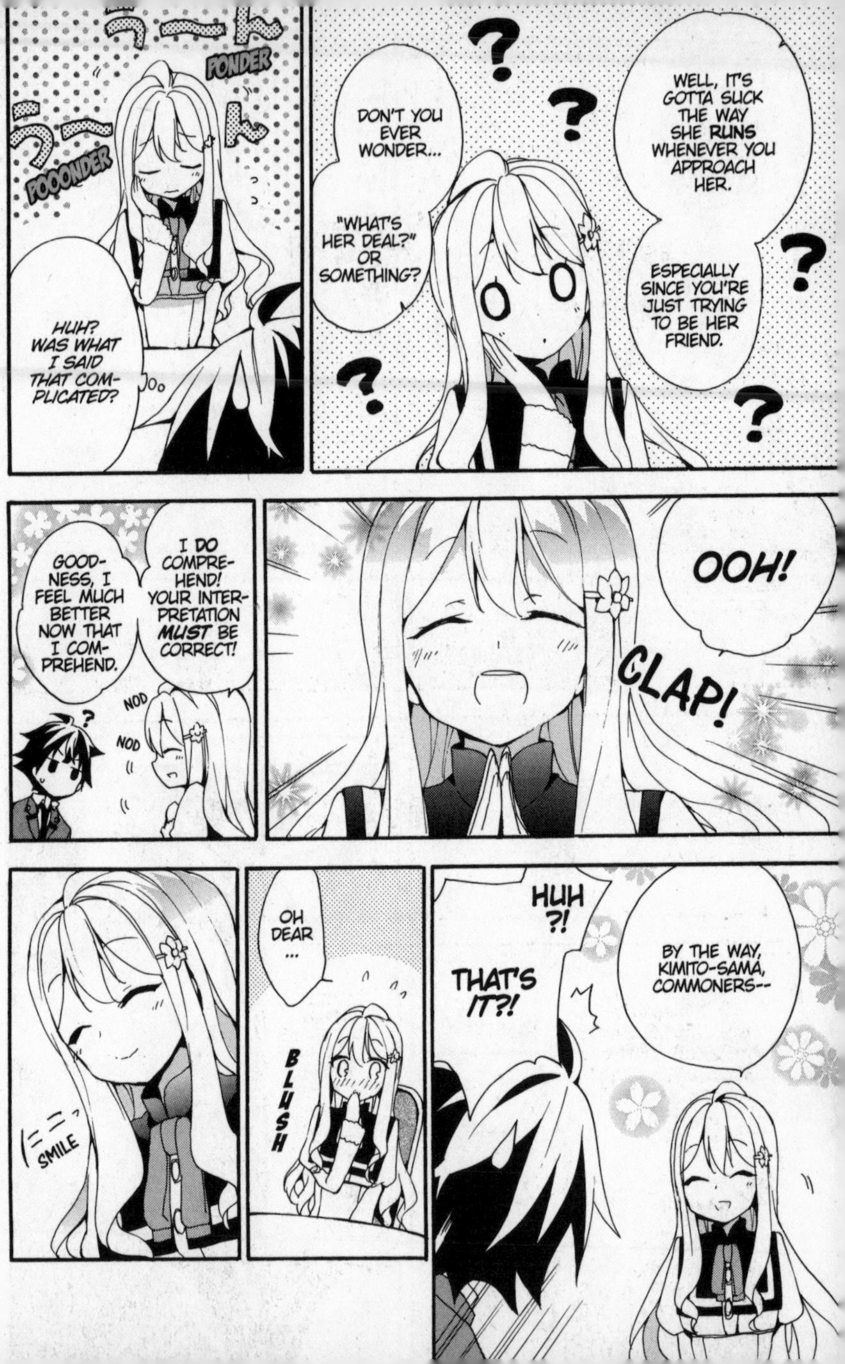
WELL, IT'S GOTTA SUCK THE WAY SHE RUNS WHENEVER YOU APPROACH HER.
ESPECIALLY SINCE YOU'RE JUST TRYING TO BE HER FRIEND.
DON'T YOU EVER WONDER...
"WHAT'S HER DEAL?" OR SOMETHING?
うーん
PONDER
うーん
POOONDER
HUH? WAS WHAT I SAID THAT COMPLICATED?
OOH!
CLAP!
I DO COMPREHEND! YOUR INTERPRETATION MUST BE CORRECT!
GOODNESS, I FEEL MUCH BETTER NOW THAT I COMPREHEND.
NOD
NOD
BY THE WAY, KIMITO-SAMA, COMMONERS--
HUH?!
THAT'S IT?!
OH DEAR...
BLUSH
SMILE

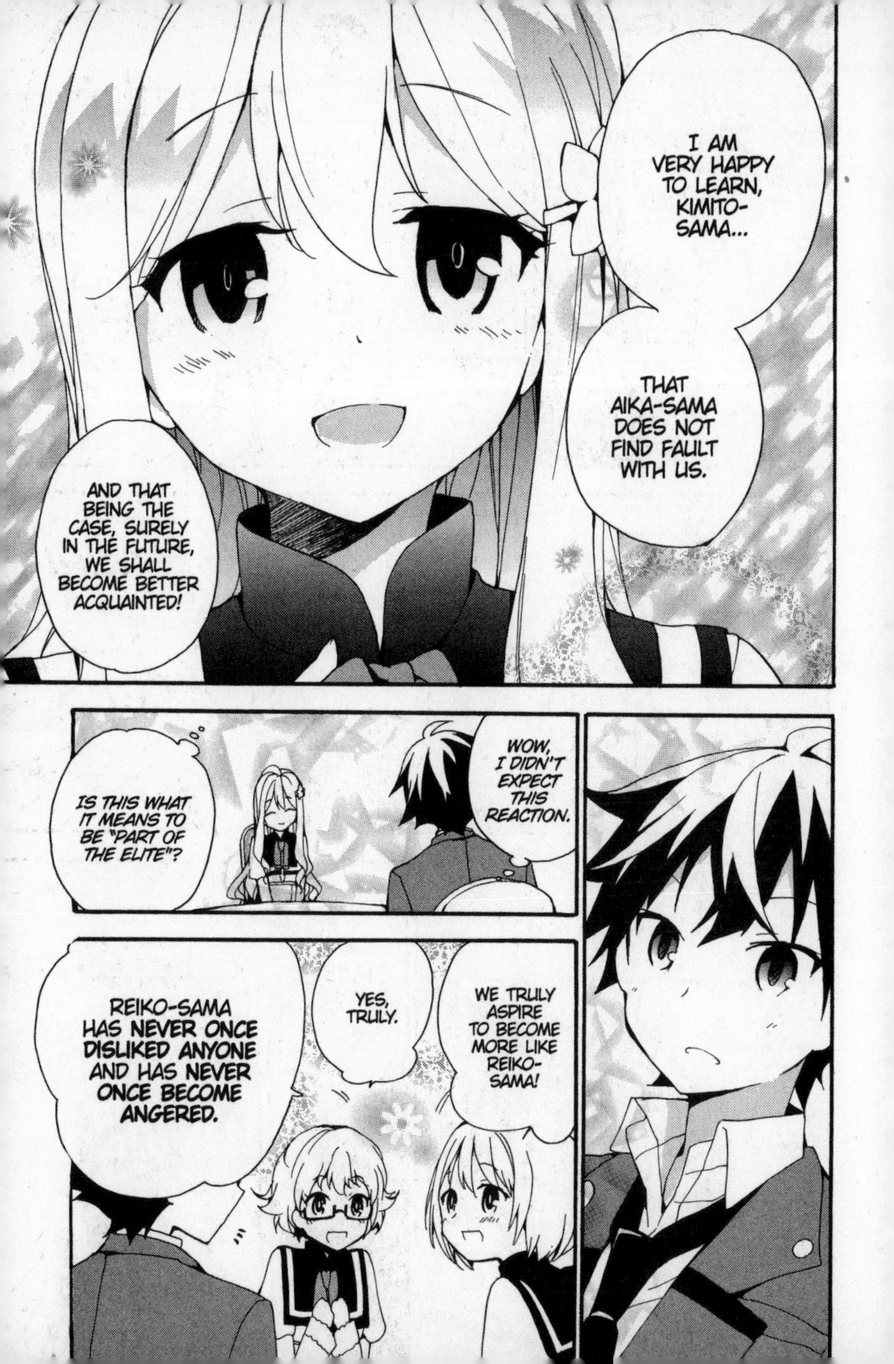
I AM VERY HAPPY TO LEARN, KIMITO-SAMA...
THAT AIKA-SAMA DOES NOT FIND FAULT WITH US.
AND THAT BEING THE CASE, SURELY IN THE FUTURE, WE SHALL BECOME BETTER ACQUAINTED!
WOW, I DIDN'T EXPECT THIS REACTION.
IS THIS WHAT IT MEANS TO BE "PART OF THE ELITE"?
WE TRULY ASPIRE TO BECOME MORE LIKE REIKO-SAMA!
YES, TRULY.
REIKO-SAMA HAS NEVER ONCE DISLIKED ANYONE AND HAS NEVER ONCE BECOME ANGERED.

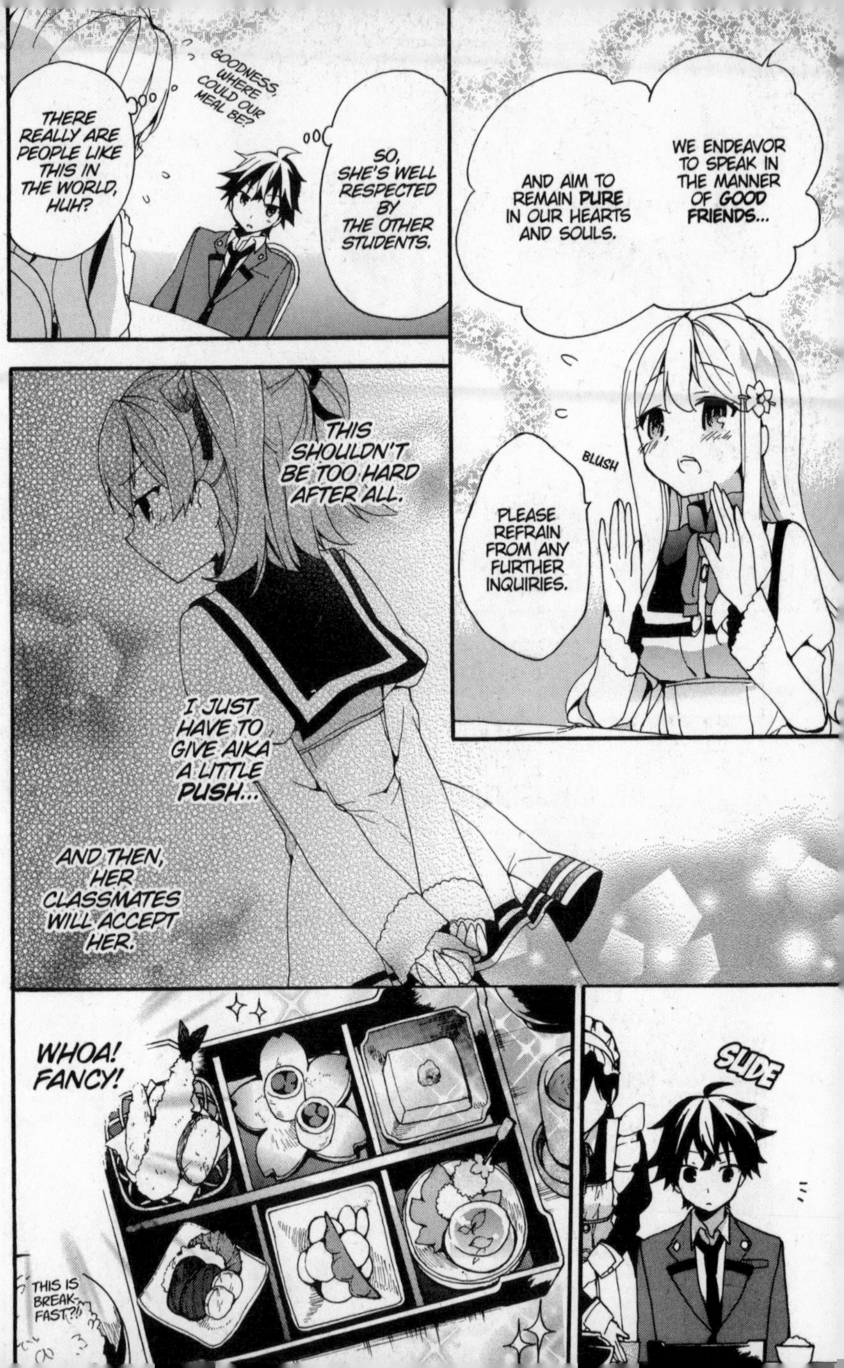
WE ENDEAVOR TO SPEAK IN THE MANNER OF **GOOD FRIENDS**...
AND AIM TO REMAIN **PURE** IN OUR HEARTS AND SOULS.
BLUSH
PLEASE REFRAIN FROM ANY FURTHER INQUIRIES.
SO, SHE'S WELL RESPECTED BY THE OTHER STUDENTS.
GOODNESS, WHERE COULD OUR MEAL BE?
THERE REALLY ARE PEOPLE LIKE THIS IN THE WORLD, HUH?
THIS SHOULDN'T BE TOO HARD AFTER ALL.
I JUST HAVE TO GIVE AIKA A LITTLE PUSH...
AND THEN, HER CLASSMATES WILL ACCEPT HER.
SLIDE
WHOA! FANCY!
THIS IS BREAK-FAST?!

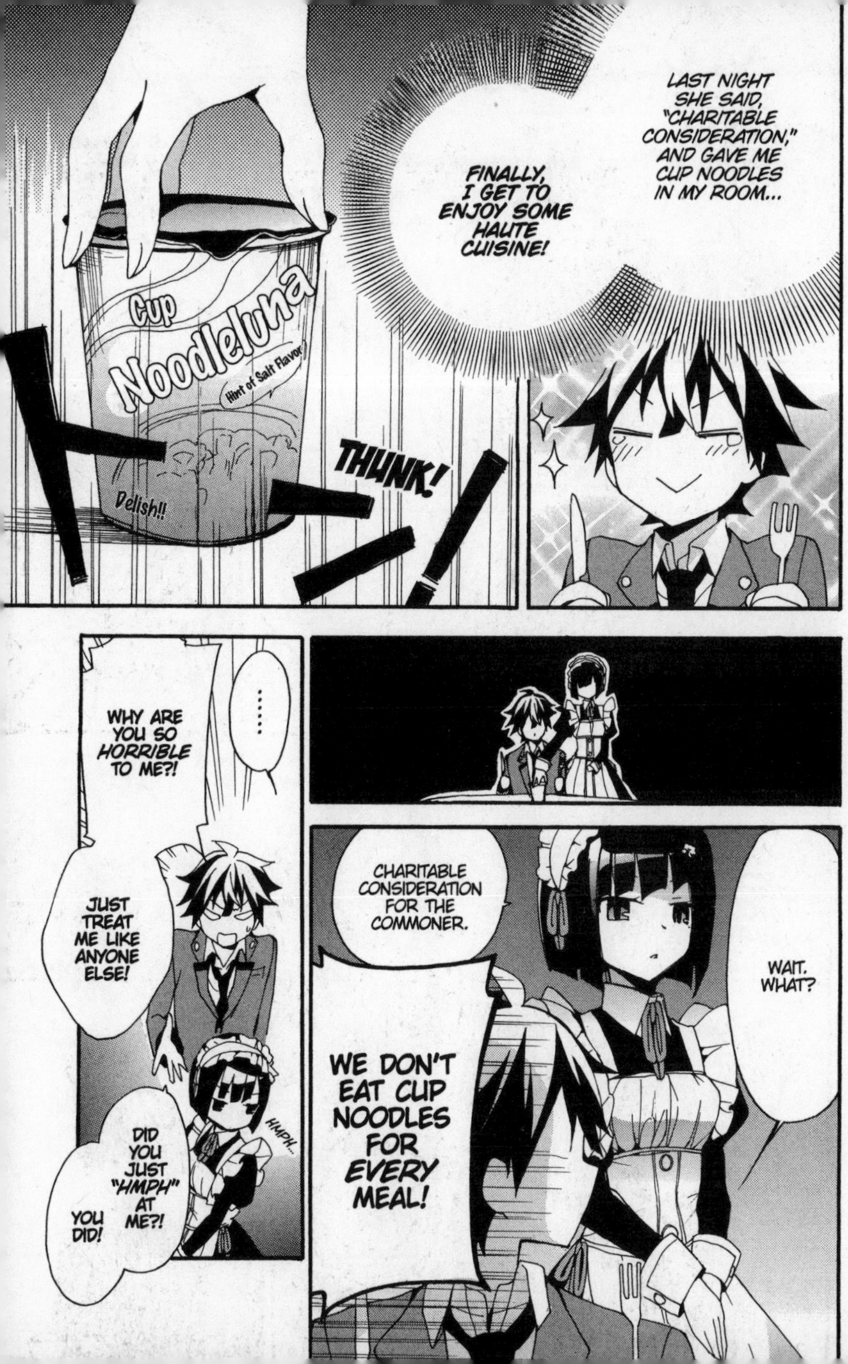
LAST NIGHT SHE SAID, "CHARITABLE CONSIDERATION," AND GAVE ME CUP NOODLES IN MY ROOM...
FINALLY, I GET TO ENJOY SOME HAUTE CUISINE!
THUNK!
Cup Noodleluna
Hint of Salt Flavor
Delish!!
WAIT. WHAT?
CHARITABLE CONSIDERATION FOR THE COMMONER.
WE DON'T EAT CUP NOODLES FOR EVERY MEAL!
......
WHY ARE YOU SO HORRIBLE TO ME?!
JUST TREAT ME LIKE ANYONE ELSE!
HMPH...
DID YOU JUST "HMPH" AT ME?!
YOU DID!

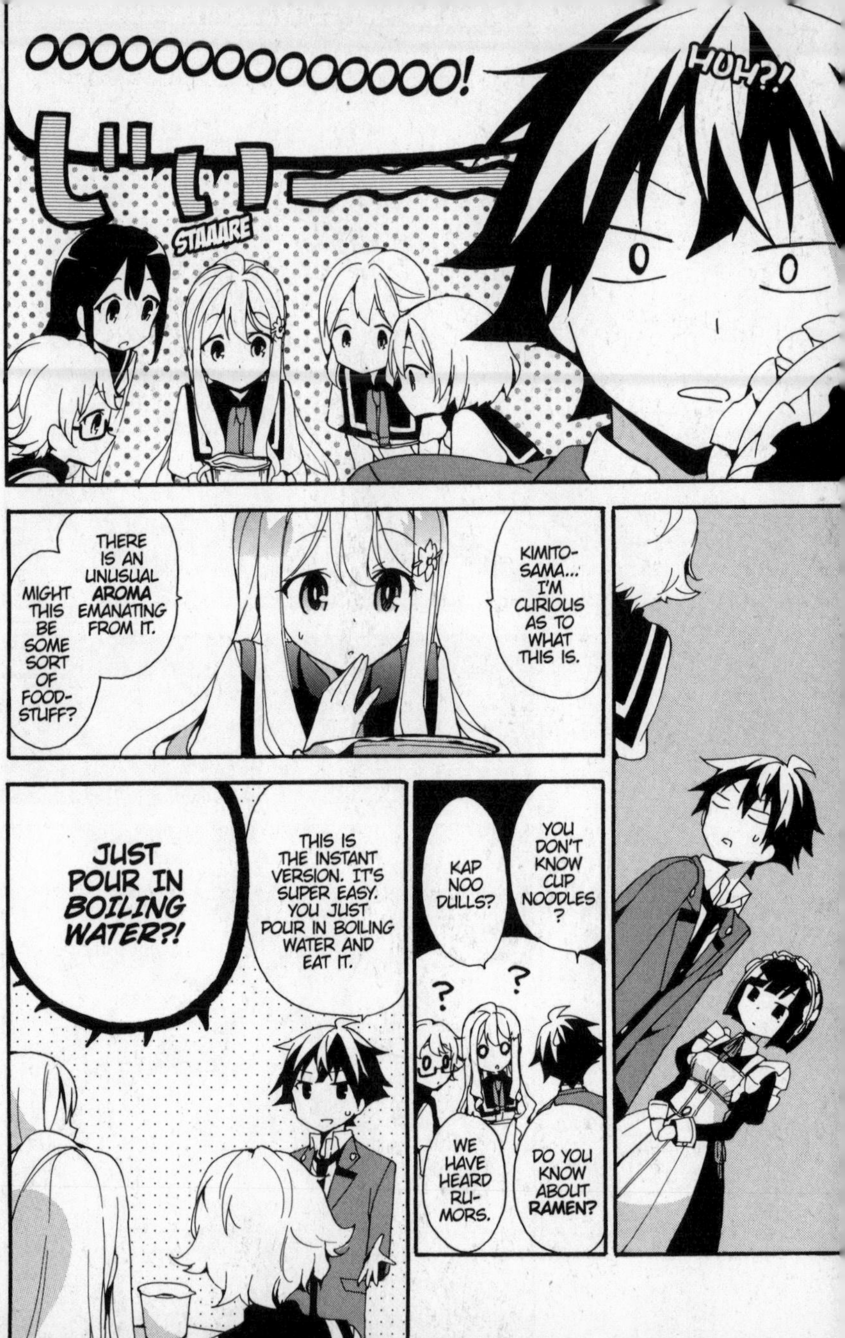
HUH?!
OOOOOOOOOOOOOO!
じぃぃー
STAAARE
KIMITO-SAMA...! I'M CURIOUS AS TO WHAT THIS IS.
THERE IS AN UNUSUAL AROMA EMANATING FROM IT.
MIGHT THIS BE SOME SORT OF FOOD-STUFF?
YOU DON'T KNOW CUP NOODLES?
KAP NOO DULLS?
?
?
DO YOU KNOW ABOUT RAMEN?
WE HAVE HEARD RU-MORS.
THIS IS THE INSTANT VERSION. IT'S SUPER EASY. YOU JUST POUR IN BOILING WATER AND EAT IT.
JUST POUR IN BOILING WATER?!

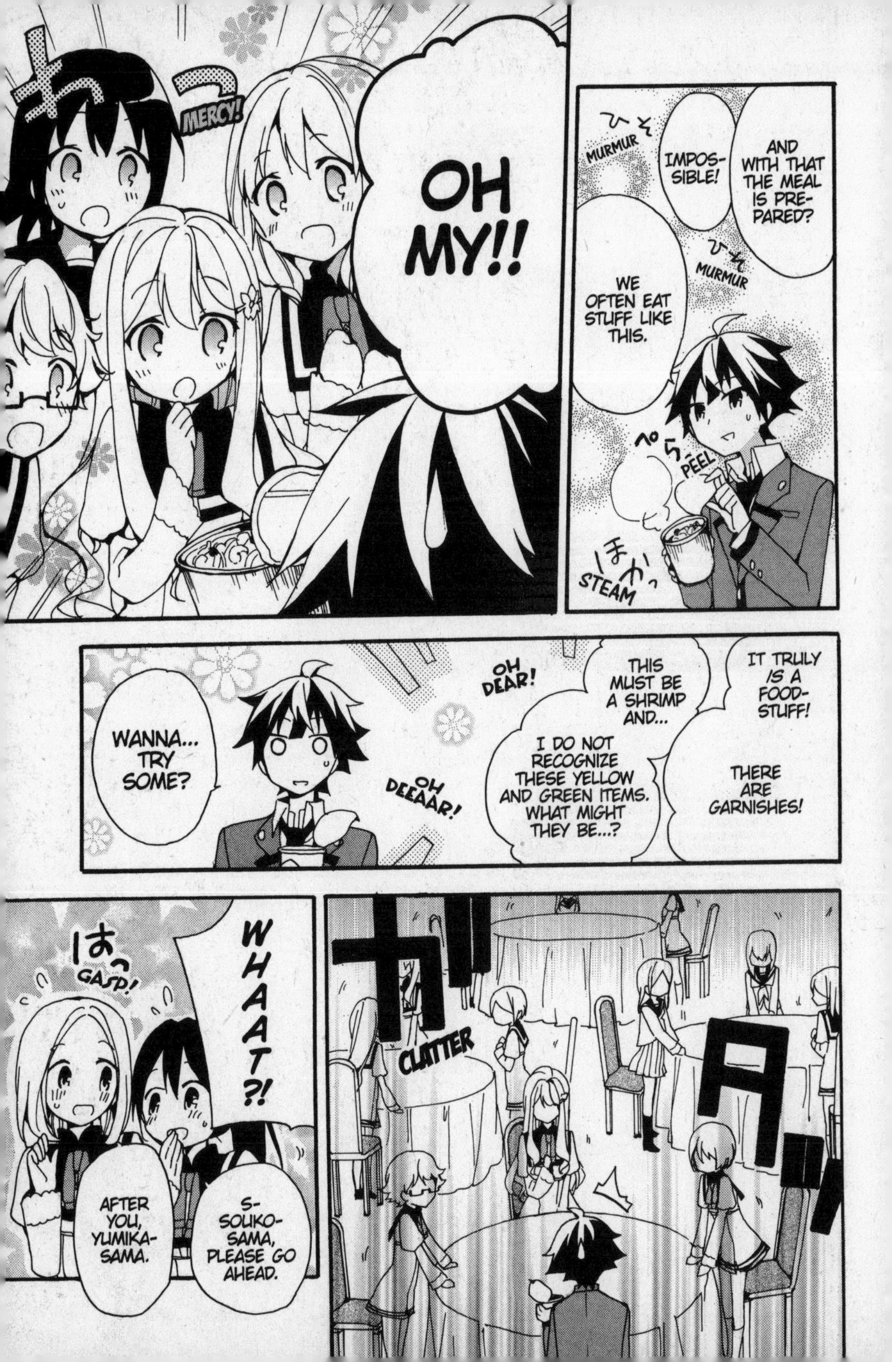

AND WITH THAT THE MEAL IS PREPARED?
IMPOSSIBLE!
ひそ
MURMUR
ひそ
MURMUR
WE OFTEN EAT STUFF LIKE THIS.
ぺら
PEEL
ほわっ
STEAM
OH MY!!
わっ
MERCY!
IT TRULY IS A FOODSTUFF!
THERE ARE GARNISHES!
THIS MUST BE A SHRIMP AND...
I DO NOT RECOGNIZE THESE YELLOW AND GREEN ITEMS. WHAT MIGHT THEY BE...?
OH DEAR!
OH DEEEAAR!
WANNA... TRY SOME?
CLATTER
WHAAT?!
はっ
GASP!
S-SOUKO-SAMA, PLEASE GO AHEAD.
AFTER YOU, YUMIKA-SAMA.

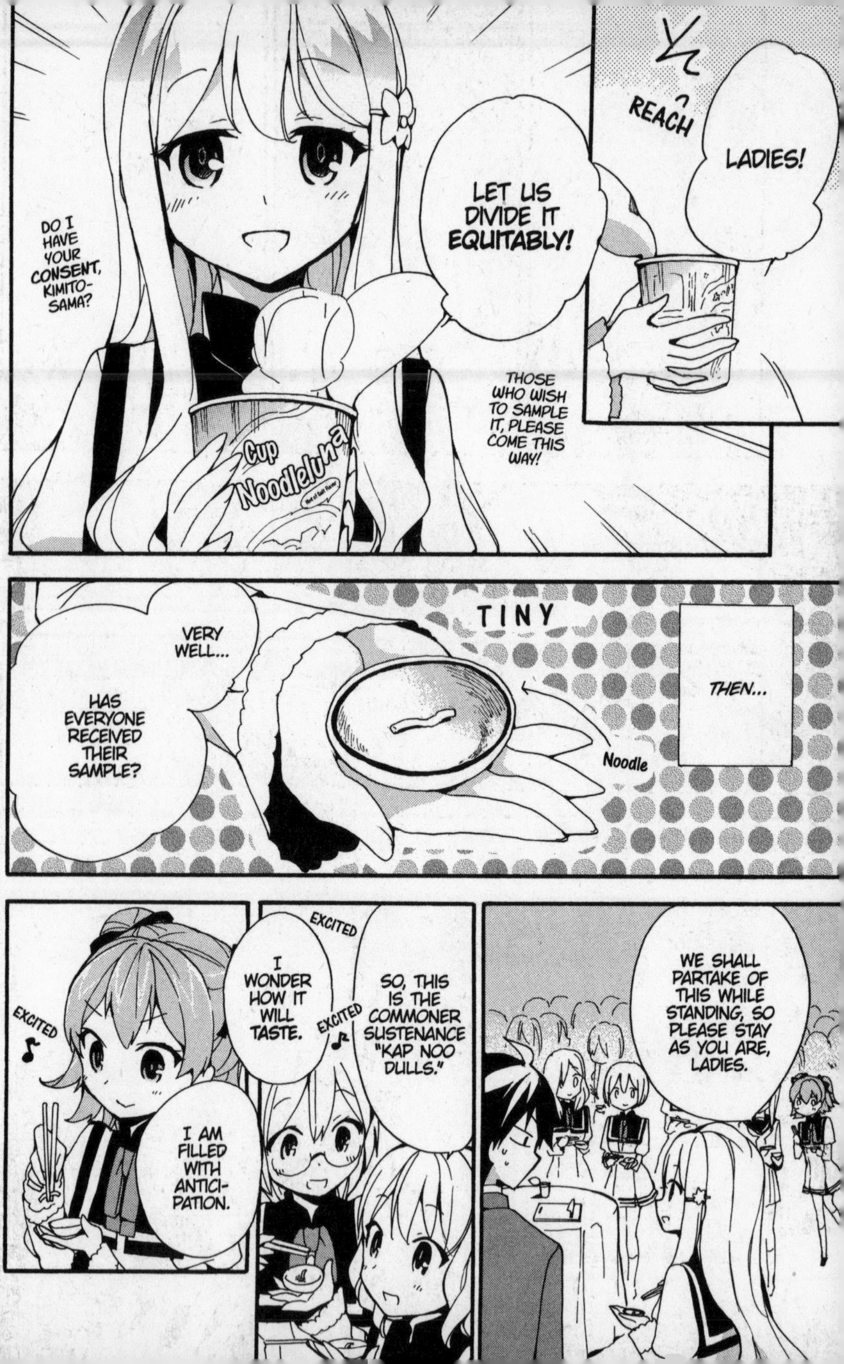
REACH
LADIES!
LET US DIVIDE IT EQUITABLY!
THOSE WHO WISH TO SAMPLE IT, PLEASE COME THIS WAY!
DO I HAVE YOUR CONSENT, KIMITO-SAMA?
Cup Noodleluna
THEN...
TINY
Noodle
VERY WELL...
HAS EVERYONE RECEIVED THEIR SAMPLE?
WE SHALL PARTAKE OF THIS WHILE STANDING, SO PLEASE STAY AS YOU ARE, LADIES.
EXCITED
SO, THIS IS THE COMMONER SUSTENANCE "KAP NOO DULLS."
EXCITED
I WONDER HOW IT WILL TASTE.
EXCITED
I AM FILLED WITH ANTICIPATION.

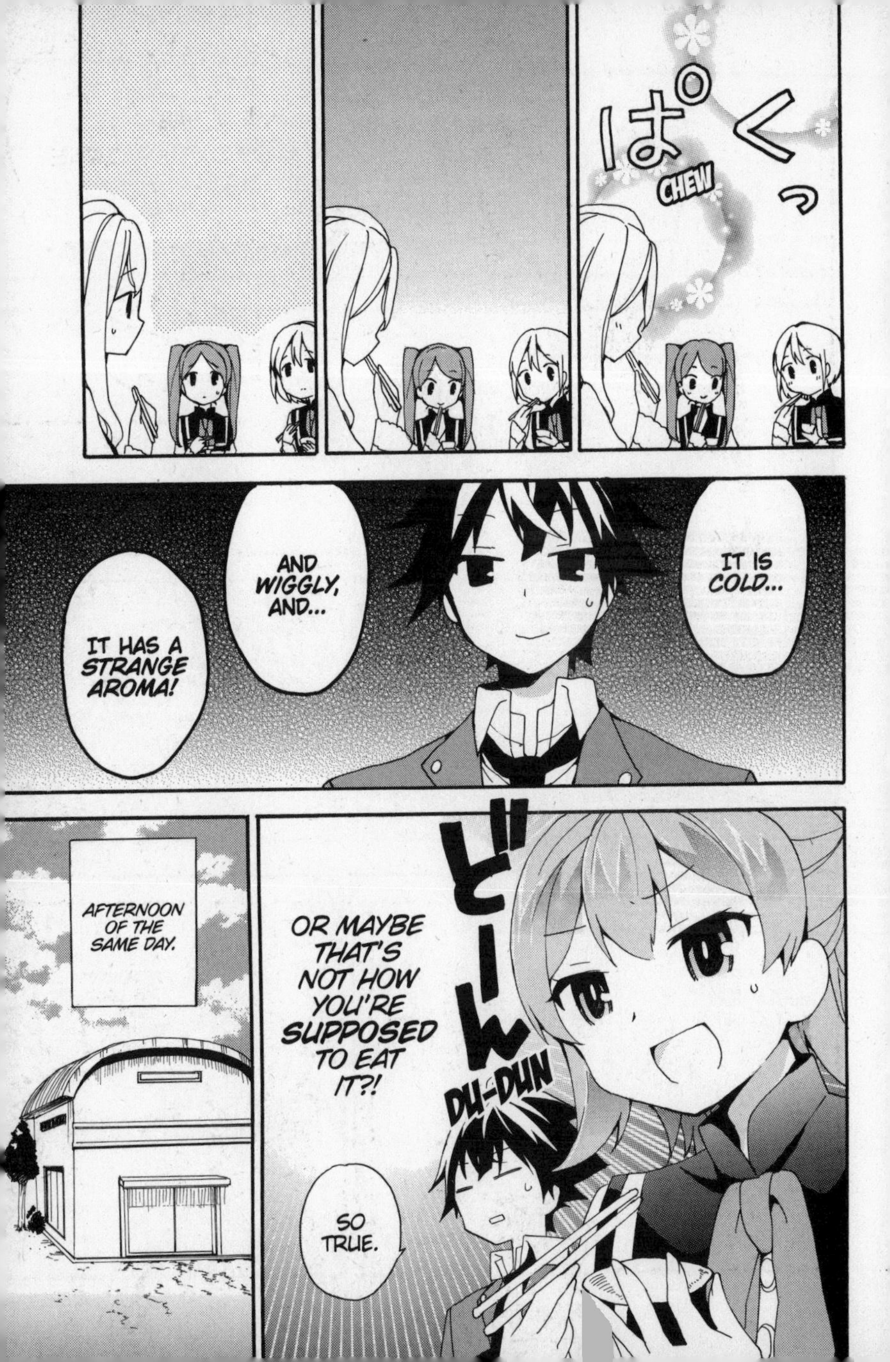
ぱくっ
CHEW
IT IS COLD...
AND WIGGLY, AND...
IT HAS A STRANGE AROMA!
どーん
DU-DUN
OR MAYBE THAT'S NOT HOW YOU'RE SUPPOSED TO EAT IT?!
SO TRUE.
AFTERNOON OF THE SAME DAY.

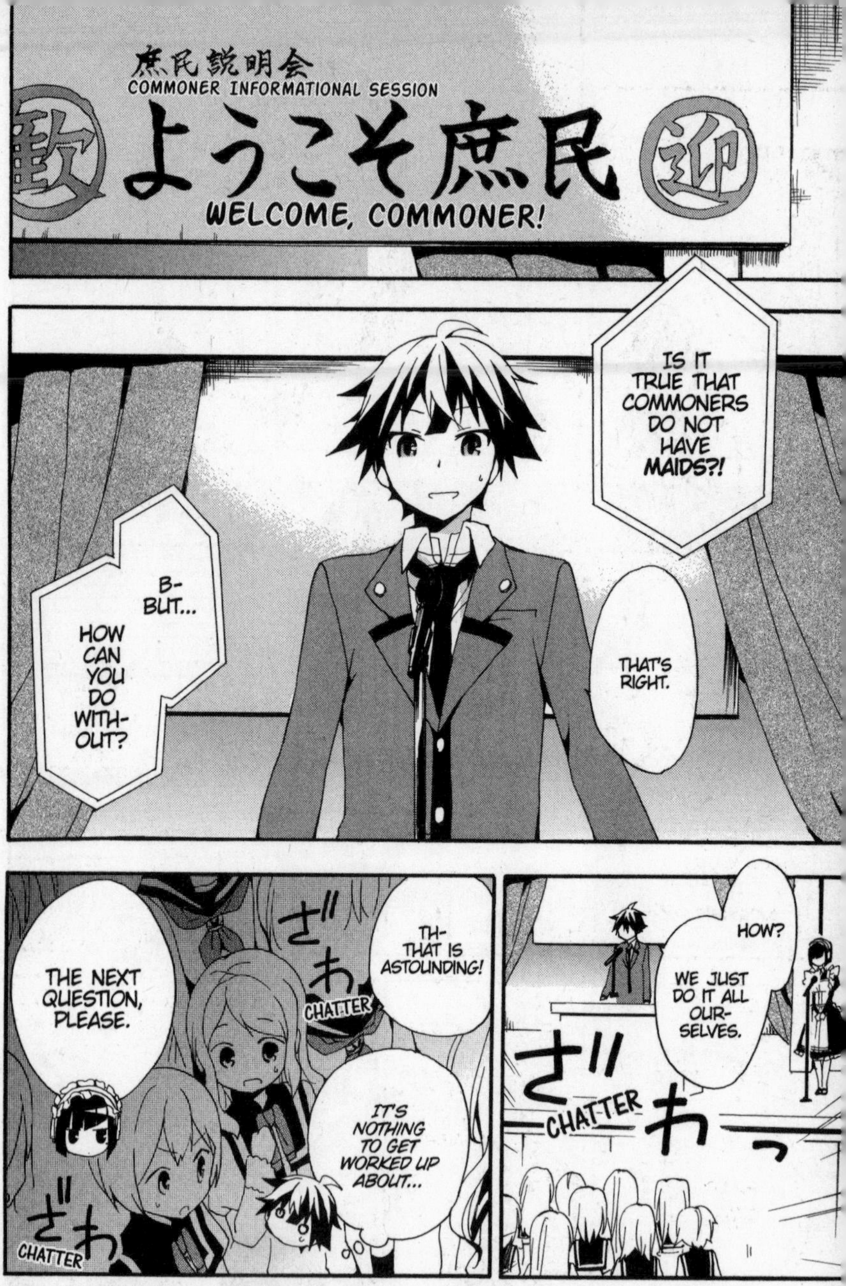
庶民説明会
COMMONER INFORMATIONAL SESSION
歓 ようこそ庶民 迎
WELCOME, COMMONER!
IS IT TRUE THAT COMMONERS DO NOT HAVE MAIDS?!
THAT'S RIGHT.
B- BUT... HOW CAN YOU DO WITH- OUT?
HOW? WE JUST DO IT ALL OUR- SELVES.
ざわっ
CHATTER
TH- THAT IS ASTOUNDING!
ざわ
CHATTER
IT'S NOTHING TO GET WORKED UP ABOUT...
THE NEXT QUESTION, PLEASE.
ざわ
CHATTER

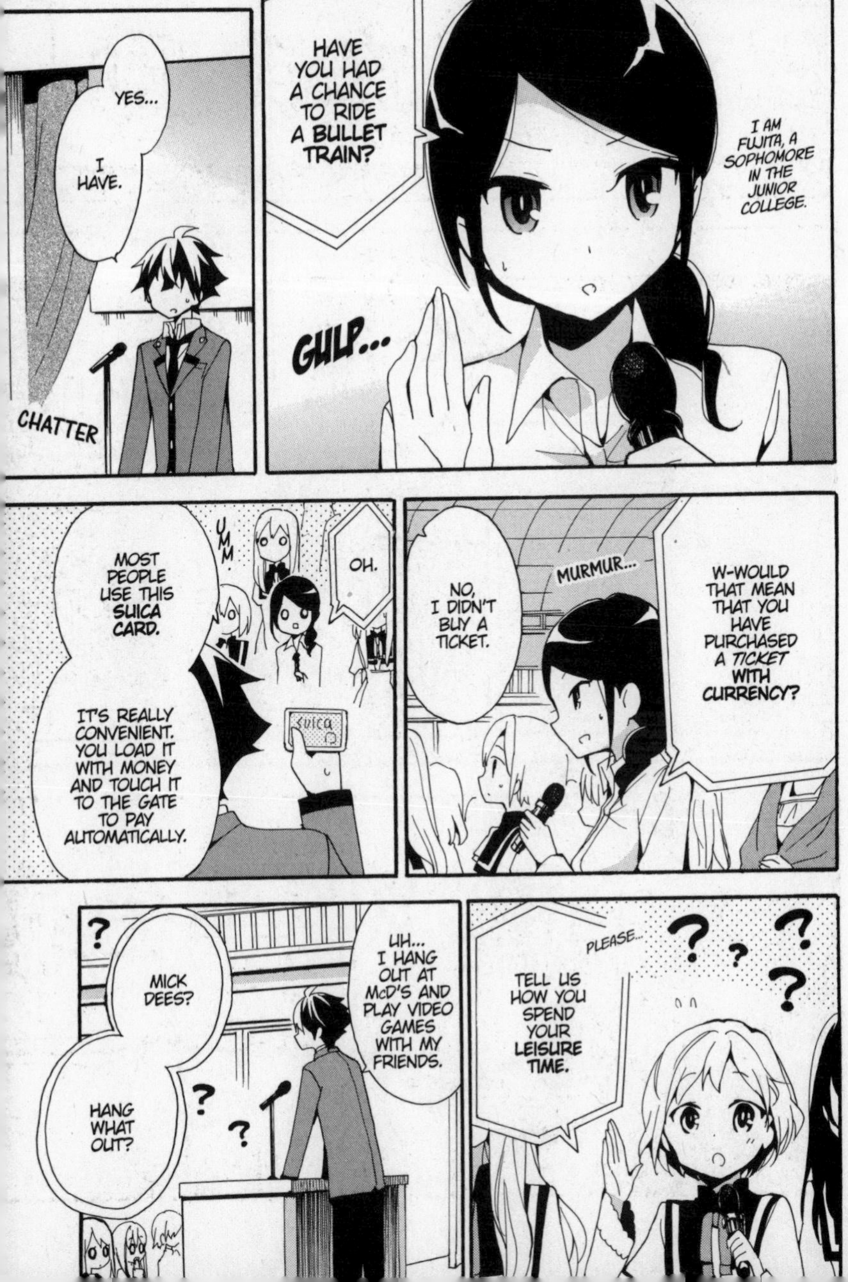
I AM FUJITA, A SOPHOMORE IN THE JUNIOR COLLEGE.
HAVE YOU HAD A CHANCE TO RIDE A BULLET TRAIN?
GULP...
YES...
I HAVE.
CHATTER
W-WOULD THAT MEAN THAT YOU HAVE PURCHASED A TICKET WITH CURRENCY?
MURMUR...
NO, I DIDN'T BUY A TICKET.
OH.
UMM
MOST PEOPLE USE THIS SUICA CARD.
SUICA
IT'S REALLY CONVENIENT. YOU LOAD IT WITH MONEY AND TOUCH IT TO THE GATE TO PAY AUTOMATICALLY.
PLEASE...
TELL US HOW YOU SPEND YOUR LEISURE TIME.
UH... I HANG OUT AT McD'S AND PLAY VIDEO GAMES WITH MY FRIENDS.
MICK DEES?
HANG WHAT OUT?

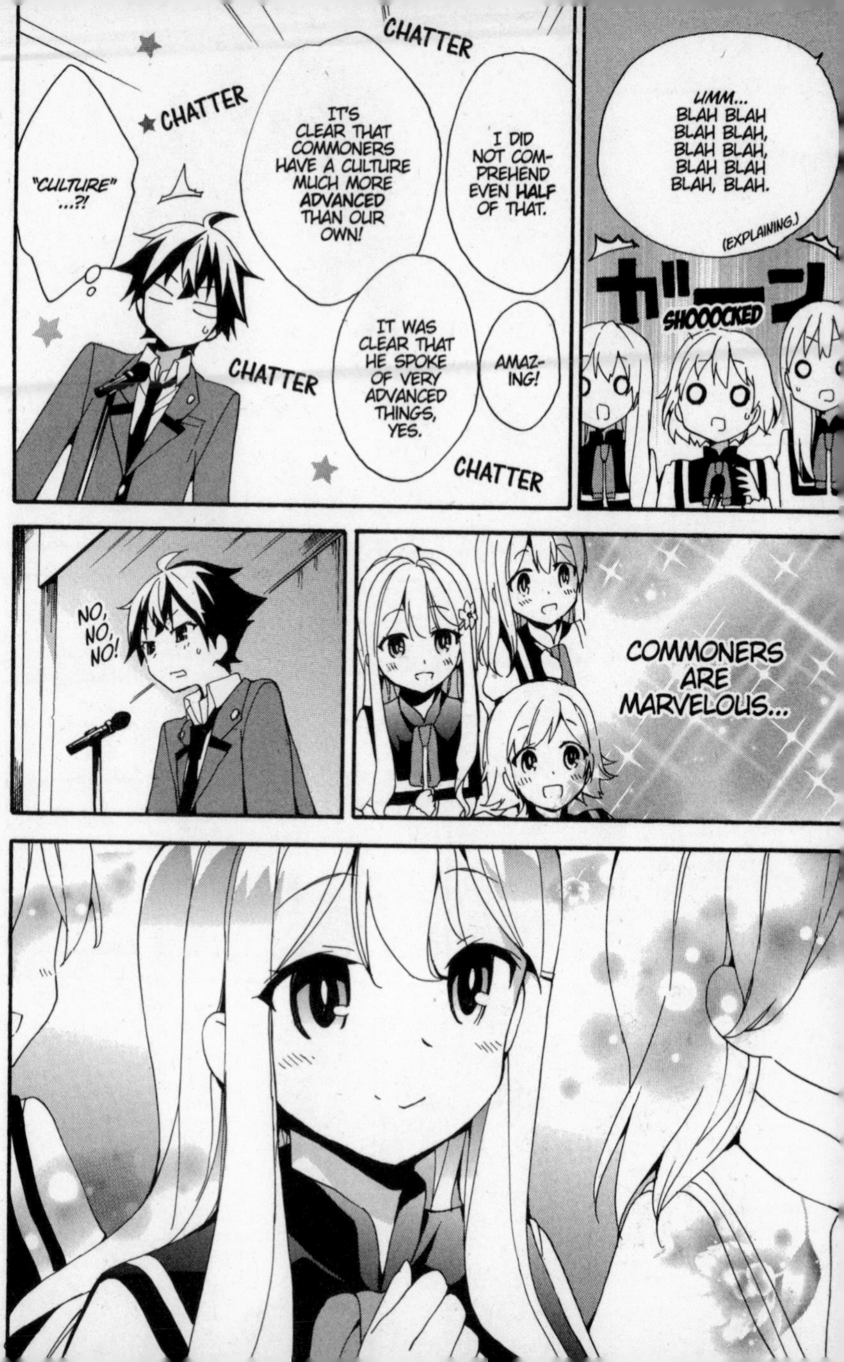
UMM... BLAH BLAH BLAH BLAH, BLAH BLAH, BLAH BLAH BLAH, BLAH.
(EXPLAINING.)
ガーン
SHOOOCKED
CHATTER
I DID NOT COMPREHEND EVEN HALF OF THAT.
IT'S CLEAR THAT COMMONERS HAVE A CULTURE MUCH MORE ADVANCED THAN OUR OWN!
CHATTER
AMAZING!
IT WAS CLEAR THAT HE SPOKE OF VERY ADVANCED THINGS, YES.
"CULTURE" ...?!
CHATTER
CHATTER
COMMONERS ARE MARVELOUS...
NO, NO, NO!

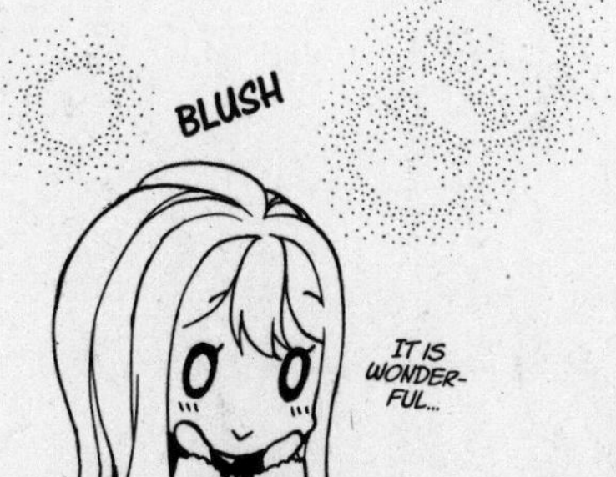
BLUSH
IT IS WONDER-FUL...

SHŌMIN
SAMPLE ❶

I Was Abducted by an Elite All-Girls
School as a Sample Commoner

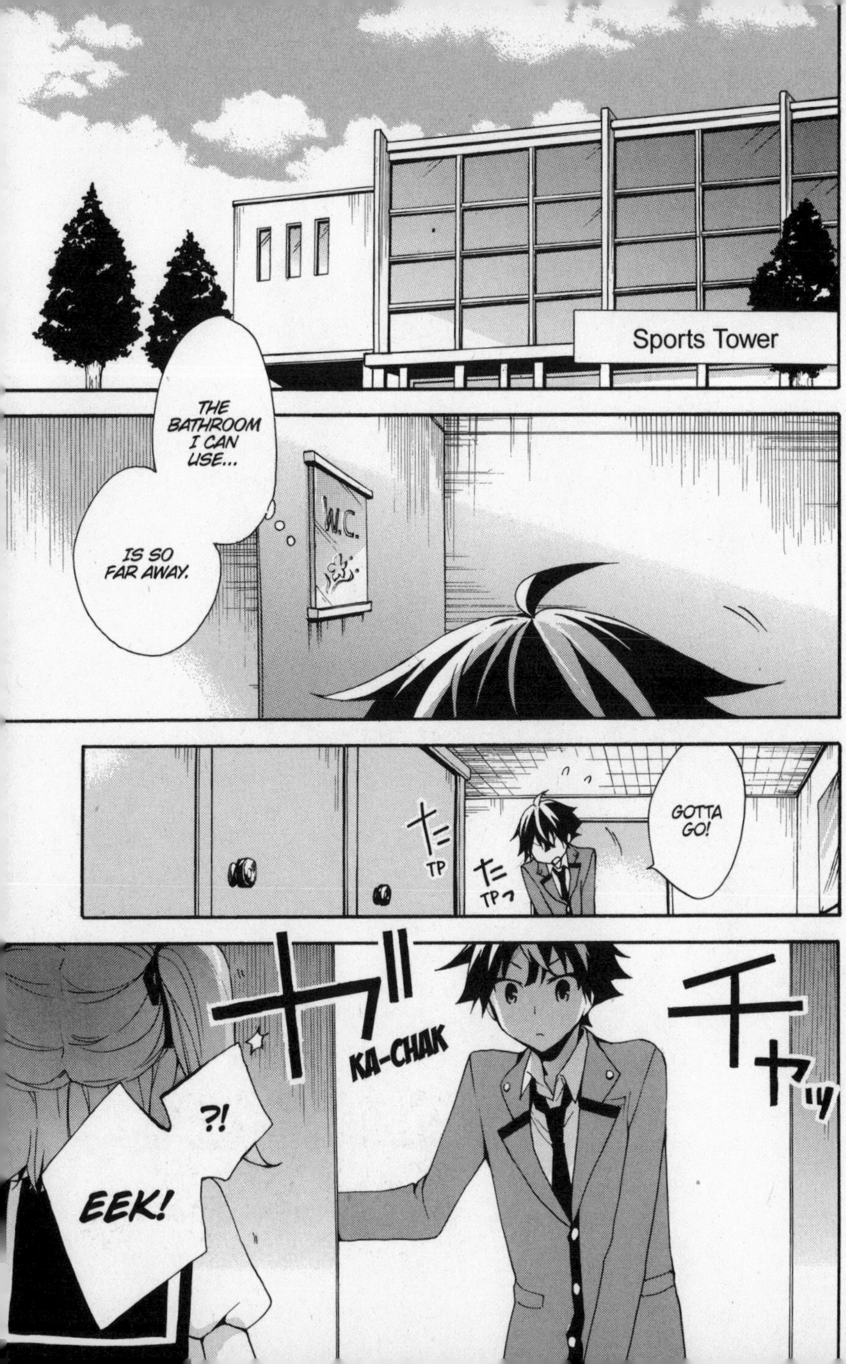
Sports Tower
THE BATHROOM I CAN USE...
IS SO FAR AWAY.
W.C.
GOTTA GO!
TP
TP
KA-CHAK
?!
EEK!

✕ Chapter 4 ✿ Gotcha!

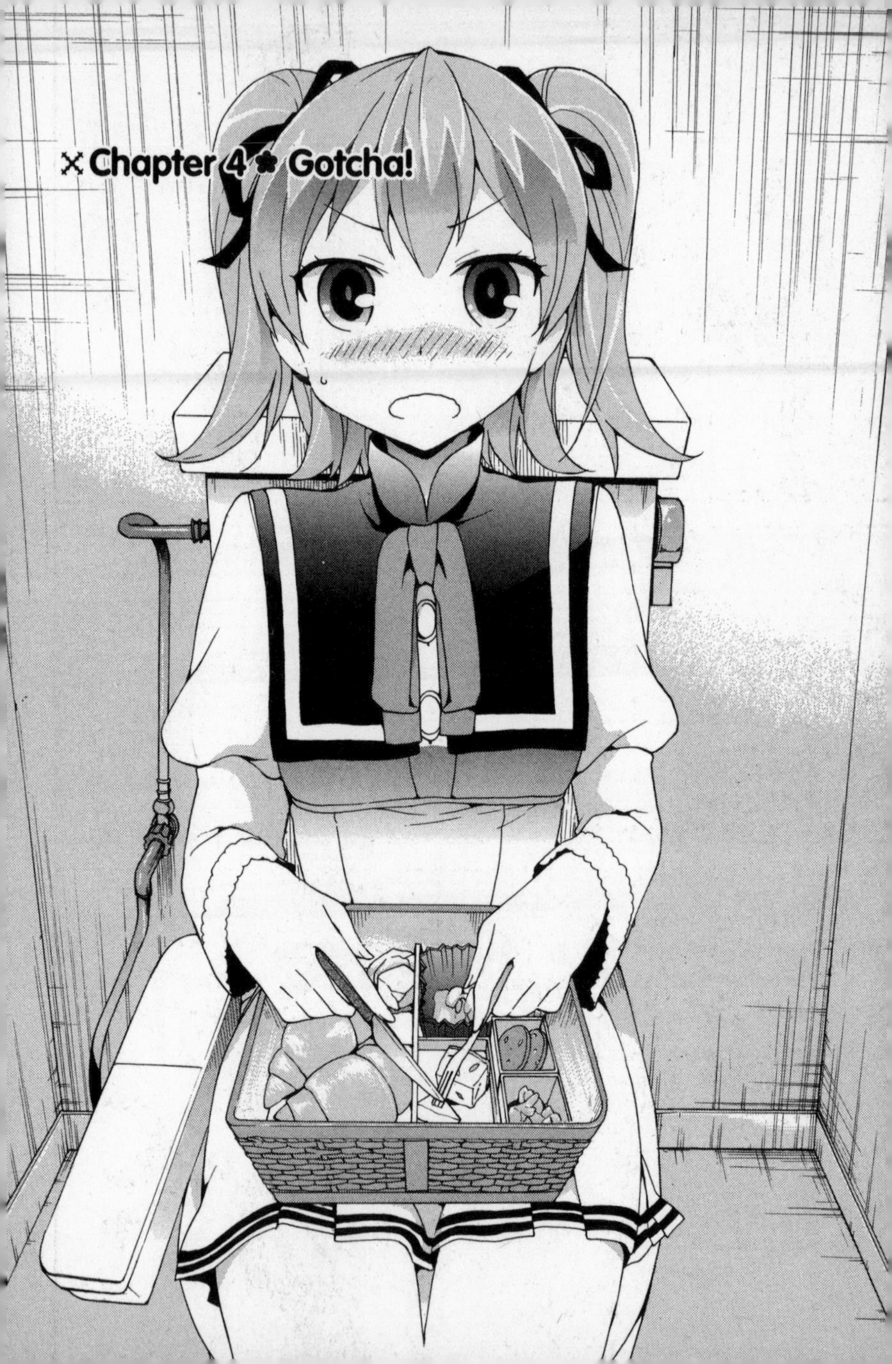

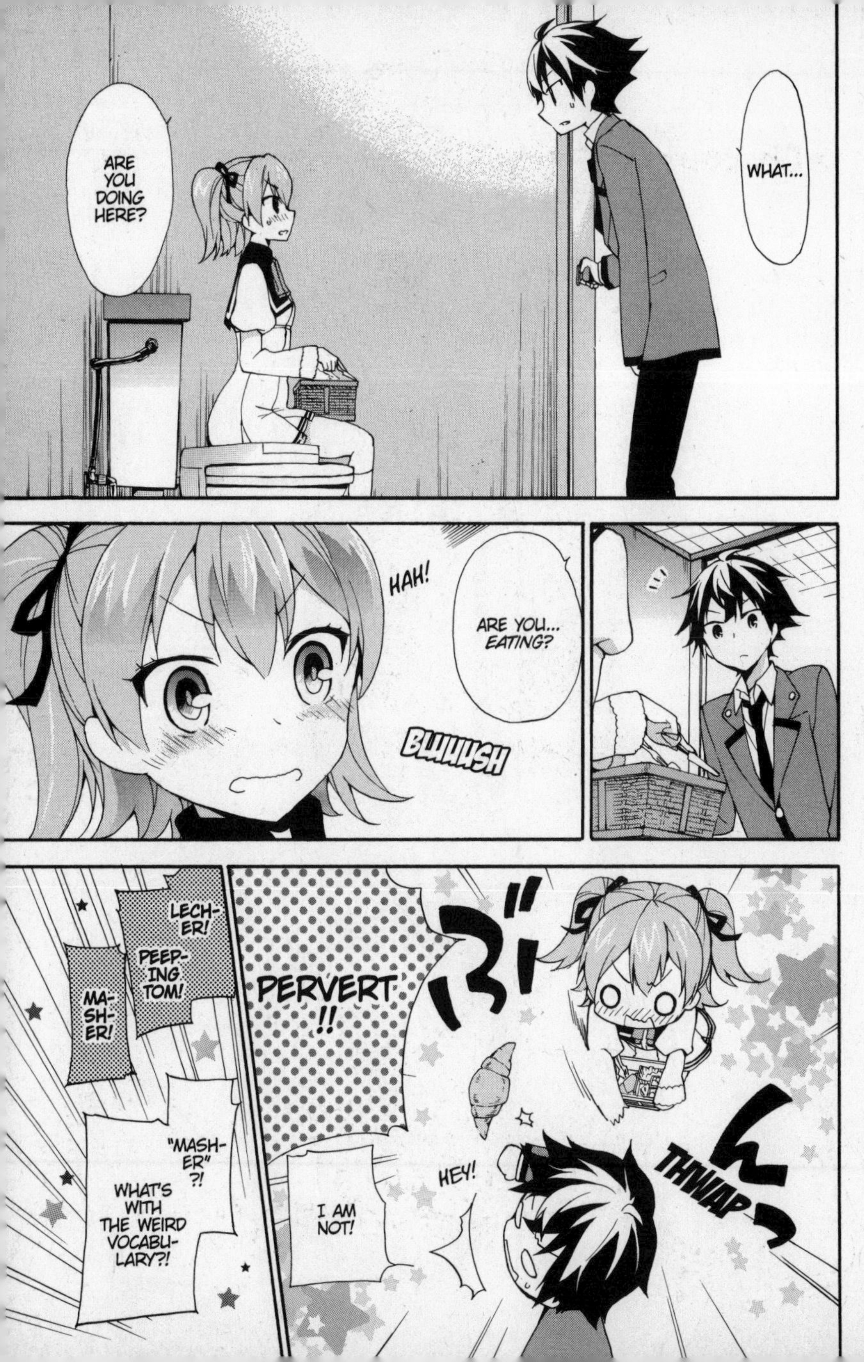
WHAT...
ARE YOU DOING HERE?
ARE YOU... EATING?
HAH!
BLUUUSH
THWAP
HEY!
I AM NOT!
PERVERT!!
LECHER!
PEEPING TOM!
MASHER!
"MASHER"?! WHAT'S WITH THE WEIRD VOCABULARY?!

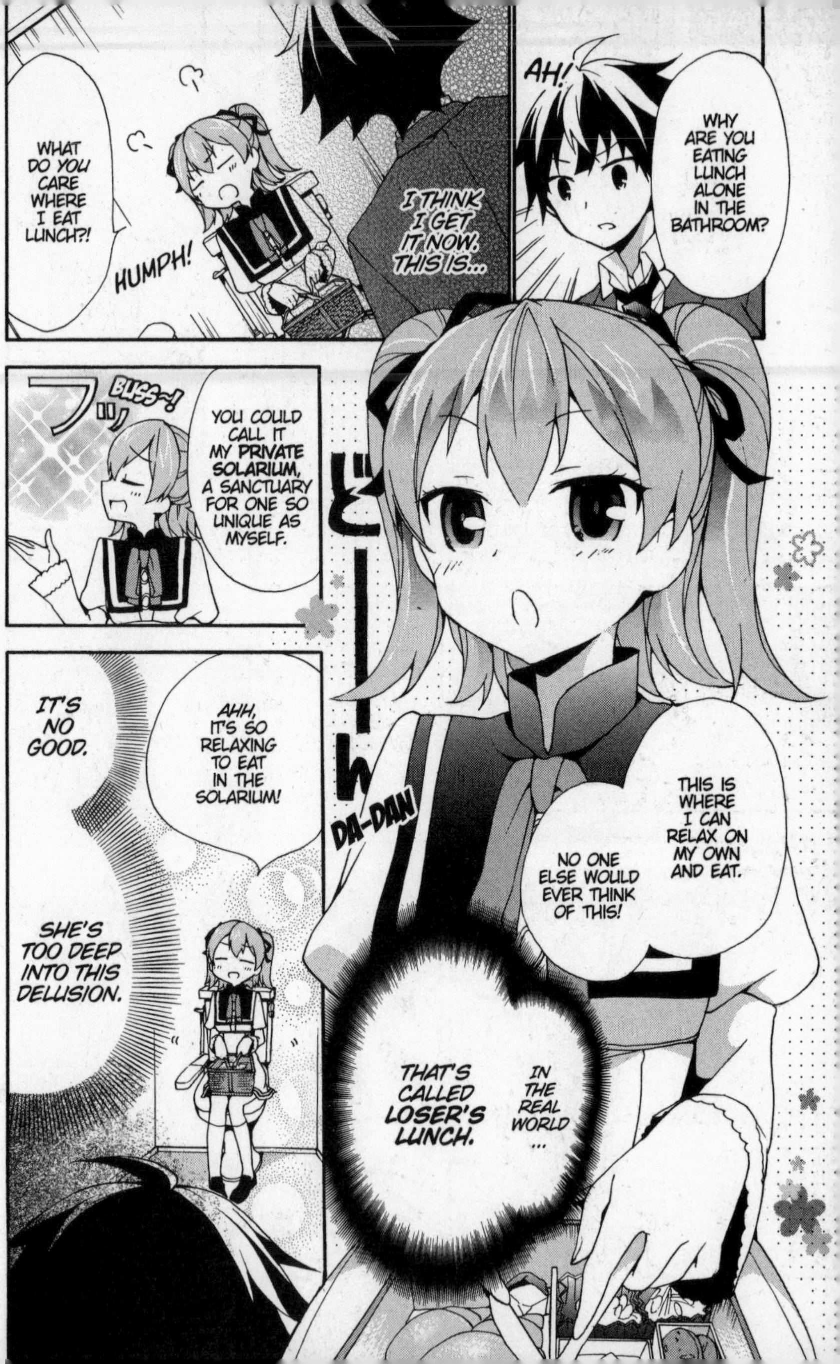
AH!
WHY ARE YOU EATING LUNCH ALONE IN THE BATHROOM?
WHAT DO YOU CARE WHERE I EAT LUNCH?!
HUMPH!
I THINK I GET IT NOW. THIS IS...
DA-DAN
THIS IS WHERE I CAN RELAX ON MY OWN AND EAT.
NO ONE ELSE WOULD EVER THINK OF THIS!
IN THE REAL WORLD...
THAT'S CALLED LOSER'S LUNCH.
BUSS~!
YOU COULD CALL IT MY PRIVATE SOLARIUM, A SANCTUARY FOR ONE SO UNIQUE AS MYSELF.
AHH, IT'S SO RELAXING TO EAT IN THE SOLARIUM!
IT'S NO GOOD.
SHE'S TOO DEEP INTO THIS DELLUSION.

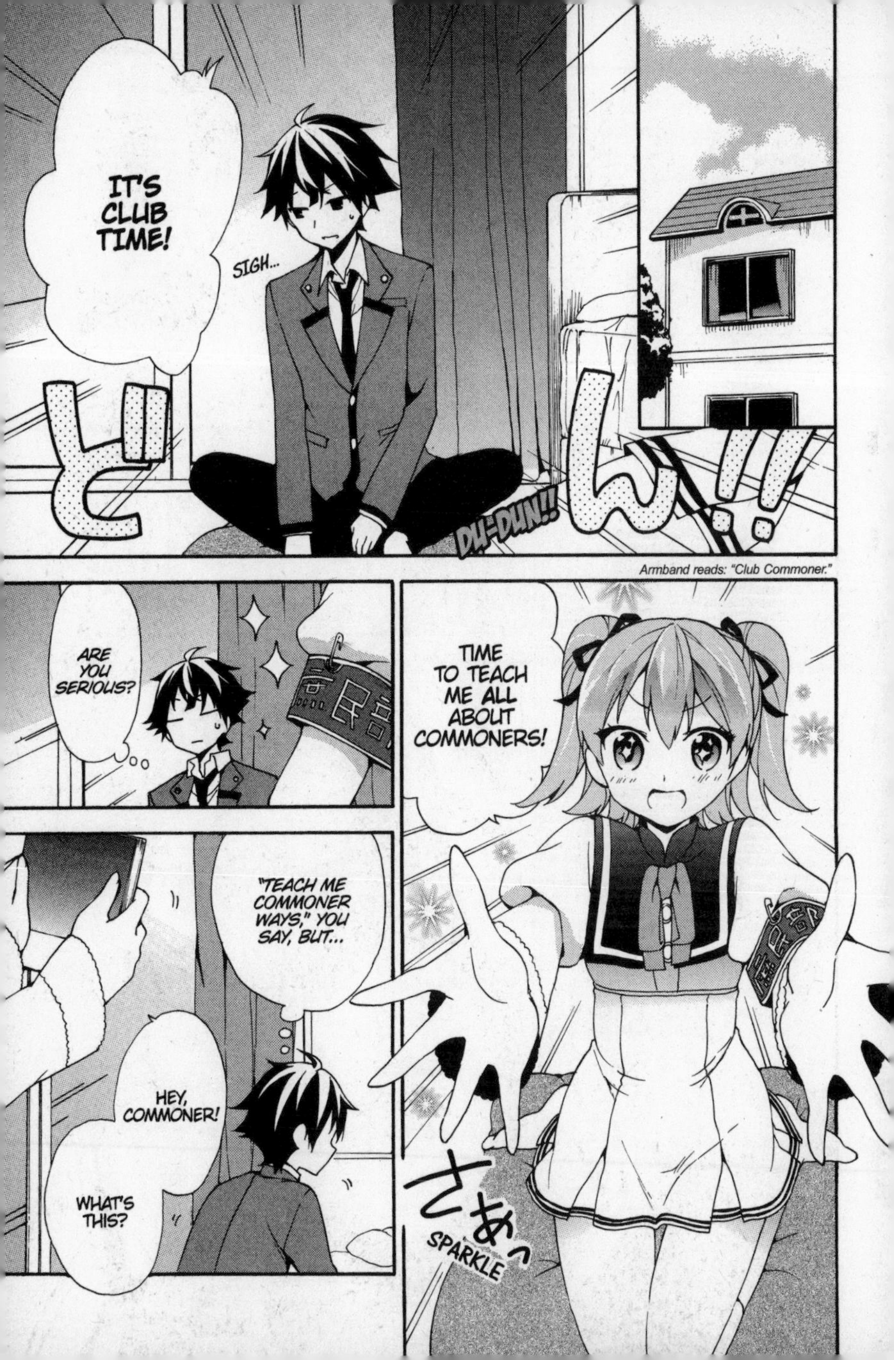

IT'S CLUB TIME!
SIGH...
どん!!
DU-DUN!!
Armband reads: "Club Commoner."
TIME TO TEACH ME ALL ABOUT COMMONERS!
さあっ
SPARKLE
ARE YOU SERIOUS?
"TEACH ME COMMONER WAYS," YOU SAY, BUT...
HEY, COMMONER!
WHAT'S THIS?

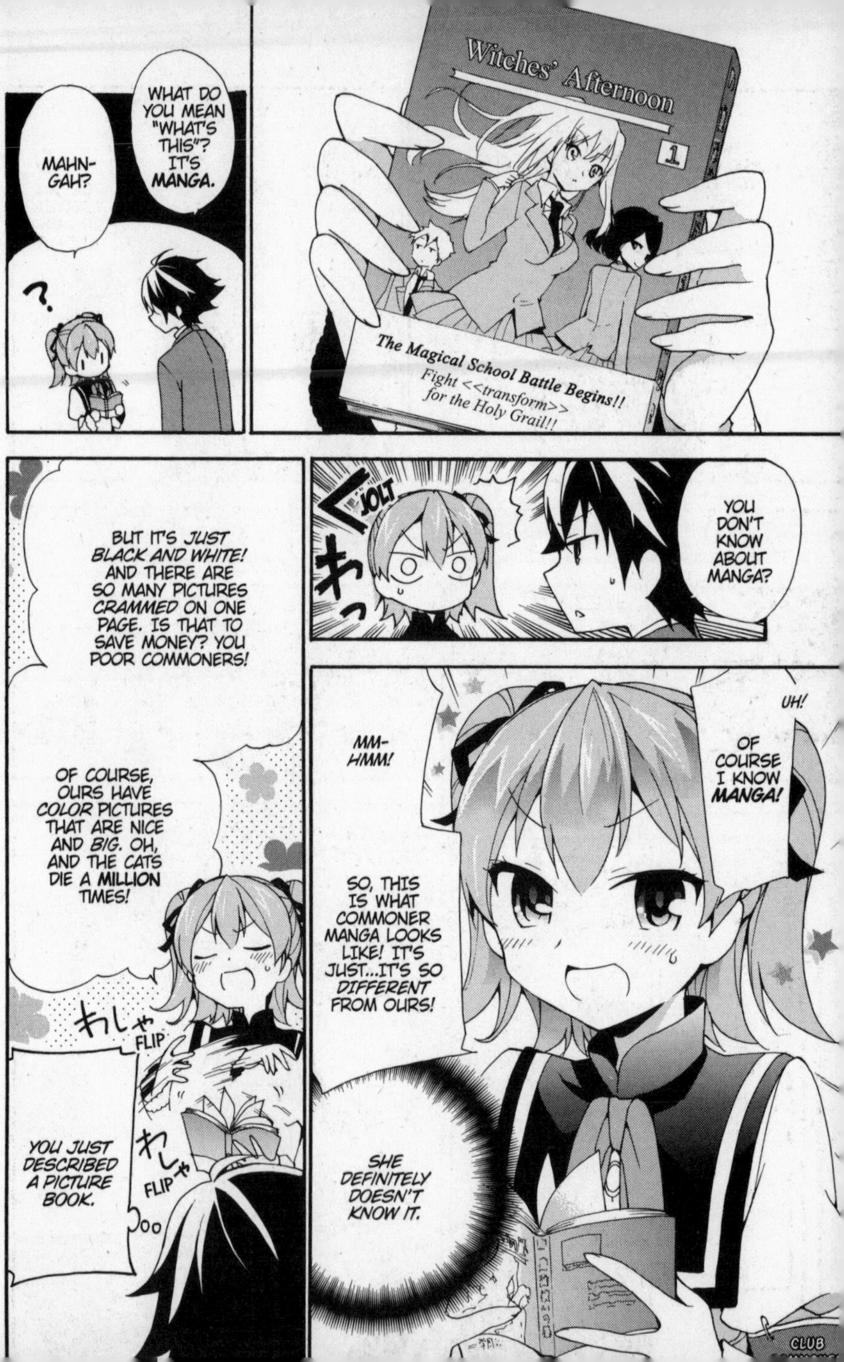

Witches' Afternoon
1
The Magical School Battle Begins!!
Fight <<transform>> for the Holy Grail!!
WHAT DO YOU MEAN "WHAT'S THIS"? IT'S MANGA.
MAHN-GAH?
?
JOLT
わっ
YOU DON'T KNOW ABOUT MANGA?
UH!
OF COURSE I KNOW MANGA!
MM-HMM!
SO, THIS IS WHAT COMMONER MANGA LOOKS LIKE! IT'S JUST...IT'S SO DIFFERENT FROM OURS!
SHE DEFINITELY DOESN'T KNOW IT.
BUT IT'S JUST BLACK AND WHITE! AND THERE ARE SO MANY PICTURES CRAMMED ON ONE PAGE. IS THAT TO SAVE MONEY? YOU POOR COMMONERS!
OF COURSE, OURS HAVE COLOR PICTURES THAT ARE NICE AND BIG. OH, AND THE CATS DIE A MILLION TIMES!
わしゃ FLIP
わしゃ FLIP
YOU JUST DESCRIBED A PICTURE BOOK.
CLUB

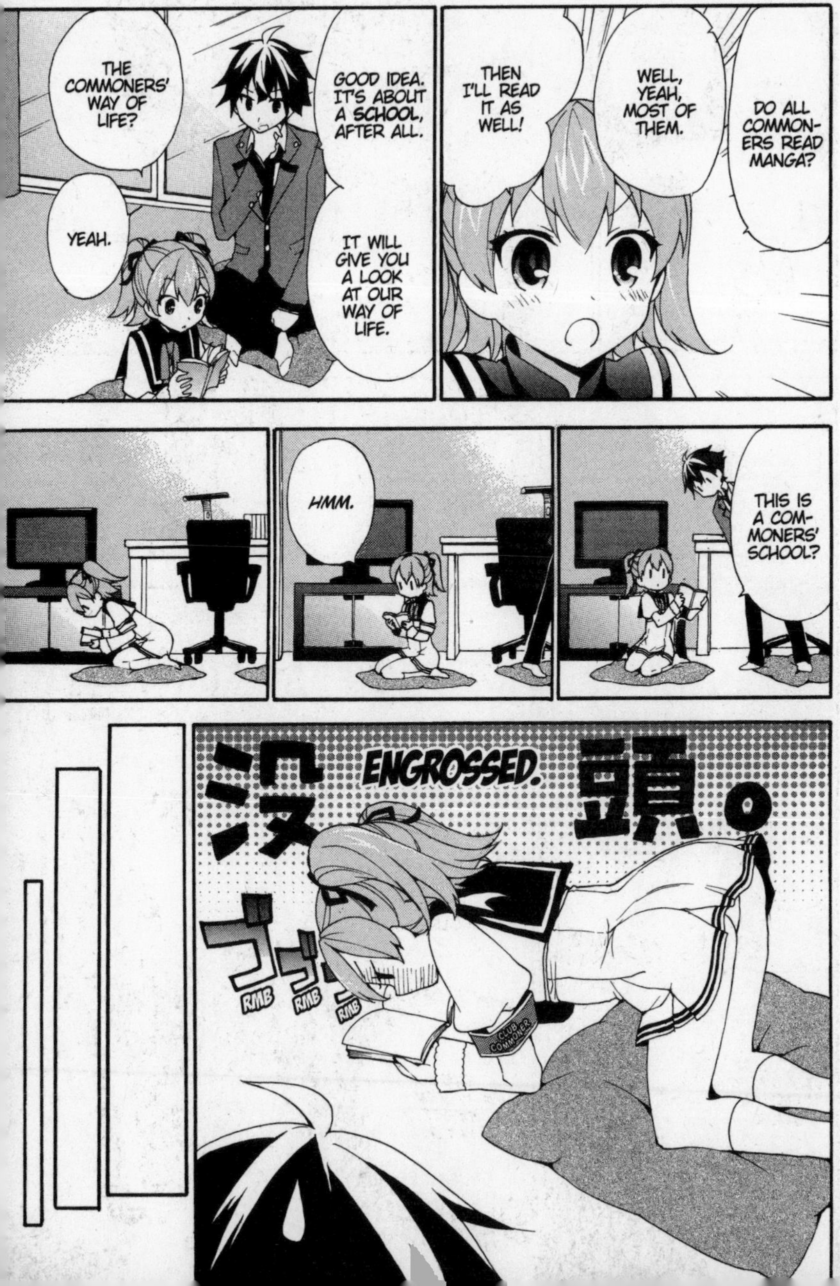
DO ALL COMMONERS READ MANGA?
WELL, YEAH, MOST OF THEM.
THEN I'LL READ IT AS WELL!
GOOD IDEA. IT'S ABOUT A SCHOOL, AFTER ALL.
IT WILL GIVE YOU A LOOK AT OUR WAY OF LIFE.
THE COMMONERS' WAY OF LIFE?
YEAH.
THIS IS A COMMONERS' SCHOOL?
HMM.
ENGROSSED.
RMB RMB RMB
CLUB COMMONER

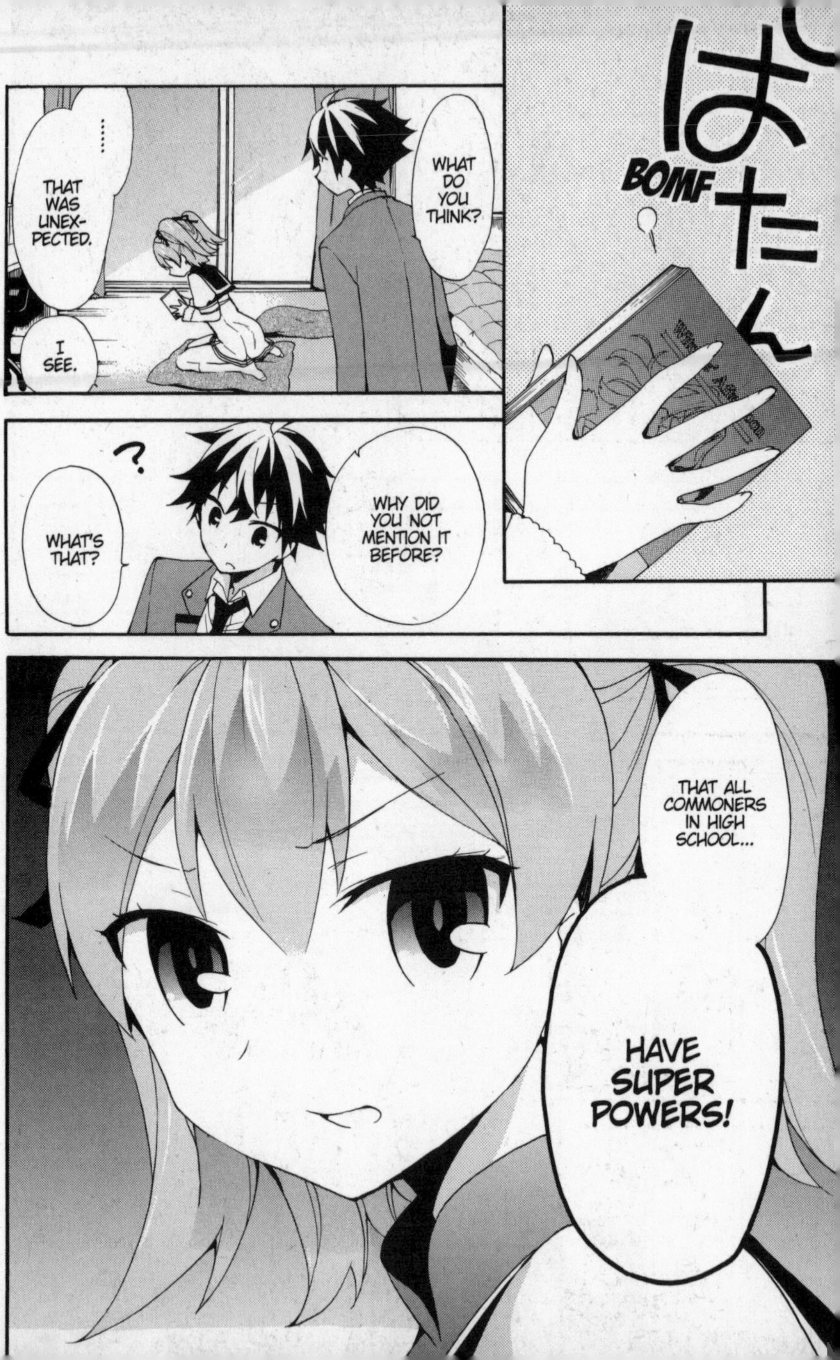
ばたん
BOMF
WHAT DO YOU THINK?
...... THAT WAS UNEXPECTED.
I SEE.
WHY DID YOU NOT MENTION IT BEFORE?
?
WHAT'S THAT?
THAT ALL COMMONERS IN HIGH SCHOOL...
HAVE SUPER POWERS!

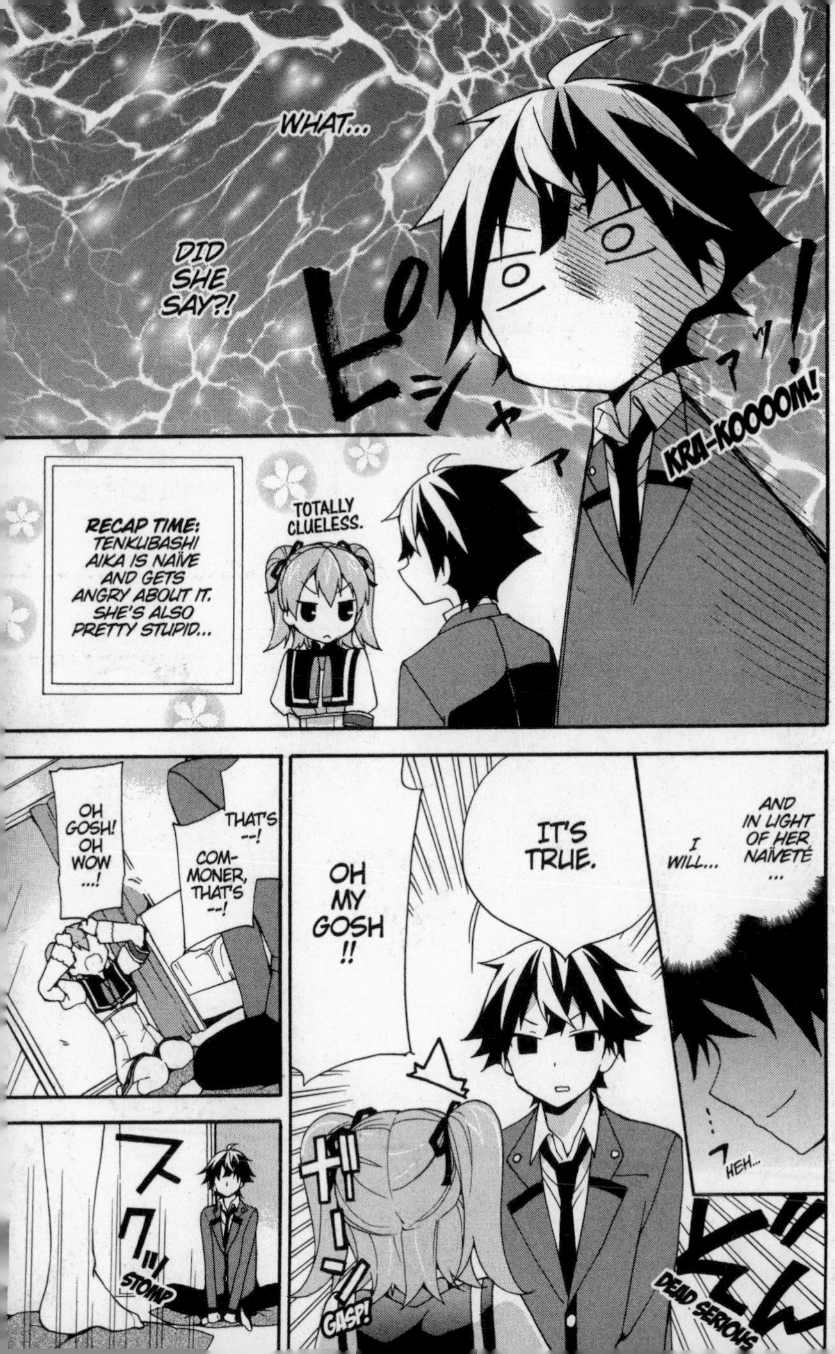
WHAT...
DID SHE SAY?!
KRA-KOOOOM!
TOTALLY CLUELESS.
RECAP TIME: TENKUBASHI AIKA IS NAÏVE AND GETS ANGRY ABOUT IT. SHE'S ALSO PRETTY STUPID...
AND IN LIGHT OF HER NAÏVETÉ ...
I WILL...
...HEH...
DEAD SERIOUS
IT'S TRUE.
OH MY GOSH !!
GASP!
THAT'S --!
COMMONER, THAT'S --!
OH GOSH! OH WOW ...!
STOMP

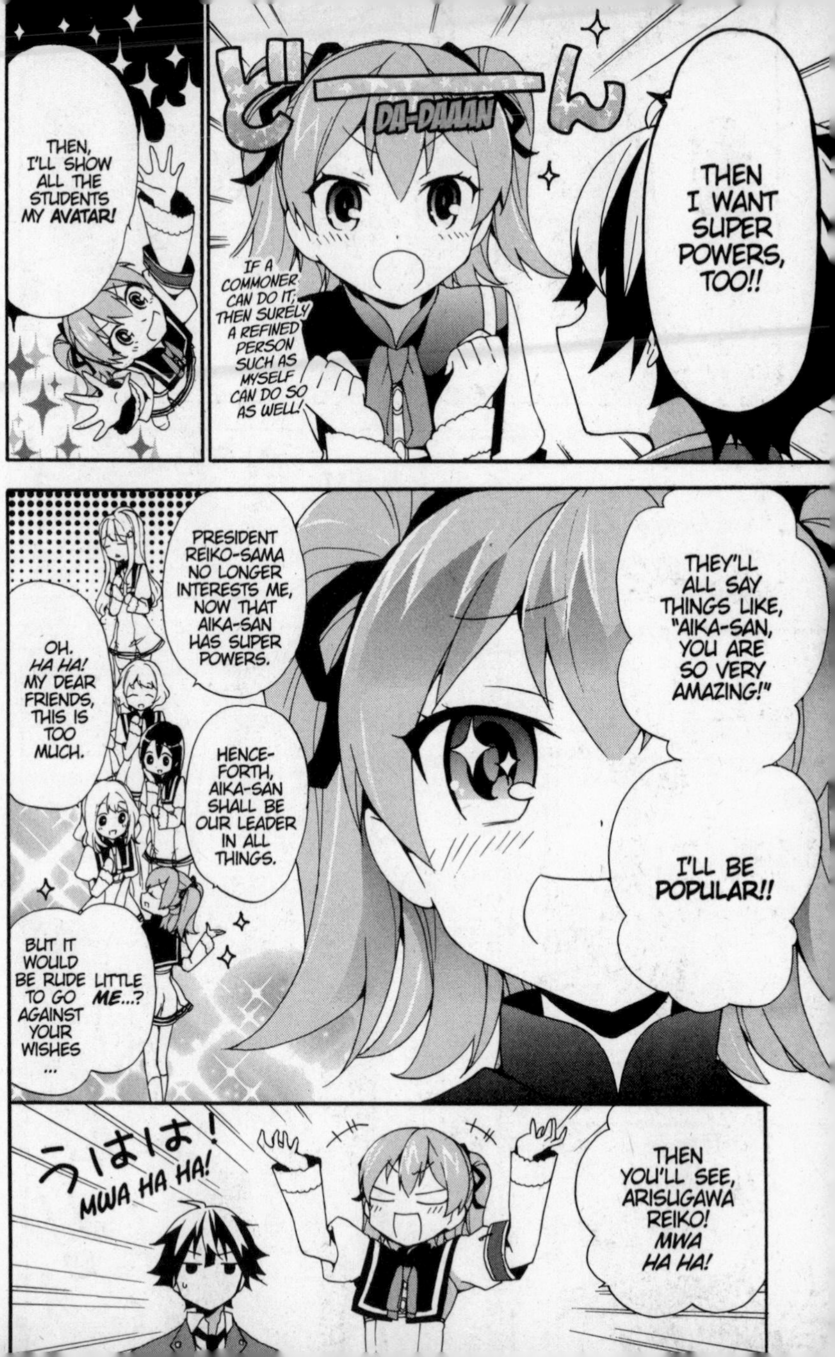
THEN I WANT SUPER POWERS, TOO!!
どーーん
DA-DAAAN
IF A COMMONER CAN DO IT, THEN SURELY A REFINED PERSON SUCH AS MYSELF CAN DO SO AS WELL!
THEN, I'LL SHOW ALL THE STUDENTS MY AVATAR!
THEY'LL ALL SAY THINGS LIKE, "AIKA-SAN, YOU ARE SO VERY AMAZING!"
I'LL BE POPULAR!!
PRESIDENT REIKO-SAMA NO LONGER INTERESTS ME, NOW THAT AIKA-SAN HAS SUPER POWERS.
HENCE-FORTH, AIKA-SAN SHALL BE OUR LEADER IN ALL THINGS.
OH. HA HA! MY DEAR FRIENDS, THIS IS TOO MUCH.
LITTLE ME...?
BUT IT WOULD BE RUDE TO GO AGAINST YOUR WISHES ...
THEN YOU'LL SEE, ARISUGAWA REIKO! MWA HA HA!
うはは!
MWA HA HA!

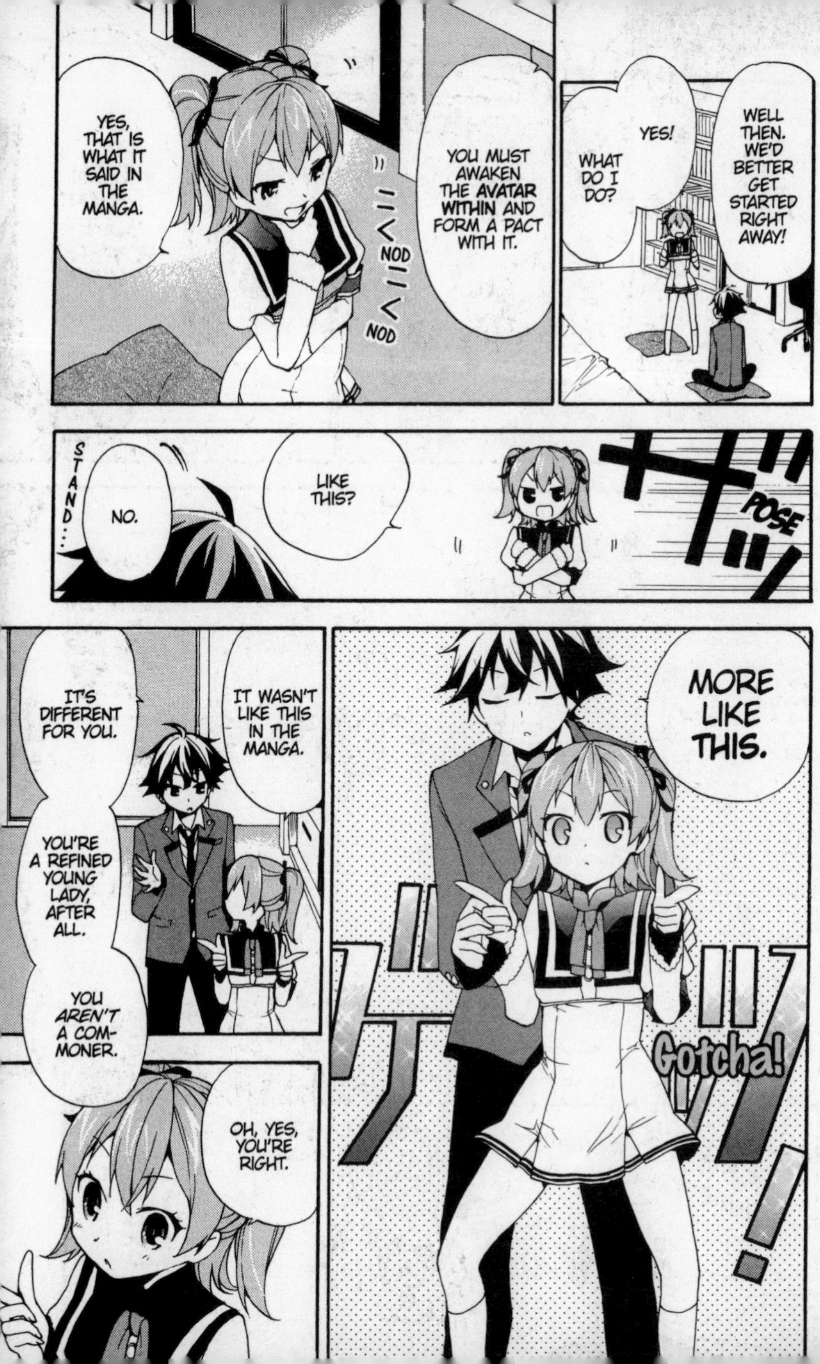
WELL THEN. WE'D BETTER GET STARTED RIGHT AWAY!
YES!
WHAT DO I DO?
YOU MUST AWAKEN THE AVATAR WITHIN AND FORM A PACT WITH IT.
NOD
NOD
YES, THAT IS WHAT IT SAID IN THE MANGA.
POSE
LIKE THIS?
NO.
STAND...
MORE LIKE THIS.
Gotcha!
IT WASN'T LIKE THIS IN THE MANGA.
IT'S DIFFERENT FOR YOU.
YOU'RE A REFINED YOUNG LADY, AFTER ALL.
YOU AREN'T A COM-MONER.
OH, YES, YOU'RE RIGHT.

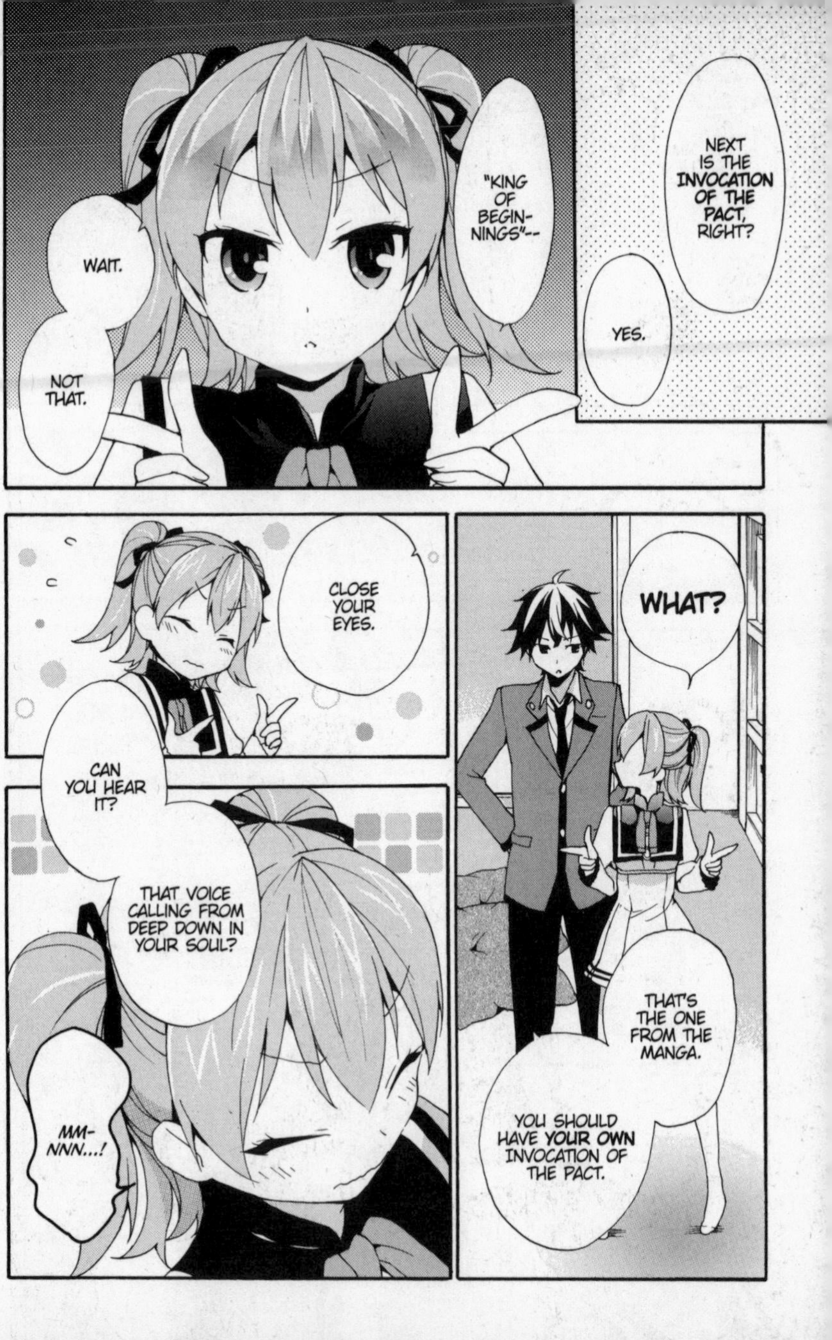
NEXT IS THE INVOCATION OF THE PACT, RIGHT?
YES.
"KING OF BEGINNINGS"--
WAIT.
NOT THAT.
WHAT?
THAT'S THE ONE FROM THE MANGA.
YOU SHOULD HAVE YOUR OWN INVOCATION OF THE PACT.
CLOSE YOUR EYES.
CAN YOU HEAR IT?
THAT VOICE CALLING FROM DEEP DOWN IN YOUR SOUL?
MM-NNN...!

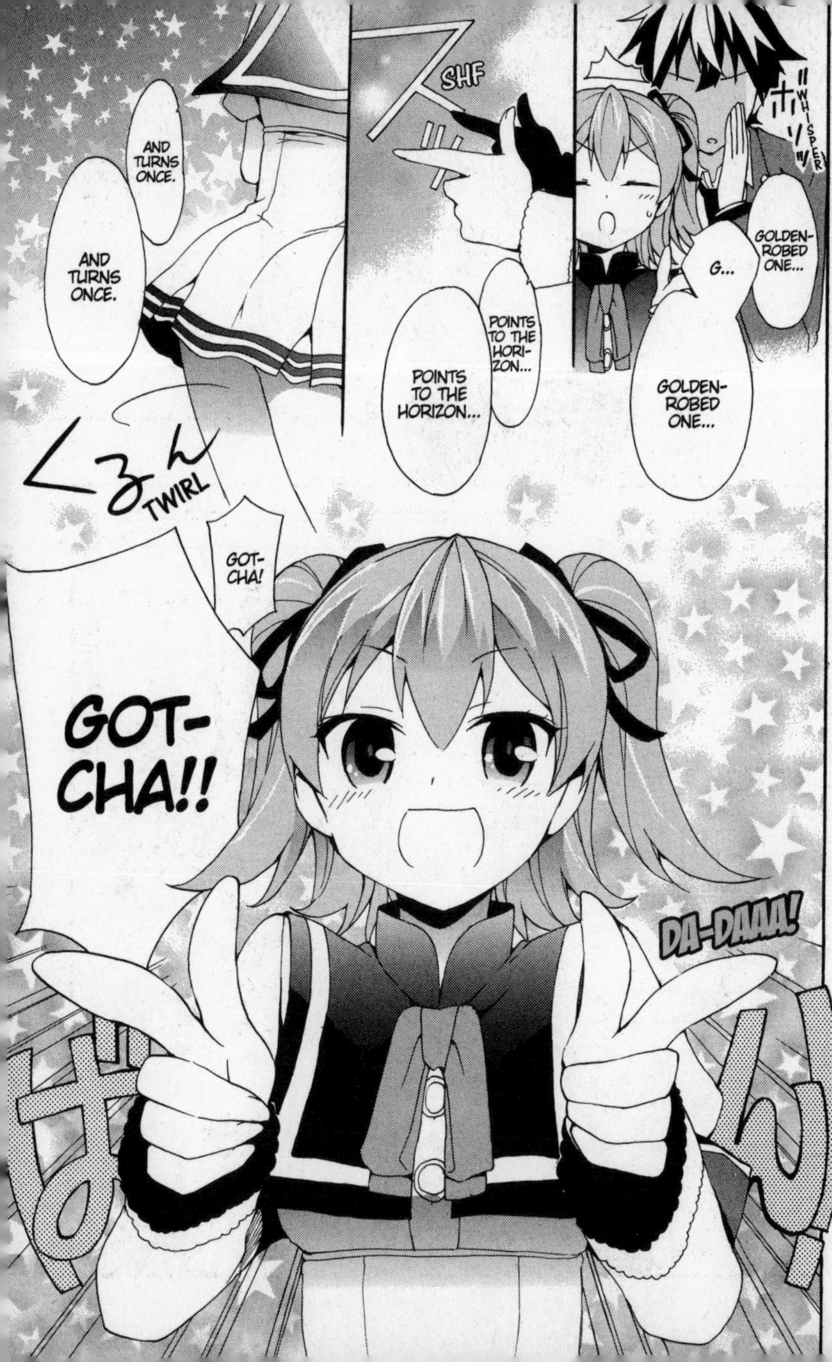
WHISPER
GOLDEN-ROBED ONE...
G...
GOLDEN-ROBED ONE...
SHF
POINTS TO THE HORI-ZON...
POINTS TO THE HORIZON...
AND TURNS ONCE.
AND TURNS ONCE.
TWIRL
GOT-CHA!
GOT-CHA!!
DA-DAAA!

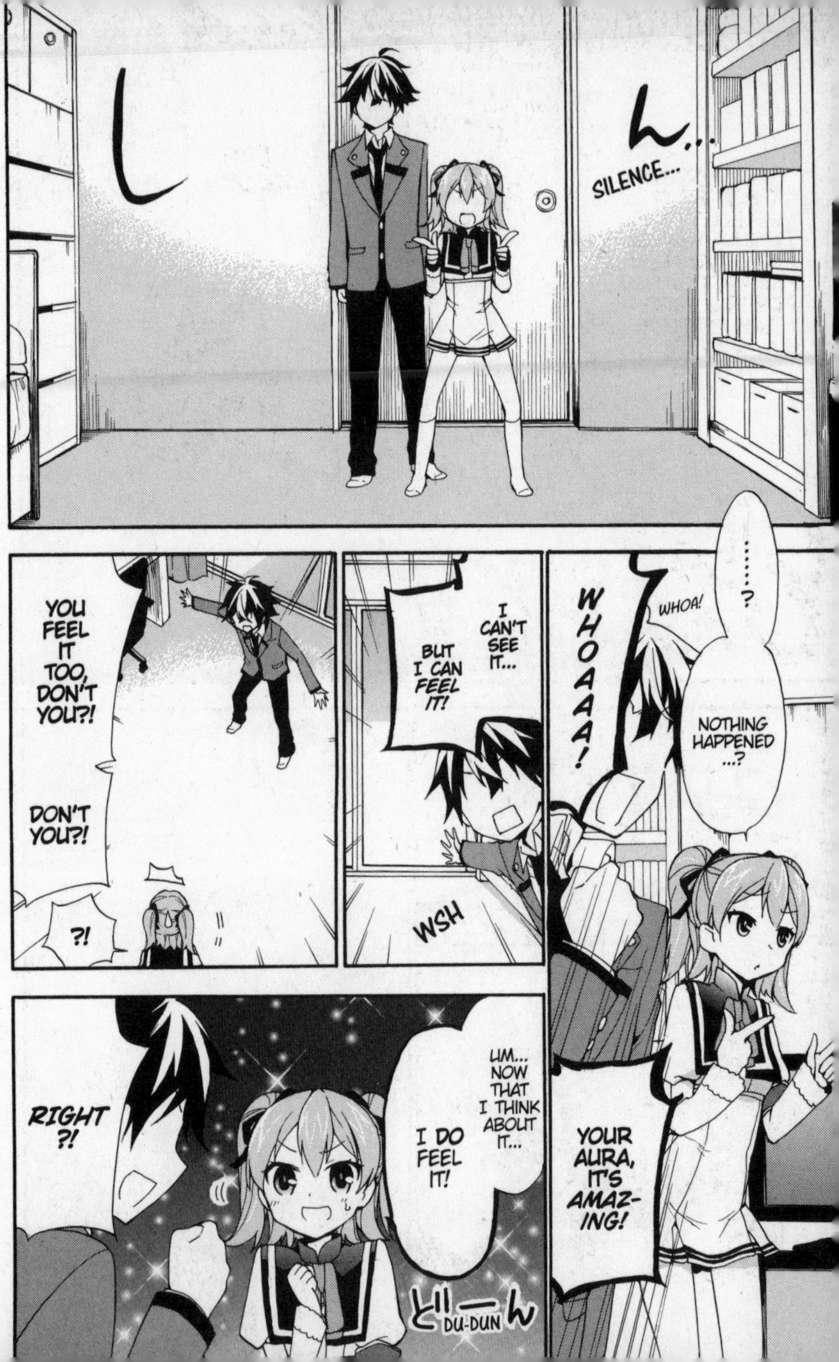

しーん...
SILENCE...
......?
NOTHING HAPPENED ...?
WHOA!
WHOAAAA!
YOUR AURA, IT'S AMAZ-ING!
I CAN'T SEE IT...
BUT I CAN FEEL IT!
WSH
YOU FEEL IT TOO, DON'T YOU?!
DON'T YOU?!
?!
UM... NOW THAT I THINK ABOUT IT...
I DO FEEL IT!
RIGHT ?!
どーーん
DU-DUN

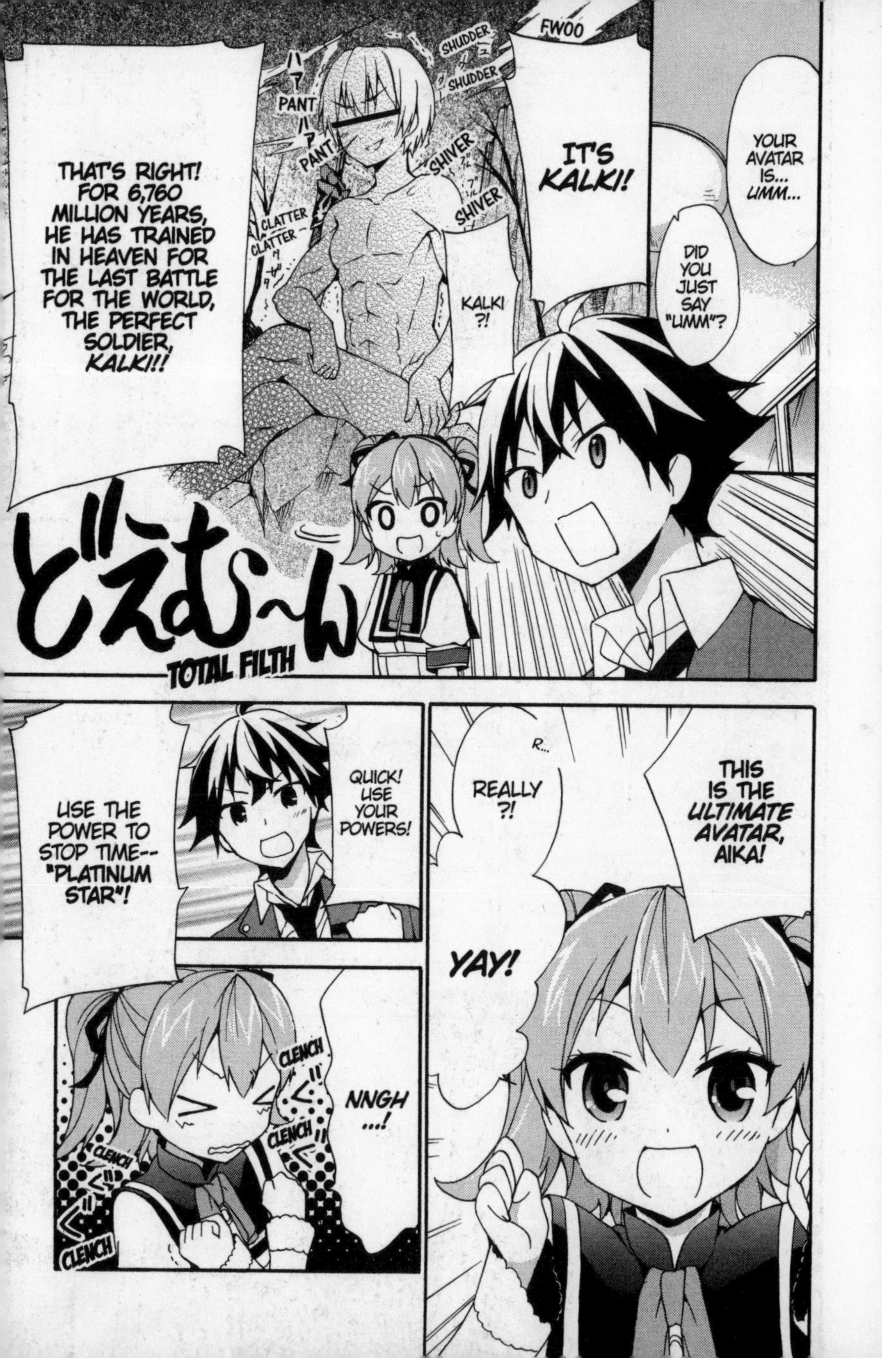
YOUR AVATAR IS... UMM...
DID YOU JUST SAY "UMM"?
FWOO
IT'S KALKI!
KALKI ?!
SHUDDER
SHUDDER
SHIVER
SHIVER
PANT
PANT
CLATTER
CLATTER
THAT'S RIGHT! FOR 6,760 MILLION YEARS, HE HAS TRAINED IN HEAVEN FOR THE LAST BATTLE FOR THE WORLD, THE PERFECT SOLDIER, KALKI!!
どえむ～ん
TOTAL FILTH
THIS IS THE ULTIMATE AVATAR, AIKA!
R...
REALLY ?!
YAY!
QUICK! USE YOUR POWERS!
USE THE POWER TO STOP TIME-- "PLATINUM STAR"!
NNGH ...!
CLENCH
CLENCH
CLENCH
CLENCH

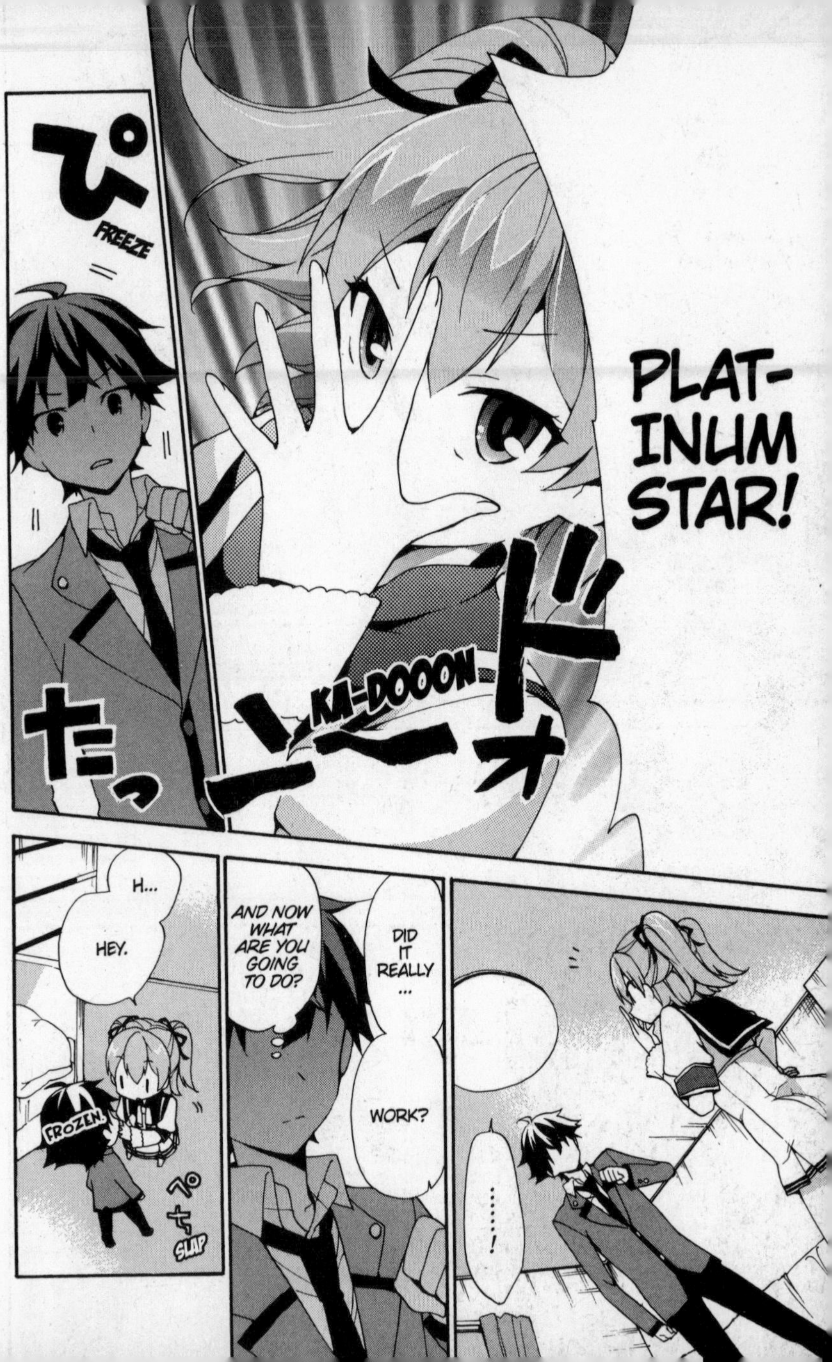
PLAT-INUM STAR!
KA-DOOON
ぴ
FREEZE
たっ
......!
DID IT REALLY ... WORK?
AND NOW WHAT ARE YOU GOING TO DO?
H... HEY.
FROZEN.
ぺち
SLAP

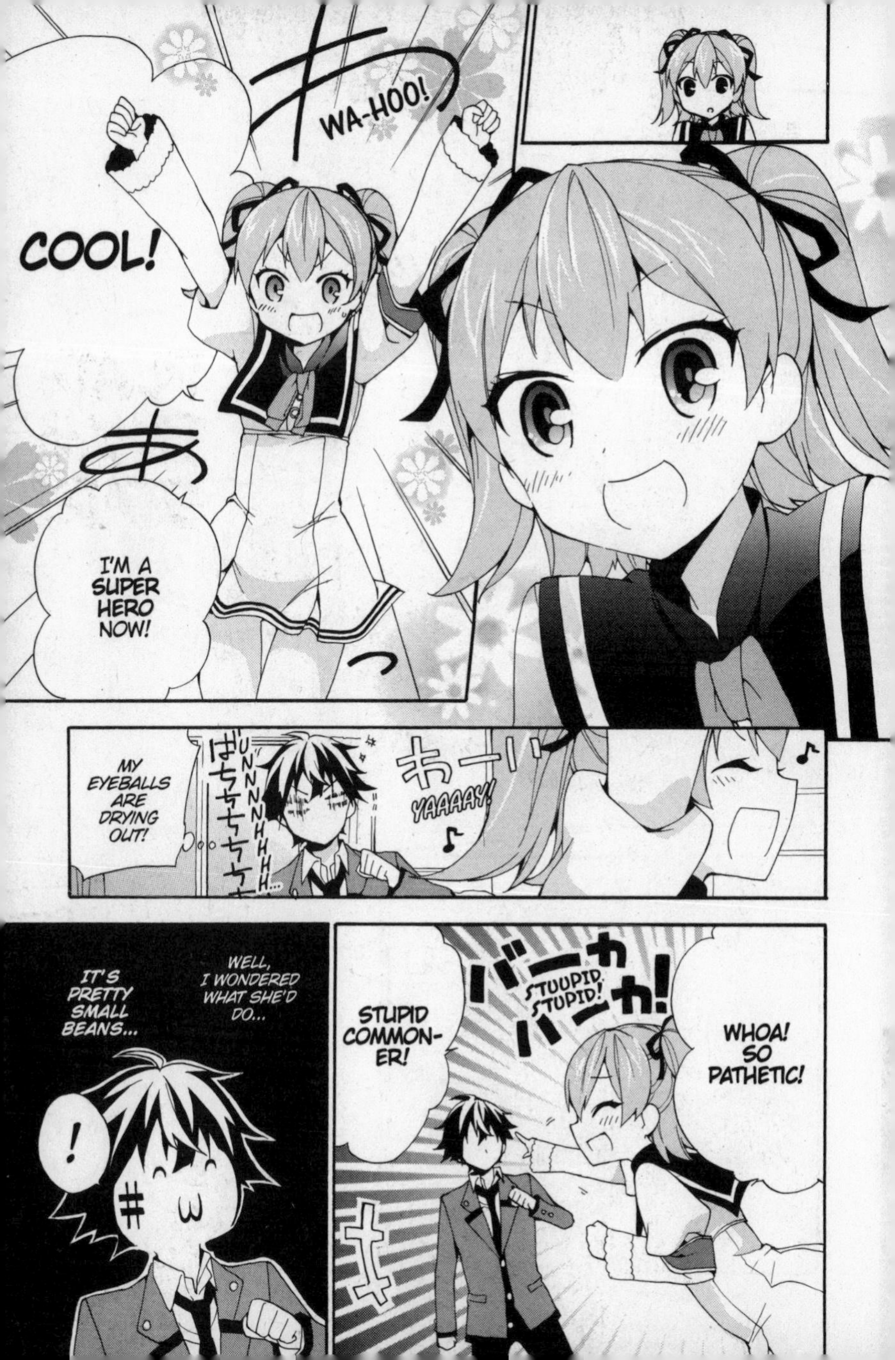
WA-HOO!
COOL!
I'M A SUPER HERO NOW!
YAAAAY!
UNNNNHHHH...
MY EYEBALLS ARE DRYING OUT!
WHOA! SO PATHETIC!
STUUPID, STUPID!
STUPID COMMONER!
WELL, I WONDERED WHAT SHE'D DO...
IT'S PRETTY SMALL BEANS...
!

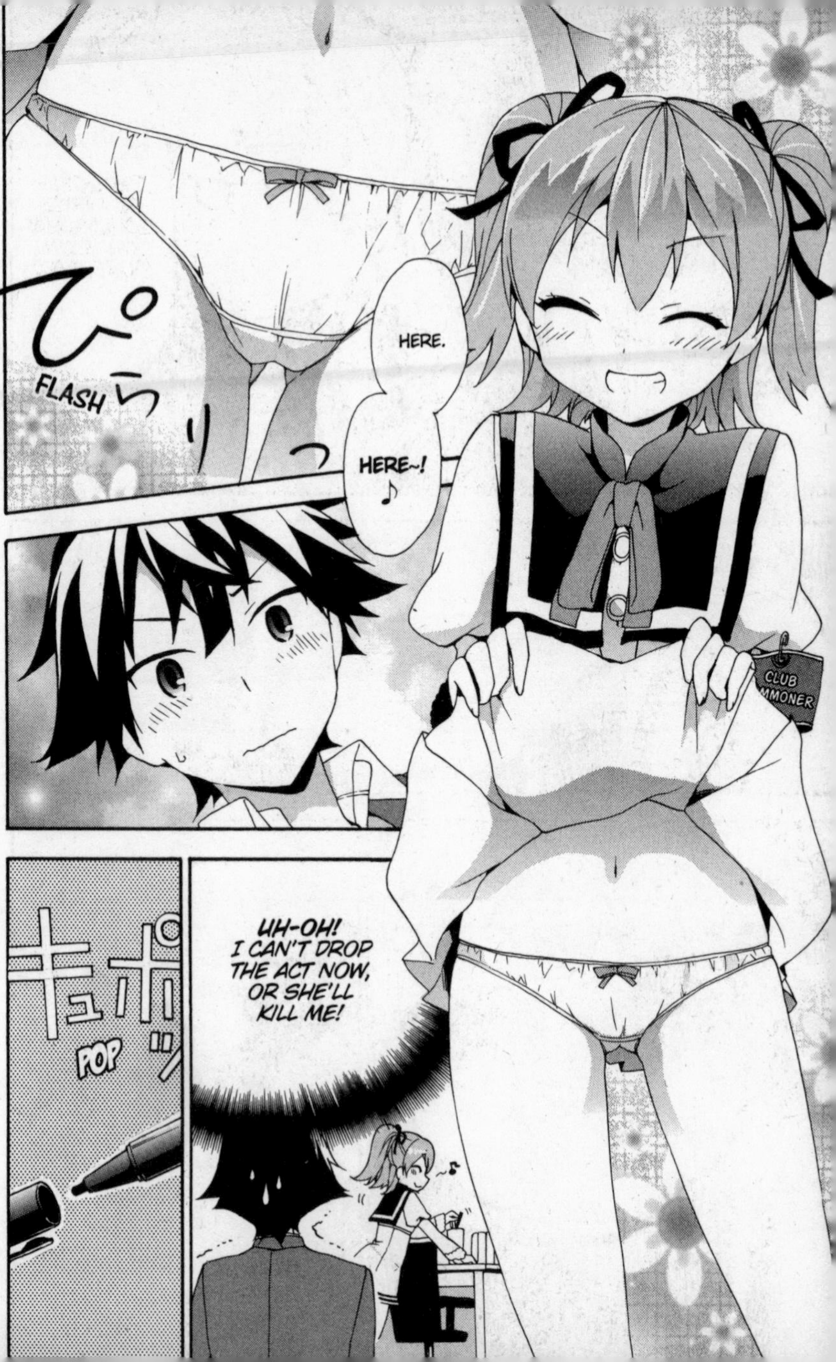

HERE.
HERE~! ♪
CLUB
ぴらりっ
FLASH
UH-OH! I CAN'T DROP THE ACT NOW, OR SHE'LL KILL ME!
キュポッ
POP

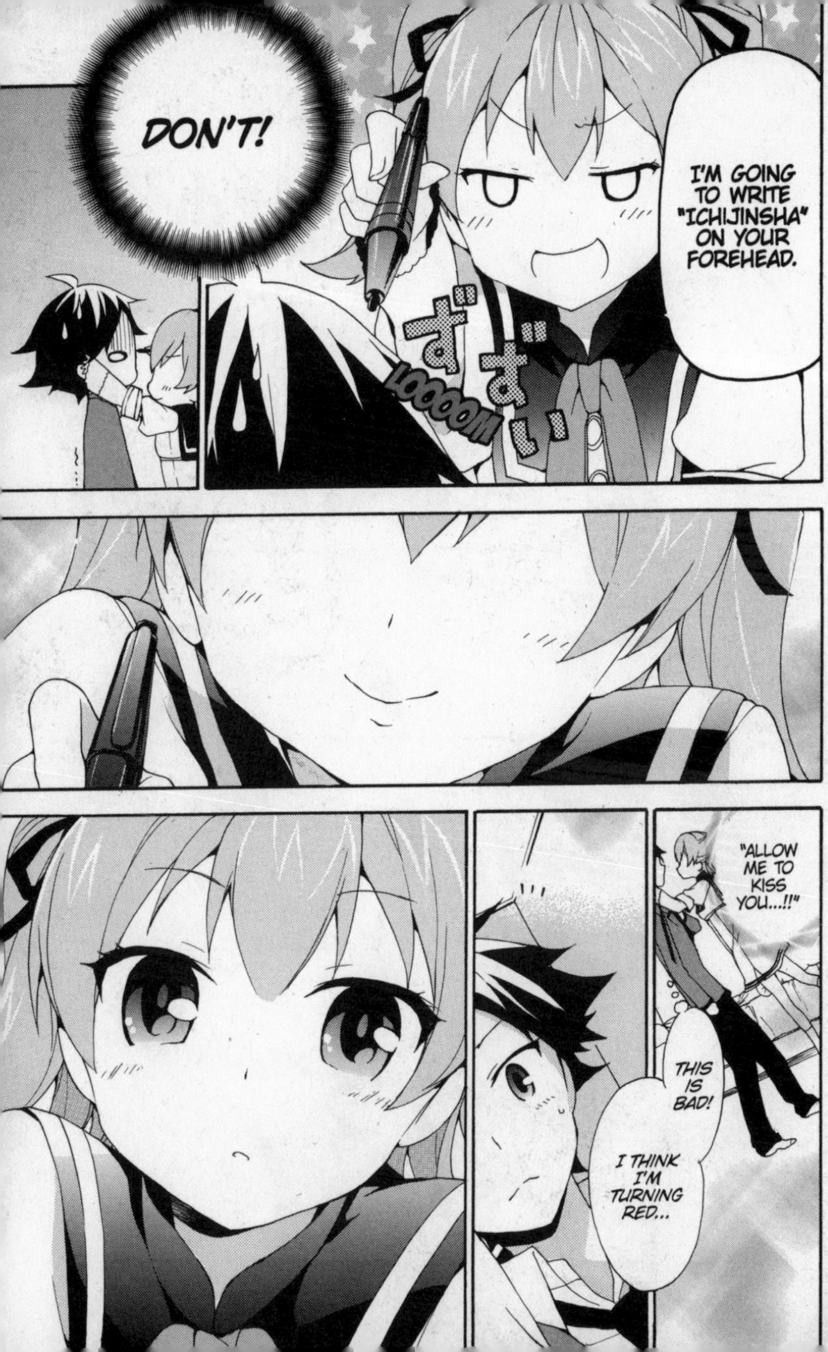
I'M GOING TO WRITE "ICHIJINSHA" ON YOUR FOREHEAD.
ずずい
LOOOOOM
DON'T!
"ALLOW ME TO KISS YOU...!!"
THIS IS BAD!
I THINK I'M TURNING RED...

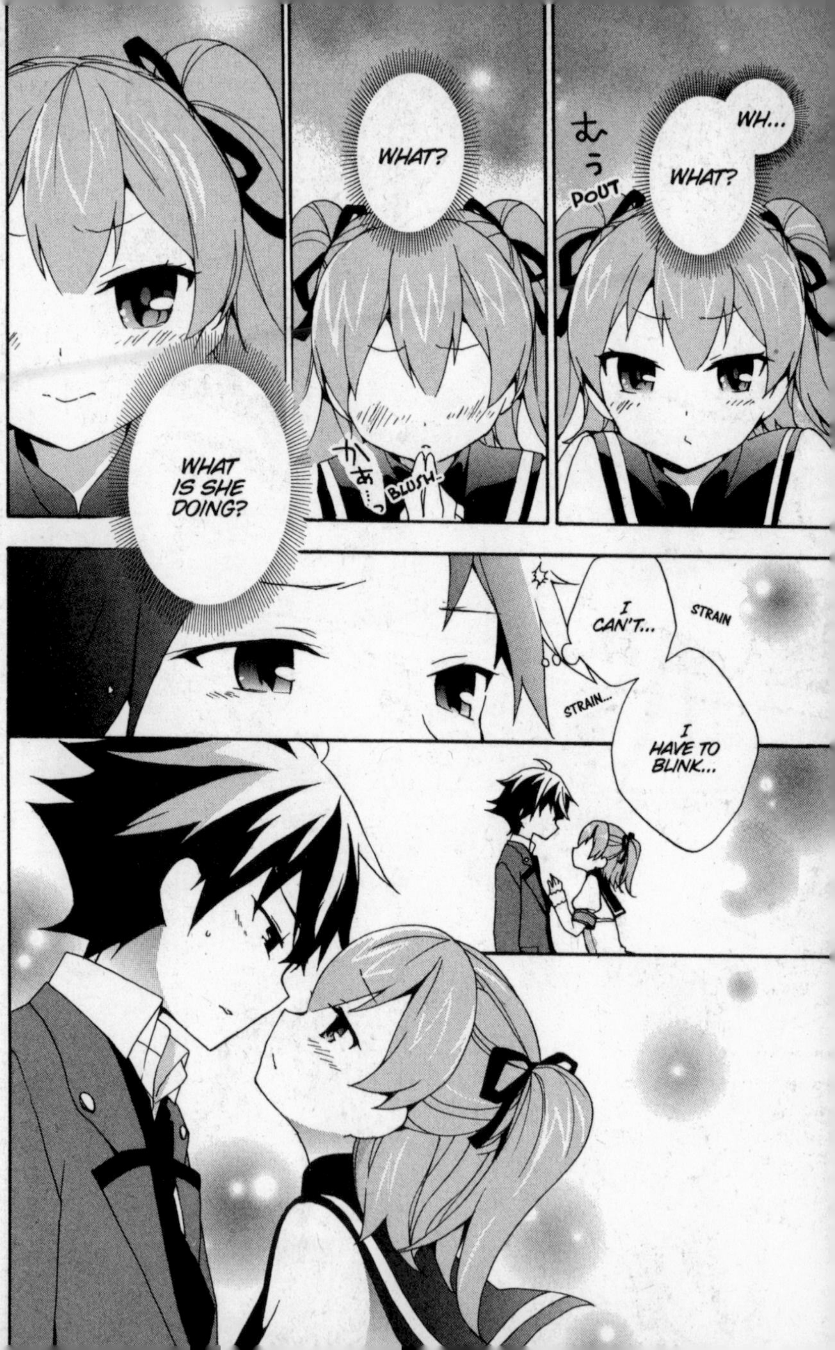

WH... WHAT?
むう
POUT
WHAT?
かあ…っ
BLUSH
WHAT IS SHE DOING?
STRAIN
I CAN'T...
STRAIN...
I HAVE TO BLINK...

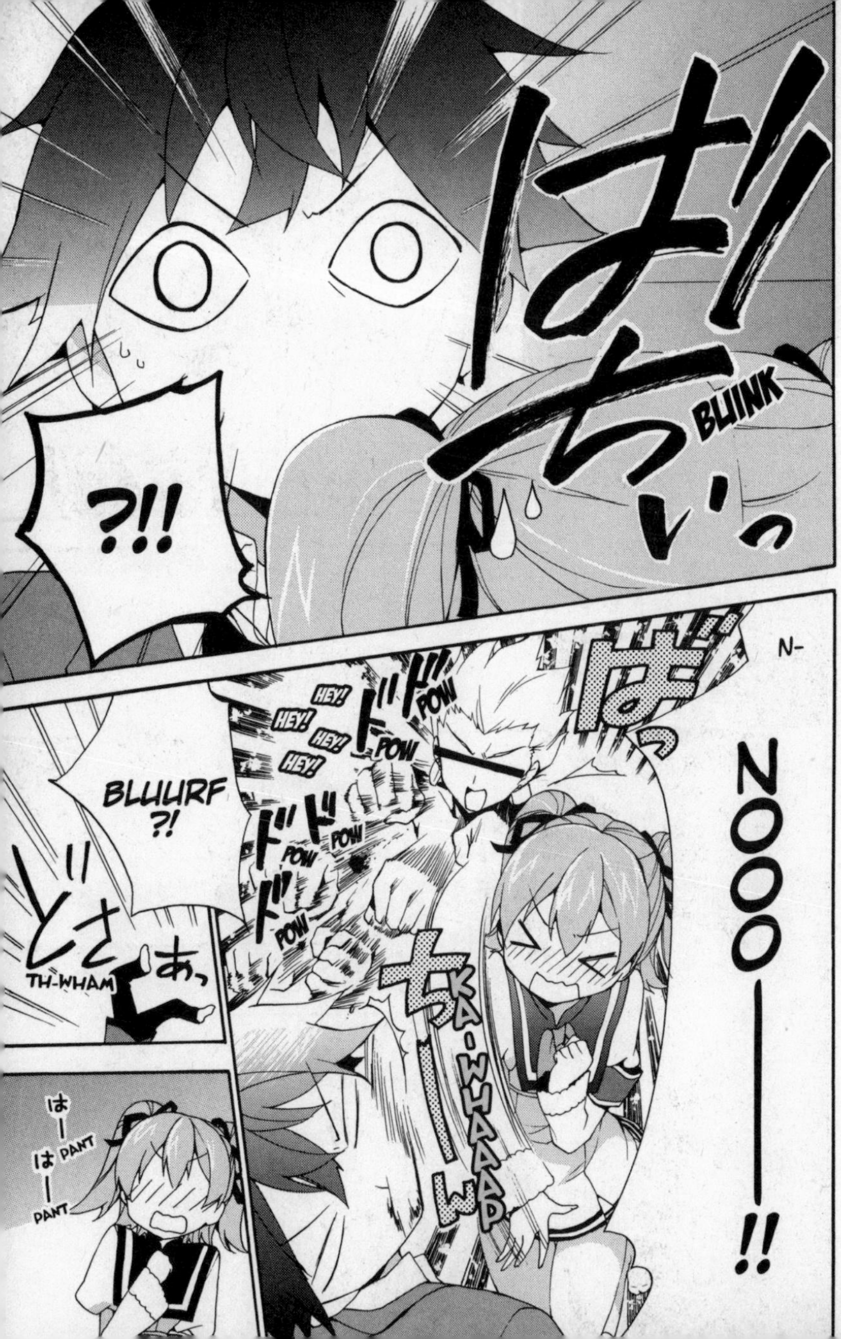
はわいっ
BLINK
?!!
N-
NOOO——!!
ばっ
HEY!
HEY!
HEY!
HEY!
ドドドド
POW
POW
POW
POW
POW
BLUURF ?!
とさ
TH-WHAM
あっ
KA-WHAAAP
はー
PANT
はー
PANT

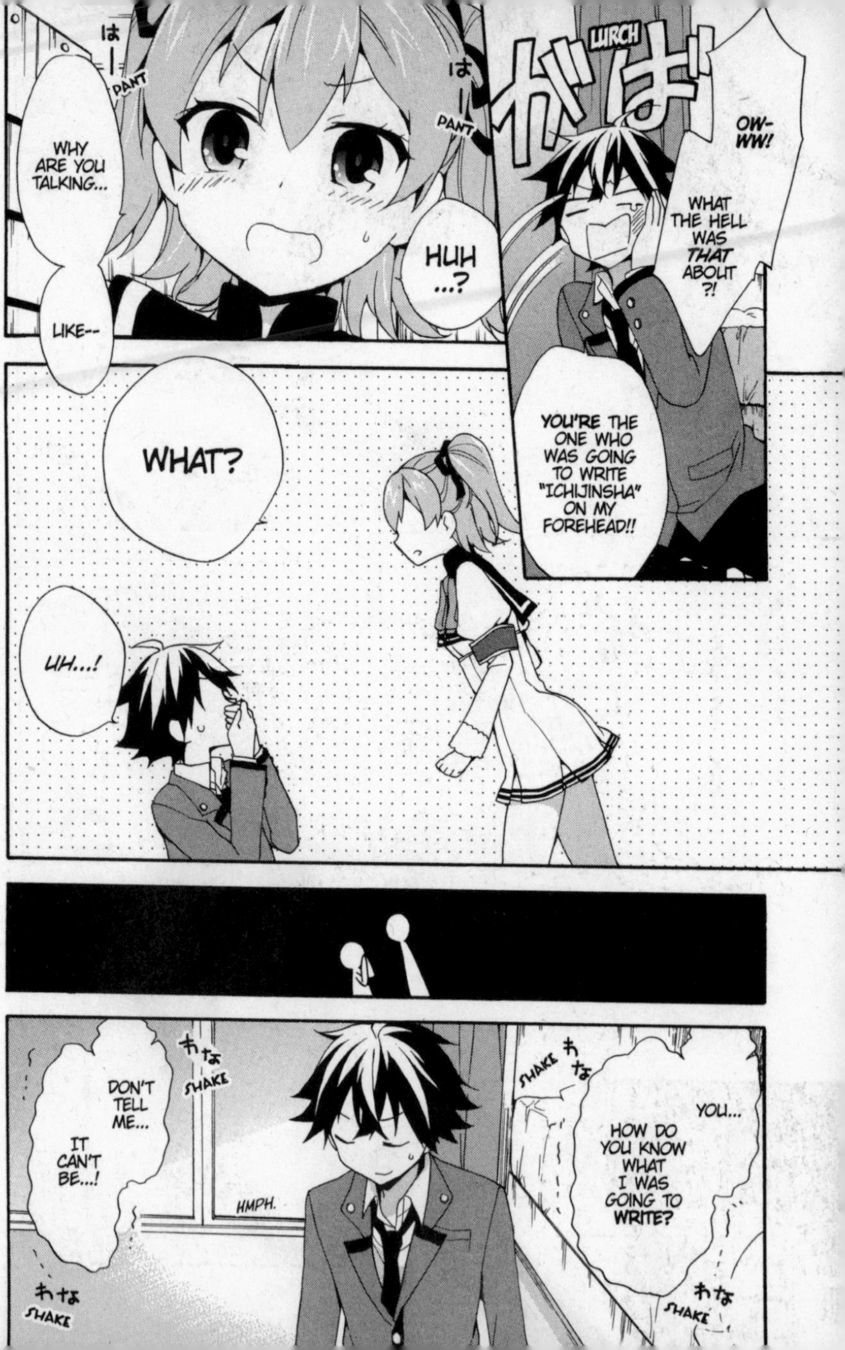

LURCH
がば
OW-WW!
WHAT THE HELL WAS THAT ABOUT?!
YOU'RE THE ONE WHO WAS GOING TO WRITE "ICHIJINSHA" ON MY FOREHEAD!!
はー
PANT
HUH ...?
はー
PANT
WHY ARE YOU TALKING...
LIKE--
WHAT?
UH...!
SHAKE わな
YOU...
HOW DO YOU KNOW WHAT I WAS GOING TO WRITE?
わな
SHAKE
わな
SHAKE
DON'T TELL ME...
IT CAN'T BE...!
HMPH.
わな
SHAKE

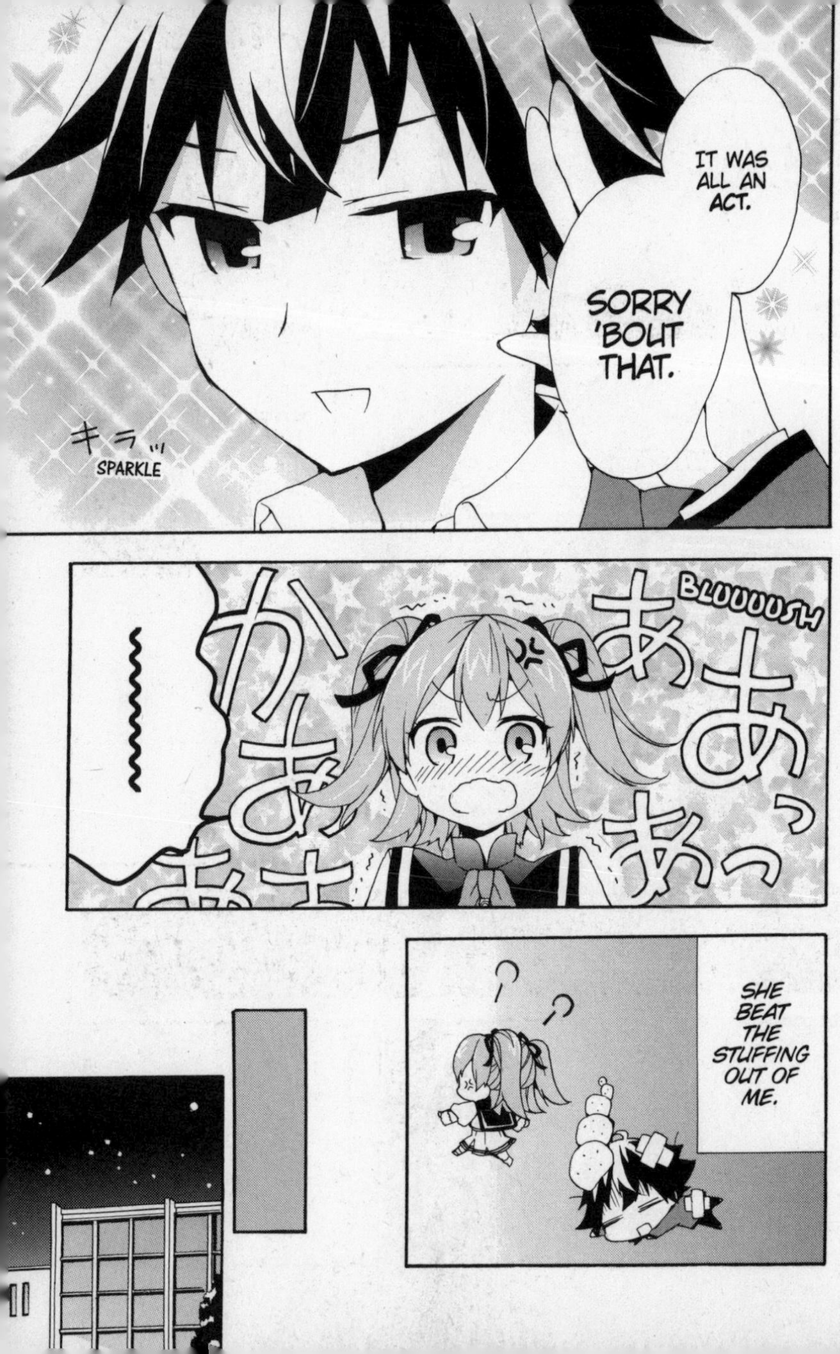
IT WAS ALL AN ACT.
SORRY 'BOUT THAT.
キラッ
SPARKLE
BLUUUUSH
SHE BEAT THE STUFFING OUT OF ME.

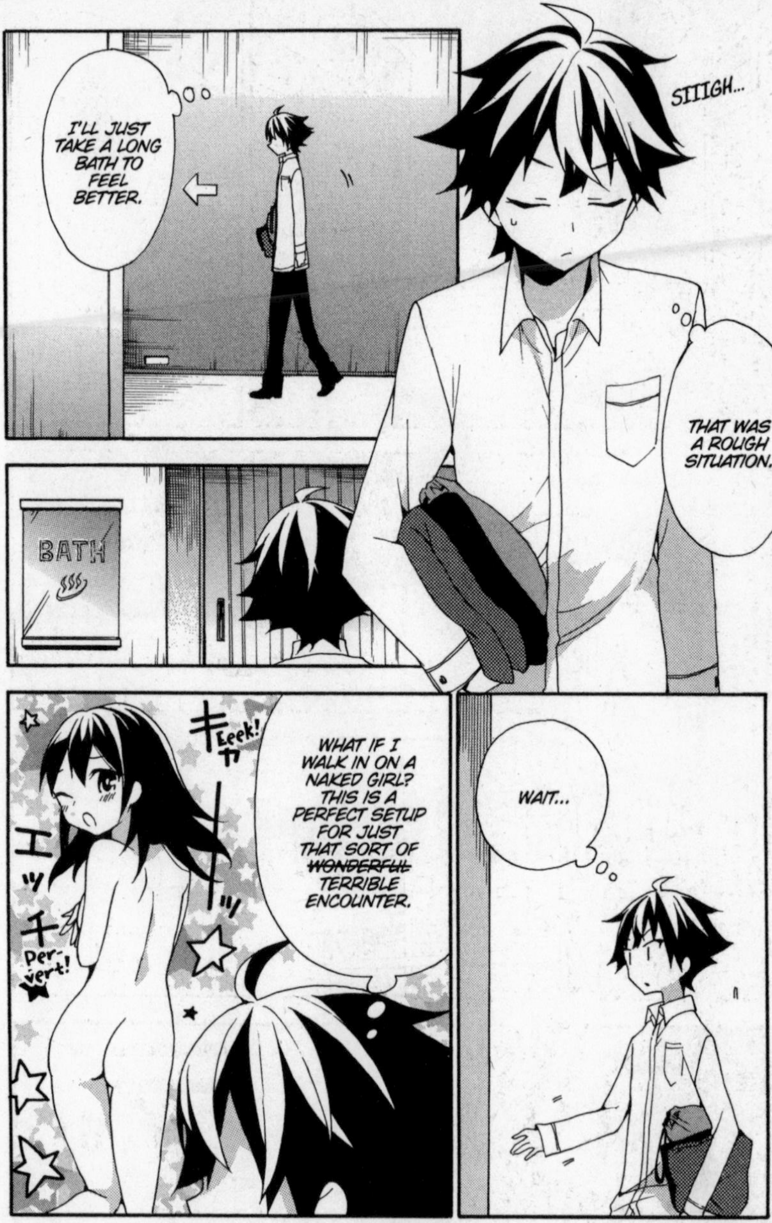
SIIIGH...
THAT WAS A ROUGH SITUATION.
I'LL JUST TAKE A LONG BATH TO FEEL BETTER.
BATH
WAIT...
WHAT IF I WALK IN ON A NAKED GIRL? THIS IS A PERFECT SETUP FOR JUST THAT SORT OF ~~WONDERFUL~~ TERRIBLE ENCOUNTER.
キャ
Eeek!
エッチ
Per-vert!

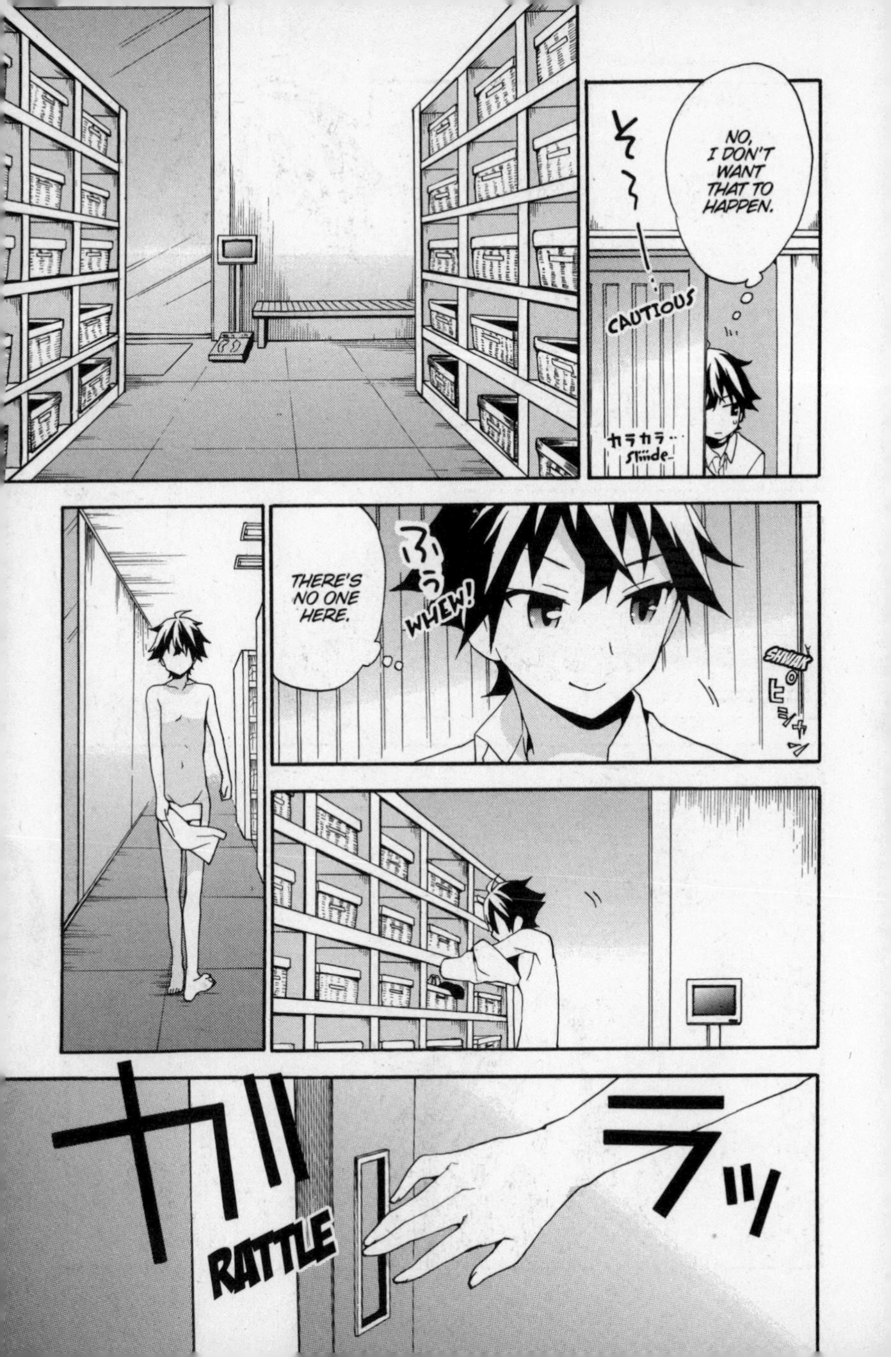

NO, I DON'T WANT THAT TO HAPPEN.
CAUTIOUS
カラカラ..
Sliiide
SHWAK
ピシャッ
ふぅ
WHEW!
THERE'S NO ONE HERE.
ガラッ
RATTLE

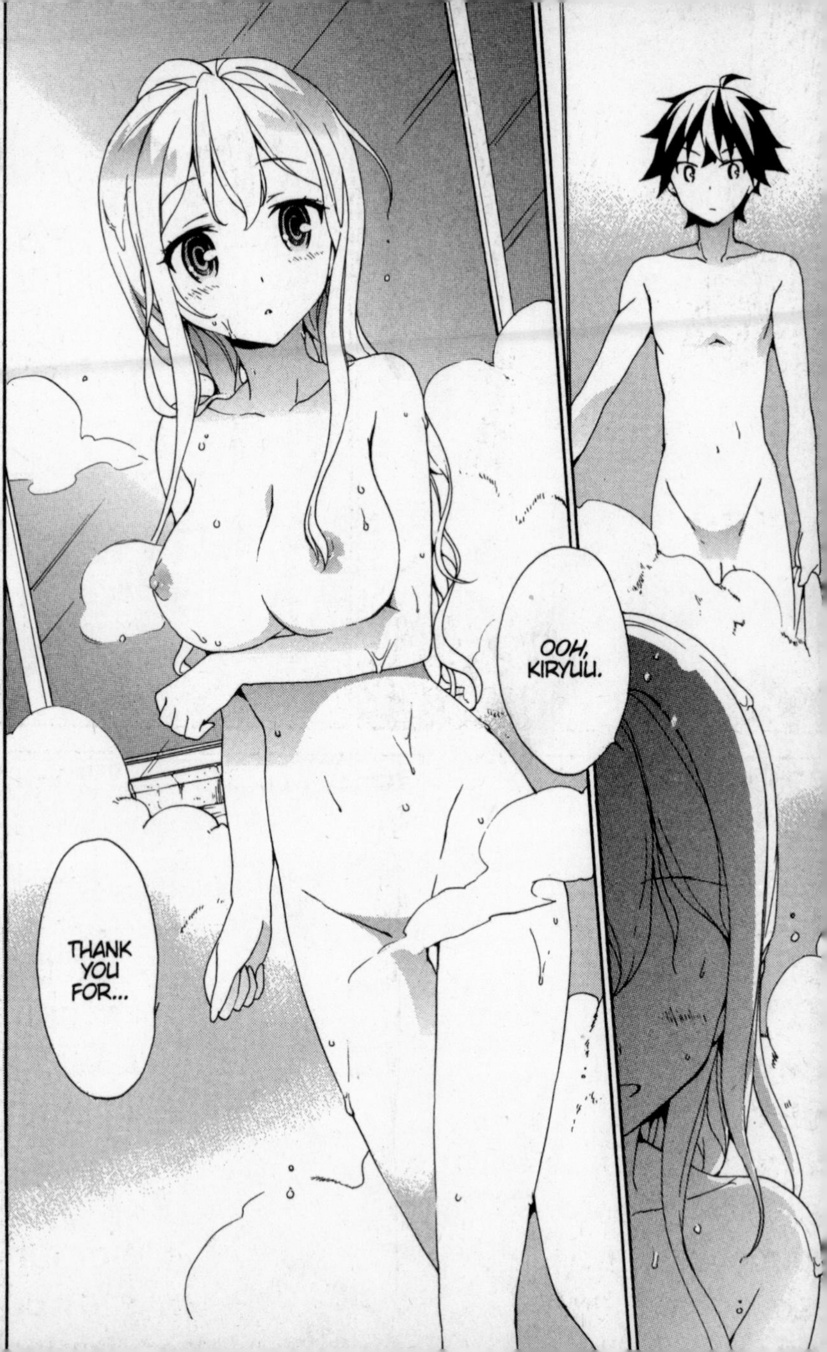
OOH, KIRYUU.
THANK YOU FOR...

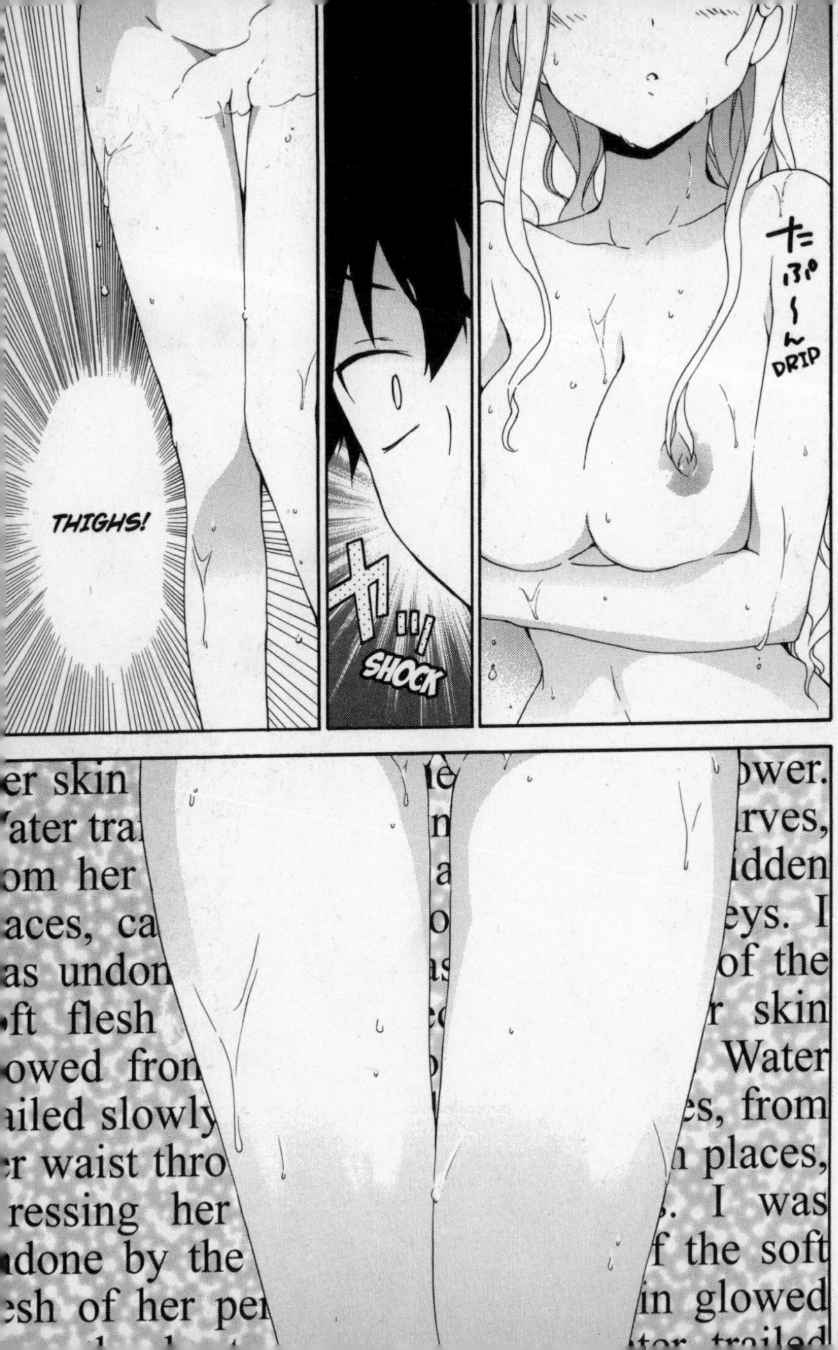
たぷ〜ん
DRIP
SHOCK
THIGHS!

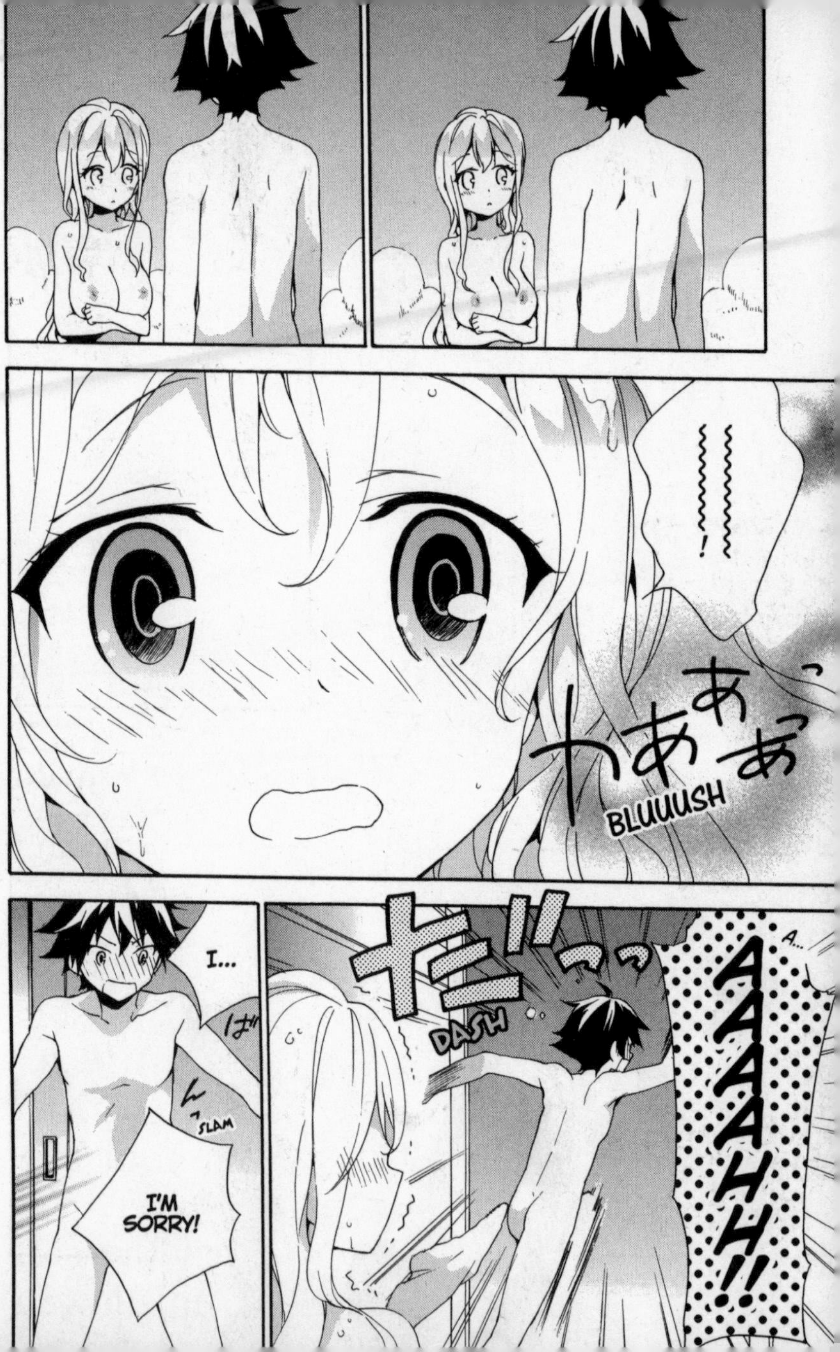
BLUUUSH
A...
AAAAHH!!
DASH
I...
SLAM
I'M SORRY!

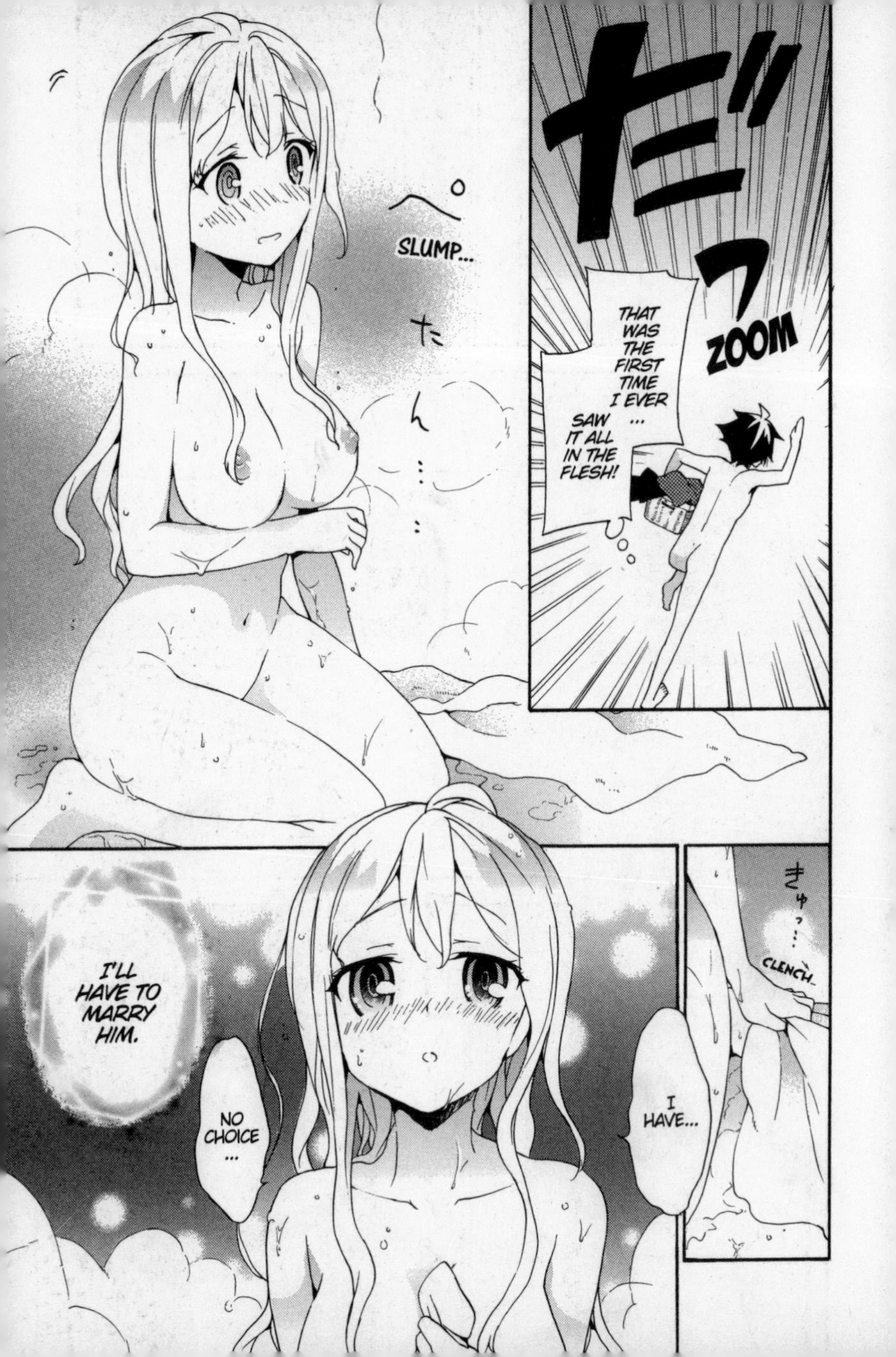
ダッ
ZOOM
THAT WAS THE FIRST TIME I EVER...
SAW IT ALL IN THE FLESH!
へ。
SLUMP...
たん……
きゅっ…
CLENCH
I HAVE...
NO CHOICE...
I'LL HAVE TO MARRY HIM.

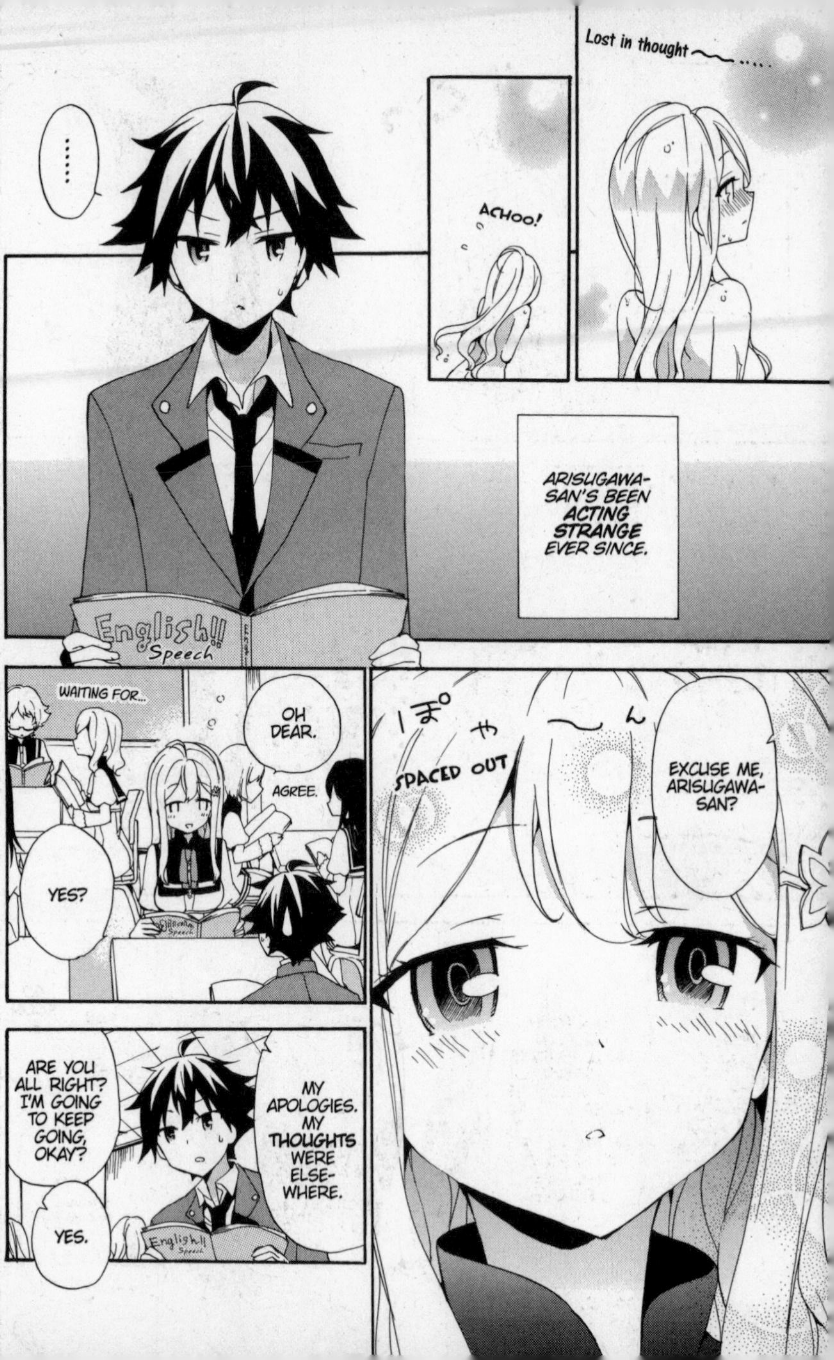

Lost in thought~~.....
ACHOO!
ARISUGAWA-SAN'S BEEN ACTING STRANGE EVER SINCE.
......
English!! Speech
ぽやーん
SPACED OUT
EXCUSE ME, ARISUGAWA-SAN?
OH DEAR.
WAITING FOR...
AGREE.
YES?
MY APOLOGIES. MY THOUGHTS WERE ELSEWHERE.
ARE YOU ALL RIGHT? I'M GOING TO KEEP GOING, OKAY?
YES.
English!! Speech

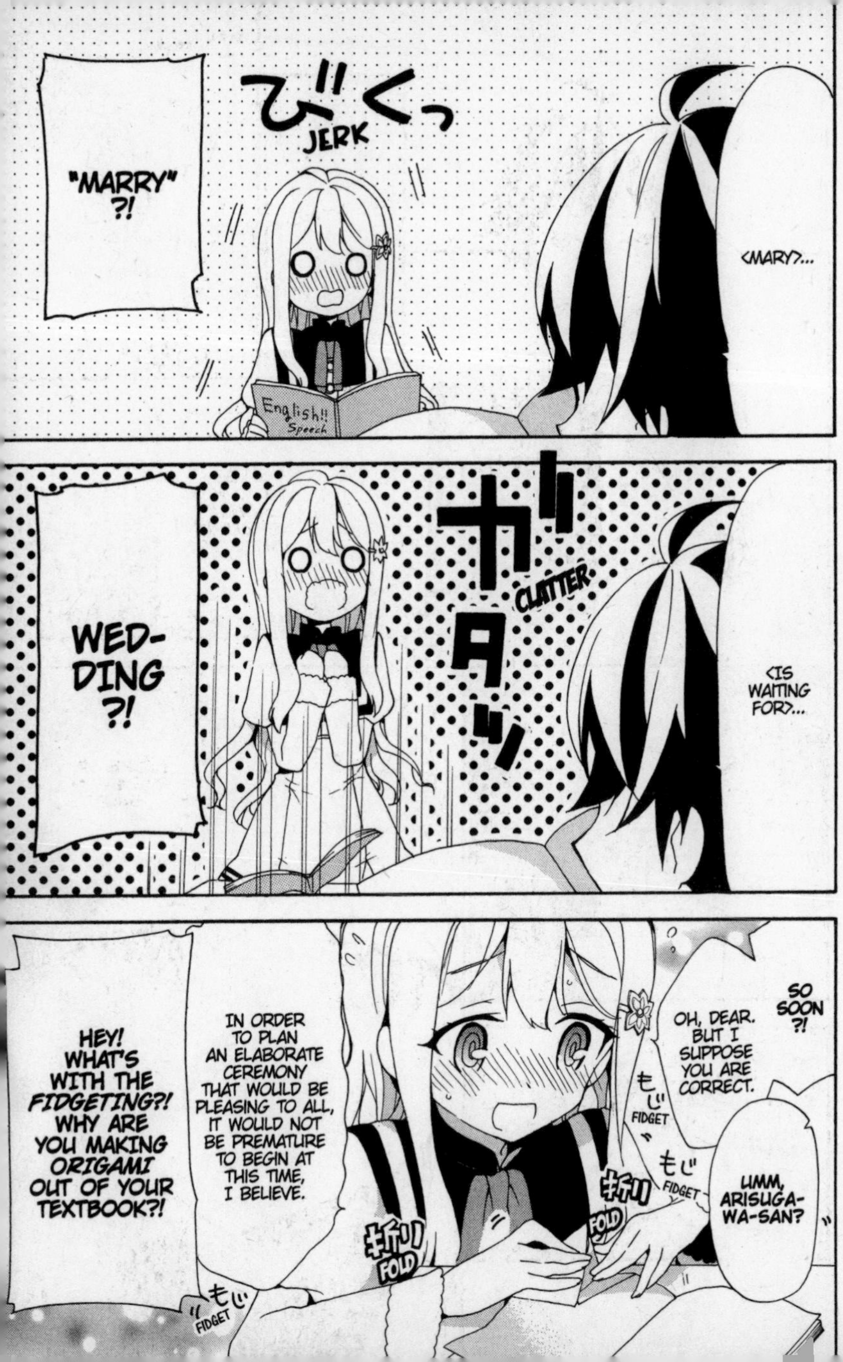
<MARY>...
びくっ
JERK
"MARRY" ?!
<IS WAITING FOR>...
ガタッ
CLATTER
WED-DING ?!
SO SOON ?!
UMM, ARISUGAWA-SAN?
OH, DEAR. BUT I SUPPOSE YOU ARE CORRECT.
もじ
FIDGET
もじ
FIDGET
折り
FOLD
折り
FOLD
IN ORDER TO PLAN AN ELABORATE CEREMONY THAT WOULD BE PLEASING TO ALL, IT WOULD NOT BE PREMATURE TO BEGIN AT THIS TIME, I BELIEVE.
HEY! WHAT'S WITH THE *FIDGETING?!* WHY ARE YOU MAKING *ORIGAMI* OUT OF YOUR TEXTBOOK?!
もじ
FIDGET

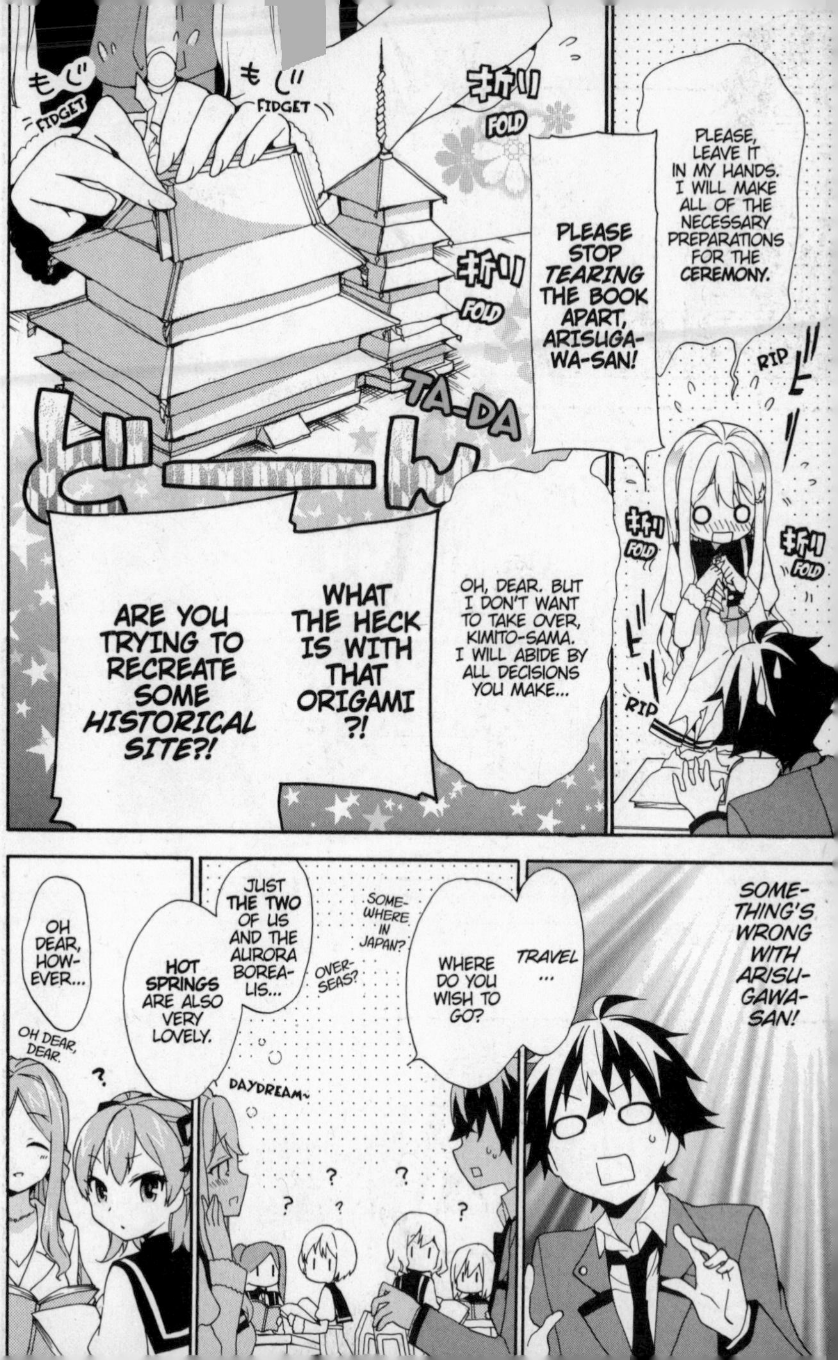
PLEASE, LEAVE IT IN MY HANDS. I WILL MAKE ALL OF THE NECESSARY PREPARATIONS FOR THE CEREMONY.
RIP
FOLD
FOLD
RIP
FIDGET
FIDGET
FOLD
FOLD
TA-DA
PLEASE STOP TEARING THE BOOK APART, ARISUGA-WA-SAN!
OH, DEAR. BUT I DON'T WANT TO TAKE OVER, KIMITO-SAMA. I WILL ABIDE BY ALL DECISIONS YOU MAKE...
WHAT THE HECK IS WITH THAT ORIGAMI ?!
ARE YOU TRYING TO RECREATE SOME HISTORICAL SITE?!
SOME-THING'S WRONG WITH ARISU-GAWA-SAN!
TRAVEL ...
WHERE DO YOU WISH TO GO?
SOME-WHERE IN JAPAN?
OVER-SEAS?
JUST THE TWO OF US AND THE AURORA BOREA-LIS...
HOT SPRINGS ARE ALSO VERY LOVELY.
DAYDREAM~
OH DEAR, HOW-EVER...
OH DEAR, DEAR.

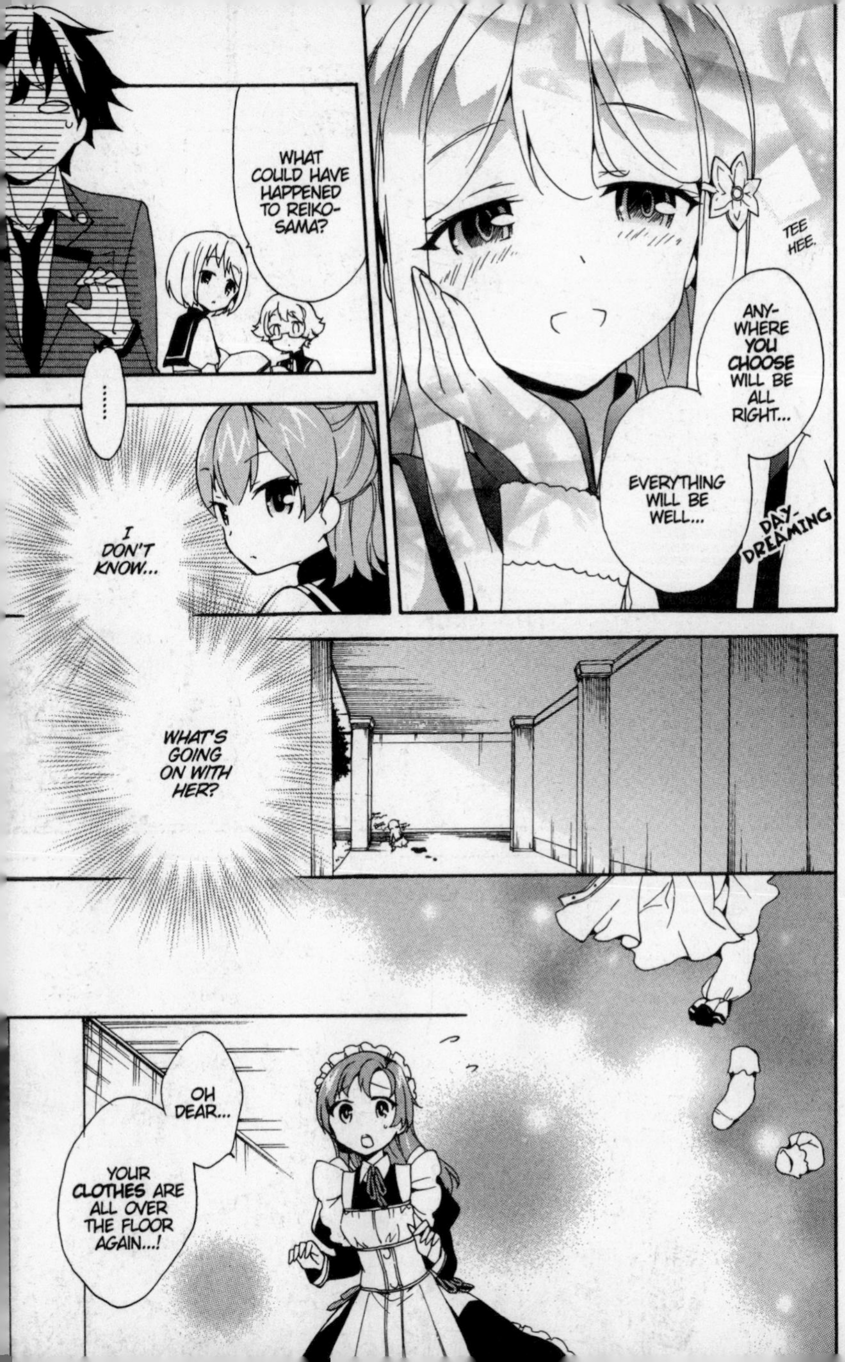
TEE HEE.
ANYWHERE YOU CHOOSE WILL BE ALL RIGHT...
EVERYTHING WILL BE WELL...
DAY-DREAMING
WHAT COULD HAVE HAPPENED TO REIKO-SAMA?
......
I DON'T KNOW...
WHAT'S GOING ON WITH HER?
OH DEAR...
YOUR CLOTHES ARE ALL OVER THE FLOOR AGAIN...!

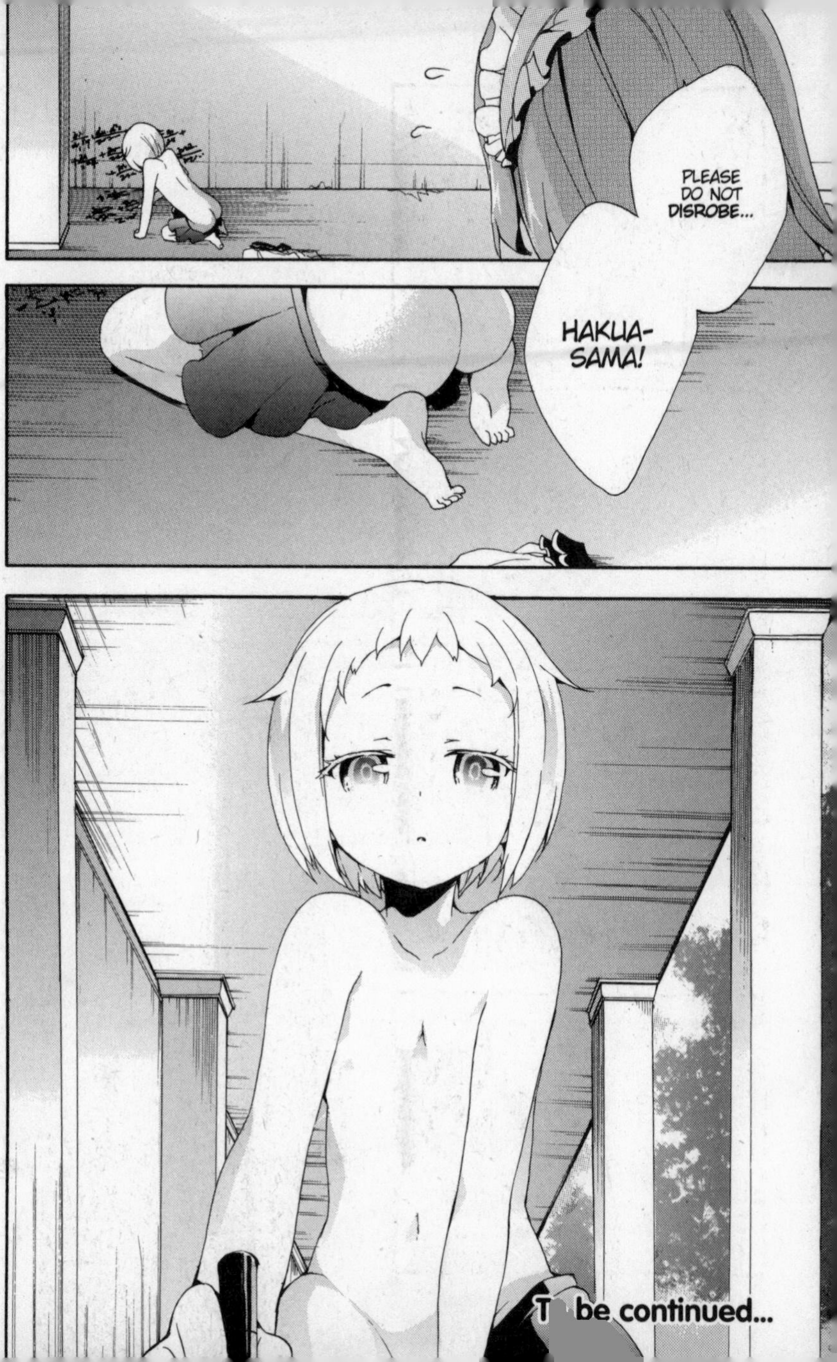
PLEASE DO NOT DISROBE...
HAKUA-SAMA!
T be continued...

Extra Manga ① Chapter Kimito

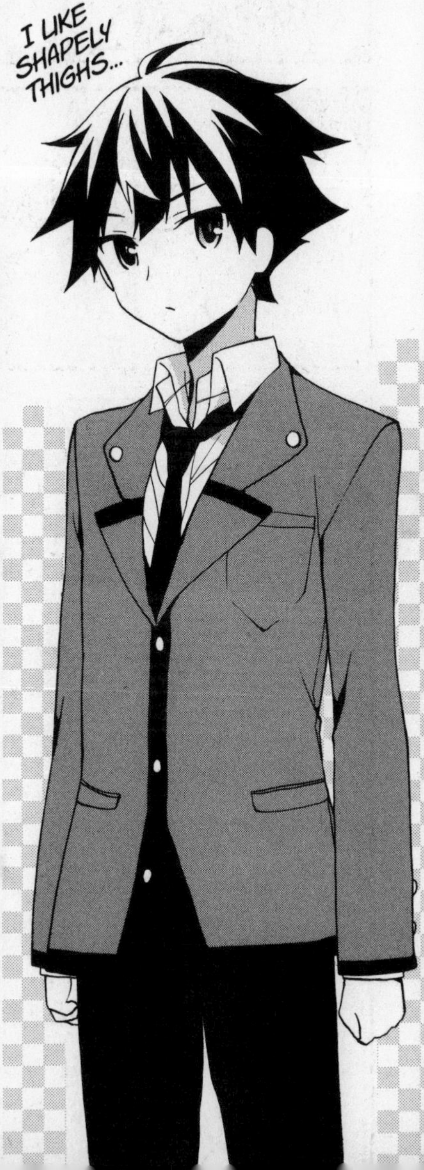
I LIKE SHAPELY THIGHS...

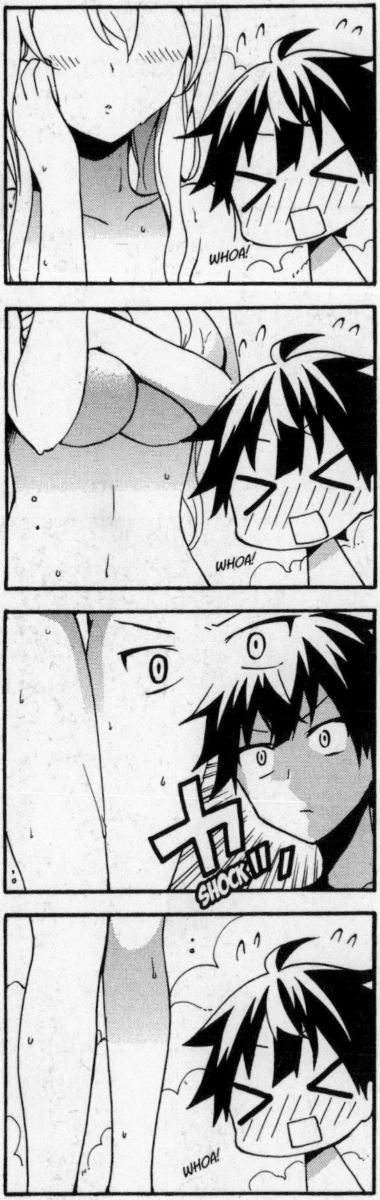
WHOA!
WHOA!
SHOCK!!
WHOA!

Extra Manga ② Chapter Aika

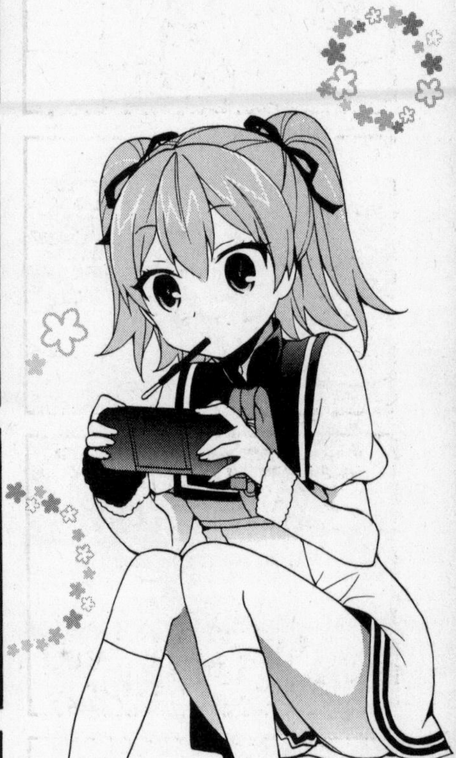
Pokkk

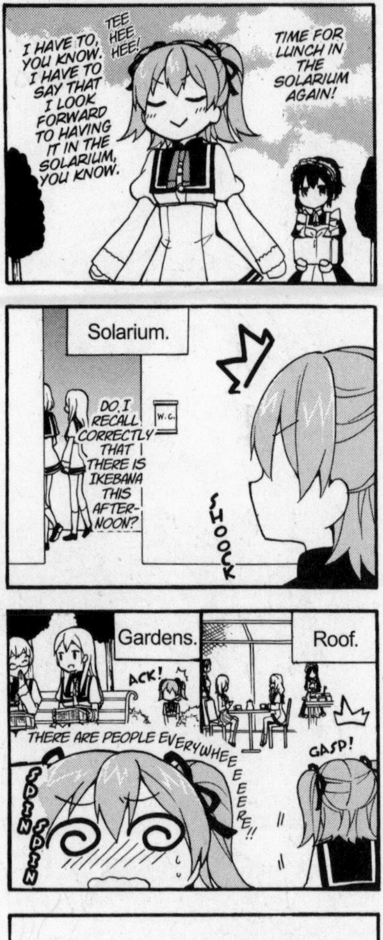
TIME FOR LUNCH IN THE SOLARIUM AGAIN!
TEE HEE HEE!
I HAVE TO, YOU KNOW. I HAVE TO SAY THAT I LOOK FORWARD TO HAVING IT IN THE SOLARIUM, YOU KNOW.
Solarium.
SHOOCK
W.C.
DO, I RECALL CORRECTLY THAT THERE IS IKEBANA THIS AFTER-NOON?
Roof.
GASP!
Gardens.
ACK!
THERE ARE PEOPLE EVERYWHEEEEEERE!!
SPIN SPIN SPIN
UNNHH...
Growl~...

Extra Manga ③
Chapter Reiko

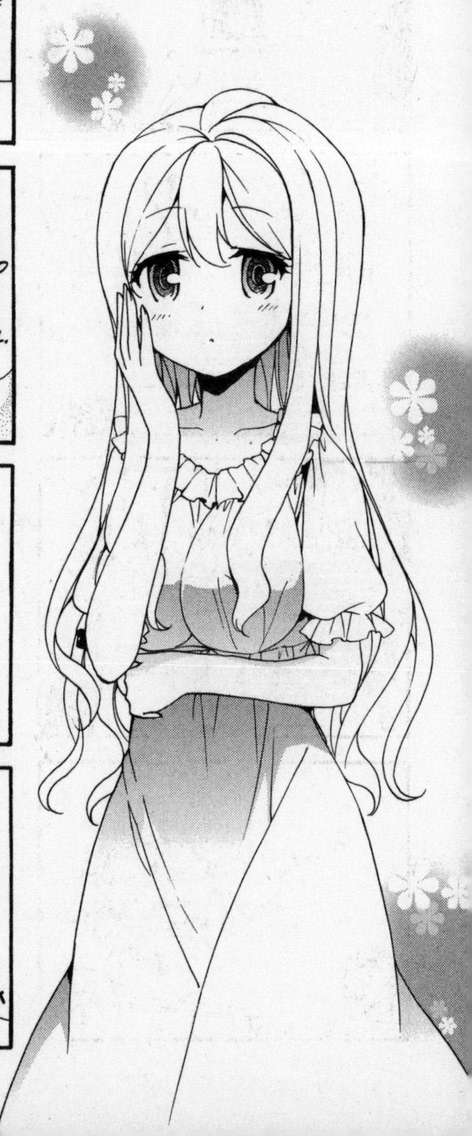

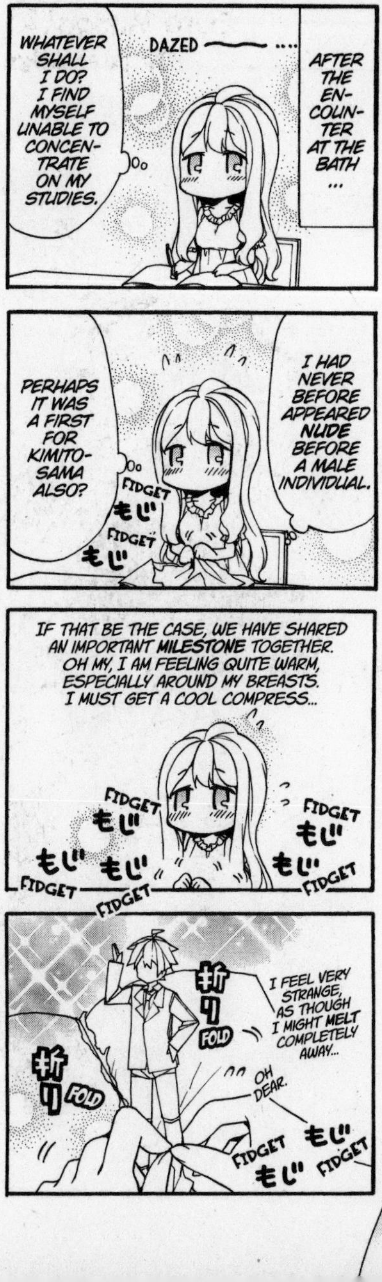
AFTER THE ENCOUNTER AT THE BATH...
DAZED —— ....
WHATEVER SHALL I DO? I FIND MYSELF UNABLE TO CONCENTRATE ON MY STUDIES.
I HAD NEVER BEFORE APPEARED NUDE BEFORE A MALE INDIVIDUAL.
PERHAPS IT WAS A FIRST FOR KIMITO-SAMA ALSO?
FIDGET もじ
FIDGET もじ
IF THAT BE THE CASE, WE HAVE SHARED AN IMPORTANT MILESTONE TOGETHER. OH MY, I AM FEELING QUITE WARM, ESPECIALLY AROUND MY BREASTS. I MUST GET A COOL COMPRESS...
FIDGET もじ
もじ FIDGET
FIDGET もじ
FIDGET もじ
FIDGET もじ
I FEEL VERY STRANGE, AS THOUGH I MIGHT MELT COMPLETELY AWAY...
折り FOLD
折り FOLD
OH DEAR.
もじ FIDGET
FIDGET もじ

Risumai-san, congratulations
on the sale of the manga!
And congratulations
to me too! Thank you!
And again, thank you!

Author
TAKAFUMI
NANATSUKI

Takafumi Nanatsuki

AIKA

Character
Designer
URUU
GEKKA

Congratulations on
the sale of the manga!
Thank you so much for
always drawing such
cute characters!!

Gekka

COMMENT

Artist
RISUMAI

THANK YOU VERY MUCH
FOR BUYING SHOMIN SAMPLE:
I WAS ABDUCTED BY AN
ELITE ALL-GIRLS SCHOOL
AS A SAMPLE COMMONER
VOLUME 1!

I AM RISUMAI! I'M
VERY GRATEFUL
FOR HAVING BEEN
ENTRUSTED WITH
THE MANGA VERSION!

WHILE ILLUSTRATING THIS,
I WAS MOVED BY AIKA'S
CUTE NAÏVETÉ.

I STILL HAVE A LONG WAY
TO GO, BUT I AM GLAD IF
I AM ABLE TO EXPRESS
THE APPEAL OF THESE
CUTE AND FUNNY
YOUNG LADIES.

SEVEN SEAS ENTERTAINMENT PRESENTS

SHOMIN SAMPLE

I Was Abducted by an Elite All-Girls School as a Sample Commoner VOL. 1

story by TAKAFUMI NANATSUKI / art by RISUMAI / character design by GEKKA URUU

TRANSLATION
Beni Axia Conrad

ADAPTATION
Lee Otter

LETTERING AND LAYOUT
Alexandra Gunawan

LOGO DESIGN
Karis Page

COVER DESIGN
Nicky Lim

PROOFREADER
Janet Houck
Patrick King

PRODUCTION MANAGER
Lissa Pattillo

EDITOR-IN-CHIEF
Adam Arnold

PUBLISHER
Jason DeAngelis

SHOMIN SAMPLE: I WAS ABDUCTED BY AN ELITE ALL-GIRLS SCHOOL AS A SAMPLE COMMONER VOL. 1

First published in Japan in 2012 by ICHIJINSHA Inc., Tokyo.
English translation rights arranged with ICHIJINSHA Inc., Tokyo.

ISBN: 978-1-626923-21-8

Printed in Canada

First Printing: May 2016

10 9 8 7 6 5 4 3 2 1

READING DIRECTIONS

This book reads from ***right to left***, Japanese style. If this is your first time reading manga, you start reading from the top right panel on each page and take it from there. If you get lost, just follow the numbered diagram here. It may seem backwards at first, but you'll get the hang of it! Have fun!!

1
2
3
4
5
6
7
8
9

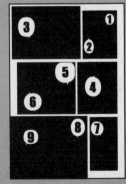